The

POWERFUL

and the

DAMNED

The

POWERFUL

and the

DAMNED

Private Diaries in Turbulent Times

LIONEL
BARBER

2

WH Allen, an imprint of Ebury Publishing,
20 Vauxhall Bridge Road,
London SW1V 2SA

WH Allen is part of the Penguin Random House group of companies
whose addresses can be found at global.penguinrandomhouse.com

Penguin
Random House
UK

First published by WH Allen in 2020

www.penguin.co.uk

A CIP catalogue record for this book is available from the British Library

Hardback ISBN 9780753558188
Trade Paperback ISBN 9780753558195

Printed and bound in Italy by Grafica Veneta S.p.A.

Text design by Couper Street Type Co.

Penguin Random House is committed to a sustainable future
for our business, our readers and our planet. This book is made
from Forest Stewardship Council® certified paper.

MIX
Paper from
responsible sources
FSC® C018179

To Victoria

CONTENTS

CONTENTS

DRAMATIS PERSONAE

Bob Diamond, CEO Barclays Bank (2011–12)
Mathias Döpfner, CEO Axel Springer (2002–)
John Fallon, CEO Pearson (2013–)
Dick Fuld, CEO Lehman Bros (1994–2008)
Sir Philip Green, chairman Arcadia Group (2002–)
Tsuneo Kita, chairman and group CEO Nikkei (2015–)
Sir Terry Leahy, CEO Tesco (1997–2011)
Marjorie Scardino, CEO Pearson (1997–2012)
Steve Schwarzman, co-founder, chairman and CEO
    Blackstone (1985–)
Robert B. Zoellick, president of the World Bank (2007–12)

ROYALTY

HRH Prince Charles, Prince of Wales
HRH Prince Andrew, Duke of York
Mohammed bin Salman, crown prince of Saudi Arabia

JOURNALISM

Paul Dacre, editor of the *Daily Mail* (1992–2018)
Roula Khalaf, deputy editor of the *Financial Times* (2016–20),
    editor (2020–)
Alan Rusbridger, editor of the *Guardian* (1995–2015)
Martin Wolf, chief economics commentator of the *FT* (1996–)

DIPLOMACY

Sylvie Bermann, French ambassador to UK (2014–17)
Fu Ying, Chinese ambassador to UK (2007–9)
Liu Xiaoming, Chinese ambassador to UK (2009–)
Louis B. Susman, US ambassador to UK (2009–13)

PREFACE

My favourite history book is *Present at the Creation*, Dean Acheson's 1969 account of how American leadership forged a new world order after World War II. These private diaries do not pretend to match Acheson's majestic memoir, but they do draw inspiration from his sweep and style in our own time of momentous change.

As editor of the *Financial Times* between 2005 and 2020 – the pre-Covid years – I had a front-row seat observing the economic and political aftershocks triggered by the global financial crisis. I was an interlocutor to dozens of people in power around the world, each offering unique insights into high-level decision-making and political calculation. And I was an agent of change at the *FT*, leading the transformation of a print-based product to a fully digital, award-winning news organisation.

The Powerful and the Damned is an eyewitness account of the crisis years when the world's financial system almost melted down; when liberal democracies were storm-tossed by waves of immigration, populism and terrorism. During this period, traditional media experienced wrenching change as power concentrated around a handful of tech giants led by Apple, Facebook and Google; China, with its own tech giants

Alibaba, Tencent and Huawei, emerged as the second super-power alongside the US.

These forces – cultural, economic, social and political – combined to present a mortal threat to the post-war international order, Acheson's order. They eroded public support for traditional parties and institutions in liberal democracies in Europe and the US. And they challenged the *FT*'s own core values of pro-market liberal internationalism and democratic capitalism.

This book aims to convey a sense of these epochal changes through individual portraits of power, via conversation and observation. As editor of the *FT*, I was privileged to gain access to world leaders in capitals ranging from Beijing, Moscow and Riyadh to Tehran, Tokyo and Washington. I interviewed presidents (Obama, Putin, Trump) as well as leading businessmen and financiers on Wall Street and in the City of London. And I was granted audiences with royalty such as Prince Charles, Prince Andrew and Mohammed bin Salman, the strongman of Saudi Arabia.

These men of power – and they are almost all men rather than women – are accustomed to wrapping themselves in protective bubbles, surrounded by armies of administrative aides, PR advisers and security guards whose job is to keep prying journalists and the public at a distance. Thanks to my position and the prestige of the *FT*, I was able to puncture the bubble and engage, up close and personal, with the Powerful and the (occasionally) Damned.

As may be deduced, I chose at the outset to be a working journalist and reporter, close to the news rather than being cooped up in the editor's office. My every hour in London was devoted to producing 'gold standard' journalism. But I also consciously made time to travel, working with members of the *FT*'s network of more than 100 foreign correspondents, to broaden my perspective.

During my editorship, the *FT* won acclaim for its journalism and its ever expanding readership, but we also made mistakes. We fell short – I fell short – in failing to appreciate popular disenchantment with authority and elites in the wake of the financial crisis. Identity politics and resentment over entrenched economic inequality paved the ground for Brexit. We were not responsible for losing the 2016 referendum, but by and large we missed the story. Being an 'establishment' newspaper is no excuse. It was a failure of imagination, and we learnt our lesson.

Nevertheless, I would maintain, many of the *FT*'s big calls were right, on markets, the euro and a series of high-risk, high-reward investigations which culminated in the exposure of Wirecard, Germany's equivalent of the Enron scandal. Wirecard's collapse, six months after I stepped down as editor, vindicated three years and more of original reporting which exposed abuse of power and deep-rooted fraud in a Dax 30 company. Perhaps even more significantly, it established the importance of facts in a supposedly post-truth age.

During my editorship, I did not keep a daily diary, but I did keep extensive notes of interviews, conversations and encounters. This book is based on those notes and published material, often complemented by passages in italics which provide personal commentary and context, often with the benefit of hindsight.

The book is divided into five sections. The first stretches between 2005 and 2007 when the global economy was living in a credit bubble, oblivious of the impending financial crisis. I saw first hand 'peak' City of London, when hedge funds and private equity ruled the roost and Royal Bank of Scotland (RBS), soon to go spectacularly bust, ranked in the top ten biggest banks in the world. Yet there were clues to the coming crisis, notably the excess leverage in the system highlighted by the *FT*'s Gillian Tett, the paper's award-winning financial markets reporter and commentator.

The second section, covering the years 2008–9, conveys the drama of the Great Crash of 2008 when the collapse of Lehman Brothers triggered a crisis of confidence in the credit markets and the wider banking system. For a brief few weeks it felt as if the global financial system was melting down. Passages draw on conversations with some of Wall Street's players such as Lloyd Blankfein of Goldman Sachs, Jamie Dimon of JPMorgan Chase, Steve Schwarzman of Blackstone and Dick Fuld of Lehman Brothers. It also features exchanges with and impressions gleaned from the politicians and technocrats tasked with managing the crisis such as Mario Draghi, president of the European Central Bank, a lifelong friend and source.

This section highlights the crisis of modern capitalism, but also draws on interviews with Chinese premier Wen Jiabao in London (a notable first with a Chinese leader) and President-elect Dmitry Medvedev in Moscow and two interviews with Chancellor Angela Merkel in Berlin. Shortly after Lehman collapsed, I witnessed the aftershocks in the United Arab Emirates when Abu Dhabi had in effect to bail out debt-laden Dubai. This was part of a wider tour of the Middle East, including four days in Syria and an interview with Benjamin Netanyahu in Jerusalem where the future Israeli prime minister prefigured the end of a separate Palestinian state.

The third section focuses on the digital revolution in media in the period 2010–14 which accelerated the decline in newspapers and ushered in a new age of fragmentation. In the UK, I watched an 'old media' phone-hacking scandal unfold which forced the closure of Rupert Murdoch's saucy tabloid, the *News of the World*. This led to the Leveson inquiry into the conduct and regulation of the press which consumed my attention for almost two years. Throughout this period, I also saw the rise of 'new media' first hand, through regular trips to Silicon Valley. An important subtext is the 'asymmetric information flow' and 'open-source journalism' symbolised by WikiLeaks, Julian Assange and the Snowden affair, all of which presented ethical and professional dilemmas for the press.

The fourth section begins with the terrorist attack in 2015 on the offices of *Charlie Hebdo*, the Parisian satirical magazine – the first wave of a series of violent Islamist acts of terror in Europe's major cities. It documents events leading up to the Brexit earthquake: Cameron's fatal gamble on a referendum, the third of his premiership, and the destruction of the Lib Dem coalition. It also features pen portraits of key actors such as Dominic Cummings and Lynton Crosby as well as George Osborne and David Cameron, and the shock and aftermath of the Brexit referendum which damned Cameron and Osborne's political careers.

Looming large is the story of the sale of the *Financial Times*, which ended up improbably in Japanese (Nikkei) hands rather than those of the seeming favourite bidder, Axel Springer, the German publishing giant. The section also includes the election of Donald Trump, which I covered with my colleagues from the *FT*'s New York newsroom. Finally, it includes, among other intimate portraits, a rare conversation in Riyadh with Mohammed bin Salman, then a mere 30 years old, destined to be the most powerful figure in Saudi Arabia and one of the richest men in the world.

Shortly after the acquisition of the *FT*, Nikkei invited me to serve a 'third term' as editor, beyond the customary tenure of ten years. This was an unexpected bonus. It gave me an opportunity not just to cement the new global media alliance between the *FT* and Nikkei (which involved 14 trips to Tokyo between 2015 and 2019) but also to gain a unique insight into Japanese business, culture and journalism.

During this period, I was privileged to serve as editor during an extraordinary period of upheaval with Brexit, Trump, the US–China trade war and the fraying of the post-war alliance system. The final section reflects on these events and features exchanges with Prime Minister Theresa May and other political actors leading up to her exit and the arrival of Boris Johnson, someone I have known since my days in Brussels as a correspondent for the *FT* almost 30 years ago.

Other power portraits include a three-hour interview in Kigali with President Paul Kagame; a conversation with Carrie Lam in Hong Kong; an interview with Donald Trump in the Oval Office (March 2017) and a rare interview in the Kremlin with Vladimir Putin (June 2019), which made world headlines. Finally, just as the first reports of coronavirus appeared, I ended my editorship with an interview with Chancellor Angela Merkel in Berlin, a political testament of the greatest defender of the old liberal order. Within weeks, the world was gripped by the coronavirus pandemic.

This once-in-a-century phenomenon seems to draw an even heavier line under the years 2005–20, adding an even greater unpredictable element to a world already in disarray, to borrow the phrase of Richard Haass, the scholar, diplomat and president of the Council on Foreign Relations. I have therefore written an epilogue which attempts to assess Covid-19's impact on the way we live now, and how it will reshape the world in future. Beyond the speculation, it is surely safe to say that Acheson's world is over. He was 'present at the creation'. And I was present at the destruction.

SECTION ONE

WE LIVE IN FINANCIAL TIMES

INTRODUCTION

THURSDAY, 20 OCTOBER

Sir David Bell would like lunch. No specific agenda. Seriously? I've known David for 20 years and he *always* has an agenda. He is an agent of influence with two intersecting roles: director for people at Pearson* which owns the *Financial Times* and non-sitting chairman of the *FT*. I've never been entirely clear how that all works. In power, but rarely in the office, I guess. If he's come all the way from London to New York to see me, something's up.

We meet at Remy's, an Italian restaurant tucked away on 53rd Street, just across the road from our New York headquarters at 1330 Avenue of the Americas. That's the skyscraper with the pink *FT* logo slapped on top to mark the moment, back in 1999, when we arrived in force in Manhattan to take on the giants of American media. I found the *FT*'s US invasion inspiring. We were the scrappy underdogs determined

---

* Founded in Yorkshire in 1844, Pearson had a long history as a hodge-podge conglomerate. When it bought the *FT* in 1957 its interests ranged from construction to merchant banking but latterly focused on education.

to make our numbers count. I was less convinced by the marketing campaign led by *Ghostbusters* star Dan Aykroyd cruising down Sixth Avenue on a pink motorbike.

David is wearing his usual rumpled dark suit, white shirt and tie. Chumminess is off the menu today, replaced by a studied formality. 'Well, you've got the job,' he says, extending a plump hand across the table. 'Congratulations!'

Editor of the *Financial Times*. It takes a few seconds to grasp that I've been handed one of the best jobs in world journalism. My mind flashes to my late father Frank who grew up in Leeds and left school at fifteen knowing that all he ever wanted to be was a newspaperman. Journalism wasn't a job, he used to tell me, it was a vocation. That's how I feel about the *FT*. I've had a wonderfully stimulating career as a reporter and foreign correspondent. I never planned to be editor. I don't even have an economics degree, but I do know the craft of journalism. At 50, I feel, in my bones, that all my earlier roles as a reporter, news editor and manager have built to this moment. I'm ready to take on the top job.

Rumours of a change have been circulating for weeks. We've lost £60m in the past three years, and advertising is down 50 per cent since the peak of 2000. Circulation is falling, particularly in the UK, our home market. The business has never really recovered from the dotcom crash of 2000–2001; but there's a problem with our journalism too. It lacks consistency and it has lost quality. For a premium brand, that's potentially fatal.

As David and I clink our glasses of water *(where's that bottle of champagne?)*, I mumble a few words of gratitude and start tucking into my favourite Italian penne pasta with the spicy arrabbiata sauce. Then David, genuinely curious but ever so mischievous, hits me with the question to which every decent editor must have an answer: 'What are you going to do now?' I fall at the first hurdle.

My appointment, while never assured, was not entirely out of the blue. Back in 2001, Pearson chose Andrew Gowers* to be the FT editor, passing over Robert Thomson's† and my own bid for the top job. I was disappointed but not enough to leave the FT. When Rupert Murdoch lured Robert to become editor of The Times, I moved from London to New York to replace him as US managing editor. For the next three and a half years, I drove our America coverage and learnt more about the commercial realities of running a modern news business and the challenges of hiring and keeping top talent. I also watched with mounting frustration the missteps in London.

In the summer of 2005 my patience snapped over Andrew's decision to make the news editor — the anchor role in the newsroom — a job share on the grounds it had become too hard for one person to manage. I asked to see Marjorie Scardino, chief executive of Pearson and the FT proprietor, in her seventh-floor office at 1330 Avenue of the Americas.

LB: 'You have to make a change.'

MS (silent, but watchful)

---

* Andrew Gowers, *FT* editor 2001–5, turned to public relations after journalism. He worked for Lehman Brothers up until its collapse in 2008 and for BP during the Deepwater Horizon disaster before joining Trafigura, the commodities trader.

† Robert Thomson began as a copy boy on the *Melbourne Herald* and rose swiftly at the *FT* from foreign correspondent in Beijing to editor of *FT Weekend* and US managing editor. He left in 2002 to edit *The Times* of London, and later ascended in the Murdoch empire to be editor of the *Wall Street Journal* and CEO of News Corporation.

LB: 'I don't care whether you appoint me or someone else. You have to change the editor . . . Otherwise this sucker's going down.'

Marjorie hated being put on the spot but thanked me — I believe sincerely — for my candour. Maybe she thought I had been watching too many Hollywood movies. I never heard another word until the Bell lunch.

WEDNESDAY, 26 OCTOBER

At David's suggestion, I've been drafting a manifesto for root-and-branch change at the *FT* that I plan to launch when I take over as editor. I want to focus not just on key questions about editorial coverage and personnel, where we have fallen down, but also on the big picture. 'Cyclical shifts do not explain why we have struggled. We are in the middle of a structural change driven by the internet which is revolutionising reading habits and turning established business models upside down.'

I set out five strategic imperatives: develop the newspaper and website in tandem; build on the international audience which is our future; rescue the UK newspaper which has drifted away from business coverage; redouble our efforts to deliver the sharpest financial news coverage to serve our readers; and lift the debilitating hiring freeze and reinvest in people and talent.

The memo concludes: 'We need to move the *FT* to the next level as a newspaper which is authoritative, credible and above all distinctive. It is time to return to the gold standard.'

MONDAY, 31 OCTOBER

To lunch at Harry Evans and Tina Brown's, New York's media power couple, at their midtown triplex on Sutton Place near the

East River. Harry made the *Sunday Times* a world-class newspaper through groundbreaking investigations like Bloody Sunday and thalidomide. My father worked for him every Saturday for fourteen years, rewriting the main story on page one, the so-called 'splash sub' role. Frank adored Harry. His gift to me when I graduated from Oxford to become a journalist in 1978 was Harry's four books on editing, writing, typefaces and photo-journalism. My favourite volume was *Pictures on a Page*, a homage to the men and women behind the camera. When I arrived in New York, my first move was to wangle an invitation to a book launch at Harry and Tina's. Once I made their A-list, my wife Victoria and I were regular guests at power receptions in their back garden. I stuck close to Harry wherever I could, ever hopeful that a little magic dust might rub off on me.

Harry would have a dozen brilliant ideas on what makes a great editor. But I'm sworn to secrecy so it's small talk only with my tablemates Joan Juliet Buck and Vicky Ward, two *Vanity Fair* contributors from Tina's days as editor (in retrospect her finest hour). Vicky hints she would like to write a column for the *FT* about New York high society, including a businessman called Jeffrey Epstein.* Never heard of him. Right now all I care about is making the evening flight to London and my imminent appointment as editor.

THURSDAY, 3 NOVEMBER

It's been 48 hours since I went undercover at the Howard Hotel near Aldwych waiting for confirmation of the terms of Andrew Gowers's departure. Matters have dragged on. Now the hotel front desk has informed me that, as of tonight,

---

* Jeffrey Epstein, New York financier, philanthropist and sex offender.

there are no more free rooms. I phone Victoria in New York who suggests switching to my fraternal twin Stephen's house in Notting Hill, but only on condition he stays shtum. Finally my Blackberry buzzes. Marjorie says an official statement will go out tomorrow referring diplomatically to 'strategic differences' between Andrew and Pearson as the reason for his untimely exit.

Next morning, Marjorie and I meet for an early breakfast near her flat in Whitehall. We go over the timetable for internal and external communication, and our surprise appearance at *FT* headquarters at One Southwark Bridge at 9am where we will be joined by Olivier Fleurot, the French CEO of the *FT*.

We arrive via the back entrance, ascending by a rickety lift to the second floor. The doors open to a startled *FT* veteran reporter who remarks – with stunning incuriosity – that it's 'unusual' to spot Marjorie, Olivier and me at the same time at OSB. *(Mental note: he's changing jobs once I take over.)* As we walk into a hastily assembled meeting of top editors, the internal message goes out: Andrew Gowers is stepping down and I am the new editor. The news flashes through the news-room like wildfire.

Marjorie speaks briefly to the top team of assistant editors, announcing the change in a matter-of-fact voice which delib-erately downplays the significance of the occasion. Her original choice of editor – the most important decision a proprietor can make – was wrong. Now she's bet the farm on me. Mar-jorie takes no questions and leaves the room with Olivier. I shoot a glance round the table, trying to read the room. Many colleagues are staring down at the rectangular table in shock. One or two are fighting back tears. There's a sense of dread but also relief that change has come after months of drift.

That's what I want to play on: to show colleagues that I'm the guy who's going to get a grip, shake things up and restore the *FT* to its rightful leadership position in British media. We can do it, I say, but make no mistake it will involve painful changes. Then I take the lift to the newsroom on the first floor, rejoined by Olivier and Ben Hughes, my old rugby buddy from Oxford days who is head of *FT* advertising.

Instinctively I gravitate to the main news desk, the place I had previously occupied seven years ago as the *FT*'s news editor – the job I'd loved most of all until this one. The news editor is the 'conductor of the orchestra', driving and guiding reporters to bigger, better stories. My presence at the news desk immediately after Marjorie's announcement is a statement of intent. Deep and original reporting must be at the heart of everything we do – a point reinforced in the speech I've been honing for the past fortnight.

From this day on, I declare, the *FT* focus will be on quality journalism with a global perspective. No more shrunken vision of 'Britain's business newspaper'. There's also a new rule for reporters: in future, all *FT* stories must be based on two independent sources. I want to be first with the news, but it's more important to be right rather than first. As a crescendo, I restate our core mission, drawing on the words of Sir Gordon Newton, the greatest *FT* editor who served from 1950 to 1972. The *Financial Times* will appeal to 'those who make or influence decisions on business, finance and public affairs in the world'. Finally, my new tagline: it's time to return to the gold standard.*

---

* Return to the gold standard: a return to linking domestic currency supply to bullion holdings, last practised in 1971, was not what I had in mind. The metaphor turned into a watchword for quality during my editorship.

The applause is polite. A few colleagues come up and wish me well. I'm pumped and deadly serious, but ready to offer reassurances to the people I'm going to need in the coming weeks. One is Mark Alderson, a fine subeditor and production journalist who will later play a vital role in our transition to fully-fledged digital journalism.

'Don't worry,' I tell him, 'we're going to have fun.'

In the afternoon, I call Ben Bradlee, the legendary editor of the *Washington Post*. I was lucky enough to observe him in action in the summer of 1985 when I was a Laurence Stern fellow at the *Post*, an annual award for promising young British journalists. Barrel-chested, cocksure and impossibly handsome, he turned the *Post* from a provincial also-ran into a national must-read that ended up toppling President Nixon in the Watergate scandal. Like Harry Evans, he has been a mentor. Now I'm editor of the *FT*, both will be role models; brilliant newsmen but also journalists 'in the mix' with access to power and influence.

Any advice, Ben?

'Walk the floor,' he replies, in the familiar gravel tone made famous by Jason Robards in *All the President's Men*.

LB: 'Anything else?'

BB: 'The day you finish as editor, that's when you find out who your real friends are.'

There is life after editorship. The difference is people don't always return your calls.

WEDNESDAY, 16 NOVEMBER

My first meeting with Tony Blair in Downing Street. I've been doing some background reading on the Blair years, thanks to a colleague lending me a copy of *The Insider*, the private diaries of Piers Morgan, the roguish ex-editor of the *Daily Mirror* and *News of the World*. Piers appears to have enjoyed considerable sofa time with TB, a mildly incestuous relationship which later soured over the Iraq war. I had resolved to keep my distance from the government, but Downing Street called seeking a meeting within days of my appointment. Now I am sitting opposite Blair, flanked by his bald middle-aged PR flak-catcher Dave Hill.

LB: 'Thank you for seeing me, Prime Minister.'

TB: 'Call me Tony.'

LB: 'That's OK, Prime Minister.'

TB (persistent): 'Call me Tony . . . I mean, we *do* know each other.'

I remind the PM we've only met once before, in the summer of 1998 at the UK ambassador's residence in Brussels. Blair looks a tad deflated.

I ask the PM about the government's defeat in Parliament a few days ago when MPs voted down proposals to allow terrorist suspects to be held for 90 days without charge. Labour holds a 66-seat majority. This was the government's first Commons defeat. What went wrong? Blair says after eight years in power the Labour party has become 'ungovernable'.

TB: 'There are three camps. The hard left and disaffected; New Labour;* and the rest who are simply confused.'

LB: 'So where would you put Gordon Brown?'

---

* New Labour: the centre-left, pro-market moniker which helped Tony Blair and Gordon Brown return the Labour party to power in 1997 after 18 years in the wilderness. In 2015, after election defeat, Labour swung back to the old hard left under Jeremy Corbyn.

TB: 'He's New Labour, I think. At least, he says he is. You better ask him.'

No worries, Prime Minister, I'll be sure to do so at the first opportunity.

Blair turns to the *FT*. How much do I intend to change things? My first reaction: none of your goddamn business. My second response: play for time. I tell him the *FT* has a consensual culture. Any new editor needs to tread carefully.

'In that case,' says the architect of New Labour and three-time general election winner, 'you won't get anything done.'

Blair was dead wrong on invading Iraq, but on the FT *and change he's dead right.*

FRIDAY, 18 NOVEMBER

The editor's waterfront corner office overlooking the Thames feels like a railway station. People are streaming in and out, some auditioning for jobs, some appealing for clemency. David Bell suggested I ask every assistant editor for their resignation, allowing me a free hand to make the changes I want. I thought that was harsh, but in retrospect it would have been a good idea. Now I'm negotiating moves and exits individually, starting with Chrystia Freeland,* deputy editor under Andrew Gowers. She's agreed to go to New York to

---

* Chrystia Freeland's relentless energy took her from her remote home town of Peace River, Alberta to Harvard and Oxford. At the *FT*, she began as a stringer in Ukraine, rapidly rising to Moscow bureau chief, *FT Weekend* editor and deputy editor.

take my old job. That's something of a reprieve, but she's Canadian so North America is her chance to shine. The rest of the Gowers inner circle will either have to move to new jobs or leave.

The power to shape a newspaper through appointments is never greater than in those first few weeks and months. It's immensely satisfying but emotionally draining. The good news is that my top team is taking shape. I've been fishing around for a deputy and finally I've landed the right guy: Martin Dickson, a veteran *FT* financial editor and columnist. He's loyal and unthreatening, a class act who looks vaguely like Timothy Dalton in his (brief) role as James Bond. Martin was my first boss in March 1985 when I joined as a rookie business reporter. He tells me he's been disillusioned by the *FT*'s drift, but he's open to a new challenge – at a price. Locking in Martin as my deputy is a big boost, especially now I've picked Robert Shrimsley as my news editor after an audition which lasted barely ten minutes. I showed Robert a copy of the newspaper and asked what was wrong with it. He unerringly picked out sloppy headlines, captions and stories which had been underplayed. I gave him the job on the spot. Robert is my kind of newsman: a hard-nosed reporter with a great sense of humour. He's the finished article who just loves being a journalist, just like his illustrious father Anthony and his uncle Bernard, both national newspaper editors.

Gordon Brown calls seeking a meeting. Obviously, he's been tipped off about my conversation with the PM. I've known Gordon since my days as a cub reporter on the *Scotsman* in Edinburgh so our working relationship should be solid. That's assuming I don't find myself sandwiched between the prime minister and chancellor – along with the rest of the Cabinet.

WEDNESDAY, 23 NOVEMBER

A clandestine meeting with Terry Smith, the boss of Collins Stewart, the London stockbroking firm, which has sued the *FT* for libel. Heather McGregor, City headhunter and the *FT*'s 'Mrs Moneypenny' columnist, has brokered a meeting at her office in Queen Anne Street, Mayfair. Most *FT* colleagues have been dead against, fearing any contact would signal we're about to capitulate. Marjorie Scardino won't be happy either, but at this stage I'm keeping her out of the loop. This is primarily an editorial matter. I spent my first weekend examining the files and nothing about the case makes me comfortable. Our stories were based on the account of a former employee dismissed for misconduct. We assumed – wrongly – that some of our material was legally privileged. Smith warned us not to publish but we went ahead. More than two years on, and a mountain of legal correspondence later, we're facing a claim for damages amounting to £37m. Smith is an East End grammar school boy made good, a multimillionaire analyst who boxes in his spare time and loves taking a swing at the establishment. I'm intrigued by my opponent, wondering whether he will be susceptible to a bit of Barber charm.

Smith greets me courteously. He's about my age, trimly built and dressed in a suit and tie. Nothing flashy, understated if anything. He listens carefully to my opening arguments and protestations that I am the new guy who had nothing to do with the original story. Naturally, I tell him, the *FT* is prepared to make a contribution to his costs and to a charity of his own choosing. We are also prepared to publish an apology, subject to an agreement over the wording. Aside from the occasional grunt of disapproval, Smith says nothing. When I am finished, he stares at me and says: 'Bullshit!'

Terry has no interest in making a fresh start with a new editor. At one point, he compares himself to a medieval warlord laying siege to a castle, populated by *FT* journalists and Pearson executives. It might take days or even weeks but eventually he *will* starve everyone into submission. When the white flags are raised, he will enter the town, triumphant. 'And then, guess what I'll do, Lionel,' he says, fixing me again in the eye. 'I'll cut every one of your fucking heads off and stick them on poles.'

MONDAY, 12 DECEMBER

Cathy Newman's* leaving party at St Stephen's Tavern in Westminster. She is off to Channel 4. I spotted Cathy's talents when I was news editor and helped her to secure a Stern Fellowship at the *Washington Post*. She's a loss. So is Peter Spiegel, our defence correspondent. He is an ace reporter, an Arizona native who joined the *FT* as part of our American invasion force. Peter got all emotional in my office saying how sorry he was to leave. I want him back. *(It took five years but I got my man.)* These departures were in train well before I arrived but they are still a blow. *Somehow I have to stop taking them personally.*

FRIDAY, 16 DECEMBER

Olivier Fleurot's been pressing me for my plan to reorganise the newsroom, taking full advantage of our new editorial

---

* Cathy Newman, Channel 4 news anchor, formerly *FT* media and political correspondent.

publishing system. There's worrying talk about bringing in management consultants. *Over my dead body.* I promise Olivier to carry out an ambitious restructuring plan but decline to guarantee him specific job cuts. Now I need some advice on how to save money. Who better to turn to than Stan O'Neal, CEO of Merrill Lynch? Stan, the sharecropper's son from Alabama, took out $7.5bn in annual costs at Merrill after the dotcom crash.

I got to know Stan when I was in New York. When we meet in his downtown office overlooking the Hudson River, his advice is simple: don't bother cutting the little things like office potted plants and travel budgets, because 'it just pisses people off.' The only way to get real savings in an organisation is through structural change. Then hire an enforcer, someone who can be a lightning rod deflecting criticism from the leader/CEO.

'And one other thing,' warns deadpan Stan. 'The enforcer may not survive the process.'

2006

BUBBLE TROUBLE

TUESDAY, 3 JANUARY

From now on, the *Financial Times* will no longer be described just as a newspaper. The *FT* is a 'news organisation' working seamlessly in print and online. It isn't exactly poetry but it's my personal statement for 2006. The *FT* is too print-centric. I need a plan to drive digital transformation, and make it easily understood by the newsroom. Sir Howard Stringer,* an old friend and fellow rugby fan in New York, has offered me useful advice about communicating change in an organisation: 'You may think people are listening. They're not. You need to say the same thing over and over again. Finally, the message might sink in.'

The Collins Stewart libel case is proving a huge distraction. I've had three secret meetings with Terry Smith in Mrs Moneypenny's Mayfair office. If anything, he's hardened his position. Advised by Rod Christie-Miller at Schillings law firm, he wants a full-page apology, costs fully reimbursed

---

* Howard Stringer, a native Welshman and former head of CBS news, was the first executive from outside Japan to lead Sony, the Japanese electronics and entertainment giant.

and damages running into seven figures. When I talk about a new editor needing to protect his 'constituency' (my fellow *FT* journalists), he laughs in my face. Several times. Clearly, he doesn't think that's his problem.

Matters are turning complicated on our side, too. Lawyers are hedging their bets on the odds of winning in court. One of our reporters has been branded 'suggestible', a legal euphemism for naive. Another can't decipher his contemporaneous notes. Our insurers, initially supportive, are getting nervous. The trial date is just a fortnight away and now Pearson wants to get involved. 'There is a point when it is better for the *FT* to lose in court than apologise,' says one well-meaning executive. 'Maybe it's better to go down fighting.'

I'm all for occupying the moral high ground, but this is insane. Media reporters in Fleet Street are queuing up to cover a (likely) two-week court case where *FT* journalism will be on trial. Any half-decent QC will rip holes in our reporting and editing process. I am determined to instil a culture of excellence in the newsroom. But that's for the future. For now I'm acutely aware that even if we win on a defence of qualified privilege (a damned thin reed in libel cases), Terry Smith will not go away. The costs and negative publicity will skyrocket.

There's no option but to admit our mistakes and settle. Draw a line under the affair, rebuild trust with our City readers. How I persuade my colleagues (and Marjorie) is another matter. And I've still to agree terms and costs with El Tel.

WEDNESDAY, 4 JANUARY

Martin Dickson drops by my office. He reports that Sir James Crosby, chief executive of HBOS, the high-flying UK retail bank, has announced he's stepping down in six months. His replacement will be Andy Hornby, a 38-year-old former executive at Asda, the UK grocer.

Crosby, 49, led the merger of Halifax building society and Bank of Scotland in 2001 to create HBOS. This stodgy combination turned into a high street bank on steroids. Crosby presided over a breakneck expansion in lending and, latterly, a doubling of profits. If everything is going swimmingly, why is Crosby calling it quits? 'Something does not add up,' says Martin.

How right he was! Crosby exited at the top of the market. His successor Hornby was ill-equipped to deal with the aftermath. So was the board, led by Sir Dennis Stevenson, until recently chairman of Pearson. This was no conspiracy of silence on our part. We simply missed the story because we lacked curiosity, the essential quality in a reporter.

HBOS's rapid growth was based on access to the wholesale markets rather than customer deposits. When the credit crunch took hold, the bank blew up and had to be rescued by Lloyds Bank and a government bailout. In 2009, Crosby was censured in a Bank of England report, and later forfeited his knighthood and part of his pension.

MONDAY, 16 JANUARY

The deal is done. After a weekend of brutal haggling, replete with four-letter words, I have agreed terms of a settlement with Terry Smith. There's no full-page apology, which would have been a humiliation. But the rest is painful to swallow. We're paying him £300,000 in damages and legal costs of £2.2m. Added to our own slightly lower legal costs, that's a total bill of more than £4m, thankfully mostly covered by our insurers. And we're publishing an apology making clear we never endorsed the allegations against Collins Stewart made by its former employee, James Middleweek.*

Our lawyers are now saying they're disappointed we did not test our case in court. Really? A legal battle was always high-risk and this was not my story to defend at all costs. I want to open a new chapter with higher standards in the newsroom, starting with the appointment of our own in-house lawyer.† I've also ordered an audit of all corrections published in the paper and a repeat instruction that every story in future must be based on two independent sources. No more sloppiness and excuses. This is about getting a grip. That's my job as editor.

TUESDAY, 17 JANUARY

I've been so bound up with the Terry Smith affair that I plain forgot my first lunch at MI5, with its imposing director Dame Eliza Manningham-Buller. En route by taxi, I'm reading a background note from my reporter-colleague Jimmy Burns. He says relations have been strained since Dame Eliza came to lunch for an off-the-record session and found

---

* In 2010, Terry Smith set up his own fund management firm – Fundsmith. He moved to Mauritius, managing a highly successful business from his house and his boat, aptly named *Thunderer*. Terry also became a good friend and fellow cyclist.

† The decision to appoint an in-house lawyer at the *FT*, latterly Nigel Hanson, was one of the best decisions of my editorship.

herself portrayed in the *FT* as 'Person in the News' a few days later.*

Stephen Fidler, a veteran reporter, is accompanying me on a mission to restore diplomatic relations. As we step out of the taxi, the surroundings appear unfamiliar. Stephen approaches the entrance and announces that the *FT* has arrived to have lunch with the director.

Security guard (baffled): 'Lunch with who . . . ?'

Fidler: 'Dame Eliza Manningham-Buller.'

Security guard: 'We don't have anybody under that name.'

Fidler (baffled): 'You must have. She's the director.'

Security guard: 'I'm afraid this is MI6, Sir – not MI5.'

My instinct is to fire Fidler on the spot. But we're already running late and until now he's been a rock-solid reporter. A taxi ferries us from Vauxhall across the Thames to MI5 headquarters near Millbank.

Barely six months have passed since the 7/7 suicide bombings in London, but the shock lingers.† 'Home-grown' terrorists are a new phenomenon. They operate in fluid cells rather than the hardened 'dartboard' structure of the IRA, the old enemy. Lunch offers insights on the current threat level and the security services' response. There's a lot of acronyms such as AQ (Al-Qaeda) and CBN (chemical, biological and nuclear weapons). I had little notion of the pressure on MI5 resources, especially the numbers required

---

* 'Person in the News': a profile slot in the Saturday features pages, accompanied by a sometimes less than flattering caricature, is reserved for the biggest mover and shaker of the week – or, occasionally, for a Villain in the News.

† The bombings on 7 July 2005 on the London public transport system were the most deadly terrorist attack on British soil, killing 52.

for round-the-clock surveillance of suspects. By the end, I feel reassured by Manningham-Buller's stern professionalism, leavened by an impish humour. On leaving, I spot a copy of *Private Eye* discreetly placed on a table outside the dining room.

WEDNESDAY, 8 FEBRUARY

Sir Fred Goodwin has dropped in for lunch, along with his top team at Royal Bank of Scotland. There's something bloodless about this ex-chartered accountant from Paisley. He's pale, with short, prematurely grey hair – a man hell-bent on building RBS into the biggest bank in the world.

My reaction is half-admiration, half-disbelief. Back in 1980–81, as a cub reporter on the *Scotsman* in Edinburgh, I revealed the secret (and ultimately successful) plan by Scottish nationalists to block the takeover of RBS by Hongkong & Shanghai Bank, later abbreviated to HSBC.* It was my first big break as a journalist. When I mention my (inflated) contribution to the independence of Scotland's premier bank, Goodwin looks supremely uninterested. He recites instead the litany of RBS acquisitions: the takeover of National Westminster Bank, followed by a string of regional banks in the US, all accompanied by ruthless cost-cutting which has earned him the nickname 'Fred the Shred'.†

As a parting gesture, the banking titan with the tartan tie

---

* Hongkong and Shanghai's hostile bid for Royal Bank in 1980 was opposed by Scottish politicians and the Bank of England and later blocked by UK competition authorities as against the public interest.

† After the 2000 hostile £22 billion takeover of NatWest, three times its size, RBS briefly became the largest bank in the world. In 2008, after the financial crisis, it received one of the biggest taxpayer bailouts on record.

invites me to tour RBS's new headquarters at Gogarburn near Edinburgh airport, a 78-acre campus opened by the queen last September. *I later paid a visit to talk to senior RBS bankers but unaccountably failed to check out Sir Fred's office's gold carpet and the private jet sitting on the tarmac.*

TUESDAY, 21 FEBRUARY

My mission to repair relations with the movers and shakers in British business is gaining momentum. Breakfasts, lunches and dinners have been booked for bankers, traders and assorted City professionals. Now comes the hard part: lunch with Sir Terry Leahy, long-serving CEO of Tesco, the UK retail giant.

Tesco has just unveiled the biggest gamble of Leahy's career: a $250m down payment on a bid to break into the US convenience-store market, starting with California and the western states. Leahy hopes his legacy will be Tesco's transformation into a truly global player. Tesco has moved into Poland, Thailand and South Korea; but America has traditionally been a graveyard for British high-street retailers like Marks & Spencer and WH Smith. And Tesco will have to take on the toughest competitor of all: Walmart.

Lucy Neville-Rolfe, Tesco's chief of PR and government relations, has insisted I travel to Tesco headquarters in Cheshunt, an hour's train ride from London Bridge. En route, I ponder how to handle Leahy, a prickly Liverpudlian who has little time for journalists.

Our lunch takes place in the no-frills staff restaurant with Tesco food and self-service. Leahy proudly shows off his latest range of ready-made dishes before probing the *FT*'s commitment to covering business 'seriously'. I bang on about mixing with hard-boiled capitalists like Lloyd Blankfein and Jamie Dimon.* Leahy is unmoved. His manner is mildly intimidating: soft voice, plenty of pauses and lots of blank stares. He's waiting for me to fill the silence – the oldest power play in the book.

On the train back to London, I feel deflated. As an emissary bearing the message of a new *FT*, I half succeeded. As a journalist, I've failed the basic test of a good reporter: get the subject talking. I came away with little information or insight into Tesco's US venture, Leahy's management style or his succession plan. Memo to self: all future 'power lunches' must generate tips or stories.

Tesco's expansion in the US under the Fresh & Easy brand proved to be a £1bn disaster. Leahy was a force in British retailing but he mismanaged his succession, underestimated the threat of online retailers like Amazon and bet the company on hubristic American expansion.

FRIDAY, 3 MARCH

Jimmy Cayne, the CEO of Bear Stearns and one of the wealthiest financiers in America, has come to the *FT* for breakfast. We're in the Bracken room, the boardroom named after Winston Churchill's Irish-born consigliere and founder of the modern *Financial Times*.†

---

* Lloyd Blankfein, chairman and CEO, Goldman Sachs (2006–18); Jamie Dimon, chairman and CEO, JPMorgan Chase (2005–).

† As Minister of Information, Brendan Bracken was Churchill's top wartime propagandist. He is said to have inspired the brash and dynamic Rex

With its spectacular view of the old Square Mile* over-looking the Thames, the Bracken room is the ideal reception for power-players like Cayne, a lugubrious 72-year-old and a paper billionaire, thanks to his stock in Bear. Today, he cannot stop raving about London. Great food, great people, great place to make money. This is his first trip in ages. He can't believe how much has changed.

Cayne is one of the scrappiest operators on Wall Street, a man who always has one eye on Bear's share price on the Bloomberg terminal on his desk. He likes his routine: a cigar in the office, a few rounds of bridge at the tables in Detroit and Las Vegas (he's a world-class player). His happy-go-lucky behaviour at breakfast was curiously out of character.

Cayne's appearance in the Bracken room was in hindsight a giveaway. He had come late to the credit party. One year later, Bear collapsed, the first domino to fall in the global financial crisis.

TUESDAY, 7 MARCH

My regular weekly breakfast with Olivier Fleurot, our French CEO. I like his good humour and methodical approach to business. Olivier has always been a champion of charging for content. Like me, he does not believe that 'information wants to be free' – a glib observation, usually parroted by columnists who want to use the internet to attract a bigger audience,

Mottram in Evelyn Waugh's *Brideshead Revisited*. Bracken piloted the 1945 merger of the *Financial News* and the *Financial Times*.
* The Square Mile is synonymous with the old City of London financial district with modern skyscrapers towering over medieval alleyways.

maximising their personal reach with no return to their employer.

We agree the best way forward is to build the *FT*'s subscription business. Right now, online subs have stalled around 80,000, while the newspaper still accounts for circulation of more than 400,000, albeit in a shrinking market where the costs of printing and distribution are fixed and advertising is in decline. Our business model, we agree but cannot say, is no longer fit for purpose.

Olivier is pressing me for budget savings based on the introduction of the new publishing system. My response is 'The New Newsroom' which will streamline workflows in print and online. That's a job for Dan Bogler, a slightly humourless Anglo-German who will be my enforcer on this initiative.* Dan will have to spend weeks consulting with the union, but ultimately 50 jobs need to go, reducing editorial numbers to just above 500 journalists. No compulsory redundancies, just 'agreed departures'. In return, I want a budget to hire a handful of star writers and reporters. People like Gideon Rachman† of *The Economist* who will have *impact* (my new favourite word). Content will drive value. Value will drive subscriptions.

Olivier appears satisfied. His relationship with Andrew Gowers was strained. He didn't have confidence in the editor and the editor didn't have confidence in him. I've vowed to be an agent of change and a credible partner for Olivier and the board. As long as they stay out of my knickers – in Marjorie Scardino's phrase – this will be a marriage made in heaven.

---

* As managing editor, Dan Bogler was my right-hand man for budget and personnel in the newsroom.

† Gideon Rachman, chief foreign affairs commentator of the *FT* (2006–), one of the most versatile and humorous writers in the business.

THURSDAY, 20 APRIL

One of my 'transformational hires' is Paul Murphy of the *Guardian*, a business journalist with a network of contacts nurtured over many years in City restaurants and watering holes. Initially I offered him a newspaper column, but he said he was only interested in web-based journalism. At my request, Paul has produced an excellent note on editorial strategy in the age of the internet.

> *Paul's memo laid the foundation for the groundbreaking financial blog* FT Alphaville. *But it also encouraged a step change in my thinking. In the past,* FT *journalists would hand out tablets of stone, like Moses, to a receptive audience. But, increasingly, the news business was 'democratising'. Readers could answer back. Our job as expert curators and editors would remain vital. But, in the future, we would use technology to engage* FT *readers as never before, thereby driving subscriptions onward and upward.*

FRIDAY, 28 APRIL

To Rome for a flying visit to attend the 50th birthday party of Alan Friedman,* former *FT* foreign correspondent turned TV celebrity in Italy. We've known each other for 20 years,

---

* Alan Friedman, best-selling author and TV personality, formerly *FT* Milan and New York correspondent. Based in Italy, he straddled the line between journalism and business, sometimes awkwardly. After 2006, Friedman worked controversially for Najib Razak's government in Malaysia and with US super-lobbyist Paul Manafort to help bolster Viktor Yanukovich, Ukraine's president.

having worked together on investigations including illegal US arms sales to Saddam Hussein's Iraq. Alan is prone to conspiracy theories and at times plays a little fast and loose with the *actualité*; but he's always great fun. His top-floor apartment in a palazzo on the Via Giulia is a monument to late 20th-century decadence, full of monstrous art, extravagant, colourful furniture and beautiful people, all swimming in a sea of alcohol.

As I am preparing to dress appropriately for the evening's entertainment, my mobile phone rings. It is David Bell. He's proved a useful bridge-builder and guide in my first months, but he's always within an inch of meddling, despite the usual disclaimer 'You must do what you think fit', followed by the inevitable 'but if I were in your shoes, which of course I'm not . . .' Tonight, David is lobbying on behalf of James Harding who has apparently been unsettled by the change in editor and the rush of senior appointments.

Harding is a Bell protégé, a good reporter who oozes charm. He has left his job as DC bureau chief and is on book leave. What am I supposed to be offering him? David says James wants a place at the top table and the news editor job is very appealing. Well, that's not a runner. Robert Shrimsley is my man. I commit to a conversation with James. My suspicion is he's finished with the *FT* and already looking to the next rung on the ladder.

James soon left the FT *to become business editor of* The Times. *In late 2007, he was appointed editor of* The Times *until he was sacked by Rupert Murdoch in 2012. He then became head of news at the BBC before embarking on a new media venture called Tortoise, an odd title for someone who's always approached life as something of a Hare.*

FRIDAY, 12 MAY

Roula Khalaf, our long-time Middle East editor, has asked to see me. She's been practising 'strategic patience', waiting for six months for a one-on-one audience with the new editor. Roula was born in Lebanon. She knows all about political intrigue and survival. 'What is your plan?' she asks me.

Well, I do have a plan for further reshuffling the top ranks but I'm not sharing, yet. Roula is definitely someone to watch.

MONDAY, 15 MAY

A management shake-up at the *FT* and at Pearson which oversees our operation. Olivier Fleurot is out, replaced by John Ridding, previously *FT* Asia editor and chairman of Pearson Asia. I've known John for 15 years. We can work together. I'm sorry about Olivier, who clearly didn't see this coming. We shared a passion for sport and a commitment to make the *FT* the most trusted business news organisation in the world. Olivier stopped the losses and steadied the ship. He loved working for *Le FT*. His departure seems to have been driven in part by internal Pearson politics.

John Ridding will report to Rona Fairhead, a potential successor to Marjorie Scardino. Rona, until now chief financial officer at Pearson, is coming in as CEO of a revived entity called FT Group with a mandate to make acquisitions. My sole concern is maintaining my reporting line to Marjorie as proprietor and now John Ridding on day-to-day matters and the budget. Rona does not come into the equation. *On that point I'm immovable.*

THURSDAY, 18 MAY

Lunch at the Bank of England with the governor, Mervyn King. It's my first serious encounter with King and we bond rapidly over our mutual interest in cricket. The governor is wearing a dark suit and tie, formal City attire in the marbled splendour of the Bank. In the summer, he turns out in flannels as an artful left-arm spin bowler, a sprightly 58-year-old still capable of claiming scalps. King also prides himself on his elegant prose, often using sporting metaphors which deflect attention from his status as an unabashed intellectual, a brilliant, if occasionally prickly economist who has taught at Harvard, MIT and the London School of Economics. Lunch soon turns into a tutorial on our extraordinary financial times.

For most of his lifetime, King says, the most important challenge facing central bankers and policy-makers was the scourge of inflation. More recently, the world has experienced the 'Great Moderation'. China and India have massively increased the supply of labour available to industry around the world. Labour-intensive goods have become more abundant and also cheaper. 'China has exported deflation to the rest of the world.'

This is a new paradigm of sorts. Inflation appears to have been tamed.

'What could possibly go wrong?' asks King, peering mischievously across the white tablecloth at me through his spectacles.

I am lost for an answer.

The governor had earlier provided an answer, flagging concerns about the fall in long-term interest rates and 'global imbalances'

between countries with a propensity to save (China and Germany)
and those with a propensity to spend (the UK and the US).*

TUESDAY, 30 MAY

Hank Paulson, somewhere in the sky en route to Washington, calls from his private jet to tell me he's accepted President Bush's offer to nominate him as US treasury secretary. Paulson, 61, is one tough hombre, a devout Christian who has run Goldman Sachs for the past seven years and escapes on bird-watching trips on the weekend.† I can barely hear his husky voice over the roar of jet engines, but we promise to keep in touch.

Paulson is adapting the old Goldman maxim of being the first client of choice for the rich and powerful. Once installed as US treasury secretary, he wants to use the *FT* as a means of communicating to an influential worldwide audience. But his phone call also signals my own personal invitation to *access power*. In future, I should be able to see him in Washington, host him in London or talk to him on the phone. Having an ever expanding group of high-level contacts like Paulson – real power-players – will prove a vital part of my editorship.

Taking the *FT* to the top of the premier division, I'm

---

* Speech in Ashford, Kent, 16 January 2006. However, King had yet to connect the dots between the dispersal of risk through sophisticated financial instruments, the 'search for yield' and the general expansion of money and credit driving asset prices up and interest rates down. The word 'bankers' never came up in our conversation.

† Hank Paulson would prove an inspired choice in the financial crisis. He had an instinctive feel for markets and excellent high-level contacts in China, though he was open to criticism that he was too close to Goldman.

starting to understand, is not just about nuts and bolts – great reporting, intrepid investigations, majestic commentary. It's also about being 'in the mix', meeting and dining with the movers and shakers, detecting the big economic, financial and political trends. That's what Ben Bradlee did every night in Washington, holding forth with senators, Supreme Court justices, even presidents. I'm no Bradlee and Marjorie Scardino is more Kay Graham-lite. But as editor I reckon I *can* make a difference, by encouraging the powerful – and, yes, the damned – to pay attention to me and, by extension, the *FT*.

FRIDAY, 16 JUNE

A mid-term report from the *UK Press Gazette* on my term as editor delivers a B grade. That's better than the C+ handed out to the editors of the *Daily Telegraph* and *Daily Mirror* and matches Simon Kelner, the experienced editor of the *Independent*. The *Press Gazette* notes the cost of the Terry Smith settlement and our return to (notional) profit. Concluding verdict: 'Lionel is a very serious individual who could possibly lighten up a little, but his teachers have been very impressed at the way he schmoozes around the newsroom.'

The good news is the FT *is no longer seen as a failing product. The bad news is that, eight months into the job, I've yet to put my stamp on the paper. Memo to self: we need a big story. With impact. Before year's end.*

MONDAY, 19 JUNE

Sir Martin Sorrell is the suitor who never takes no for an answer. Night or day, Shanghai or Seattle, he's always pitching for business, via email, text or phone call, a man in perpetual motion, always looking for an edge for his clients – and himself.

Sorrell took a controlling stake in Wire and Plastic Products, a British wire shopping basket manufacturer in 1985 shortly after I joined the *FT*. Through a spate of bold acquisitions, he built WPP into the biggest advertising agency in the world, a tribute to his single-minded pursuit of fame, influence and wealth. One of his many ad agencies has now joined a 'beauty parade' auditioning to design the *FT*'s new brand campaign highlighting a fresher, sharper newspaper. Sorrell tells me we would be mad to drop the iconic slogan 'No *FT*, no comment'. I'm not so sure. 'No *FT*, no comment' sounds stuffy and supercilious; it's more than 20 years old and it doesn't translate for an international audience, something I am determined to grow during my tenure.

WPP failed to win the mandate. Sorrell was miffed but we moved on. Over the years, we enjoyed a 'push-me, pull-you' relationship, swapping gossip about people in media and politics. Then, in 2018, Martin Sorrell's world fell apart and I found myself present at the implosion.

THURSDAY, 29 JUNE

An embossed invitation from the All England Lawn Tennis Club arrives in the editor's office. Two seats in the Royal Box at Wimbledon. Does this fall under an improper benefit in kind? Surely that would be a smoked-salmon sandwich too far. Victoria and I are long-standing tennis fans, regularly attending the US Open during our stint in New York.

Victoria has magnanimously handed over her seat to our daughter as a high school graduation present. We are greeted by RAF staff and escorted upstairs to drinks and lunch. We scour the room for celebrities, but this year most of the guests are businessmen, serving military commanders and a smattering of Fleet Street editors. Strawberries and cream, champagne and chocolates are available on demand. The tennis is eminently watchable. No pangs of guilt about being away from the office. The goodie bag features white chocolate and an All England lapel badge.

The Royal Box invitation became a highlight of the year, a chance to schmooze during a great sporting occasion. As long as Roger Federer was on Centre Court, Victoria was happy.

FRIDAY, 14 JULY

The first pitch for a new marketing campaign to accompany our planned 'rebrush' of the *FT* is from DDB advertising agency in London. Stephen Woodford, the tall, blond, tieless CEO, is no 'Mad Man'. He's cool, slightly detached and prepared to listen. I tell him the *FT* is far bigger (and better) than 'Britain's business newspaper'. I want us to be 'the paper of globalisation'. Woodford and his team get the message. From that opening exchange a new marketing slogan will be born: 'We Live In Financial Times'.

MONDAY, 7 AUGUST

A big story has broken overnight in Alaska. BP says it is shutting down its Prudhoe Bay oil field, the largest in North America. Tests ordered by regulators have discovered 'severe corrosion' in the pipeline. As Sheila McNulty, our Houston correspondent, writes: 'The shutdown is embarrassing for the UK oil major which has been attempting to portray a March spill – the largest ever at Prudhoe Bay – as a one-off and not indicative of the state of the Alaska field.'

For several months, Sheila has been hearing, via union sources, that BP has a safety problem in the US. We've nibbled but failed to nail the story – an outcome all too common over the last few years. I order Sheila to work exclusively on an investigation, starting with the explosion at BP's Texas City terminal in 2005 which killed 15 and injured an estimated 500 people. I'm determined this will be our marquee business story of 2006.

TUESDAY, 5 SEPTEMBER

After a four-year absence in New York, the family has moved back into our house in south London. My own daily routine has also settled by now. A car arrives at 7.10am for the 35-minute journey to the *FT* headquarters on Southwark Bridge. The car initially seemed like a luxury – I used to bike to work – but I need time to read and think ahead of the 12- to 15-hour day ahead. Once in the office, I head for the sixth-floor staff canteen for porridge or oat bran with a cup of Assam tea, followed by a cappuccino or caffè latte as I read the news.

By 9.30am, I've read the *FT*, *Wall Street Journal*, *The Times*, the *Guardian* and the *Daily Telegraph* – and browsed the web to check the *New York Times*, the *Washington Post* and Bloomberg. By now I'm ready for the 10.30am news conference, my chance to engage in a bit of theatre and to shape coverage over the next day. Like Ben Bradlee, whom I watched in action every night at the *Washington Post*, I always try to single out people or stories for praise and bring two or three ideas for stories of my own, only rarely mentioning the competition. Public moaning is a morale-sapper; in private that's another matter.

The work hours are physically draining, and I've found staying fit is a crucial part of the job so I block out an hour of gym time twice a week. The highlight is a 4km run, with a personal goal of running under 18 minutes. Abandoning the run — which only happens after a late night out — I count as a personal failure.

TUESDAY, 19 SEPTEMBER

Black-tie dinner at the Banqueting House in Whitehall for the board of AIG, the American insurance giant. Back in January 1649, after the end of the Civil War, Charles I was beheaded on a nearby scaffold. Tonight I'm witness to a coronation — not an execution. Martin Sullivan, the silver-haired Essex boy made good, is hosting a dinner to mark more than a year in office as AIG president and chief executive. He succeeded Maurice 'Hank' Greenberg, an industry legend forced out in 2005 after an accounting scandal. Sullivan, an insurance industry lifer, is being feted as one of Britain's most successful businessmen in America. When I met him in New York, he looked like an improbable successor to Greenberg, the seemingly indestructible hero on Utah beach during the Normandy landings. Sullivan accepts my congratulations with a broad grin. For the son of a foreman at the Ford plant in Dagenham who left school at 16, it doesn't get much better than tonight.

This was peak AIG. Almost two years to the day later the insurance giant collapsed, culminating in a government bailout costing $182bn. The fatal flaw was a series of credit derivative contracts of more than $1 trillion. When Goldman Sachs made billions of dollars of collateral calls after the Lehman Brothers collapse, AIG went down. Sullivan, who was an insurance man not a capital markets expert, later claimed he had no idea about Goldman's demands until after the event.*

27 SEPTEMBER–8 OCTOBER

At the start of my editorship, I made a personal vow not to travel overseas, bar visiting my family in New York. It was important to remain in London, establishing myself as a leader determined to recreate a culture of excellence on the ground at the *FT* office. Almost one year on, I feel confident enough to venture abroad to spend ten days in India. Victoria will join me on what an envious rival calls my 'proconsular visit'. These trips overseas would become an annual routine. True, there was always the risk of the editor 'bigfooting' colleagues. Against that, my job title opened doors and the trips offered a chance to work with local correspondents, promote the *FT*'s brand and, hopefully, produce some great journalism.

This will be my first trip to India, a chance to glimpse the economic transformation of the subcontinent first hand. Jo Johnson, younger brother of Boris Johnson, is our bureau chief in New Delhi. He's polished and well connected, an

---

* Financial Crisis Inquiry Commission interview with Martin Sullivan, 7 June 2010

ambitious 35-year-old often described as the real brains in the Johnson clan.*

Jo has drawn up a mouth-watering schedule which balances high-level business and political appointments with cultural and social delights. We'll be dropping in to see Manmohan Singh, the Indian technocrat prime minister in his official residence at 7 Race Course Road. We're also visiting the Taj Mahal in Rajasthan, touring Mughal temples and spending a night in Jaipur. Then on to Mumbai for meetings with a handful of billionaires, headed by the feuding Ambani brothers.

My warm-up meeting is with P. Chidambaram, the bumptious, Harvard-educated finance minister from Tamil Nadu. His opening words are a flattering endorsement of the *Financial Times* as a global business newspaper. I'll take the compliment, albeit with a counterpunch: 'Well, minister . . . it's a pity we're not allowed to print the *FT* in India *(because of a dispute over our trademark)*. If we could print, you'd be able to read all the news in the *FT* on the same day.'

Chidambaram takes my cheeky rejoinder in his stride. He's chipper about the economy's stellar growth rates – 8.9 per cent in the second quarter. India appears to be on a roll.

A more nuanced picture emerges after our interview with the Indian PM. Singh is a softly spoken Sikh, a Cambridge-educated economist who moved to Oxford for his doctorate. There he became lifelong friends with Martin Wolf, our chief economics commentator. In the early 1990s, Singh, then finance minister, dismantled the command economy,

---

* Jo earned a first-class honours degree in Modern History at Balliol College, Oxford. Boris, a fellow Balliol graduate, fell short with a second.

unleashing a period of sustained growth. Now he's pressing for a second round of reforms in the financial sector to boost support for infrastructure, India's Achilles heel. But left-wingers in his ruling Congress party are putting the brakes on.

'Politics is the art of the possible and I have to live with the situation I inherited,' says the serene PM. 'There have been difficulties [with the left] but I have not given up hope. We've only completed half the term.'

After dinner, Victoria and I go out for a midnight walking tour in Old Delhi. When she first broached the idea in London, the *FT* was opposed on the grounds it was too dangerous. Tonight, we head off with a surly driver who says little and sticks to the main roads. All of a sudden, he stops the car and declares it is safe to get out.

The night air is steamy. Sleeping bodies litter the pavements. Our guide takes us to his favourite restaurant, one of several still open. He insists the food is fresh and tasty, but we're not keen on eating and confine ourselves to jasmine tea. After a 25-minute stroll, it's time to go home. En route back to the hotel, our driver points to a spot where a Muslim was hanged a few days before. Only then do we discover that he's a Muslim too, a belated explanation for why he was so reluctant to move off the main road into the Hindi backstreets. These are life-and-death decisions in India.

After a day in Bangalore, India's Silicon Valley, we fly to Mumbai, financial centre, heart of the Bollywood film industry and India's most populous city. First sight is the Mumbai slums, later immortalised by Katherine Boo in her book *Behind the Beautiful Forevers*. The gap between abject poverty in the urban ghetto and the naked opulence of India's merchant class is hard to reconcile. Over the next four days, the assault on the senses – sight, smell, taste, touch – is invigorating, if overwhelming. Never in my life have I seen so many people.

Early one morning, Jo and I clamber into a helicopter owned by Anil Ambani, billionaire chairman of Reliance Group, the telecoms-to-financial-services conglomerate, to take a trip over the bay to his James Bond-style corporate headquarters. As the helicopter banks left, the vast metropolis moves into full view. I look nervously at Jo who gives me an 'aw shucks' look, as if to say it won't be his fault if anything untoward should happen mid-flight.

As the helicopter nestles on a landing pad, I spot the thickset figure of Anil Ambani waiting for us. Months earlier, after the intervention of their mother, the brothers Ambani divided the estate of their father Dhirubhai, a one-time yarn trader who founded Reliance Industries and became one of India's most powerful tycoons. Anil won't talk about the feud with his brother Mukesh, but he makes it pretty clear he thinks he got the better part of the deal, especially with his stake in the mobile telecoms business.

How wrong he was! Anil took the glamorous parts of Reliance, but Mukesh built up the industrial side before making a daring multi-billion-dollar move into mobile phones, under the brand Jio. Anil's empire slowly crumbled before he was forced into a fire sale, coupled with a financial rescue by his elder brother, whom I would meet on several occasions on his path to becoming one of the world's richest men. By 2019, Anil's net worth had fallen from $50bn to a point in February 2019 where he claimed he was broke. On his way down, he sued numerous Indian publications and the FT over negative coverage. His libel suit against the FT was dropped just before I stepped down as editor.

THURSDAY, 19 OCTOBER

To the Oxford Union to debate the motion 'This House believes the tabloids run the country'. Back 30 years ago, when I was a student, the Oxford Union was the hang-out for the soon-to-be-powerful and those who had already made it to the top. Fresh-faced undergraduates like me swooned in front of Benazir Bhutto.* Tonight, I am greeted by students, each eager to polish their CVs and build their networks. It's my first experience of a live debate and I'm curiously short of breath.

'Ladies and gentlemen, I come before you as a man of print, not the spoken word' – self-deprecating humour which achieves the most important goal in public speaking: get the audience onside, early. Adam Boulton, Sky News anchor, and Simon Kelner, editor of the *Independent*, join me in opposing the motion. Denis MacShane, ex-Fleet Street journalist and union activist, Labour MP and junior minister, leads the defence. They lost, we won.

The assumption that successive British governments were held hostage by tabloids like the Sun *and the* Daily Mail *was common currency in Blair's Britain. The role of phone-hacking in obtaining 'dirt' on politicians had yet to be fully exposed. In reality, tabloid circulation was in terminal decline. The motion was revealing in another way. It foreshadowed the 'fake news' debate a decade later, underlining how young people had lost confidence in mainstream media and were increasingly gathering information online.*

---

* Benazir Bhutto, daughter of Pakistan's leader in the 1970s and former president of the Oxford Union, became the first woman to be elected the Muslim nation's prime minister.

WEDNESDAY, 22 NOVEMBER

Angela Ahrendts, CEO of Burberry, one of Britain's top fashion retailers, has asked to see me for a one-on-one. For the past few months, Burberry's PR advisers Brunswick have been pestering us about our coverage. Burberry hates our constant references to the popularity of its trademark camel check among so-called chavs. I was unfamiliar with the term until a colleague explained it was a pejorative description of people of limited means who are obsessed with brand names, cheap jewellery and football.

I'm sympathetic but don't want to be viewed as a push-over. Ahrendts, an elegant American from the Midwest, has been joined by Susan Gilchrist, a top Brunswick executive. I've nothing against Susan, but two's company and three's a crowd. Irritated, I undertake to look into the chav matter. On the way out, Ahrendts asks me if anything is wrong. Well, I prefer talking to principals directly, I tell her. She gives an undertaking that all future meetings will be one-on-one, without minders. They were.

As editor, I always tried to avoid PR people mediating between me and the powerful. A small number could be a useful bridge to CEOs, helping me to prepare for an interview or the occasional bollocking. Too many were no more than suits. Angela Ahrendts was a useful guide to retail trends and management before she moved to Apple where she was kept well under wraps.

MONDAY, 11 DECEMBER

To Stephanie Flanders and John Arlidge's annual Christmas party in west London. Earlier this year, I tried to poach

Stephanie from the BBC. The offer was to run the *FT*'s opinion and commentary. She would have been in charge of big *FT* brands like Martin Wolf, John Gapper and our new foreign affairs commentator Gideon Rachman. But she wanted to stick to a TV career. Stephanie worked for us a decade ago, and she would have been an ideal fit for the new *FT*. Of all the people I tried to hire this year, she was the one that got away.

THURSDAY, 14 DECEMBER

My soon-to-be-regular quarterly lunch with Marjorie in her office at Pearson headquarters in the art deco Shell Mex House, next to the Savoy hotel overlooking the Thames. Our meal at 80 Strand is a chance to share worries, swap gossip and talk about my own performance, invariably with the same abstemious menu: salad, fruit dessert and mint tea. My first full year as editor has passed all too quickly, but there's plenty to be proud of. We've taken the first steps towards the digital transformation of the newsroom. We've also sharpened our journalism, summed up by our (later award-winning) investigation of BP's lamentable safety record in the US. Being editor of the *FT* is a huge privilege, and I intend to make the most of every minute in the job.

CREDIT CRUNCH

'We live in Financial Times', our new marketing slogan, was more revealing than we ever imagined. The world was living through the 'Wile E. Coyote moment' when everyone was rushing to access cheap credit, oblivious to impending disaster.* Easy credit had led to all sorts of aberrant behaviour, exacerbated by flawed regulation and valuation models. A reckoning was due. The only issue was the timing.

MONDAY, 15 JANUARY

Gillian Tett's nickname at the *FT* is 'the Tett offensive'. When she spots a story, she's unstoppable. A former PhD in social anthropology at Cambridge, she took a course which, she often reminds us, included studying goatherds in Tajikistan. As capital markets editor of the *FT*, her speciality is talking to 'geeks', people trading in exotic financial instruments whose value is determined by complex mathematical

---

* Wile E. Coyote, hapless antagonist of the Road Runner in Chuck Jones's iconic Looney Tunes cartoons. The scheming coyote famously does not fall until he looks down and sees that he's run off a cliff.

risk modelling. Today she's reporting disturbing developments in the credit markets.

Gillian's article zeroes in on a subject I've barely heard of: collateralised debt obligations (CDOs). She cites one eye-popping statistic: total CDOs in global credit markets are believed to have topped $2,500bn in 2006. These financial instruments allow one asset – like a mortgage loan – to be used and reused many times over to create new trading and hedging opportunities. 'A small amount of sugar spun into a huge cone of candy floss,' she explains.

Something else caught my eye. Northern Rock, the 150-year-old high-street lender, is increasing its lending by 20 per cent a year. The UK bank, once a nondescript building society based in Newcastle upon Tyne, is issuing mortgage-backed bonds on a vast scale. At a glitzy dinner at a Mayfair hotel, Gillian reports, Northern Rock grabbed the prize of 'best financial borrower'. Apparently this means being the most creative in raising funds.

Creative. An interesting use of the word.

TUESDAY, 16 JANUARY

Still savouring last night's performance at the Gielgud theatre of *Frost/Nixon* by Peter Morgan, later turned into a movie by Ron Howard. Michael Sheen is delicious as Frost, Frank Langella suitably sinister (and vulnerable) as Nixon. Frost's interview technique made him special. He was a great listener, always interested in other people. That could easily be mistaken for modesty. Frost once told me he felt very proud that the chosen title for both movie and play was *Frost/Nixon*. Not vice versa.

23–27 JANUARY

To Davos, the annual schmoozefest for the world's elite in business, finance and politics. Davos Man *(and they are largely men)* has long been the *FT*'s natural audience. This is my second trip as editor and I've lined up meetings with the world's top bankers, starting with Dick Fuld, chairman and CEO of Lehman Brothers.

Fuld took over at Lehman in 1994 and is the longest-serving CEO on Wall Street. He's survived mergers, spin-offs and the 1998 Asian financial crisis. A big man with jet-black hair and a beak, Fuld cuts an intimidating figure – maybe that's why he is known as the Gorilla of Wall Street. My experience of seeing him in New York was almost always favourable. He was courteous and pleasant, once agreeing to chair the annual fund-raising dinner for the Knight-Bagehot fellowship programme at Columbia Journalism School for mid-career journalists.

Conventional wisdom suggests that Fuld runs a tight operation. But the Lehman event at the Belvedere hotel doesn't feel right. Maybe it's the fact that my predecessor Andrew Gowers has turned up in his new incarnation as chief PR man for Lehman's international operation based in London; maybe it's Fuld's refrain that things have never been so good in the financial markets.

I feel the same giddy sensation listening to Steve Schwarzman, the co-founder of Blackstone, the private equity powerhouse. He's hosting a breakfast for movers and shakers, including Sir Martin Sorrell. Steve is one of the smartest businessmen around, a former high-school track star with a ruthlessly competitive streak. Sometimes he cannot stop talking and today is no exception. He is musing about credit terms that are almost too good to be true: 'I mean, it's like we almost don't have to repay . . .' I'm writing down Steve's words in my little black notebook in disbelief. I suspect he knows, too, this is unsustainable. Something's got to give.

After Davos, I approached FT *colleagues and we agreed the world was in a credit bubble. How and when it would burst was another matter. In June, Blackstone went public, selling a 12.3 per cent stake in the company. Schwarzman had gone through the dotcom bubble and knew he needed capital. His market timing was exquisite, just before the music stopped. He would become a billionaire many times over. Our relationship, occasionally fractious, became one of the most important of my editorship.*

MONDAY, 19 MARCH

Gordon Brown is weeks away from taking over from Tony Blair as prime minister. What will he do? What's he like as a leader? These are the questions *FT* readers want answers to. Months ago, I assigned one of our most experienced reporters, Nick Timmins, to dig deep into Brown's record in government, focusing on his uninterrupted near-ten-year stint as chancellor of the exchequer in charge of the UK treasury. Timmins is a seasoned operator with a wispy ginger beard rapidly turning grey. He is one of the most reliable story-producers in the *FT* newsroom. Understated and easily underestimated.

Today, Timmins has come up trumps. During his many interviews, he spoke to Andrew Turnbull, former Cabinet secretary and permanent secretary of the treasury.* Lord

---

* Cabinet secretary is the most senior role in the UK civil service, immortalised by the fictional Sir Humphrey Appleby in the 1980s TV series *Yes, Prime Minister.*

Turnbull, astonishingly, described Brown as running the treasury with 'Stalinist ruthlessness', treating Cabinet colleagues 'with more or less complete contempt' and having 'a Macavity quality' like the criminal cat from T.S. Eliot's poem who always manages to escape blame.

I want more Turnbull. Timmins obliges with more quotes from his notebook. 'Do those ends justify the means? It has enhanced Treasury control but at the expense of any government cohesion and any assessment of strategy. You can choose whether you are impressed or depressed by that, but you cannot help admire the sheer Stalinist ruthlessness of it all.' Brown, the ex-mandarin concludes, has 'a very cynical view of mankind and his colleagues'.

LB: 'Brilliant story. Was it all on the record?'

NT: 'Well, he never said it was off the record.'

Turnbull is a man of integrity and discretion. He also happens to be my south London neighbour. Nick argues he's known Turnbull for 20 years. He's been a regular source, providing insight and judgement. Nick never sought to mislead him about the object of the story: the definitive portrait of Gordon Brown in government. Turnbull's words are devastatingly revealing, coming from a man who observed Brown at close quarters for a long time.

The FT *has to publish.*

TUESDAY, 20 MARCH

Two satellite television trucks are parked outside in our street. Reporters are camped outside Turnbull's door. Victoria is worried about neighbourly relations and, more pressingly, the well-being of Ali G, our male cat named after

Sacha Baron Cohen's comic hip-hop stereotype. Lord Turnbull looks after Ali G when we are travelling overseas, feeding him and talking to him. Ali G is family, you see. We had him 'chipped' so he could spend four years with us in our New York apartment. His black coat and white fluffy chest give him a tuxedo look, marking him out as one of the more distinguished characters in the street.

At 7.15am, I skulk out of the front door to my car which is waiting at a discreet distance down the street, well away from reporters unaware that the perpetrator/publisher has been hiding in plain sight. On my way to work, I rehearse in my mind the sequence of events, aware of the need for a sound defence in the likely post-mortem to such a big story.

In my favour, I did attempt to tip off Andrew about the coming story, but only after a prompt from Michael Spencer, the City financier with whom I was having dinner at the Groucho club. Michael was right and I was wrong to delay the courtesy call to a good neighbour. Unfortunately, Andrew failed to answer the house phone. (He did knock on my door later, but my teenage son Dash pleaded ignorance.) Just before midnight, Nick called me to report that Turnbull was 'incandescent'. The good news comes later. 'There's only one thing you really need to know and that is three words from Andrew Turnbull: it is true.'

After publication our story dominates the airwaves, overshadowing Gordon Brown's 11th and final budget as chancellor. It's a high-impact story, the biggest political scoop we have had in years. On Budget Day, Brown calls me.

GB: 'You've been having quite a week.'

LB: 'Nothing personal, Gordon. This is business. One day I'll tell you the whole story over a glass of whisky. Or maybe not quite the full story . . .'

GB: 'What did you think of the budget?'

LB (unsighted): 'The *FT* is broadly supportive.'

Brown, apparently satisfied, pays tribute to the many civil servants who helped him forge his last budget. He calls them his 'comrades', mercifully his only reference to the Stalin story.

SATURDAY, 24 MARCH

Our Brown scoop is running out of steam. It's time to talk to Turnbull. I walk across the road like a naughty schoolboy summoned to the headmaster's study for a good thrashing. Andrew, 62, tall and broad-shouldered, opens the front door and directs me to his living room. He is still incandescent. The damage done by the *FT*'s story is substantial, he says. It's damaging to him, to me and to the *FT*.

Agreed on the first count. Brown is about to become prime minister with the power and patronage that comes with office; Turnbull, once the most powerful civil servant in the country, stands damned, at least for a while. My own reputation may take a hit in Whitehall among those who believe he was stitched up, but I can live with that. On the last count, I fundamentally disagree: our Brown-as-Uncle-Joe story is deeply revealing and it has got everybody talking about the *FT* as a hard-hitting newspaper.

Turnbull would still like an apology. I try to be gracious but I'm not backing down. But I do offer to have a quiet word with Brown. This appears to placate Turnbull, who ushers me to the door with one rueful afterthought: 'At least there's no danger of me putting your cat in the microwave.'

Lord Turnbull remained a devoted friend of Ali G who passed away aged 18½ in November 2018. He remains a great neighbour

*and an acute observer of business, economics and politics. He does
not regularly read the* FT.

Whenever I've needed a little morale booster, I take a look at a
framed picture in our downstairs loo at home in London. It's
a copy of the front page of the *Washington Post* dated 31 August
1985. It was a report on South Africa's central bank governor
Gerhard de Kock's emergency mission to Washington to head
off his country's financial crisis. The headline – 'South African chief gets little encouragement' – was hardly a humdinger;
but I didn't care. I had my first ever front-page byline.

Twenty-two years later, I am on my way to South Africa,
my first trip. The *FT* has a new correspondent, Alec Russell,
a veteran *Daily Telegraph* foreign correspondent and the latest
among my 'transformational' hires. Alec covered the transition from apartheid under Nelson Mandela. He remains on
first-name terms with almost everyone who matters in the
ruling African National Congress party. On my week-long
tour I can watch Alec in action and learn a lot about a vitally
important country and economy on the continent. There's
also the small matter of paying a weekend visit to my daughter, Francesca, who is spending a gap year teaching in a small
village in neighbouring Botswana.

Alec has set up a first-rate schedule in Cape Town and
Johannesburg. Meetings and dinners with the business elite,
including the union boss turned tycoon Cyril Ramaphosa;
and an overnight stay at Tswalu, the Kalahari desert retreat
of the Oppenheimers, the diamond mining family. To cap
the trip, Alec has arranged an interview with President
Thabo Mbeki.

Storm clouds are gathering around Mbeki, the hard-headed technocrat chosen in 1999 to succeed Mandela, an unenviable task given 'Madiba's' personal charisma and moral authority. At home, Mbeki is facing a challenge to his leadership of the ANC from Jacob Zuma, the firebrand deputy president, while neighbouring Zimbabwe is sliding into chaos under its ageing dictator Robert Mugabe. Each week, hundreds more refugees from Zimbabwe are pouring in across the Limpopo River to escape hyperinflation and the regime's violent crackdown. I want to find out how Mbeki plans to respond to these twin challenges.

We meet on a cool Monday morning at Mbeki's official residence in Pretoria, a 45-minute drive from Johannesburg. The elegant white house, surrounded by sweeping lawns and gardens, was formerly called Libertas. It was built in 1940 in the Cape Dutch style of Afrikaner architecture, but after the end of apartheid changed its name to Mahlamba Ndlopfu, the Tsonga term for 'New Dawn'. Mbeki arrives on time for our interview, asks politely about my weekend in Botswana and orders English tea for his two guests.

Over the next two hours, the president reveals many of the strengths and weaknesses of his leadership. He has been a shrewd steward of the economy working with finance minister Trevor Manuel. But he is tone deaf on issues such as crime and public health, especially AIDS which has decimated the black community. A rare flash of anger appears as he addresses – in convoluted terms – white fears about rising crime. These fears are largely driven by lingering racism, he claims.

'The people who built the apartheid system say, "We did all of this to try and build a wall around ourselves, because here we are sitting in this continent surrounded by black hordes and we don't know what they are going to do, so we needed to protect ourselves" . . . It all had to do with a fear that "one day we would be swamped, that one day they would just come and devour us". It would seem to me that some of the communication you get around crime is driven still by this notion of fear.'

Mbeki is also prickly when talking about Zimbabwe. He avoids all direct criticism of Mugabe, implausibly claiming that the octogenarian dictator may in future give up power after free and fair elections. The ties that bind former liberation movements are too strong. Later that afternoon, as I watch Alec writing up our interview at speed by his home swimming pool, I reflect that Mbeki has neither the charisma nor the moral authority to exercise power like Mandela, the power to move a nation towards reconciliation and the world towards universal admiration.

South Africa did not need another saint after 'Madiba' and Mbeki was a competent technocrat, but there was something missing in his political make-up. Ultimately, Mbeki was a prisoner of his past, an anti-apartheid campaigner who fought on the student campus in England rather than in the African bush or suffering like Mandela for 27 years in prison.

The Mbeki interview provided many clues to South Africa's precipitous decline over the next decade. He was complacent about Jacob Zuma, who first ousted him as ANC leader and later won the presidency, ushering in an unparalleled period of corruption and looting of the state. He was also excessively indulgent towards Mugabe who, aged 93, was finally forced from power in 2017.

FRIDAY, 20 APRIL

A lightning trip to Washington, starting with an interview with Condoleezza Rice, US secretary of state. I've known 'Condi' for almost 20 years, going back to her days as a Soviet expert on the National Security Council staff under President George H.W Bush. In George W. Bush's first term, she served as national security advisor. Her job was to broker differences and unify policy during the 'global war on terror' and the invasion of Iraq. She often ended up as a marble between the elephants of Dick Cheney, Donald Rumsfeld and Colin Powell.

Rice has enjoyed a seamless rise to the top since growing up in segregated Birmingham, Alabama. She receives us in a newly upholstered State Department room, with a prominent portrait of Dean Acheson, to my mind her most illustrious predecessor alongside James A. Baker III. Rice is dressed in a beige suit and exudes poise and discipline, avoiding any hint of spontaneity. Her answers on Iran, Iraq and North Korea are formulaic. I goad her by asking if she still stands by her 2005 pro-democracy speech in Cairo? Would arch-realist Henry Kissinger (whom we've just spotted slipping into the State Department) approve?

Rice insists her speech was 'one of the most important statements I could have ever made'. She called out President Hosni Mubarak for holding 'an old-style Egyptian election'. As for the recent Palestinian elections, where Hamas won a majority, she is adamant that she was right to support the poll – even if Hamas have not lived up to their responsibilities. 'Under no circumstances will this president or this administration turn its back on what we believe to be the essential fact about the Middle East, which is that without reform and democratisation you're going to have a false stability which will continue to give rise to extremism.'

I remain unconvinced. Elections mean little unless they are underpinned by strong institutions of government. That was not the

case in the Palestinian territories. In the run-up to the Iraq war,
Brent Scowcroft, the elder Bush's national security advisor and
mentor to Rice, told me that neoconservatives were deluded in their
campaign to turn the Middle East into 'a garden of democracy'.
Rice was no neocon but her Cairo speech, while well meaning, gave
succour to pro-democracy movements which ended in despair in the
Arab Spring. The US under President Obama was neither willing
nor able to offer sustained economic, financial and political support.
Inevitably, the autocrats reasserted control, in Egypt and in Syria.

SATURDAY, 21 APRIL

The annual White House correspondents' dinner at the
Washington Hilton used to be the hottest ticket in town.
Tables cost $2,500, each seating eight guests, preferably the
rich, famous and powerful. In recent years, the quota of Hollywood celebrities has gone up and the quality of conversation
has gone down. Tonight, I'm hosting Hank Paulson, US
treasury secretary. He's a big, bald man who speaks in a
hoarse, halting voice barely audible above the raucous noise
of the gala dinner, broken only by an expectant silence when
President Bush begins the traditional roasting of political
opponents and the press.

Paulson is one of numerous Goldman Sachs alumni who
have ended up in Washington. Officially, this is known as
'giving back to public service'. There's no reason to question
the motives of Paulson, who is independently wealthy and a
generous philanthropist, having sold $500m of Goldman
stock before taking up his role. Critics are less generous,
describing the Goldman power network as 'Government
Sachs'.

I want to know Paulson's views on the future of Paul

Wolfowitz, the neocon defence strategist and strong advocate of the Iraq war whom Bush successfully nominated as president of the World Bank. Wolfowitz is under pressure to resign. Based on two independent sources, the *FT* has reported that he ordered a Bank employee to give a female friend a large pay rise and promotion when she moved from the Bank to the State Department. Paulson is cagey, noting that the two people who matter – Bush and Vice President Cheney – have yet to make their views known. My takeaway: Paulson wants Wolfowitz out but he's not going to be the one to push him.*

That night, Victoria and I head up Connecticut Avenue to an afterparty hosted by Christopher Hitchens at his 12th-floor apartment in the Wyoming building, built at the end of the 19th century. His 'hood' is located between the stiffly elegant diplomatic quarter in Kalorama and the more bohemian Adams Morgan, sometimes called 'Madam's Organ', as Hitchens drily observes.

His apartment wraps around the whole of the top floor, with magnificent views of the Naval Observatory (home of the US vice president), the British embassy and, less congruously, the Russian trade mission. There is next to no furniture in the rooms, a decision justified by Christopher's love of the ornate, original wooden flooring designed by the architect of the building himself. The white walls are lined with bookshelves, featuring everything George Orwell wrote (including his BBC expenses), most of Marcel Proust, James Joyce and

---

* Wolfowitz resigned in May 2007. A World Bank statement accepted his assurance that he had acted ethically and in good faith in the treatment of his friend.

P. G. Wodehouse, as well as Evelyn Waugh, Karl Marx and Vladimir Nabokov.*

Victoria met Christopher, then a precocious young student at Oxford, in the late 1960s. We became friends when I was a reporter at the *Washington Post* (Christopher invited me to lunch after reading an article I wrote on the Irish-American lobby). We renewed contact when V and I moved back to Washington in 1986 – the beginning of a new three-way friendship.

Gin and tonic in hand, Christopher greets us with a big smile. The crowd includes familiar faces like investigative journalist duo Andrew and Leslie Cockburn and assorted media literati. Carol Blue, Hitch's partner, hovers in the background. Slowly the room fills to capacity, boosted by power-players such as Richard Holbrooke, one of America's top diplomatic troubleshooters. Almost invariably, Hitch feigns surprise that the VIPs should have bothered to turn up at such a modest occasion.

By midnight, the rooms are packed. Christopher ambles over and we exchange thoughts about the conflict in Iraq which he supported, to the outrage of many liberal friends, on the grounds that Saddam Hussein was a murderous dictator. Several glasses of wine later, I recount my conversation with Hank Paulson and the future of the World Bank. 'I want that story nailed – and Wolfowitz too.'

Unbeknown to me, and much to the amusement of my conversation partners, Wolfowitz is standing right behind me.

---

* I owe the detailed description of Hitch's apartment to an interview and tour he gave to C-Span on 28 August 2007, now available on YouTube.

When I told Christopher about the drunken encounter a few days later, he emitted a wry chuckle. 'Good story,' he said. 'I must assume it's true.'

MONDAY, 23 APRIL

Day One of the *FT* newspaper's 'rebrush'. The PR team has advised against calling it a redesign because it suggests that something was wrong with the original. *There was, but that was then and this is now.* I've approved a new typeface, a new running order for the first section and sharper labelling for fact boxes and 'background' elements. My personal highlight is the revival of the *FT*'s original motto: 'Without fear and without favour'. This sums up my approach to *FT* journalism. We're independent, we won't be pushed around and, beyond our basic commitment to capitalism and wealth creation, we'll give everyone a fair crack of the whip.

My commitment to fair and impartial reporting would remain a constant during my editorship, though it was severely tested during the hyper-partisanship of the Brexit–Trump era.

TUESDAY, 1 MAY

John Browne, the dapper oil man who turned BP from a second-tier natural resources company into one of the global giants, has abruptly resigned. He has lost his injunction against the *Mail on Sunday* to prevent the newspaper publishing allegations that he handed numerous cheques to his lover Jeff Chevalier over the past four years.

This is a tricky story for the *FT*. Browne is a business icon, but he has acknowledged offering 'an untruthful account' of the circumstances in which he met Chevalier. It was via a gay male escort agency rather than while jogging in Battersea park. I first heard rumours about a court injunction covering Browne's closet relationship months ago. That prevented us writing about the case but now it's gone public. How much detail should we publish about a private consensual relationship? Should we comment on the story? How to get the tone right?

I'm dreading my phone call with Browne. He sounds crushed when we finally speak. I reassure him that his role as the outstanding businessman of his age stands (though I skirt over BP's safety record in the US which we highlighted just months ago). Instead, I accentuate the positive, noting how he transformed BP and pioneered the visionary marketing slogan 'Beyond Petroleum' which anticipated the debate on climate change. Browne thanks me and asks how he can help.

What follows is less interview, more confessional. After 20 minutes, I put the phone down, deflated. This is a sad story of a world-class businessman unable to live openly with his sexuality. We publish a full story and a letter to the editor, signed by a dozen or so of Browne's many admirers in the City and business. One day, I hope he will write the story.*

Two hours later, an even bigger story breaks. Rupert Murdoch has bid $5bn for Dow Jones, the financial publishing empire which owns the *Wall Street Journal*. This is an even trickier story for the *FT*. The *WSJ* is a direct competitor. Media consolidation on this scale threatens us and rivals like the *New York Times* and the *Washington Post*. Murdoch has

---

* In 2014, Lord Browne published *The Glass Closet*, a short, forthright book which documented the pressure he felt to conceal his sexuality as he rose to the top of BP.

struck with lethal intent, offering a knockout cash bid which will make it hard for the controlling Bancroft family to resist.

There's a personal interest too. Marcus Brauchli, a close friend, has just been appointed managing editor of the *WSJ*, the top job in charge of the newsroom. When I reach Marcus on the phone, he's distinctly nervous about Murdoch. I tell him not to be fooled by the pixie dust which Robert Thomson, the old *FT* hand and now *Times* editor, is spreading about protecting editorial independence. Marcus knows it's rubbish too but the *WSJ* editorship is the job he's sought all his career. He knows the *Journal* has to change. And Murdoch will demand it. He is in a tight spot.

Known as the Rocket, Marcus was destined to rise to the top. As a foreign correspondent for the Wall Street Journal *in Shanghai and Tokyo, he was a sharp reporter on business and financial trends with a strong sense of the absurd. He once joined a group of Hong Kong people who spent five days throwing dummy hand grenades and shooting AK-47s at a People's Liberation Army camp in China. The exercises were designed to foster patriotism and Marcus later published a colour feature. When he was appointed managing editor of the* WSJ, *I thought that two friends running the world's two best business newspapers was too good to be true. It was.**

FRIDAY, 4 MAY

Martin Sorrell says Rupert will eat us alive once he gets his hands on the *Wall Street Journal*. He'll pump in money, hire

---

* Marcus Brauchli was later appointed executive editor of the *Washington Post*, the last before the Graham family sold the paper to Amazon founder Jeff Bezos.

talent and target the *FT*. That's not my view. I reckon he will go for the *New York Times*. 'He won't be able to resist taking on the liberal establishment in New York,' I tell Martin. 'The *FT* will be collateral damage, at worst.'

I was right, Martin was wrong. Under Murdoch, the WSJ *became a more general newspaper, adding a special New York section of metropolitan news. The shift in focus helped the* FT, *even though the attempts to poach our staff remained the pain that never went away.*

MONDAY, 14 MAY

To Frankfurt for an interview over lunch with Jean-Claude Trichet, president of the European Central Bank. Trichet is a French technocrat who thinks and speaks in neutral, tightly structured paragraphs. Over many years of on/off-the-record going back to our first conversation in the autumn of 1993 walking around Lake Genval outside Brussels, in the margins of some Euro-gathering or another, I've never got a story out of him.

We meet in his office on the 35th floor of the Eurotower in central Frankfurt, a brutalist monument to Europe's single currency. Trichet is dapper, wearing a dark grey suit and tie to match his coiffed silver hair. I'm accompanied by Ralph Atkins, our ECB correspondent. The conversation is polite but leaden. My attempts to divine the future direction of interest rates and monetary policy are politely rebuffed. On the credit bubble, he offers Delphic platitudes. His basic position is that the euro is Europe's anchor. Unmentioned is that Europe's single currency is also the culmination of his life's work. This is personal for him.

The Trichet interview was a missed opportunity. We should have probed harder on pressures building in the financial markets. Instead, we focused on tensions with the newly elected French president, Nicolas Sarkozy. This was politics, no-go territory for a central banker. I should have known better.

WEDNESDAY, 16 MAY

Eye-opening article in the *FT* today on Moody's, Standard & Poor's and Fitch, the credit-rating agencies known as 'the high priests of finance'. Our markets team is again asking hard questions: can ratings agencies be trusted to assess correctly the value of financial products? We point out a blatant conflict of interest: banks – not investors – pay for the ratings service. We also quote analysts questioning whether the agencies are up to the job of assessing rarefied 'structured finance' products such as credit derivatives and mortgage-backed securities. The conclusion is dynamite: Triple A credit ratings may not be all they seem.*

Bruce Page, the swashbuckling Insight editor at the Sunday Times, *used to say there were only two types of investigative journalism: 'Arrow points to the defective part' or 'We name the guilty man'. Our article did both. The whole credit rating system rested on flimsy, conflict-ridden foundations.*

---

* Triple A is the highest rating for creditworthiness awarded by the rating agencies. Low-grade 'sub-prime' mortgages were packaged up into complex financial instruments that were awarded high credit ratings. The theory that you could engineer the risk out of products proved to be dead wrong.

James Murdoch has agreed to speak to the *FT*'s senior management group. These meetings are usually a bit ho-hum but the younger Murdoch is a breath of fresh air. For the past four years, he's run BSkyB, the satellite broadcaster whose money-spinner is Sky Sports, chief broadcaster for Premier League football. James is being touted as the heir apparent to the Murdoch empire. That may not be in his best interests.

Murdoch jnr casts himself as a 'cheerleader for change' in the digital age. His speech delivery is crisp and relevant. Should content be free? If so, how much? How should companies manage the shift from satellite to cable? How best to deliver content to the 'iPod generation' that wants 'news on demand'? These are all questions highly relevant to the *FT*. Do we have the answers?

No one really had the answers. But I was impressed James M. was asking the right questions.

My old friend Bob Zoellick is the front runner to succeed Paul Wolfowitz at the World Bank. Zoellick has worked as a top adviser to Bush snr and Bush jnr. He's been deputy White House chief of staff, US trade representative and deputy US secretary of state. And he's been a mentor and friend of mine for 20 years. Now he's poised to take on one of the top jobs in international finance and public service. *Great news for him – and me.*

THURSDAY, 14 JUNE

Gordon Brown has summoned me to 11 Downing Street* at 6pm for a one-on-one meeting which I'm fairly sure will feature our story about his Stalinist tendencies.

To my surprise. Brown looks more chipper than he has in a long time. The portrait of former prime minister David Lloyd George offers a clue. Brown is ready to assume the job he has so long coveted, having felt cheated back in 1994 when Tony Blair ran for the Labour leadership and won. In a fortnight, Brown will move next door to Number 10. Is he ready, I ask?

Brown launches into his manifesto for change: a 'new national consensus', a more diversified Cabinet, a Whitehall shake-up featuring a Government of All the Talents. *The GOAT acronym is unfortunate but we'll leave that for now.* Brown is unstoppable, expounding on UK economic policy, Europe and the US. He does not want a referendum on the Lisbon treaty,† declaring that he's been unfairly branded anti-European because he was against the UK joining the euro. Well, he was dead right on that count, I say, and now the *FT* has declared so too.

Brown is guarded about an early election. He wants to establish his own record in government. The risk is that the economy turns down after ten years of economic growth

---

* 11 Downing Street is the official residence of the chancellor of the exchequer. Tony Blair claimed the larger flat in Number 11 for his family, displacing Gordon Brown to the smaller residence above Number 10. The apartment swap has continued since.

† The Lisbon treaty, which entered into force in 2009, amended and updated the Maastricht treaty of 1992. Eurosceptics insisted it was a further step towards federal integration in Europe.

and he is left stranded. When Brown asks me what the *FT* is focusing on, my response is the American economy and the world economy because 'it doesn't get much better than it is at the moment'.

Brown was an unofficial member of the east coast establishment, invariably well informed about America. Peter Mandelson once explained to me: 'Gordon is not pro-American, he is pro-Cape Cod.'

FRIDAY, 15 JUNE

Lunch at Le Pont de la Tour with Michael Grade, executive chairman of ITV and former chairman of the BBC Board of Governors. Grade, son of the great cigar-chomping TV impresario Sir Lew, is looking a lot happier now he's out of the BBC. He is a slightly roguish character with a mischievous sense of humour. He asks lots of questions about the *Wall Street Journal* and the future of newspapers. I predict Rupert Murdoch will get his hands on the *Journal* and Dow Jones. Grade turns to politics. He predicts Brown won't go for an early election and won't last as PM: 'He doesn't have the "make you feel happy after seeing him" factor that Blair has.'

Brown was intellectually brilliant but his two weaknesses were indecision and a short fuse. His outbursts were like a summer storm: lots of dark clouds, flashes of lightning followed by a torrential downpour. Then the sun would come out and everything was supposed to be normal again. Some saw his rage as driven by the intense frustration at waiting so long for the top job. Others who knew him well said he was a great leader as long as he didn't think about politics.

MONDAY, 18 JUNE

There's a spate of rumours and a report in the *Wall Street Journal* that Pearson is trying to organise a bid for Dow Jones using support from GE, owner of NBC, the US TV network. Marjorie Scardino is not returning my calls. Rona Fairhead is fussing in the wings. To make this deal work, it would need significant cost savings, maybe via the *FT* closing its American operation and the *WSJ* shutting down in Europe. This would sink my hopes of making the *FT* a truly global news organisation. *It's a non-starter for me. I will say so, if and when the time comes (which I seriously doubt).*

The rush to media consolidation and mega deal-making is one more sign that markets are on a sugar high, fuelled by cheap money. Martin Wolf has written a weighty commentary today, headlined 'The New Capitalism'. According to Martin, the world has entered a revolutionary period marked by 'the transformation of mid-20th century managerial capitalism into global financial capitalism'.

Martin describes an explosion of new products like credit derivatives, and a shift from traditional commercial banking to transaction-based investment banking. The results are vast new regulatory, social and political challenges. Optimists argue that the new system combines efficiency and stability to an unprecedented degree. Pessimists like Mr Wolf are not so sure. 'Monetary conditions have been so benign for so long that huge risks are being built up, unidentified and uncontrolled, within the system.'

Martin's article on 'unfettered finance' called the top of the market. All the ingredients of the global financial crisis were laid out in a newspaper costing less than a cafe latte. Cheap at the price.

TUESDAY, 19 JUNE

To 10 Downing Street for a final interview with Tony Blair as prime minister. He's wearing a sharp dark suit and a bold pink tie – an ageing rock star, eager to try out his repertoire one last time.

As usual we talk about Europe, our common preoccupation. What prospects for ratification of the Lisbon treaty, I ask? Blair runs through the pros and cons, the opt-outs and the obstacles. 'If we screw this up,' says TB, 'this will be bad for Britain.'

Blair insists that Europe has moved our way. The idea of a federal superstate run out of Brussels is a myth. Enlargement to central and eastern Europe 'has made alliances more fluid so there's no chance of a Franco-German alliance dominating in the way it used to in a smaller union. People just haven't woken up to this.'

I agree, but the public are indifferent to or ignorant about the EU. The *Daily Mail* and *Daily Telegraph* are campaigning on European issues such as immigration and the charter of fundamental rights. Blair claims the UK has opt-outs in areas like asylum including a 'gold-plated emergency brake' to deal with illegal immigrants.

This sounded impressive but later proved to be singularly lacking. Even at the height of his popularity, after two crushing election victories over the Conservatives, Blair never succeeded in convincing the British press or the public that Europe was 'moving our way'. He failed to persuade newspaper editors and his charm had little effect on the owners. Blair told me he always liked Rupert Murdoch, whom he found much more trustworthy than other proprietors. But, on Europe, 'I never moved him an inch.'

THURSDAY, 21 JUNE

Louis Susman, my old contact at Citigroup who raised millions of dollars for Senator John Kerry's presidential campaign in 2004, is now backing Barack Obama. They share a Chicago connection. Lou has another piece of news: he's told clients to sell anything that's not core because private equity 'is buying everything'. There's cheap money everywhere. 'It's a doddle,' says Lou.

In hindsight, one more sign that we had hit the top of the market.

SUNDAY, 8 JULY

To the wedding of Jonathan Powell and Sarah Helm, his long-time partner.* New Labour is out in force, led by Tony Blair. Sarah and I first met as reporters for the *Sunday Times* in the early 1980s and fellow Washington and Brussels correspondents. Powell, a trained diplomat, is a newer acquaintance. A cool, unfussy presence with a laser-like intellect. He and TB deliver eloquent tributes but Sarah steals the show with her opening line: 'There've been three people in this marriage: Jonathan, Tony . . . and me.'

---

* Jonathan Powell was chief of staff to Tony Blair throughout his premiership and co-architect of the Good Friday Agreement in Northern Ireland. He later founded Inter Mediate, a firm dedicated to conflict resolution, and took part in many negotiations between governments and insurgents in Europe and Asia.

MONDAY, 9 JULY

Chuck Prince, CEO of Citigroup, has delivered the quote of the year – maybe the decade – in an interview with the *Financial Times*. Speaking in Japan, Prince denied that Citigroup, one of the biggest providers of finance to private equity deals, was pulling back. 'When the music stops, in terms of liquidity, things will be complicated. But as long as the music is playing, you've got to get up and dance. We're still dancing.'

Prince was not a renegade. He was doing his best to express, a little too plainly as it turned out, the strategy pursued by the Wall Street banks. They continued their leveraged lending and 'structured credit' because to have done otherwise would have curtailed their revenue growth and offended clients such as private equity firms who were on an acquisition spree. Wall Street's game was akin to musical chairs. The trick was not only to keep dancing but to get out in time to grab the last stool. Prince forgot that lesson and lost his job soon afterwards.

THURSDAY, 9 AUGUST

Two disturbing items on ft.com today. The French bank BNP Paribas has closed three funds because it could not be sure of their value. The problem is linked to sub-prime mortgages. An unnamed German regional bank is also said to be in trouble. The European Central Bank has intervened in the money markets.

Alistair Darling, chancellor under Gordon Brown, later revealed in his book Back from the Brink *that he had picked up a copy of the* FT *while on holiday in Mallorca on this same day. This was the moment he grasped that a serious financial crisis was under way, though there was no sign that any British bank was in trouble. It might have made a great* FT *marketing campaign. Sigh.*

THURSDAY, 13 SEPTEMBER

A bombshell scoop from Robert Peston, BBC business editor and a former *FT* journalist: Northern Rock is seeking emergency funding from the Bank of England. This is the first sign that the credit crunch is spreading into core sectors of the economy. A market story has suddenly gone mainstream. This must be our moment.

FRIDAY, 14 SEPTEMBER

Gordon Brown has ordered the rescue of Northern Rock. The British taxpayer is on the hook for several billion pounds and people are raging about an irresponsible financial sector. John Gapper reminds *FT* readers that operating an open economy carries risks.

'Until the August financial shock, the world was enjoying an era of enormous financial liquidity, driven by low interest rates and high commodity and property prices. A lot of it flowed into the UK, in the form of both corporate investment and Middle Eastern and Russian billionaires buying big houses. Everyone from Northern Rock to investment banks, ministers and regulators enjoyed the knock-on effects while they lasted.

'It is therefore a bit rich for the British, who have been basking in the heat of hot money, to turn around and blame foreigners when things suddenly get chilly. That was what some Asian governments did after the 1997 financial crisis and it was equally unattractive and unjustified. Together with sterling and house prices, British self-regard has become unnaturally inflated. It is due for a correction.'

23–25 SEPTEMBER

Election fever is coursing through the Labour party conference in Bournemouth, dampened only by a light south coast drizzle. Sunday dinner is with John Hutton, the über-Blairite business minister who's somehow survived into the Brown Cabinet. He's a World War I buff and has just finished the draft of *Kitchener's Men*, a history of the King's Own Royal Lancasters in France during the Great War. Hutton is pushing for an early election. 'The Tories are in disarray . . . People are being marched up the hill. What's the point if there's no early poll? Go early, go all out.'

Next day, we meet Ed Balls, Brown's right-hand man, now in the Cabinet as secretary of state for children, schools and families. Balls is an ex-*FT* man who combines laddish humour (he's a brutish football striker and Norwich City supporter) with a first-class brain honed at Oxford and Harvard. He teases us about an election date, but on balance would prefer a delay until May when Brown can build a record in government and Labour could develop a proper policy agenda. On the other hand, an early election would help create a new mandate for change.

It's infuriatingly fuzzy – a reflection of Brown's indecision. But Balls does reveal one important nugget. Mervyn King at the Bank of England has been 'too out in front' on ruling out future bank bailouts.

The issue of 'moral hazard' – in effect, rewarding bad behaviour – would provoke serious debate. Mervyn King was convinced that bankers like Fred Goodwin had behaved recklessly and there had to be a price – financial or otherwise – for bailouts. The government was sympathetic but nervous about appearing anti-business. The bankers remained unrepentant.

WEDNESDAY, 10 OCTOBER

The formula for Lunch with the *FT* is deceptively simple: a conversation-cum-interview over an agreeable meal with personalities like presidents, playwrights, tycoons, film stars and the occasional oddball. Martin Amis, England's one-time *enfant terrible* novelist, is my guest today at Odette's, a hang-out for patrons of the arts and theatre in Primrose Hill, conveniently near the Amis residence.

I'm running slightly late, having spent 45 minutes in front of a House of Lords select committee on media ownership, a light grilling which produced no great insights. Amis, a slight figure in a black waistcoat, is plainly irritated at being made to wait. For several minutes, he stares silently at the menu. Finally, he speaks: 'The menu is very pig-oriented.'

Our conversation feels a bit scattergun. We talk briefly about his running public feud with Terry Eagleton, the Marxist English literary professor, who has accused him of Islamophobia, a charge he somewhat flippantly denies. I ask Amis about Kingsley, his father. 'He wasn't an invigilator,' Amis replies. 'It was nice having a kind of lazy father, a very soft, sweet father.' Finally, too hurriedly, he talks about his lifelong friendship with Christopher Hitchens going back to

their time at the *New Statesman* and their 'low-bohemia prom-
iscuity' in 1970s London.

Writing up Lunch with the *FT* is usually a pleasure, less so
this time. I cannot match Amis's sledgehammer prose. After
several drafts, I hand in the 2,000-word feature to the editors, knowing that I have failed to do justice to my subject.
Post-publication, I write to the Hitch in search of a compliment. He's polite but non-committal. *Not a bad job, but you've
missed Martin's sense of humour.* Funny, but I laughed aloud
reading *Money* in my mid-twenties. In person Martin Amis
was hardly a bellyful of laughs. *Memo to self: when in doubt, go
with the gut.*

31 OCTOBER–3 NOVEMBER

Here's my secret confession: I'm old media desperate to be new
media. For a guy who grew up in print, this is not just a technological challenge. It requires a change of mindset, a willingness
to embrace collaboration, disruption, participation and open-
source information like Wikipedia. This feels liberating but
also threatening. What better place to learn how best to adapt
than Silicon Valley, birthplace of the digital revolution.

Marjorie Scardino, who faces her own challenges in Pearson's high-margin but text-heavy education business, has
chosen Google headquarters in Mountain View to open this
year's 'Brighton' meeting, the annual shindig for top Pearson
and *FT* executives. Over the next two days, we will be introduced to the world of the mobile web, where technologies
are rapidly converging and mobile apps are proliferating at
warp speed.

Marissa Mayer, Google's 20th employee and a star software engineer who developed its world-beating search engine,

opens the presentations. She is a tall 32-year-old blonde who speaks in slogans like 'launch early and often' and 'innovation not perfection'. The world comes down to 'users, users, users'. She displays the confidence of a multimillionaire and the certainty of someone who's cracked the code; but there's also a child-like naivety, summed up by her casual assertion that 'data is apolitical'. Eric Schmidt, Google's hard-nosed CEO, proffers the same soundbites and the odd jarring note. In the middle of his talk about Google's ambition to organise the world's information, in front of an audience of 100 publishing executives, Schmidt muses about 'the oddness of copyright law'. *Duh.*

Google's boot camp convinced me more than ever of the need for faster digital change at the FT. *The* FT *would never be able to embrace the freewheeling Silicon Valley culture fully, but we had so much to learn. Yet Google's success was not without its defects. Software engineers like Mayer lived in their own virtual worlds where they figured that they — not governments — should determine the rules, preferably by algorithm. Therein would lie the seeds of future conflict.*

FRIDAY, 23 NOVEMBER

Another prescient column from Gillian Tett, reporting that Gulf investors are about to ride to the rescue of US credit markets. With oil touching $100 a barrel, Gulf investors are awash with cash. This looks like a perfect moment for cash-rich investors to grab distressed assets.

The world had entered a new phase in the financial crisis as hard-pressed western banks turned to Qatar, UAE and China for funds to shore up their balance sheets. For Barclays Bank, which was determined to avoid taking government money, Middle East funding proved to be a fateful move.

THURSDAY, 29 NOVEMBER

Sir Fred Goodwin greets me with a forced smile. A few weeks ago, he was one of the world's top bankers, having pulled off a daring consortium bid for ABN Amro, the Dutch bank, beating off a rival offer from Barclays. Today, as credit markets have tightened, the Scots swagger has vanished.

We meet one-on-one for lunch at 280 Bishopsgate, the London office of Royal Bank of Scotland near Liverpool Street station. Goodwin's message is unequivocal: RBS has no trouble accessing credit in the markets. I've been told the opposite, but Goodwin remains adamant that the bank's capital buffers are adequate. He looks like a desperate man in denial.

TUESDAY, 4 DECEMBER

An invitation from Lord Snowdon to take part in a group photograph of UK national newspaper editors for *Vanity Fair* magazine. I arrive diplomatically early at the master portraitist's Holborn studio, wearing a dark suit, blue shirt, orange tie (a favourite Ferragamo) and a Burberry scarf, a birthday gift from Angela Ahrendts, the Burberry CEO. Snowdon greets me himself, a well-preserved 77-year-old with a twinkle in his eye, a reminder that this was the man who seduced Princess Margaret in her prime. *Or was it the other way round?*

The shoot is due to take place at 2.30pm. One by one, the editors dribble in, a collection of 11 middle-aged white men joined by one woman: Tina Weaver, editor of the *Sunday*

Mirror. A slightly bedraggled Alan Rusbridger of the *Guardian* turns up, late as usual. Paul Dacre, the longest-serving editor in Fleet Street, is absent.

Dacre preferred to exercise power outside the public eye. One day, I resolved, I would meet the man whose dark demeanour inspired terror (and a measure of respect) among colleagues and politicians alike.

As we pose for the camera, I cheekily try to sneak a copy of the *FT* into the frame. Snowdon politely asks me to remove it. A few more 'cheeses', a few more adjustments. Finally, he pronounces himself satisfied.

Snowdon's photograph offered a snapshot of power in decline. Fleet Street editors, including several in the shot, were soon sacked, moved or embroiled in the tabloid phone-hacking scandal. A copy of the photograph hangs in my downstairs loo. Private viewing only.

MONDAY, 17 DECEMBER

I've obtained an advance draft of Howard Davies's essay on the future of financial regulation. It's a brilliant summary of the key questions surrounding the financial crisis and – just maybe – an audition for the post of governor of the Bank of England when Mervyn King steps down.*

Davies raises awkward questions about Alan Greenspan and the Federal Reserve's role in inflating the credit bubble after the dotcom crash and the 9/11 terrorist attacks. Were

---

* Sir Howard Davies was director of the London School of Economics (2003–11), after serving as head of the Financial Services Authority, the now-defunct UK financial regulator.

other central banks 'accessories after the fact', he wonders? Davies also suggests that Northern Rock has highlighted flaws in the UK regulatory system, specifically the separation of banking supervision from the Bank of England. Finally, he wonders whether the crisis shows that liberalisation in financial markets has gone too far. Are there fundamental flaws in the Anglo-Saxon model?

These are the critical questions for the *FT*. This is a story about financial capitalism in the 21st century. When I became editor, I pledged to restore the gold standard in our core areas of business and finance. This is an opportunity to tell the story in a manner more authoritative, more compelling than our rivals. It's our chance – my chance – to make a global mark.

SECTION TWO

———

'THE WORLD FELL OFF A CLIFF'

———

LEHMAN DOWN

Throughout 2008, until the cataclysmic events in mid-September when Lehman Brothers collapsed, the financial crisis was like a gathering storm, ominous but not entirely visible. Credit markets tightened, the system creaked, confidence slowly evaporated. As editor, I faced a dilemma. If the FT *overplayed the story, we risked being accused of fomenting speculation and eventually panic. If we underplayed the story, we would be charged with a dereliction of duty covering the biggest story on our patch in two generations.*

Powerful actors – banks, politicians and technocrats – continued to insist that the crisis was manageable. This was particularly true in the UK and US, the epicentre of the crisis. Many countries believed the financial crisis was an Anglo-American problem, as I discovered during trips to the European continent, Russia and China. They assumed they were relatively insulated. This was a misreading, though it did not compare to the self-delusion which I witnessed at times in London and New York.

WEDNESDAY, 9 JANUARY

To David and Samantha Cameron's for dinner, courtesy of George Osborne. En route to the Cameron home in west

London, George sends a message. Her Majesty's Leader of the Opposition is looking forward to meeting me and Victoria, but this will be a 'get to know you' session only. There will be no discussion of British politics.

If 'Dave' is nervous about inviting a journalist into his home, why bother? For the first 15 minutes I'm pouting as we try to engage in small talk. The caterers serve something turkey-like and tasteless. Finally, we turn to Barack Obama's rise from near nowhere. It seems politics is up for discussion – as long as it's America. When I tell Cameron that some big-money donors have told me they're backing Obama, he wants to hear more.

Can Obama build on his victory in the Iowa caucuses? Could he beat Hillary Clinton? Is America ready for a black president?

My view is that he definitely has a chance. Obama has charisma aplenty (I was in the room watching his career-defining Red–Blue speech at the 2004 Democratic convention in Boston). Obama comprehensively out-organised Clinton in Iowa. Her campaign staff are for the most part arrogant, bloated and smug. I can't figure out where husband Bill – the big dog on the porch – fits in. Hillary's campaign slogan amounts to little more than 'It's my turn'.

Cameron the politician is riveted. He doesn't seem to be much interested in discussing policy but he sure as hell wants to know what it takes to win an election.

TUESDAY, 19 FEBRUARY

I have written a pompous letter to the *Guardian* complaining about a Polly Toynbee column which suggested our reporting on non-doms* was polemical, spurious, unsourced, unchecked and disreputable. Marjorie sends me a scribbled note asking why I rose to her bait.

That was the last letter to an editor I ever wrote. Letters to the FT *editor were generally more amusing, as I discovered while working with Heather Davidson, the long-time letters editor.*

THURSDAY, 28 FEBRUARY

José Manuel Barroso greets me like an old friend *(we don't really know each other but my name apparently counts for something in Euroland)*. The Portuguese president of the Commission is a thickset man with a full mop of black hair, with streaks of grey. His suit is impeccably cut, matched by a blue shirt and tie. Barroso is markedly less chippy than his predecessor Jacques Delors, the philosopher king who would explode with rage if he considered the questioner ignorant or impertinent. Delors, who suffered from sciatica, once waved his walking stick at me, mouthing epithets in rapid French. Barroso, who speaks English fluently, albeit with a heavy Portuguese accent, is altogether an easier proposition.

I've come to Brussels with two questions in mind: if the financial crisis is largely driven by the failure of regulation, what are the rule-makers intending to do? And, second, how bad could it get? Barroso is damning about the sophisticated debt packages which banks are peddling in the market,

---

* Alistair Darling sought to reform the tax treatment of wealthy 'non-domiciled' foreigners living in the UK. The *FT* favoured closing loopholes but criticised muddled policy-making.

especially mortgage-backed securities. He blames poor risk modelling, which means the credit-rating agencies. 'Mathematical models are *not* the answer to everything,' he tells me. Yet Barroso is keenly aware of the benefits of free capital flows and wary about imposing new regulations. 'We're trying to avoid it but we don't exclude it.'

How much worse things could get is hard to figure. There are rumours of Spain getting support from the European Central Bank, and the European economy is slowing down. Yet Barroso and others seem to think the euro will provide protection against financial chaos, allowing Europe to 'decouple' from America.*

> *After the dotcom crash in 2000–2001, I had made the same 'decoupling' argument to the international advisory board of Salomon Smith Barney headed by former US treasury secretary Bob Rubin. When I finished my presentation, Rubin thanked me and said: 'I think your point is 100 per cent wrong.' Then, he paused: 'I'm sorry, Lionel, that was rude of me: 99 per cent.'*

5–7 MARCH

Robert Dilenschneider is a grizzled overweight bear of a PR man in his mid-sixties whose offices sit in the shadow of the MetLife building in mid-town Manhattan. He's a big Barber supporter who talks to me in the third person, as in 'Barber

---

* In 2016, two years after Barroso stepped down from the Commission, he became chairman of Goldman Sachs International. He succeeded Peter Sutherland, who had been responsible for competition and trade policy in the Commission.

should do this, Barber should do that.' Marjorie says she doesn't trust Bob and has advised me to keep my distance. But he's a valuable market source who also keeps an eye on Chrystia Freeland, who heads our New York operation. Today, Bob is gushing with information.

Bear Stearns is 'dressed for sale'. Jimmy Cayne 'lost a lot of money' and the traders are unhappy. John Mack at Morgan Stanley is in trouble. Vikram Pandit is struggling at Citigroup. There's going to be a wave of consolidation in the US banking sector. *This is gold dust, but how to turn it into a story without being accused of spreading panic?*

First stop is Dick Fuld at Lehman Brothers. The Gorilla of Wall Street is wearing a starched white shirt without a suit jacket, and is giving me the Big Stare. (I had the nerve to ask him about his balance sheet and his bank's exposure to mortgage-backed securities and other 'counterparties' like hedge funds.)

'I've got $100bn of collateral to deploy,' says Fuld, jabbing his finger towards my face, 'we're whipping hedge funds like dogs.'

In Davos this year, at a lunch in a hotel room with walls covered with mink-like fur, Fuld promised he was going to 'take some money off the table'. *Rough translation: I'm going to be more responsible.* Lehman has been a huge investor in real estate, betting that prices would continue to rise. They were then engaged in bigger, riskier trading games off this real-estate base. This is a new version of the Greater Fool Theory, which states that people can make money by buying securities, whether or not they are overvalued, by selling them for a profit at a later date. The gamble is that there will always be a bigger fool willing to pay a higher price. Fuld is no fool but he's gotten greedy. Now he wants help from the Federal

Reserve, through lower interest rates. 'The Fed is way behind the curve,' he tells me.

As a parting shot, I asked Fuld how he squared his own prospective $100m-plus remuneration package with Lehman's expected loss in the second quarter. He gave me a mouthful. I never saw him again.

Early breakfast next day with John Mack, the embattled CEO of Morgan Stanley. He confirms – as I suspected – that things are a lot worse than everyone's letting on. Speaking in the lilting tones of his native North Carolina, Mack says the peak of the credit boom last summer was 'like getting high'; now the downer's arrived. 'We're dealing with ten LTCMs,' he says, an ominous reference to the super-leveraged Greenwich-based hedge fund which had to be bailed out by Wall Street banks exactly a decade ago.*

John Thain, the ex-Goldman executive now running Merrill Lynch, confirms that financial markets are under stress. I've known Thain for ten years, latterly as chief executive of the New York Stock Exchange. He's accompanied by his new chief PR Margaret Tutwiler, an Alabama native and long-time aide to James A. Baker III, then US treasury secretary and secretary of state. Tutwiler eats journalists for breakfast – and lunch and dinner. She's a smart hire by Thain, a short, wiry man with an unsettling intensity level. In his view, there's a 'crisis of confidence' rather than a 'crisis of liquidity'. Fed monetary policy won't help. The US

---

* Long-Term Capital Management (LTCM), founded by Nobel Prize-winning economists, was the subject of a Wall Street bail-out in 1998 coordinated by the Federal Reserve to prevent an explosive collapse. A forerunner of the 'too big to fail' doctrine.

treasury (under his old Goldman boss Hank Paulson) is insufficiently active. 'We're dealing with a broken transmission system,' says Thain.

At Goldman, Lloyd Blankfein, the one-time precious-metals trader, is hoping for the best but planning for the worst. The son of a postal clerk, Blankfein grew up in the Brooklyn housing projects and went to a rough-house state school. His smarts took him to Harvard and Harvard Law School. Lloyd has always offered an oblique perspective on life, musing in an ironic tone and often drawing on historical analogies. He likes to remind colleagues: history is current.

Today, he's turned to the Bible to explain what's going on in the financial markets. 'It's like three days of rain before the Great Flood. It's bad but it could get a lot worse.' What he means but does not say is that there is no way people could guess on Day Three what actually happened on Day Forty. They were preoccupied with that day's downpour; after 37 more days of rain Noah would discover the world had been wiped out.

Unlike Lehman, Goldman was aggressively hedging at both the short and long ends of the market. I missed that story and the bigger picture. Investors and traders could no longer be confident about the value of assets on the balance sheets of major banks. Until the banks came clean, normal buying and selling would be suspended. The problem was made vastly more complicated by excessive borrowing, known as leverage.

FRIDAY, 14 MARCH

Bear Stearns is no more. The Federal Reserve Bank of New York has stepped in with a $25bn loan, soon to be swapped for Bear's sale to JPMorgan Chase. Bear has survived every financial crisis since the stock-market crash in 1929. We knew Bear was in deep trouble, but the demise still comes as a shock. John Gapper, our chief business columnist, captures the moment. 'The US has acquired its own version of Northern Rock.'

SUNDAY, 16 MARCH

A coup to be celebrated in our drive to attract big-name contributors to the debate on the financial crisis. Alan Greenspan, former Fed chairman, offers half a mea culpa for his own role which he attributes to inadequate risk modelling. He predicts the crisis will be the most wrenching since World War II. Home prices will fall, the pace of liquidation will increase. Greenspan does not mention the Fed's cheap-money policy but blames human nature instead: what Keynes called 'animal spirits' and the rest of us would call greed. He ends with a sombre prediction: 'If, as I strongly suspect, periods of euphoria are very difficult to suppress as they build, they will not collapse until the speculative fever breaks on its own.'

17–23 MARCH

To Moscow, my first trip since the collapse of the Soviet Union. Victoria has come along as co-ambassador on her first visit to Russia. We begin with a tour of Vladimir, one of the medieval capitals of Russia, a three-hour drive from Moscow. Our guide says she preferred life under the Communists. Why, I ask?

Guide: 'I would like to tell a joke.'

LB: 'Be my guest.'

Guide: 'Oligarch walks into shop and wants to buy a boat.'

LB (intrigued)

Guide: 'Shop says we don't sell boats. We only sell cars. Like Volga.

Oligarch replies: I don't need the water. I just want to buy a boat.'

Early breakfast next morning with Garry Kasparov, the former world chess champion and Kremlin critic, in his Moscow apartment. His mother looks on, saying nothing. As the tea warms up on the samovar, Kasparov thinks and talks rapidly, like he's playing chess against the clock. The Soviet regime was morally and financially bankrupt. Vladimir Putin was the 'President of hope' but the tone has since changed. Putin was unnerved by Nato's assault on Kosovo* and by US plans for a new missile defence system. The regime has become harder edged but corruption is as bad as ever. Now Putin has (temporarily) moved aside for Dmitry Medvedev. 'At least Putin had some legitimacy. Medvedev has none.'

Kasparov says Russia needs political renewal, a new grass-roots movement and a national assembly which will challenge what he describes as 'the system', the new *nomenklatura* in league with Putin.

My trip has been arranged by Neil Buckley, the *FT*'s Moscow bureau chief, a cautious, thoughtful Mancunian who has never knowingly oversold a story. Our six-day agenda is

---

* The 11-week campaign of NATO air strikes against Serbian forces in Kosovo represented a new interventionist doctrine championed by Tony Blair and others under the 'right to protect' against human rights abuse. Putin saw Kosovo as the prelude to regime change beyond the Balkans.

packed with appointments featuring an extraordinary group of characters who wield – or once wielded – power in post-Communist Russia. Billionaire oligarchs like Mikhail Fridman and Vladimir Potanin who made their fortunes in oil and mining; securocrats like Alexander Voloshin; conservative nationalists like Vyacheslav Nikonov, Molotov's* grandson, and washed-up liberals like Grigor Yavlinsky and Yegor Gaidar from the Gorbachev years. These meetings underline the *FT*'s pulling power as well as the Russian elite's interest in engaging with one of the world's premier capitalist news organisations.

Midway through the trip, our interview with President-elect Medvedev comes through. We enter the Kremlin, walking down a hall with prints depicting Napoleon's retreat from Moscow in 1812 before entering a small green room, crammed with flunkeys. Medvedev, a 42-year-old lawyer, backroom operator and native of St Petersburg, speaks slowly and precisely through an interpreter whose English he frequently corrects. His goal, he declares, is to embed the rule of law in Russian society. 'It is a monumental task,' he agrees, momentarily switching into English. 'Russia is a country where people don't like to observe the law. It is, as they say, a country of legal nihilism.'

Does this mean he will order the *siloviki* (the hard men) in the Kremlin to stop interfering in the courts? Does the Russian definition of democracy allow for individual rights and limited state power? Would he describe himself as a democrat?

Medvedev says he won't be categorised as a liberal or a

---

* Vyacheslav Molotov (1890–1986) was a long-serving Soviet diplomat and foreign minister who negotiated a notorious non-aggression pact with Nazi Germany in 1939 which partitioned Poland.

conservative but he does say he supports 'the values of democracy'. He won't accept the notion that Russia is not capable of democracy. 'Russia is a European country and Russia is absolutely capable of developing together with other states that have chosen this democratic path of development.'

Medvedev was the Potemkin* president, in office but not in power. Those who wielded real power were the super-rich oligarchs, shadowy securocrats often operating with commercial interests, and Putin himself. This was what Garry Kasparov called 'the system', a complex series of arrangements and transactions virtually impenetrable to the outside eye. Putin would gradually assert more control. Five months after my visit, Russian troops invaded Georgia, signalling a decade of adventurism which later included the annexation of Crimea and the invasion of eastern Ukraine.

THURSDAY, 27 MARCH

Nicolas Sarkozy has been caught posing on camera too many times with his supermodel wife, Carla Bruni, earning him the nickname 'President Bling'.

After a night at Windsor Castle, 'Sarko' and his wife are attending a white-tie dinner at the Guildhall. The French presidential couple enter the banquet hall to the blare of trumpets, the diminutive Sarko cutting a dash with a bright red sash slanted across his white dress shirt. Bruni is wearing

---

* The name of Grigory Potemkin (1739–91) – soldier, powerful adviser and lover to the Russian empress Catherine the Great – is synonymous with the false portable villages he allegedly constructed to disguise the true state of the countryside in Crimea during her visit in 1787.

an elegant strapless maroon gown dress, a Franco-Italian version of Jacqueline Onassis.

Sarko doesn't speak English and looks bored over dinner. He pays tribute to the vibrancy of the UK economy. No mention of the credit crunch. Maybe France feels it's safe. A Foreign Office mandarin confesses sheepishly he enjoyed being sandwiched between the stack-heeled president and his statuesque bride. 'You might say I was stuck between a rock and a soft place.'

Sarko later suggests that the old *entente cordiale* could develop into an *entente amicale* with Gordon Brown. 'It is not a one-night stand,' he declares. 'I would say we could even go together into the next day's breakfast.' *Brown as Bruni? An unlikely pair. But Sarkozy later formed a common front with Brown in tackling the financial crisis within the forum of the Group of 20 industrialised countries. It was Brown's finest hour.*

TUESDAY, 8 APRIL

The *Financial Times* has won newspaper of the year in the British press awards, a resounding endorsement of our return to the gold standard, pledge one in my manifesto as editor. It vindicates our shift to digital subscriptions, a decisive change in our business model underpinned by higher prices. My only concern is complacency amid the gathering storm in the markets. We're sitting on a huge story. If we get it wrong, we'll be written off as a one-trick pony. If we get it right, we're off to the races.

TUESDAY, 22 APRIL

Marcus Brauchli has been ousted at the *Wall Street Journal*. We arrange to meet for a drink in a dingy bar at the Carlyle

Hotel. Marcus has a look which says 'Well, that was inevitable but good luck to them'; but he's still disappointed at what might have been. This was his dream job. I feel sorry for my friend – and genuinely lucky still to be in my job at the *FT* where Marjorie remains loyal and respectful of editorial independence.

THURSDAY–FRIDAY, 24–25 APRIL

Jamie Dimon is the uncrowned King of Wall Street. Silver-haired with Hollywood good looks, Dimon combines charisma with a mastery of managing complex organisations and risk. At 52, he's in his prime, respected among his peers and ready to take the lead in the coming banking consolidation, having just snapped up Bear Stearns. Maybe he even sees himself as a modern incarnation of John Pierpont Morgan, who, during the Panic of 1907, organised a coalition of financiers to save the US economy. I've dropped by to see Dimon at his office on Park Avenue, a discreet setting with a firefighter's axe framed on the wall, a gift from the fire brigade in Chicago. Along with family photographs sitting on the mantelpiece, there is a portrait of Abraham Lincoln, Dimon's favourite president, on the grounds that 'Honest Abe' emancipated slaves and saved the Union. Dimon reckons he got a good deal with the Bear purchase. 'The financial part is almost done,' he tells me, 'all the crap is on the table.'

Dimon would later acknowledge that the Bear deal was nowhere near as favourable as he first thought because the US government deemed JPMorgan liable for some of Bear's bad bets. At the time, Dimon was looking at markets from a different angle: what he called 'Chapter Two', the impact of the credit crunch on the real economy. 'The real issue is jobs,' he told me.

Alan Greenspan enjoyed near papal infallibility during his 17 years at the Federal Reserve but his legacy doesn't look so pristine now the credit crunch has cut off funding to many banks and financial institutions. Greenspan did not just neglect the bubble, he stoked it with policies intended to boost home-equity withdrawals and consumer spending. His successor is Ben Bernanke, an economics professor and expert on the Great Depression – an ominous qualification.

Krishna Guha, the *FT*'s cerebral US economics correspondent, has arranged an audience with Dr Bernanke at his modest office in the Federal Reserve building in Washington. Bernanke is bald with a trim black beard, a soft-spoken man who explains complex economics as if he were lecturing one of his old student classes at Princeton. *(I cannot speak for Krishna, but that's fine by me.)*

The Fed chair describes the credit crunch as sinister. 'It's not like appendicitis. It's spread through the body and you don't know what it is.' He is more certain on two counts. First, 'We're still early in the housing crisis' (an implicit recognition that real-estate prices have yet to hit bottom). Second, financial institutions are now at risk of not being able to repay their debts.

This is a revelation. Wall Street bosses have insisted to me that they are financially sound and that the crisis is largely about liquidity, the temporary provision of funding. Bernanke is saying that the lack of confidence in assets held on banks' balance sheets is creating a solvency issue. This is not a temporary problem; it is an existential one.

The key question, Bernanke says, revolves around whether the Fed should intervene more aggressively to stabilise the financial system. But at what point and by how much? What will be the impact on the 'real' economy such as industrial output and jobs? And how will the banking system respond? To what degree have the banks passed on risk to other actors such as monoline insurers, who guarantee corporate bonds?

In the end, Bernanke says the future of the global economy will depend on America, whether it's 'decoupling or recoupling' to the rest of the world. Central banks are not necessarily in control – a point he reinforces by quoting a conversation between Stalin and Churchill during World War II. The Soviet leader told Churchill that once upon a time villagers were being terrorised by a bear which was stealing their chickens. They tried shooting the bear but failed. So the villagers decided to make some poison powder and blow it in the bear's face. 'But', said Stalin, 'the bear blew first.'

The Fed's official mandate was to manage inflation and minimise unemployment. Bernanke was signalling to the FT *that the Fed was prepared to move into a larger, uncharted role as a central player in the economic crisis, a role it had never played before.*

THURSDAY–FRIDAY, 5–6 JUNE

I've been plotting for weeks to land an interview with Angela Merkel, working with Bertrand Benoit, our French bureau chief in Berlin (the *FT*'s modest contribution to the Franco-German alliance). Finally it's come through.

We are sitting around a large rectangular wooden table in

Merkel's private office at the top of the Bundeskanzleramt near the Reichstag. Bertrand, a fluent German-speaker, has joined me, along with Hugh Williamson, the *FT* Berlin correspondent who is married to a German. Two Merkel aides look on.

Merkel appears to be heavily made up, a rotund, almost unnaturally brown face with large, friendly eyes. But there's a steeliness about this daughter of a Lutheran pastor raised in Communist East Germany, the most unforgiving regime under Soviet occupation in Europe. Her manner is *sachlich* – businesslike, with an attention to facts not opinions.

Tim Geithner, US treasury secretary, once said privately that Merkel was the only leader during the financial crisis who was 'numerate'.

Her message carries an unmistakable moral authority: it is time to challenge the dominance of 'Anglo-Saxon' thinking and the wholesale deregulation of finance. The banks don't seem to know what product they're selling or how to value it. Then her political point: 'When things go wrong, suddenly the state is back in favour.'

We turn to America. Merkel is impressed, if puzzled by Barack Obama's rock star status*. 'Who is he? What does he stand for?' She is wary of his Republican opponent Senator John McCain who is 'worryingly Cold War'.

The bigger point, she says, is that Hillary Clinton's defeat shows that the US political landscape is shifting, profoundly.

---

* Obama visited Berlin in July 2008, an unusual move for a US politician running for president and intentionally evocative of John F. Kennedy's famous 'Ich bin ein Berliner' speech.

A prescient remark which pointed to American voters' rejection of the establishment candidate. This would be true in 2008 with the Obama victory, but even truer with the election of Donald Trump.

After 45 minutes, the conversation is over. Merkel agrees, slightly reluctantly, to a photo-opportunity with the editor. An aide encourages Merkel to engage in small talk. 'I have nothing to say,' she responds. Then, as the cameras flash, she asks how Gordon Brown is doing.

LB (in German): 'Not so good. He finds it hard to make big decisions.'

AM: 'Why is that? He comes across well in European summits.'

LB: 'He's struggling because of the economy.'

AM: '*Dann kommt Cameron.* Then Cameron's coming [to power].'

Unprompted, Merkel lambasts Cameron's decision to withdraw the Conservative party from the centre-right European People's party in the European Parliament. Team Cameron have insisted to me this was a sop to Eurosceptics but Merkel says it gives succour to people who want to 'tear down' Europe. Her parting shot: she will have little to do with Cameron for now, apart from matters like environmental policy.

Cameron argued that to remain inside a federalist EPP grouping in the European Parliament would have been hypocrisy. He did not grasp the importance of the centre-right 'family'. Merkel would later tell me that the EPP decision marked the beginning of the end of the Conservative party's support for EU membership. Yet Cameron and Osborne continued to believe that Merkel would help them out of scrapes, including the biggest scrape of all: the Brexit referendum.

SATURDAY, 26 JULY

Barack Obama is on a flying visit to London. Gordon Brown has decided a Downing Street cook-out is the best way to bond with the man who would be US president. On his trip, Obama has also met with Tony Blair and David Cameron.

A few days later, a close friend of Obama's (and mine) offers the Democratic candidate's verdict on the trip.

On Blair: Sizzle and substance.

On Brown: Substance.

On Cameron: Sizzle.

20–31 AUGUST

Over the summer, there was a sense of foreboding but no evidence of panic in financial markets. Rumours circulated about stronger banks taking over weaker institutions, like JPMorgan's purchase of Bear Stearns. On balance, I judged it safe to go ahead with a trip to China to attend the closing ceremony of the Beijing Olympics and on to Denver for the Democratic convention where Obama would accept his party's nomination to run for president.

Victoria and I received VIP treatment in Beijing, temporarily under blue skies. (The authorities had closed down smoke-spewing factories around the capital.) Highlight was a trip to the Bird's Nest stadium and the 100m final where Usain Bolt triumphed; less uplifting was the eight-course lunch hosted by the People's Daily *and the nationalist* Global Times. *I was talking so much I failed to notice Victoria's warning signal about the sea slug. Chewy. Very chewy.*

The Olympics closing ceremony was Oscar-grade choreography, with a British coda looking ahead to the 2012 games. David Beckham featured, backed up by Jimmy Page on the guitar, a red double-decker bus and Mayor of London Boris Johnson, hands in pocket, jacket flapping, bounding on stage to wave the Olympic flag. The Chinese media later upbraided Johnson for ignoring protocol. As usual he had an excuse, declaring he was merely following 'a policy of openness, transparency and individual freedom'.

The Beijing Olympics marked the moment when China opened its capital to the world, showcasing the nation's athletic prowess but also the capital's magnificent modern architecture. Openness, transparency and individual freedom were, however, tightly constrained within Communist party rule. This was true under President Hu Jintao; even more so under his successor Xi Jinping.

Attending Barack Obama's coronation as the Democratic candidate for president was never in doubt. I wanted to be able to say to any future grandchildren: we were there. Plenty of media celebrities felt that way too. Tina Brown, the Queen of Buzz, was present. So was Arianna Huffington, promoting her news site, the Huffington Post. *In baking heat, we watched Obama's speech before an 84,000 crowd in the Invesco stadium, home of the Denver Broncos football team. It failed to match his 2004 Red–Blue stem-winder, the one that made his name. But he was the first African-American to be nominated for president by any major US party. And 'Yes We Can' captured the spirit of optimism in America.*

At Denver Airport, TV screens flashed breaking news. John McCain had nominated Sarah Palin, governor of Alaska, as his running mate. My immediate thought: this is either a game-changer which kickstarts the leaden McCain campaign or it's a mad bet which puts a kooky right-winger from the Land of the Midnight Sun within a heartbeat of the presidency. It turned out to be neither.

MONDAY, 8 SEPTEMBER

A prescient piece today in the *FT*'s Lex Column on tensions in the eurozone, specifically Portugal, Italy, Greece and

Spain, often dismissed as the 'Club Med' countries. The author is John Paul Rathbone who has come up with a new acronym for the southern Europeans: the PIGS. And he's written a mischievous headline: 'Pigs in Muck'.

JP's prose is damning: 'Eight years ago, Pigs really did fly. Their economies soared after joining the eurozone. Interest rates fell to historical lows – and were often negative in real terms. A credit boom followed, just as night follows day. Wages rose, debt levels ballooned, as did house prices and consumption. Now the Pigs are falling back to earth.'

The current account deficits in Spain and Portugal are now equivalent to 10 per cent of GDP. Greece's is a whopping 14 per cent, while Italy's is 'relatively respectable' at about 3 per cent. The usual response to a yawning current account deficit is a stiff devaluation; but the Pigs are members of the euro so that route is closed.

Another option for the debtor countries is to try to finance the deficit, but the credit crunch is making that harder to do. Spain's municipal banks – the *cajas* – have been using low-quality asset-backed collateral to raise cheap funds from the European Central Bank. The trouble is the ECB plans to tighten its lending rules.

The last, most painful solution is restoring competitiveness through a drop in real wages. In other words, a deep recession. JP concludes: 'Some now wonder if the Pigs, as part of the euro, risk turning into bacon.'

The Spanish embassy in London complained that 'pig' was one of the most pejorative terms in the Spanish language. Several readers said the FT *had sunk to the level of the* Daily Mirror *and the* Sun. *'You clearly feel you are much cleverer than the Mediterranean countries,' wrote one (Spanish) investment banker. 'Now the crisis is just showing what you are about.'*

In fact, JP had identified the fatal flaw in the eurozone: the imbalances between fiscally orthodox northern economies like Germany and fiscally profligate countries in the south. He had, in effect, predicted Europe's sovereign debt crisis, a brilliant piece of detective work which served readers and investors well.

WEDNESDAY, 10 SEPTEMBER

The chancellor Alistair Darling* comes to lunch in the Bracken room. The mild-mannered Scot from the Lowlands lacks authority and comes across as too reasonable in a crisis. His equivocations in response to our questions suggest he's being second-guessed by Gordon Brown.

My verdict was premature. Darling declined to grandstand, because he didn't have the answers at this stage. Nor did the prime minister. And nor did the FT.

MONDAY, 15 SEPTEMBER

RIP Lehman Brothers, one of the most fabled names on Wall Street. The federal government has stood aside and let the bank collapse. Weekend negotiations for a full sale ended in failure, though Barclays will pick up half the stricken bank. This is the biggest story in the world and it's only just

---

* Alistair Darling was born in Hendon, Middlesex but was educated in Scotland. Only one of three ministers to serve continuously in government since Labour's 1997 landslide election victory.

begun in terms of the likely 'domino effect' on other wobbly financial institutions like Merrill Lynch and Morgan Stanley, the impact on the world economy and the future shape of financial regulation.

A financial bubble is like a train of thrill seekers on a downhill stretch with no brakes. You can throw all the warning signals you want on the tracks to try to slow down the train, but the gravity of greed will always win out. In this case, the politicians and regulators thought they had matters under control and the passengers, many of them blindfold, were definitely enjoying the ride. The only way the train stops is when it crashes. That's what happened in September 2008.*

My job is to assemble an army for the battle ahead. Martin Wolf on finance and the economy; Gillian Tett and John Authers on markets. The banking team need more news-hounds like Francesco Guerrera, our US banking editor. Our US news editor Gary Silverman talks too much, like all New Yorkers; but he's a shrewd, experienced ex-Wall Street reporter who is the best rewrite man in town. Robert Shrimsley has all the skills to organise the reporting teams and manage the story with me and Martin Dickson.

I do have one nagging doubt. Roula Khalaf has put together a long-planned two-week tour of the Middle East in mid-October. We are due to interview Benjamin Netanyahu in Israel, King Hussein of Jordan, possibly Bashar al-Assad in Syria and the fabulously rich rulers of Dubai and Abu Dhabi in the United Arab Emirates, plus a host of other sources. We're bound to pick up a host of good stories.

---

* I am indebted to my friend Jim Macgregor for the train of thrill seekers metaphor. We have had several memorable rides together.

There's a sound business reason for going too: the *FT* is looking to expand readership in the region. But a prolonged absence will take me away from a huge, fast-moving story. *The dilemma highlights the tensions in my self-appointed role as editor-reporter. Fortunately, I think I know a way out.*

THURSDAY, 18 SEPTEMBER

The global financial system is in meltdown. Banks in desperate search of liquidity are cutting credit lines to hedge funds. The commercial paper market is drying up. Short sellers are rampant. The Volatility Index known as the Vix has gone haywire. Equity markets are in free fall.

I'm hovering around the main news desk, watching the TV screens flashing red sell signs. Yet, for all the buzz that afternoon and evening, I confess to feeling a bit like a bystander. As a reporter at heart, I'm tempted to work the phones. As an editor, I'm dying to get my hands on some copy. And yet, as I keep reminding myself, the editor must not be a backseat driver, especially on deadline. You have to stop fussing and let colleagues get on with the job.

Where I can exert direct influence is the mid-morning meeting of commentators and 'leader writers', where we agree on the *FT*'s editorial line on the big issues of the day. Normally, I'm light touch. But these are not normal times. Today, the question is whether regulators should impose a temporary ban on short selling. Should we back intervention, knowing that short sellers help to establish market value; or should we back a ban on the grounds that the survival of the financial system is at stake? In the end we backed a temporary ban.

The authorities simply had to intervene, a point later reinforced by Steve Schwarzman, head of Blackstone. He told me that market confidence was evaporating by the hour. He called his wife Christine who advised him to call Hank Paulson in Washington. When Steve suggested Paulson might be too busy to talk and anyway what should he say, Christine replied: 'Tell him we need a sheriff in town.'

FRIDAY, 19 SEPTEMBER

Today we published a new Friday version of *How to Spend It*, our glossy weekend luxury magazine, highlighting its launch at the top of the front page of the newspaper. It was called, laughably, *The Bonus Issue*.

'How to spend what, exactly?' asks one irate reader. Another accuses the *FT* of losing all sense of perspective. I summon Gillian de Bono, the award-winning *HTSI* editor. 'I don't give a damn what you call it. Just no more *Bonus Issue*!'

SATURDAY, 20 SEPTEMBER

John Gapper, writing from New York, has captured the momentous events of the past week, starting with the collapse of Lehman and ending with the fall of AIG, the US insurance giant.

'We are now, unquestionably, in the worst financial crisis since 1929. We do not know how many more banks and institutions will fail – Washington Mutual, the US counterpart for HBOS, is under severe pressure – but Bear Stearns, Fannie Mae and Freddie Mac, Lehman and AIG are plenty,' he says.

'There are lots of people and institutions to blame for that, from regulators to mortgage brokers to, let us admit it, all of us who decided to speculate on house prices. But AIG takes the biscuit. Here was a huge multinational insurance group with a reputation for solid underwriting and risk management that decided to diversify from insuring risks it knew well – car crashes and fires – to covering derivatives it did not understand.'

SUNDAY, 21 SEPTEMBER

A cheeky call to Andrew Gowers, who took over as communications chief at Lehman in London, only to be present at its collapse two years later. I want to hear his side of the story and so I invite myself around for coffee at his place which happens to be within walking distance of my house.

Andrew is standing in his spacious kitchen, flushed with frustration. He calls his former colleagues 'reckless, supine cheerleaders' for Dick Fuld, who insisted on keeping making money at the top of the market but was always behind the curve. Lehman's collapse was entirely avoidable, he says, 'but not after June 2008'.

The second-quarter loss reported in July was a turning point. Fuld refused to speak on the analysts' call. Ten days later, he finally admitted mistakes had been made. Andrew remembers Fuld saying: 'You're never as good as they make you out to be. But you're never as bad either.'

In August, Andrew flew to New York to try to persuade Fuld to hire some 'strategic communication'. He told him the turnaround story was no longer working and it was time to level with the markets. Fuld, surrounded by loyalists, refused to budge. The experience was 'terrible' and Andrew resigned thereafter.

This is one helluva tale. Might Andrew be prepared to write it all up for the *FT*? I've already got the headline: 'Lehman: My Part in its Downfall'.

Andrew is willing to talk – but not to tell. Yet.

28–30 SEPTEMBER

I've taken a calculated risk attending the Conservative party conference in Birmingham. The markets are still whipsawing and all eyes are on Congress where the Bush administration is trying to put together a huge rescue package for the banks. But there will be plenty of bankers and businessmen around to discuss the financial crisis. And, like me, they want to see whether the Tories are a government-in-waiting.

Tea with George Osborne, who is planning sweeping changes in economic management and financial supervision. These include a new independent Office of Budget Responsibility to assess government spending plans and tax forecasts, and a revamp of the Bank of England specifically to cover supervision of the banks. Under Mervyn King, he says, the Bank has become 'too much of a monetary institute'.

The new model would end divided responsibility for macro-prudential policy between the Bank and the Financial Services Authority where 'two fingers are on the same trigger'. *George is right. The system devised by Gordon Brown a decade ago is too siloed. Unifying responsibility will lead to a concentration of power round the governor, but it's a necessary adjustment.*

As I chair an evening fringe debate on the future of the City of London, assuming there is one, there's stomach-churning news from Washington. The House of Representatives has rejected the US government's TARP bailout for the banks. Markets have plunged. The future of the world financial system is at stake. And of all places I'm in Birmingham.

Martin Dickson later told me that the TARP story broke on deadline as he was signing off the first edition of the newspaper.

Robert Shrimsley asked him if he could, for once, insert the word 'panic' in the page-one headline. 'Print it,' said Martin. It was, he later reflected, the most exciting moment in his career.

1—13 OCTOBER, MIDDLE EAST

After more to-and-fro, I have decided to go ahead with my trip to the Middle East. This is about delegation. I trust Martin Dickson. I can call in every morning to London. If there's another Lehman or AIG, I'll be on the next plane home.

This is my first visit to Israel, though I've written intermittently about the Middle East conflict for 20 years. Victoria is accompanying me. Our guide for this leg of the trip is Tobias Buck, an Anglo-German who has just arrived in Jerusalem as the *FT*'s correspondent. Tobias and I drive an hour west to Tel Aviv for a high-level security briefing at the Israel defence ministry. A top securocrat, sitting with a photo of the Auschwitz death camp visible in his office, describes the new political reality in the Middle East. The Arab–Israeli conflict, the organising principle for foreign policy professionals, has been superseded by a broader struggle against radical Islam. Israel and the Arab autocracies now have a common enemy. The fate of the Palestinians has become secondary.

Saudi Arabia and Jordan, the senior defence official continues, have defeated the Islamist terror group Al-Qaeda thanks to their 'state-of-the-art intelligence'. *I wonder if this is a deliberate hint of Israeli assistance.* Egypt has contained the Islamist threat thanks to its tested military and security apparatus. Israel's overriding national security goal is to contain the menace of terrorism, whether A-Q, Hizbollah or

'Hamastan'.* The senior official sums up the situation: 'Stability is more important than democracy.'

The Israelis felt – for now at least – that autocrats were a safer bet than democrats in the Middle East. So much for Condi Rice's vision of democratic change in the region. By 2008, the US had spent $2 trillion trying to build democracy in Iraq and Afghanistan, with heavy loss of life. Israel, America's closest ally, was saying in effect: the mission has been a fool's errand.

Back in Jerusalem, we enter the Knesset, past numerous checks and armed guards, for our interview with Benjamin 'Bibi' Netanyahu, the Likud party hardliner tipped to return as Israeli prime minister in the coming general election. Netanyahu speaks fluent English with a heavy American accent cultivated during his time as a student at Massachusetts Institute of Technology (MIT). Eager to impress, he opens with a lecture on the causes of and remedies for the global financial crisis, addressing his visitors as if they were high-school students. Then he turns to the Palestinian issue.

Netanyahu grabs a green marker and jumps from his seat to sketch a map of the West Bank on a nearby whiteboard. With vigorous strokes, he draws a map with the West Bank divided into disconnected economic zones with dedicated business projects. The ancient town of Jericho will be a magnet for Baptist tourists from the US, he says, with thousands of jobs created. The Palestinians can hold on to their population centres, but the Judean desert and Jordan valley will remain under Israeli control.

---

* Hamastan is a disparaging portmanteau referring to the Gaza Strip under the control of the Islamist group Hamas.

This vision of Greater Israel is a world apart from the two-state solution for Israel and Palestinians supported by the international community, one based on borders in place before the 1967 war and Israeli occupation. Bibi asks me what I make of his makeshift map. 'Actually, I've seen it before,' I reply. 'It's just like a Bantustan.'

Netanyahu, momentarily taken aback, ploughed on regardless. Dore Gold,* his minder and a friend of Martin Wolf, later gave me a mild reprimand. My analogy with the apartheid era in South Africa in fact had some merit. The white nationalists in South Africa set aside territory for blacks known as Bantu homelands. Their idea was to create ethnically homogeneous statelets. More than a decade after our meeting in Jerusalem, Netanyahu, by now in his fourth term as prime minister, formally produced a similar proposal for the Palestinians.

WEDNESDAY, 8 OCTOBER

Gordon Brown is going to part-nationalise the banks, spending £50bn on equity stakes and provide money to help credit flow. This is a big move and I have a brief conversation with London. Of course we have to be supportive. The banks need a bailout, but what matters are the conditions for government support. There needs to be oversight of the banks but not daily micromanagement. My only question is: are the measures enough to turn round market confidence about the state of the banking system?

---

* Dore Gold, a pre-eminent Israeli diplomat, was ambassador to the United Nations in the 1990s and one of Netanyahu's top advisers.

The next five days in the Middle East felt like a distraction, apart from a near-death experience en route to Amman to see the king of Jordan. One of the king's security drivers swerved violently to evade an oncoming Mercedes, almost sending us over a cliff edge – a fitting parallel with the state of the financial world.

By now, Roula Khalaf had joined us. The early-morning drive from Beirut to Damascus was more relaxed, a stunning ride through the Shouf mountains, past the cedar trees and olive groves, and finally a glorious descent into the Syrian capital. President Assad declined to see us, serving up his long-time foreign minister-turned-vice president Farouk al-Sharaa who had worked for the elder Assad. It was a perfunctory conversation.

Next day, Roula and I interview the Syrian industry minister who talks about agricultural reform. He spent time studying in England and speaks with a northern accent. After half an hour, the minister breaks off. 'Mr Barber, would you like to speak to a committee of senior Syrian government ministers on the global financial crisis?'

No warning. No preparation. I ask Roula, the Syria buff, whether the request is legit. She says it's OK to accept. Victoria laughs at the notion I have much useful to say. On the principle of 'do everything once', I jot down thoughts for ten minutes. Then I am escorted into a room with eight or so officials with headphones and an interpreter in a booth. My message is that things are going to get worse before they get better. It may feel like Syria is insulated from the global financial crisis but the shockwaves will arrive soon. Any questions?

A gentleman with grey hair and spectacles raises his hand: 'Do you agree that George W. Bush deliberately caused the financial crisis, just like the invasion of Iraq?'

Three days in Assad's Syria left me with one overriding impression: the society was ossified and stuck in time. People were afraid of the state but there was no respect for it. The ingredients for the coming popular uprising must have been there, but they were impossible for me to detect.

FRIDAY, 10 OCTOBER

The world's financial markets are in turmoil but the official word in Dubai is that everything is ginger peachy. Roula and I are seated for lunch at the Burj Khalifa tower, the tallest building in the world. All the government ministers appear to be present, along with various movers and shakers. One seat remains empty, perhaps reserved for Dubai's ruler Sheikh Mohammed bin Rashid al-Maktoum. *Perhaps Sheikh Mohammed will come; but we make no promises, Mr Barber. Inshallah.*

Midway through lunch the ruler arrives and – surprise, surprise – sits next to me. He insists there are no financial problems in Dubai, whatever the rumours. Dubai is like a stallion, says the ruler, a frequent visitor to Newmarket racecourse. To change the habits of a lifetime now would damage the confidence of his hand-picked team. 'We survived the Iraq invasion of Kuwait, we survived Gulf War I and Gulf War II. We always go against the trend. In life there are lions and sheep. We want lions.' I nod politely.

The 140km drive from Dubai to neighbouring Abu Dhabi took just over an hour and a half. We're due for lunch with an old Roula contact who is running late. When he finally arrives, he looks flustered. Roula asks him what is wrong. He cannot possibly say. Is there a story? Yes but he cannot say. We press hard. Well, he says, looking at his watch, I can tell you but only under embargo. 'We have guaranteed all the banking deposits in the UAE.'

A stunning scoop which renders Sheikh Mohammed's lion assurances meaningless. I mention the Dubai ruler's words to the senior Emirati official who points to a palm tree in the courtyard opposite our restaurant. 'You see that tree,' he says. 'I would like to string them up [the Dubai elite], they're so irresponsible.'

Heavily indebted Dubai recovered but only after a painful financial restructuring. Several favoured businessmen went to jail. In 2009, the FT's *reporting from Dubai incurred the wrath of the authorities, prompting an unusual intervention by telephone from Prince Andrew to my office.*

HRH Duke of York: 'Your man in Dubai, Simon Carr, is causing a lot of trouble.'

LB: 'You mean Simeon Kerr.'

HRH Duke of York: 'Yes, Simon Kerr . . . Look, I'm just passing on a message . . . your man is causing a lot of problems.'

LB: 'Have you read any of Simeon's articles from Dubai?'

HRH Duke of York: 'No. Of course not.'

LB: 'Well, I've read every word that Simeon Kerr has written about Dubai and I don't see a problem . . .'

The conversation ended shortly thereafter.

WEDNESDAY, 15 OCTOBER

A lightning trip to New York to co-host our Business Book of the Year. Lloyd Blankfein, my co-chair, has made time to attend, despite the pressures on Goldman in the market turmoil. Lloyd is still cracking the odd joke but he looks exhausted. The judging panel end up choosing as winner

Mohamed El-Erian's *When Markets Collide*. A title for our times.

Next day I turn up for breakfast with Vikram Pandit, the cerebral Indian CEO of Citigroup, at the bank's Park Avenue headquarters. We meet in a modest guest room far from the elegant top-floor suites decorated with expensive modern art.

Citigroup is basically bust. Does Vikram, whom I first met when he was a senior executive at Morgan Stanley, have the leadership skills to turn it round? He's a picture of grim determination. He's also in despair over public ignorance about the financial crisis, what went wrong and what must now be done. The people in Congress have no clue. 'The *Financial Times* has an important role to play,' he tells me.

Vikram says modern finance has become so complex, mathematical equations modelling risk so sophisticated, that the system has become unmanageable. Even the most brilliant operators in the banks, hedge funds and private equity got their sums wrong. They had no idea of real value. On the other hand, the world cannot go back to a barter system, the most primitive form of transaction. 'There has to be a middle way between securitisation and Stone Age lending.'

Vikram's right. The FT *has an opportunity to make the case for a reformed capitalism, where modern finance is tamed and the right balance is struck between risk and reward. But how do I do it best?*

WEDNESDAY, 5 NOVEMBER

Barack Obama's election victory speech in Grant Park, in his home city of Chicago. I'm watching live on breakfast television at home in London – and I'm looking at our edition of the newspaper which went to print too early to capture the news. But we're going all in on ft.com, opening up the home page with dispatches from Washington, New York and Chicago on the one-term junior senator from Illinois who has made it to the White House. Expectations are high, way too high. Obama is taking office in the middle of the most serious financial crisis since the Great Depression.

MONDAY, 17 NOVEMBER

Glen Moreno, chairman of Pearson, calls early evening. He's an ex-Citigroup executive and former CEO of Fidelity International who is intimately familiar with financial markets. He's also got an odd sense of humour, telling me once that his favourite pastime at his cattle farm in Virginia was to climb up a tree and watch his favourite bull shag all the available cows in a nearby field.

We're at 'the beginning of the end' of a systemic crisis, Moreno says. Governments have stepped in to recapitalise AIG and the Wall Street banks but the real problems have only just begun. Banks are furiously shedding bad assets. And they're making collateral calls on other people to boost their own capital. This has exposed all the 'crap' – a technical term, I believe, which describes near-insolvent, off-balance-sheet entities such as 'conduits' and 'special investment vehicles' stuffed with poor assets like sub-prime-mortgage-backed securities. Meanwhile, private equity is 'buying back the debt of their own crummy deals', says Moreno. *What goes around comes around in modern finance, I guess.*

The Fed is doing its bit, buying commercial paper in order to free up the locked credit markets. But there's another huge risk pending. 'We're going into a recession with a financial system in crisis. This is going to impact the real economy in retail, commercial property and cars.

In short, says Moreno, with a hint of resignation, 'This ain't over.'

Glen Moreno was an invaluable financial markets mentor in the coming months. As Marjorie's nominal boss, he was also a (usually reliable) source of political intelligence at Pearson. In the next few days, I reached out to every source available in order to better understand the impact of the financial crisis. These were vital 'background' conversations which helped me to shape the tenor of news coverage and commentary.

Sir Richard Lambert, former editor of the FT *and director general of the* CBI *employers' federation, was always direct and helpful. We had enjoyed a special connection since he hired me as a young pup back in late 1984, a courtship which involved several lunches and grillings at the* FT*'s office, then at Bracken House.*

A close colleague once remarked that Richard combined three essential qualities as FT *editor: effortless superiority, childlike naivety and ratlike cunning. When a big story broke, Richard would turn Tiggerish, banishing newsroom torpor and demanding excellence from editors and reporters alike. He inspired great loyalty.*

In late November we spoke by phone. Richard sounded a little breathless to me, shaken perhaps by the gravity of the situation.

'Banks are in a state of shock. They've had a near-death experience. This is no time for business as usual. Credit risk is deteriorating. Banks have to shrink the size of their loan book, but there has to be an orderly work-out run by the Bank of England.'

Richard tells me that talk of wholesale nationalisation of

the banking industry is 'absurd'. It is critical to get credit markets moving again. He favours a temporary fiscal boost to the economy, not too much but enough to free up cash flow. A lot of good businesses are going to the wall. 'Bottom line,' he tells me, 'it's going to be bumpy.'

FRIDAY, 5 DECEMBER

I've almost finished my photojournalism essay for 2008, when the world appeared to be hurtling towards financial Armageddon. On reflection, I write, the global financial crisis is a sober reminder that the path of history is far from linear.

'Some may view events as a form of divine retribution, a punishment for a generation of excess characterised by the growing gap between the very rich and the rest of us. At the very least, they challenge two assumptions which have held good since the fall of the Berlin Wall: the innate superiority of the western model of market capitalism and the inevitable progress of globalisation.'

2009

AFTERSHOCKS

*By the turn of 2009, the global financial crisis had moved from
survival to recovery. Central banks had 'saved the system' by
injecting vast amounts of liquidity to support the banks. But
questions remained about their solvency. A serious recession was
under way, as well as a political reckoning for the model of liberal
capitalism which had held sway since the Thatcher–Reagan years.
The US, with an untested President Obama in office, would have a
vital role to play in international economic diplomacy. The Group
of 20, a new forum for the world's most important powers, would
work on a coordinated fiscal stimulus. Other groups examined
re-regulation of the financial sector. Gordon Brown would make a
significant contribution on all fronts. China, the second economic
superpower, would emerge as a global player, a theme highlighted in
the* FT's *groundbreaking interview with premier Wen Jiabao in
London.*

*Three years into the job, I wanted a renewed focus on original
reporting, especially in the financial sector; but I was also
determined to shape the debate about the future of capitalism. My
final task was to maintain the pace of digital change in the
newsroom. Robert Shrimsley's move from news editor to managing
editor ft.com was the most important appointment of the year, a
signal that one of our best journalists would lead the digital*

transformation of the FT, *a job he held until the end of my editorship.*

Editorial transformation was key to the FT*'s commercial proposition which relied heavily on business subscriptions from banks, accountancy and law firms, as well as prestigious institutions such as the IMF and World Bank. This 'B2B' business was run by Caspar de Bono, a brilliant, obdurate man who spoke in short sentences which usually started and finished with 'our contribution [profits] to the business will double this year.' Caspar's team sold subscriptions in bulk to companies, like debentures for seats at Wimbledon. Thanks to technology, we could show customers how much individuals were reading. Naturally, our new business model relied upon the companies' employees not sharing individual passwords. Some businesses understood; but there were exceptions.*

THURSDAY, 29 JANUARY, DAVOS

My appointment with Steve Schwarzman, the billionaire buy-out king of Wall Street, is late afternoon in the main conference centre in Davos. I want to talk about the US economy, but there's also the small matter of the *FT*'s lawsuit in Manhattan which alleges employees of Blackstone short-changed the *FT* on ft.com subscription payments.

I had my doubts about filing a suit against the might of Blackstone but Chief Inspector de Bono is adamant he has proof that one of the firm's employees set up an account later shared with other people at the firm. The username was 'the blackstone group' and the password 'blackstone', hardly the most imaginative codewords in the English lexicon. At any rate, thousands of articles were shared in the period 2006–8, our suit alleges, and the *FT* is seeking compensation.

Blackstone denies responsibility and says the senior employee has long since left. We are at a stand-off. At this point, I've suggested to the *FT* board that I could have a quiet word with Steve.

We meet at a small plastic table near the bar serving soft drinks, coffee and little blocks of Swiss chocolate. Steve is livid that the *FT* has had the temerity to take legal action against his firm. He's baffled by our insistence that *FT* journalism cannot be shared around the office, just like a newspaper, and he thinks our pricing is extortionate. But what's really set him alight is that the *New York Post* has picked up on the story. Every Wall Street banker reads the *Post*, mainly for the gossip. In this case, the reporter has contrasted Blackstone's alleged penny-pinching with Steve's 60th birthday party which cost $3m, closed down a lane of Park Avenue and featured Rod Stewart and $40 crab legs.

Steve believes the *FT* deliberately leaked the story to the *New York Post*. That's not true but he's not listening. He's beyond indignant that we have impugned the integrity of his firm and, by implication, him. I accept that Steve is in no way at fault. But his threats of Blackstone reprisals are endless. Bans on advertising, boycotts of reporters and more. Finally, I've had enough.

LB: 'You know, there's a lot of people who say newspapers are finished, that there's no way they can survive.'

SS (seething but listening)

LB: 'The *FT* has built a new business model based on people paying for subscriptions. We've worked really, really hard to show people that they're wrong to write off the *FT*.'

SS (still seething)

LB: 'So there comes a moment when I say: fuck you.'

SS (after a long pause): 'I get it.'

Blackstone and the FT *came to an amicable resolution of the dispute. Other businesses clamped down on password sharing and our B2B operation thrived. A generous philanthropist, Schwarzman remained an invaluable source of advice and insight, especially on US–China relations where he set up the Schwarzman Scholars programme at Tsinghua university in Beijing. In September 2019, we enjoyed a memorable Lunch with the* FT *at Claridge's, owned and refurbished by Blackstone, to mark publication of his memoir,* What It Takes: Lessons in the Pursuit of Excellence.

My trip to Davos inspires the usual mixture of fascination and dread. Journalists, even newspaper editors, are assigned rooms with tiny wooden beds and what appear to be moulded plastic showers. Some delegate or other invariably breaks an elbow slipping on ice, none of the street signs make any sense, and every room, hotel façade and street hoarding is plastered with vacuous, 'forward-looking' corporate branding. Davos founder Klaus Schwab's annual *talkfest* has turned into a giant money-making machine.

This year, I tell myself, the trip to the Swiss Alps should be useful because the cream of the capitalist world is in attendance. Then again, I won't discover much from Vladimir Putin's keynote address, 'Shaping the Post-Crisis World' – a thinly disguised obituary to western capitalism, delivered with an industrial dose of Schadenfreude. Schwab offers effusive praise and welcomes on to the stage Michael Dell, billionaire founder of the eponymous computer group.

'How can I help?' asks Dell, turning to the Russian leader.

Putin, who understands and speaks English, looks witheringly at Dell. Speaking in Russian, he replies: 'We don't need help. We are not invalids. We don't have limited mental capacity . . . Pensioners need help. Russia does NOT need help.'

An American journalist asked Putin the following day why he had humiliated Dell in public. Putin paused and then performed the equivalent of a judo throw. He asked the journalist why he was wearing such a prominent ring on his finger. Was he trying to make a statement? What kind of statement? Within a minute, the journalist had turned to jelly.

FRIDAY, 30 JANUARY

Marcus Agius,* chairman of Barclays Bank, wants a quiet word. We go back 25 years when I was a financial reporter and he was a merchant banker at Lazard. Today, Agius wants a vote of confidence in Barclays which picked up half of Lehman Brothers business and wants to be seen as one of the bigger winners in the crisis.

We meet 'off-stage' in a meeting room at Promenade 98, a house near the Congress Centre which for a small fortune the world's elite can book for the week. I'm sweating because I've been running late as usual, forgetting to remove my cool black ski jacket. Agius is dressed-down casual, the model of the gentleman banker.

He highlights 'sound' banks like Barclays, Lloyds, HSBC and Standard Chartered with strong capital buffers and contrasts them with reckless speculative operators such as

---

* Marcus Agius was a City grandee who spent more than three decades at Lazard before joining the Barclays board in 2006. He was also a director of the BBC executive board and former chairman of the trustees of the Royal Botanic Gardens.

HBOS and Royal Bank of Scotland (RBS). 'Some people are OK,' says Agius, 'and some people have done their brains in.' Barclays, he suggests, 'is a proxy for other good banks.'

Agius was skirting over an inconvenient truth. In the US, Wall Street banks were forced to take public money to recapitalise their balance sheets. In the UK, HSBC successfully argued it had no need for government support, because of its deposits in Asia. Barclays escaped too, turning instead to Qatari investors and assuming life could go on as usual. The UK authorities saw the move as ill-advised but also as a slight to their authority in a crisis.

Mark Carney, the ex-Goldman Sachs executive turned governor of the Bank of Canada with the matinee good looks, is a man to watch. He tells a Davos fringe meeting that banks 'need to get back to being the handmaidens of industry' rather than financial speculators. He's calling for new rules to bolster banks' capital buffers. The idea is to strengthen balance sheets in order to reduce risk-taking, thus providing insurance against the next crisis.

My final stop is a 'working lunch' with Gordon Brown at the Hotel Seehof, a half-hour trudge through snow and security checks from the main conference centre. I'm expecting all the summit suspects to be present: Prince Andrew, a Davos regular in his role as special UK trade envoy; Sir Mike Rake, the garrulous Europhile chairman of BT; Stephen (later Lord) Green, Anglican priest and chairman of HSBC, known as 'God's Banker'; Ian Davis, head of McKinsey, the global management consultancy; Roger Carr, the British industrialist and unofficial chairman of the Great and Good.

There's an air of expectation among the 30 or so guests crammed round a long rectangular table stacked with wine glasses. This is Brown's first Davos outing as prime minister and the business lobby is eager to hear his first-hand assessment of the crisis and the government's response. Brown, a son of the manse, is on first-name terms with the global elite. Today, he's on cracking form.

International cooperation is crucial to tackling the next phase of the crisis. He's earmarked the G-20 summit* in London in April where the UK is leading efforts to agree on a coordinated stimulus to stop the world economy going into a deep recession. The prime minister is mindful of history. In July 1933, the London economic conference tried a similar coordinated approach on exchange rates to stop competitive devaluations and pull the global economy out of depression. 'It failed,' says Brown pointedly.

Brown's economic diplomacy would bear fruit at the G-20 meeting with a co-ordinated $5 trillion stimulus to the world economy, a bigger role for the IMF and a host of regulatory reforms. His calls for a similar international response to Covid-19 in 2020 would fall on deaf ears.

SUNDAY, 1 FEBRUARY

Wen Jiabao, China's premier, is known as Grandpa Wen. Last year, after an earthquake struck northern Sichuan province, Wen became the grieving face of the nation, touring flattened villages and calling out to buried victims. He is even reported to have shed tears, a rare display of emotion from a Chinese Communist party leader.

---

* The Group of 20 was the newly configured vehicle for post-crisis statecraft including large developing economies, notably China and India.

After weeks of low-key diplomacy, I've landed an interview with the premier via Madame Fu Ying, Beijing's ambassador in London. Madame Fu is a silky operator with a cast-iron grip who served as an interpreter to Deng Xiaoping, the great reformist Chinese leader. Her role fits into Beijing's charm offensive, a decade-long effort to play down the threat associated with China's rise. The *FT* is seen as a medium to convey a bigger message: post-Olympics China has arrived on the world stage to play its role in management of the financial crisis.

The *FT*'s interview with Premier Wen is due to take place in the Mandarin Oriental hotel in Knightsbridge. Over lunch, Madame Fu sketched a portrait of Wen, 66, the trained geologist turned politician. He is apparently 'a very nice man' who loves to read Adam Smith's *Theory of Moral Sentiments* and quote ancient Chinese poetry. I've also had two briefings from the *FT*'s in-house China expert, James Kynge, who has advised me to be respectful but not supine, to listen and not interrupt. This is far from easy, because consecutive translation is bound to eat into our allotted interview time of around one hour.

Wen Jiabao arrives on time, a sprightly, dapper figure who greets me with a friendly smile. The Chinese premier has been up since dawn and even jogged around Hyde Park. The Rosebery room, usually reserved for tea and sweet-cakes, has been rearranged to fit an elaborately choreographed stage set. A young female interpreter is placed to his right. Four *FT* journalists (myself, James Kynge, Geoff Dyer, Beijing bureau chief, and Lifen Zhang, editor of *FT Chinese*) sit in tiered formation. I am placed most directly opposite Wen, who quietly but firmly sets the ground rules for the interview.

'I want to make clear here that I will be most sincere in all my answers, but I may not tell you everything,' says Wen, pointing an index finger at us.

Wen's public image at home is that of a self-effacing, frugal man (though stories would soon emerge that his son, Winston, had made a fortune as China liberalised its economy). Today, he's modestly dressed in a dark suit, white shirt and greyish tie. His message is that the Chinese government is spending untold billions on infrastructure and tax cuts to boost the domestic economy. China is doing its bit to revive demand; now other countries must respond too.

My response is that people have been telling Beijing for 50 years that only capitalism will save China and now – hey presto – China must save capitalism. The premier demurs. I try another angle. Does he accept that, while the crisis was made in America, China also indirectly contributed because of its excessive savings? Wen, stiffening, talks about 'confusing right and wrong when people who have been overspending blame those who lent them the money'. He cites a famous proverb in China about Zhu Bajie, a fictitious character in the 16th-century Chinese fable *Journey to the West*. Zhu always blames others who try to help him.

When the young interpreter translates the character of Zhu Bajie as a 'pig', a senior Chinese official stands up and says flatly, 'Wrong translation.' The interpreter flushes with embarrassment. A brief pause, and Wen continues.

At the end of the interview, I try to show off by quoting a passage from *The Theory of Moral Sentiments* and Wen smiles approvingly. After a final formal handshake, he leaves for meetings with Tony Blair and David Cameron, who've been waiting patiently in the wings.

Suddenly Madame Fu appears out of nowhere, tugging

my sleeve and remonstrating, 'No pig, no pig.' For a moment, I am baffled. Then it dawns on me: Premier Wen appears to have implied America is 'a pig'. *Maybe not a greedy pig. But, still, a pig. This could spell a major diplomatic incident.* My initial response is to play for time. But Madame Fu is insistent, 'Please, no pig!'

Back at the office, the Chinese embassy has already made several calls, warning that pigs must not appear in tomorrow's newspaper. *I hate being muscled.* My response is we need to read the transcript *and* check out exactly who this character Zhu Bajie is. After intensive research, translation and discussion, I reach a judgement: Zhu was in fact a self-righteous individual who magically assumed many identities, including a pig. So, while we will keep the reference to Zhu in our interview, pigs will not fly in the *FT.* On this day or any other day.

TUESDAY, 3 FEBRUARY

Max Hastings, former editor of the *Daily Telegraph* and *Evening Standard*, war historian and grand poobah of the shires, has invited himself to lunch. We meet at Wilton's, the fish restaurant of choice in London's St James's. Max may – or may not – be available as a contributor. It's difficult to divine between the harrumphs. Max is a very tall man with an aristocratic mien who would be unbearably intimidating were it not for his excellent sense of humour and plentiful gossip. I know he won't leave the *Daily Mail*, because it pays too well. But I know he would make a great *FT* contributor. I make him an offer.

LB: 'How about £500 to £600 per column?'

MH (mildly insulted): 'That's cartridge money.'

*We eventually settled on a slightly higher sum. Max became, with
a slight interruption, one of the very best contributors to the
Weekend FT on politics, history, travel and any other subject.
He remains one of the most versatile (and fastest) writers I've had
the privilege of working with.*

WEDNESDAY, 4 FEBRUARY

The House of Commons treasury select committee has summoned five top business journalists, including the *FT* editor,
to account for their reporting on the banking crisis. We sit
on a bench in the Wilson room at Portcullis House, the modern annexe opposite the House of Commons. There's a few
spectators, including Parliamentary sketchwriters waiting to
pounce at the first misstep.

Robert Peston takes the first question, as usual. I'm eager
to counter the lazy argument that journalists – not bankers
or regulators – contributed to the crash. We were not inno-
cent bystanders but we were certainly not accomplices to
the crime. Our job was to report and respond to unfolding
events. That's hard enough. And it's especially hard when –
as Sky TV anchor Jeff Randall says – there's an army of
people paid to stop us getting anywhere near the truth.

George Mudie, Labour MP for Leeds East, asks me
whether the financial press ignored rumours about Northern Rock's difficulties because bad news doesn't sell
newspapers. *Wait a minute.* We're usually accused of printing
bad news *because* it sells newspapers. In fact, Mudie has half a
point. We're not in the business of reproducing rumours but
we could have better flagged the risks when HBOS and
Northern Rock made their dash for growth in the credit
boom.

THURSDAY, 12 FEBRUARY

An early-evening drink at Dennis Stevenson's house near Buckingham Palace. Over a bottle of Chablis, we muse about Pearson, the *FT* and the financial crash. Lord Stevenson of Coddenham was chairman of HBOS when it was a runaway train. What are the lessons? Where did he go wrong? I'm hopeful that Dennis will write something for us. So far he's not biting. *And he never did bite, despite several more encounters over several more glasses of fine wine.*

FRIDAY, 13 FEBRUARY

Breakfast with Mervyn King at the Bank of England. The governor is irritated that the banks are pushing Gordon Brown around. They're not playing ball on lending or owning up to the toxic assets on their balance sheets. 'I always thought that banks were dangerous institutions,' says King.

King favours a measure of coercion ('Mrs Thatcher would have called them all into a room and told them: this is what is happening'). His impression is that Brown is getting conflicting advice and cannot make up his mind. The PM is fearful about the political fallout from part-nationalising the banks, a reasonable concern since one of New Labour's flagship policies was the abolition of Clause IV in the party's constitution calling for the common ownership of industry. Brown is worried about Tory attacks and negative headlines.

I say Brown is too anxious about day-to-day news stories. The financial crisis is not like fighting a battle. It's a war and we're in for the long haul. Remember Winston Churchill in 1940–41. The Blitz wasn't a turning point. We still had the North African and Italian campaigns ahead of us. King, a history buff, is too polite to rubbish my half-baked analogy.

Policy-making, he says, must be bold, clear and decisive. It's too complicated in the UK and US. He favours a proposal whereby the government guarantees to replenish bank capital ratios if they dip below a certain level, say 4 per cent, in exchange for equity. Of course, that would lead to the market wiping out shareholders in anticipation of nationalisation. *So be it.*

MONDAY, 9 MARCH

Martin Wolf has opened our Future of Capitalism series with a blistering salvo. The world has witnessed the end of the era of financial liberalisation, a moment as significant as the death of revolutionary socialism. 'Another ideological god has failed,' writes Martin, never one to miss calling a moment in history.

For the past three decades, the pro-market ideology of the Thatcher–Reagan years held sway after the perceived failure of the mixed-economy Keynesian model. Other developments played a role too: the shift from the planned economy to the market in China under Deng Xiaoping, the collapse of Communism and the end of stifling central planning in India. The global financial crisis has undermined the legitimacy of the market and the reputations of those, like Alan Greenspan, who placed their faith in its infallibility. What now?

Martin's essay predicted the return of government and regulation in the management of the economy; a huge increase in public deficits;

*and a shift in politics away from the global towards the national,
just as occurred in the 1930s after the Depression. After a brief
post-crisis interlude, the Covid-19 pandemic gave fresh impetus to
the shift towards the state.*

FRIDAY, 27 MARCH

Barack Obama has agreed to an interview with the *FT*. I'm
thrilled because he's not giving interviews to US news rivals.
I'm also intrigued to meet the man who made history, the
first African-American in the White House. *Maybe even a little
star-struck.*

Obama greets us not in the Oval Office but in the
Roosevelt room, named after Teddy Roosevelt, the progres-
sive Republican and big-game hunter, and Franklin Roosevelt,
the four-term president who saved America from the Depression and Europe from fascism. The president is wearing a dark
suit, white shirt and his favourite ruby-red tie, with just a hint
of grey around his temples.

'I read the *Financial Times* before other people read the
Financial Times [in Chicago in the 1980s],' the president says,
flattering his audience. 'Now it's trendy and everybody carries around a *Financial Times*.'

I'm joined by Ed Luce, our Washington bureau chief, and
Chrystia Freeland, our US managing editor. Both Ed and I
felt that two was company and three risked turning into a
crowd for the *FT*'s biggest interview of the year. Chrystia
was keen to attend and I don't blame her. The only remaining question was whether to ask Obama for his autograph.
No way, I ruled.

We've been preparing – *maybe over-preparing* – our list of questions. Both sides have agreed to focus on the US economy and

the financial crisis. In between the upcoming G-20 summit, the economic stimulus package and tax havens – *tax havens, seriously?* – I find myself asking whether this conversation is turning a little too comfy.

Obama projects a Zen-like calm. He comes across as eminently reasonable, calling on allies to display 'unity in the face of crisis'. Bankers, who he points out were responsible for the crisis, should show restraint on bonuses and pay. The world must resist a slide into 1930s-style protectionism. There's no hint of what he would later tell a Wall Street delegation: 'My administration is the only thing between you and the pitchforks.'

After barely 20 minutes, Robert Gibbs, the Alabama-born White House press secretary, places an hourglass on the table in front of me. For the rest of the interview I'm eyeing the sand running through the hourglass not Obama. Suddenly the time is gone. We have enough for a full-page interview but it's bloodless. I should have asked one out-of-the-box question, something irreverent like what's your management style since you've never managed anything? Just one sneaky question to prise open the new president.

In the end, the FT *got a marketing endorsement and I got an upgrade to business class on the flight home to London, thanks to a (visibly) star-struck cabin crew wanting to hear my account of half an hour in the White House with Barack Obama. With the passage of time, the interview stood up better. Here was an American president working with allies on a co-ordinated response to a crisis – a stark contrast with Donald Trump's 'America First' approach to policy.*

FRIDAY, 3 APRIL

Ambassador Richard Holbrooke, America's top diplomatic troubleshooter, has been a mentor-tormentor* for more than a decade. When I was in New York, we lunched regularly at Michael's, the power breakfast and lunch venue of choice in midtown Manhattan. Holbrooke – people called him Dick for many reasons – is a brilliant, flawed bull elephant of a man, blessed with a great intellect who taught me more about American foreign policy than almost anyone. He's also a bully. That's par for the course when facing down Serbia's president Slobodan Milošević, as he did in the Dayton peace agreement; but it's less appealing close-up.

Today, Holbrooke has invited himself for lunch at the *FT* in his new role as Obama's special envoy to Afghanistan and Pakistan, the job nobody in Washington wanted. Holbrooke long coveted the job of US secretary of state. No doubt he still does. The post of special envoy is a comedown, despite his (exaggerated) claims that he has a clear line into Obama.

Holbrooke argues, persuasively, that the Afghan conflict can only be solved in the context of Afghanistan and neighbouring Pakistan ('a fragmented state but not yet a failing state'). There's 'one theatre of war' straddling an ill-defined border between two nations where ethnic ties go back centuries. He's keen to avoid 'Americanising' the Afghan conflict, mindful of Vietnam, where he served as a precocious young

---

* I am indebted to Samantha Power, Pulitzer Prize-winning author and US ambassador to the UN (2013–17), who first used the term 'mentor-tormentor' to describe Richard Holbrooke. I have adopted it as a fellow student-sufferer.

diplomat and witnessed the slow humiliation of his country's military at the hands of guerrilla insurgents. Forty years on, he still believes that America can be a force for good. I too believe that the US, for all its mistakes and missteps, has been for the most part of the 20th century on the right side of history. But at the end of the lunch I'm more than ever convinced that this Afghan misadventure will end in failure.

Holbrooke died in December 2010, collapsing in the office of Hillary Clinton at the State Department from a torn aorta. By 2020, the Trump administration had finally given up on the war against the Taliban. It did not mark a defeat on the scale of Vietnam but it was a significant foreign policy failure.

MONDAY, 13 APRIL

A full-page *FT* editorial to conclude our Future of Capitalism series. 'Some crises spread hysteria; some clear the mind and focus attention,' the leader opens. 'This one has done both.'

Markets are not always self-correcting, the editorial argues. Unregulated markets may reduce, not improve, social efficiency, but these are indictments of capitalists, not capitalism. The main features of the liberal market economy – private property rights, smart but even-handed and arm's-length regulation and democratic politics – are uncontested. But, we conclude, keeping financial markets global while making them safe requires much tighter cooperation between countries, including China, on financial regulation, global macroeconomics and monetary policy. A new international approach is needed.

TUESDAY, 21 APRIL

Yale university has invited me to give the Poynter fellowship lecture, 'Did the media miss the crisis?' I'm still working through in my mind how we could have done a better job. Maybe we were too close to the top people in the City and on Wall Street. We failed to pay enough attention to the traders. Where were our Big Shorts,* the handful of eccentric, oddball investors who spotted that the US housing market – and, by extension, the entire financial system – was built on a foundation of sand?

The Big Shorts read the financial statements, did the due diligence and intuitively understood irrational exuberance. Journalists, like politicians and regulators, were responsible for a failure of imagination. We missed the links between easy monetary policy, the expansion of credit and the explosion of sophisticated debt instruments. We focused too much on the equity markets – equity prices, public company earnings – rather than the credit markets and the 'shadow banking system'. That was where the big money was being made. Just as in the dotcom bubble, we could have done a better job by sending clearer warning signals about risk.

On the other hand, I say to my Yale audience, business publications were pushing against a powerful force: greed. When markets are going up and credit is flowing, it's hard to be a 'perma-bear'.

---

* Michael Lewis's book *The Big Short*, later adapted by Hollywood, portrays the cast of 'misfits' who foresaw the crash. The title refers to large bets placed against the market.

MONDAY, 27 APRIL

A two-day trip to Abu Dhabi to attend the launch of the *FT* edition for the Gulf. Team *FT* is staying at the seven-star Hotel Kempinski Emirates Palace, an 850,000-square-metre gold and marble complex with vast rooms and en-suite bathrooms stuffed with goodies. I telephone Victoria saying I need a golf cart to get to breakfast at Le Café, renowned for its 23-carat gold-flaked Palace Cappuccino which is apparently both drinkable and edible.

Roula Khalaf is handling the Middle East initiative with John Ridding. We're upping our contingent of reporters in the Gulf region to four, increasing our print run ex Dubai, and joining something called the Abu Dhabi media centre. I tell Roula that I've come up with a new name for the cash-rich emirate: 'Abu Doshi'.

FRIDAY, 8 MAY

The *Daily Telegraph* has a blockbuster scoop on MPs abusing expenses claims. Will Lewis,* the ex-*FT* man in charge of the *Torygraph*, has plastered the story over page one as if World War III has broken out. The detail, which comes from a computer disk leaked to the newspaper in return for an undisclosed payment, is excruciating. MPs have been claiming expenses for items ranging from moat-clearing to a duck house and dubious second homes. The sums involved are chump change compared

---

* Will Lewis, an ebullient *FT* reporter, succeeded the author as news editor in 2000 before joining the *Sunday Times* and *Daily Telegraph*, where he soon became editor, rising to be CEO of Dow Jones and publisher of the *Wall Street Journal* (2014–20).

to the money sloshing around Washington, but that's beside the point. Britain's underpaid elected representatives have gamed an antiquated system which relied upon people doing 'the right thing'. Our democracy has been diminished.

The long-term damage to a national institution was hard to measure but beyond dispute. The more mundane question was what the FT *could add to the story. Following up other people's scoops is the most frustrating job in reporting.*

WEDNESDAY, 3 JUNE

Select briefings from Downing Street suggest that Gordon Brown intends to replace Alistair Darling as chancellor with his favourite counsellor Ed Balls. The rumours have grown following Brown's humiliating defeat in the European Parliament elections. Martin Wolf and I decide the *FT* should rally behind Darling, even though Balls is an ex-*FT* man. I approve the editorial, overlooking the mixed metaphor: 'Replacing him would be political theatre – a puppet show to distract from the [electoral] carnage . . . Mr Darling should stay.'

Darling later told me that he credited the FT *editorial with saving his job as chancellor. When Brown read it, he blinked. It was a rare political intervention for the* FT *but Darling had done nothing to deserve demotion. A Balls promotion, by contrast, would have been too clubby by half.*

FRIDAY, 5 JUNE

Evgeny Lebedev, the youthful owner of the *Evening Standard*, has invited Victoria and me to a dinner in honour of Mikhail

Gorbachev at the Jerusalem Chamber in Westminster Abbey, where Henry IV died before embarking on a planned crusade. Lebedev snr is also present, a former KGB agent turned businessman whom I met in Moscow last year. His public persona is a reformist Putin critic, but who knows?

The Lebedevs have long been supporters of the Gorbachev charity for leukaemia research, and the black-bearded Evgeny – who might easily have stepped out of a Chekhov novel – is a new star on London's social scene. David Frost, who is sitting next to me, notes that Gorbachev is looking frail these days. He then catches the waiter's eye and asks for a refill. 'The claret is most agreeable, don't you think, Lionel?'

Twenty years ago, I watched Gorbachev in action in Moscow and Washington. The charismatic Soviet reformer radiated confidence which masked his basic weakness at home. Putin despises Gorbachev as presiding over 'the greatest geo-political catastrophe of the twentieth century'. I see him more as a tragic hero who grasped that the Communist system was bankrupt but hoped he could rescue it through economic rather than political reform. He was no democrat but he changed the course of history.

THURSDAY, 11 JUNE

The *FT* is launching an automatically updating app which will enable readers to access our journalism across a wide range of tablet and smartphone devices – and we're bypassing Apple iTunes store and Google's Android market.

This was a big moment for the FT. *We were among the first news publishers to argue that our value and audience loyalty could trump even the power of Apple. We took a gamble that* FT *readers would come to us and not insist that we share revenues with a gatekeeper. Naturally, we said none of this in public. Our actions spoke louder than any words.*

MONDAY, 27 JULY

Memorial service for Eddie George at St Paul's Cathedral. The former governor of the Bank of England was, like me, a scholarship boy from Dulwich College. He was in charge of the Bank when the Blair government granted its independence, allowing it to set interest rates free of interference from HM treasury or Downing Street. This was an unholy bargain because the price was handing supervision of the banks to the newly created Financial Services Authority. George left everyone in no doubt he thought that was a mistake.

He was right. The Bank of England's more limited remit meant it focused on inflation-targeting and interest rate policy rather than broader financial stability. I couldn't help wonder whether, under the old system, 'Steady Eddie' would have spotted signs of the developing crisis earlier.

TUESDAY, 4 AUGUST

After the Gorbachev dinner, the Lebedev lunch. Evgeny has invited me to Sake no Hana, the Japanese restaurant he owns in St James's Street. He wants advice on how to improve the *Evening Standard*. My watchword is 'focus'. Like the *FT*, the *Standard* has to concentrate on a few things that it does better than everyone else. The arts, culture, the property market, Boris Johnson's mayoralty. Evgeny nods in agreement, casually dropping that his father thinks that more coverage of Russians in

London might be a winning strategy. *This is hopeless.* Then Evgeny mentions that he's thinking of turning the *Standard* into a free sheet. *Lebedev jnr may be a little more serious than I assumed.**

THURSDAY, 6 AUGUST

Baroness Buscombe, the newly appointed director of the Press Complaints Commission, wants lunch. My dealings with the PCC have been mercifully minimal. I prefer settling complaints from readers directly and promptly. And, after Terry Smith, I don't like litigation.

Buscombe has replaced Sir Christopher Meyer, formerly UK ambassador in Washington and John Major's spokesman, a chummy if bombastic man best known for his taste in red socks. The baroness has invited me to lunch at Smiths in Clerkenwell, the vaguely trendy restaurant with a terrace view of St Paul's. Buscombe is a trained barrister and Conservative peer, a little light on the charm. Our lunch is perfectly pleasant until she launches into an attack on Alan Rusbridger, editor of the *Guardian*. Rusbridger, she says, is obsessed by his paper's coverage of phone-hacking at the *News of the World*. He's trying to get the PCC involved. If the story really is true, then it's a matter for the police.

The PCC is plainly rattled. Alan later tells me that the phone-hacking story is very serious. It's a test of the PCC's credibility. He would like the FT *to follow up. This story requires serious digging and still does not feel 'core'. At this stage, it's a watching brief only.*

---

* Lebedev was nominated as a crossbench life peer by Boris Johnson in July 2020, a move which drew charges of cronyism.

6–19 OCTOBER

The *FT*'s Latin America coverage has been a source of personal frustration for some time. I want more pizzazz and I think I've found my man: JP Rathbone, half Cuban mixed with English Parliamentary stock, with a bit of acting thrown in (his father's cousin, Basil, played Sherlock Holmes). JP is understated but classy, an independent thinker with plenty of Latino charm. Three months ago, I called him into my office and hinted at promoting him to Latin American editor. A final decision would come after a joint trip to Argentina, Brazil and Colombia, his own favourite country in the region.

My verdict so far: Brazil is on course to be a regional power, a fast-growing economy with (apparently) stable politics. Under President Lula da Silva, living standards have risen, thanks in part to China's insatiable demand for commodities. Lula has chosen his charismatically challenged chief of staff Dilma Rousseff as his successor, deciding against seeking a third term which would have required a change to the constitution. By contrast, political instability and myopic economic policy in Argentina means people cannot plan from one week to the next. *Conclusion: I'm short on Buenos Aires, long on Brazil.*

Victoria and I rejoin JP in Bogotá. The highlight of our visit – apart from the weekend in Cartagena to round off the Lat-Am tour – is an interview with Álvaro Uribe in the presidential palace. Uribe is the short, silver-haired hard man who has brought the insurgent left-wing Farc movement to the brink of defeat and the world's longest-running civil war to a close. He's followed Teddy Roosevelt's maxim: if you've got them by the balls, their hearts and minds will surely follow.

Security is as tight as Israel's Knesset. Women in pale-blue uniforms patrol the corridors with heavy assault rifles. Our interview was due at 6pm. As we wait, attendants keep offering me cups of Colombian coffee. By 8pm, I'm about to be scraped off the ceiling.

A short man approaches and begins to speak.

'El Presidente, he is very busy . . . El Presidente has a big problem with Venezuela. El Presidente has to see a delegation from Washington. El Presidente see you maybe in one hour. OK?'

The short man disappears.

LB: 'Unbelievable. You mean, we're going to have to wait another hour or more. What's going on? And anyway, who the hell was that guy anyway?'

JP: 'Er, that was Uribe.'

Finally, after almost four hours waiting, we are summoned to a room painted in stunning Colombian yellow to await the president. Uribe takes his place on the opposite side of a vast mahogany table, polished like glass. After a nod to the crisis with neighbouring Venezuela – something to do with plant health standards – I lob a verbal grenade in the president's direction: if two terms was good enough for George Washington, why not for Álvaro Uribe?

Colombia's hard man leaps up and advances towards me, as if to smack me across the face for my impudence. Suddenly he stops and breaks into a smile.

'Because I'm still looking for my Thomas Jefferson.'

Uribe did finally step down, making way for Juan Manuel Santos, the former defence minister. After tortuous negotiations, Santos secured a peace agreement with the Farc. The peace deal failed the first time round in a referendum but was later ratified. Uribe turned into an embittered tweeter who nevertheless helped his protégé-puppet Iván Duque win the 2018 presidential election.

THURSDAY, 29 OCTOBER

My commission for an investigation of Tony Blair's post-Downing Street money-making has come good. We've called the feature 'Inside Blair Inc'. Publication is timed to coincide with Blair's unofficial candidacy for the role of the EU's first full-time president. On paper, he is eminently qualified, barring the Iraq debacle. But our article points out the political risks.

'EU leaders may not like the idea of nominating a man whose affairs are so complex and, some might say, so undis-criminating. He has dealings with Muammar Gaddafi and his son Saif in Libya, the governments of Abu Dhabi, Kuwait; autocrats such as Paul Kagame in Rwanda and President Nazarbayev in Kazakhstan. And that's before the seven-figure annual retainer from J P Morgan Chase.'

Blair failed to land the EU president's job. His commercial (and philanthropic) ventures only grew. I liked and respected TB personally, but ordered reporters to keep an eye on what he was up to. His business was our business.

WEDNESDAY, 4 NOVEMBER

President Lula is in London to sell the Brazil story to investors and pitch his successor Dilma. Lula, the machine worker who ran three times for president before succeeding in 2002, has a touch of Lech Wałęsa. Cheroot in hand, constantly touching the arm of the interviewer, he talks about Brazil's economic miracle which has taken millions out of poverty.

He ends with a personal invitation to me to spend time on his ranch next time I am in Brazil.

Brazil was peaking. Once commodity prices turned down, the economy's weaknesses were exposed, alongside the corruption institutionalised in Lula's first term. Our Brazil correspondent Jonathan Wheatley was always sceptical about the country's economic boom. He was right. Lula went to jail and I steered clear of his ranch.

MONDAY, 9 NOVEMBER

Simon Lewis, Gordon Brown's head of communications, calls during breakfast, Paris time. Would I please take a call from the PM? *Quel sujet?* Simon points to *FT* coverage of the weekend G-20 finance ministers' meeting in St Andrews, Scotland, hosted by Brown.

Around 9am, the PM comes on the line, spluttering with rage about our story suggesting that the government is back-pedalling on its proposal for a global financial transactions tax. I'm walking along a Paris boulevard, trying to get a word in. Voices are raised. Victoria instructs me to take a hike. Suddenly, I find myself in a cemetery, the ideal place to cool off.

Brown had floated a 'Tobin' tax* on financial transactions and appeared to have backtracked after US objections. His insistence that the story was in all respects false made me dig in. In retrospect, I might have been more generous. The PM was showing

---

* The Tobin tax was a small levy on foreign currency exchanges aimed at reducing incentives for high-frequency trading. First proposed in the 1970s by Nobel Prize-winning economist James Tobin, it was supposed to increase financial stability and make the banks pay their share.

international leadership and felt the FT *was undermining him. What we wrote mattered. On the other side, Gordon was a 'moaner'. Siding with him on a contested story was dangerous. When we were clearly in the wrong, I would always act. When in doubt, I would invariably side with the reporters.*

FRIDAY, II DECEMBER

Kevin Rudd,* Australia's bumptious prime minister, wants to talk about the Copenhagen summit on climate change. We've had one phone call which was more than useful. Rudd sees himself as a grand strategist. He also has an unerring ability to talk down to people.

LB: 'I've just been talking to Gordon Brown. He passes on his best wishes.'

KR: 'Really.'

LB: 'I was thinking Gordon Brown is the only person in the world who spends more time looking at his approval ratings than you, Kevin.'

KR (pause): 'Well, I suppose that's what happens when you wake up every morning and have to eat a shit sandwich.'

---

* Kevin Rudd, born in the small town of Nambour on Queensland's 'sunshine coast', led Australia's Labour party to victory in 2007. A fluent Mandarin-speaker, he began his career as a diplomat before switching to politics.

SECTION THREE

AUSTERITY, LEVESON AND THE AGE OF THE IPHONE

COALITION

FRIDAY, 1 JANUARY

After four years in the editor's chair, it is time to rotate the top team. My plan is to move Gillian Tett to New York, replacing Chrystia Freeland as US managing editor. Chrystia has done a good job but I suspect she wants mine. I'm offering her a new job as Washington editor – let's see if she takes it. Marjorie won't like it, but so far she's respected my right as editor to make my own appointments. *And she did so again.**

Gillian's appointment was part of a wider reshuffle of the top team. I want a new managing editor to help me drive the next phase of digital changes in the newsroom. My eye is on a promising South African production journalist, Lisa MacLeod, who is generally popular among colleagues. Dan Bogler has been a steady influence who kept a lid on costs. He will be fine in a new role supporting John Ridding on the

---

* Chrystia passed up the Washington offer and joined Reuters. She later gave up journalism for politics in her native Canada, rising rapidly to foreign minister and then finance minister, becoming a leading voice for liberal democracy in the world. She had found her second vocation.

business side. Stan O'Neal was almost spot on: the *FT* enforcer survived four years but it was time for a change.

By far the biggest story for the FT *in 2010 was the eurozone debt crisis. Greece was found to have cooked its books with debts reaching 300bn euros, the highest in modern history. Fear about a Greek exit from the eurozone ('Grexit') was spreading to other heavily indebted countries, Portugal, Ireland and Spain. In the UK general election, Gordon Brown faced a serious challenge from David Cameron's new model Conservatives. My year opened, improbably, with a three-day trip to Afghanistan in the company of British generals.*

21–24 JANUARY

The first and last time I found myself in a war zone was in Los Angeles in 1992 when the *FT* asked me to cover the urban riots triggered by the police beating of Rodney King. Now Stephen Dalton, head of the Royal Air Force, has invited me to accompany him to Afghanistan. Of course, it's a PR exercise; but my country is at war and I feel it is my duty as editor to witness the conflict first hand, however briefly. We take off in a C-17 transport plane from RAF Northolt for Kabul. In the evening, I am invited into the cockpit as we descend to the Afghan capital. City lights flicker in the night sky. Was that a rocket flare? *This is scarier than walking the streets of south-central LA in the early 1990s.*

The newly formed joint command, headed by US special forces general Stan McChrystal,* is poised to escalate the

---

* McChrystal was later forced to resign for criticising senior Obama administration officials, including Richard Holbrooke, in off-hand remarks to a *Rolling Stone* reporter.

fighting massively against a resurgent Taliban. Coalition forces have belatedly realised that hubris and ignorance doomed the allied campaign in 2006. Now they are fighting back. 'It's the last throw of the dice,' says one UK commander.

Over the next three days, we are whisked in an armed convoy around Kabul, on to Kandahar air base and then via helicopter to the giant British base at Camp Bastion in Helmand province. Jon Williams, BBC News foreign editor, and Robert Hannigan, the prime minister's chief counter-terrorism adviser,* are the other civilian guests on the trip. Amazing how quickly Jon and I bond under mortar fire, real or imagined, on a night in Kandahar.

Until we visit a military hospital, the conflict appears curiously distant. A surgeon in jeans talks about operating on soldiers torn apart by improvised explosive devices (IEDs). He mentions casually that the floor of the operating theatre has been washed of blood. That's the moment I realise the visceral reality of war.

A British commander likens the conflict to fighting the IRA in South Armagh: ethnic, tribal and irreconcilable. Another opines that 'It's all about who controls the night.' The Taliban are dogged and resourceful, targeting those members of the coalition (the Germans, apparently) whom they suspect are vulnerable. The International Security Assistance Force's (ISAF) military goals are: shape, clear, hold and rebuild territory. It sounds neat but in Afghanistan everything is a thousand shades of grey.

Much hope – *too much hope* – rests on Hamid Karzai, the elected president, a master manipulator of tribal loyalties.

---

* Robert Hannigan went on to lead GCHQ, the UK eavesdropping agency (2014–17)

'Clinton without the sex', as one British military man puts it. But Karzai is a Pashtun from Kandahar, not a wily white politician from Arkansas. He is not – and cannot ever be – his own man. In the short term, the violence is going up. The Taliban counter-insurgency risks turning into a terrorist operation against the local population.

One morning, we join Dalton's group at a high-level ISAF briefing. General McChrystal is on manoeuvres. Our host is Lieutenant General Nick Parker, a grizzled veteran whose son was grievously wounded last year by a booby-trap bomb. ISAF, says Parker, is a new command structure more like a 'forced Caesarean' than a natural birth. Reconciliation is 'a bit of a wild card'. The allies have left it a bit late: 'I'm saying "We can win", not "will win".'

Dalton congratulates Parker on his summary. Could he define what success in Afghanistan might look like?

'Well, sir,' says General Parker, 'success would be when we turn the country into a normal Third World basket case . . .'

Nervous laughter.

General Parker adds a more serious note: 'We should not be too big on democracy.'

The idea of turning Afghanistan into a democracy was always a pipe dream. It was simply too big, too poor and too ethnically diverse. I wanted to support the British military campaign, but I left Kabul with my doubts reinforced.

WEDNESDAY, 10 MARCH

A British general election is coming – soon. Gordon Brown bottled a snap election in 2007; now he's running out of time.

Labour's poll rating has dipped. David Cameron's Conservatives have a slim lead, but the race feels ever tighter. Nick Clegg, leader of the Liberal Democrats, might hold the balance of power. He is our host tonight at dinner in his west London home.

I've known Nick from my days in Brussels and always liked him. He was a super-smart member of the cabinet of Sir Leon Brittan, then EU trade commissioner. Like his old boss, he can be inflexible and a tad self-righteous. That's the Dutch blood in him. (Sir John Kerr, Britain's ambassador in Brussels, once told me that the definition of a Dutchman is someone who sees a wall and accelerates.) Clegg is a committed European who supports economic and political integration. So is Miriam, his Spanish wife, who is a top City lawyer. They have three young sons: Alberto, Antonio and Miguel. *Multilingual, multicultural, a moderate alternative for Tory voters: the Cleggs are high on the* Daily Mail's *(s)hit list.*

There's nothing fancy about Clegg's middle-class home: no ostentatious art on the walls; no bone china and crystal on the table. It's a family house that's lived in, Victoria says, approvingly. Nick and Miriam have invited Matthew Parris, the *Times* columnist, and his partner and *Guardian* commentator Julian Glover as fellow guests. We all want to know whether the Lib Dems will partner with the Conservatives or Labour. Clegg is having great fun keeping us guessing. 'Oooh, I can't possibly say. No, really, I've not made up my mind.' My bet is Clegg has made up his mind. He's a liberal on social policy and a conservative on economics. He has to choose Cameron.

Nick Clegg was a fresh face with a middle-of-the-road message. He dominated the first TV election debate but Cleggmania faded after

he said Britain suffered 'delusions of grandeur' over World War II.
The Daily Mail *savaged him for attacking national pride. Nick*
had accelerated into a brick wall of his own making.

WEDNESDAY, 31 MARCH

David Cameron breezes through the door of his private
office in the House of Commons. He is tieless, wearing a
white shirt and casual black trousers. No sign of the Eton
mess jacket he wore as a schoolboy, nor the bespoke tailored
tailcoat in navy blue, with matching velvet collar, offset with
a mustard waistcoat and sky blue tie which he wore as a member of the Bullingdon Club in his student days in Oxford.
David William Donald Cameron wants to be an Average
Dave for the day. He's preparing for power, eager to impress
the *FT*, aware that we have yet to signal our preference in the
coming election.

I'm joined in the interview by George Parker, the *FT*'s
political editor, former Brussels bureau chief and fellow cyclist. Apart from Crystal Palace football club, we have a lot in
common. We are reporters at heart, men who love chasing
the big story, swapping gossip and feeding on adrenalin to
meet a news deadline. In the coming weeks, George's day-
to-day judgements will be crucial to shaping my own views
of the campaign.

Cameron is more confident, more fluent than in previous
encounters. His big pitch is the 'Big Society'. This bears no
resemblance to Lyndon Johnson's Great Society with its
huge federal welfare programmes; in fact, it is the opposite.
Cameron is betting on a modern version of Edmund Burke's
small platoons of civic-minded volunteers and faith-based
charities. But these good people surely cannot be a substitute

for the state. George and I reckon the Big Society is a cover for cuts in welfare. *And we were right.*

On European policy, Cameron promises he will be honest, straightforward and engaged with Europe as 'friendly neighbours, not reluctant tenants'. *Another soundbite which would later crumble in the Brexit referendum.* Cameron has placed a photograph of himself with Chancellor Merkel near the entrance of the office, an unsubtle hint that the Tories are closer to the heart of Europe than the *FT* imagines. 'We get on very well,' Cameron insists, unaware that I heard the opposite at the end of the Merkel interview in Berlin two years ago. Maybe they've become chummy in the interim. Somehow I doubt it.

WEDNESDAY, 7 APRIL, MADRID

Alan Parker* is a pest. He might be best pals with David Cameron but London's top PR man is still a pest. He keeps promising to fix an interview in Madrid with José Luis Rodríguez Zapatero, the socialist prime minister of Spain. Muchas gracias, *Alan, but if Zapatero wants an interview, his people can contact my people.* In truth, I'm being a bit precious. The timing for a Zapatero interview is excellent. The risk of a debt default by Greece is increasing. Zapatero has one goal: to reassure financial markets that Spain is not Greece, and he has chosen the *FT* as the medium to deliver the message.

We meet in the Palace of the Moncloa, the official residence

---

* Sir Alan Parker, chairman of Brunswick, the global PR firm which he founded in 1987. Knighted in 2014 for services to business and charity.

and workplace of the prime minister. Zapatero, 49, is a professional politician nicknamed 'Bambi' or 'little slippers' (a pun on his name). He's a soft touch compared to his brusque predecessor José María Aznar, whom I interviewed in 2000 in the Moncloa. Zapatero's solution is to throw money at problems. That was fine when Spain was in the middle of a wild construction boom. After the spectacular bust of 2008–9, Spain needs reform badly.

'We have a plan, a credible, quantified plan,' Zapatero declares. 'If we need more austerity and more extreme measures, then we will implement them.'

Everything Zapatero says is hedged, though he is more robust when it comes to his liberal social agenda and passage of a same-sex marriage law. That's an impressive stand in conservative, heavily religious Spain, but it's a sideshow compared to the economic crisis. Exasperated, I toss a grenade his way.

'Mr Prime Minister, do you believe, when historians look back on your time in office, they will conclude this was the moment when Spain slipped from the premier league into division two in Europe?'

Zapatero is aghast. 'No, no. Spain is not going to fall back into the second division. Yes, times are difficult, but we will be in the first division with the strong countries.'

The interview closes. Zapatero, still shaken, asks me to accompany him on a walk in the woods in the grounds of the Moncloa.

PM (finally speaking English): 'How is my friend Tony Blair?'

LB: 'He's fine. Missing office.'

PM: 'I want to return to your question. Spain is not Greece. It is not in the second division.'

LB: 'Mr Prime Minister, the water is up to your neck. If you don't take action, I fear the worst.'

PM: 'Yes, yes, I understand. But Spain is a very conservative country . . . People live in their villages, they don't move. If we don't handle this properly, we will have people on the streets . . .'

Zapatero introduced austerity measures a month later, but he left it too late and paid the electoral price. His centre-right successor Mariano Rajoy looked like a plodder but took on the task of economic reform. Spain slowly turned the corner.

TUESDAY, 20 APRIL

An explosion at a BP-operated oil rig called Deepwater Horizon in the Gulf of Mexico has killed eleven people and sent millions of gallons of oil into the coastal waters off Louisiana. My mind flashes to our award-winning investigation into BP's poor safety record in the US. This 'blowout' accident is on a different scale, more like the *Exxon Valdez* spill. *Exxon Valdez* altered attitudes to environmental safety for a generation (and, incidentally, made the future Exxon Mobil combination a better, more safety-conscious company). *This is a huge story for the* FT: *one of Britain's most important companies is in deep trouble in America. I order extra reporters to be deployed.*

THURSDAY, 22 APRIL

Every once in a while, my job takes me away from business and financial news to somewhere I never dreamt of. Today, Victoria and I catch one last glimpse of the punk era: the funeral of Malcolm McLaren, manager of the Sex Pistols and inspiration behind the movement which spat in the face of the British establishment. I interviewed McLaren at the 2009 *FT*'s Business of Luxury Summit in Monaco, one of my more incongruous assignments. He was warm, thoughtful and sickly pale from the cancer which eventually consumed him.

Young Kim, his partner, has invited Victoria and me to the funeral service held at the deconsecrated church now known as One Marylebone, opposite Great Portland Street station. We take our seats behind Vivienne Westwood, the grand dame of fashion design and McLaren's former partner. She's wearing her signature headband 'chaos'. Other guests include Sir Bob Geldof, Turner Prize-winner Tracey Emin and punk-era glitterati with orange, green and jet-black hair, many decorated in chains and black leather jackets.

The service is comically unruly, marked by an inter-familial row, a wolf caller from the Arctic North and a choir from Tiffin School, McLaren's alma mater. At the end, the Sex Pistols signature song 'Pretty Vacant' blasts through the aisles. A matt-black coffin, spray-painted with 'Too fast to live, too young to die' is loaded on to a horse-drawn hearse headed for Highgate cemetery, resting place of Karl Marx. Pearly kings and queens follow in his wake. RIP Malcolm M.

MONDAY, 26 APRIL

George Osborne has agreed to see me at the Conservative party's Milbank election headquarters. The polls look tight. Osborne is not his usual laid-back self. He predicts a close election. Is a coalition on the cards? Osborne rules nothing in or out. The shadow chancellor won't ask directly for the *FT*'s support but he talks about 'being helpful'. Then, unprompted, he suggests that the Conservatives might have to do a deal with the Democratic Unionist party (DUP)* in Northern Ireland.

I call George Parker. He too finds this implausible. Our takeaway is that a tight election means a coalition looks inevitable. But will the Tories come out as the party with the most seats and the chance to form a government? Or will Gordon Brown pull off a come-from-behind victory?

TUESDAY, 27 APRIL

Time to decide which party to back in the election. In 1992, when the *FT* gave a mealy-mouthed endorsement to Neil Kinnock's Labour party, I was on sabbatical at the Institute of Governmental Studies at the University of California, Berkeley. My professor-mentor was Nelson Polsby, a heavy-weight (in every sense) with a passion for British politics. Nelson asked me who the *FT* would back. John Major's Conservatives, I shot back. My credibility on campus never recovered.

As editor, I inherited a Blairite newspaper. The *FT* backed New Labour in 1997, 2001 and 2005. Blair/Brown were responsible stewards of the UK economy, pro-European and, well, modern. We had no room for Tory Europhobes. Two decades on, I'm determined to avoid another Kinnock moment. We have to make a choice and declare with conviction.

---

* Founded in 1971 by Ian Paisley, the DUP is the major force in Northern Irish politics in favour of maintaining the UK union.

Hardly anyone among senior *FT* colleagues has a good word for Labour or the Tories. At one meeting, many speak up for constitutional reform, including the voting system* and the House of Lords. A squishy majority favours the Liberal Democrats or an unspecified coalition involving the Lib Dems. I like Nick Clegg, but there's no way the *FT* can back the Lib Dems. They don't have a hope of being the majority party. I summon Jonathan Ford, newly recruited as chief leader writer. I picked Jonathan because he was a good writer and we needed someone to balance the *FT*'s Blairite majority. I didn't really care what kind of Tory he was.

Then a colleague showed me a photograph of a youthful Jonathan in full Bullingdon dress, sitting alongside Boris Johnson on the steps of Christ Church in 1987. David Cameron is standing haughtily in the middle. *Jesus (and I don't mean the college).* Jonathan mumbles something about Bullingdon being many years ago. I agree. Jonathan may have political preferences but he has an inquiring mind. That's why I hired him. We will write the election editorial together. 'This is not a Polish parliament,' I tell Jonathan, 'everyone does not have a veto.'

After several drafts, we reach an unambiguous conclusion that it is time for a change. 'Britain needs a stable and legitimate government to navigate its fiscal crisis and punch its weight abroad. On balance, the Conservative party best fits the bill.'

---

* Liberal Democrats wanted to introduce more proportional representation in Parliamentary elections in place of the first-past-the-post system that favours the two major parties, Conservative and Labour.

FRIDAY, 7 MAY

The Conservatives are the biggest party but with no clear parliamentary majority. A coalition of some kind looks inevitable. Several conversations with colleagues confirm my view that a Tory–Lib Dem combination would be best for Britain. I call Osborne. Watch this space, he says.

WEDNESDAY, 12 MAY

David Cameron and Nick Clegg look like newlyweds in 10 Downing Street's rose garden. But this is no shotgun marriage. It's taken almost a week to agree on the terms of a new coalition government. Five Lib Dems are in the Cabinet, led by Clegg, now given the title deputy prime minister. A new fixed-term Parliament act will lock the coalition in place for five years. After 13 years of New Labour, this feels like new politics.

My bet is that this coalition can work. Clegg and Cameron are centrists so on a personal level there is no political chasm between them. The issue is whether they can control the likes of Boris Johnson, who has called the coalition a cross between a bulldog and a chihuahua. Tory instincts are for single-party rule.

To Lucy Kellaway's book launch: she's written a tale of two office romances doomed from day one. Lucy joined the *FT* in 1985, a few weeks after me, and has become one of our star columnists. A diminutive figure with an impish smile, Lucy enjoys a unique rapport with readers. She doesn't think twice about skewering the pompous, powerful – and me. The other day I said that we needed to strengthen the *FT*'s bench. Lionel, she remonstrated, this is not a bloody football team.

SUNDAY, 30 MAY

Tony Hayward, chief exec of BP, calls me. He has been fire-fighting for five weeks after the Deepwater Horizon oil-spill disaster. 'It's like a war over there,' he says; 'the rage in America is 24/7.' BP still cannot cap the well. Hundreds of millions of gallons of oil are continuing to spill along the coastline of Louisiana, Alabama and Mississippi. The other day, Hayward took a break on his private boat and ended up on the front page of the newspapers. When challenged, he said: 'I want my life back.' This is a PR disaster. BP's head of communications is Andrew Gowers. *Talk about the curse of Lehman.*

THURSDAY, 3 JUNE

Eric Schmidt, CEO of Google, has dropped by for a chat. He is the (paper) billionaire brand ambassador, the bridge between the Google software engineers in their own virtual world and the real world of politicians, journalists and the general public. Schmidt is beyond borderline arrogant. Every other sentence ends with a supercilious smile. Today Schmidt is making an effort to be charming. I suspect he's angling for more favourable coverage.

Google came up with a catch-all 'Don't be evil' company motto which gave them a near free pass on any ethical complaints for a while. Their search business has been an enormous boon for consumers; but as Google's power has grown, it has started to attract bad publicity in the UK and on the continent. People are muttering that Google doesn't pay enough tax. Privacy is an issue, too. Street View, ostensibly a product to map out streets and houses, has been accidently collecting data on Wi-Fi use by individuals. Online competitors in media complain Google is deprioritising rival search results to favour its own digital advertising business. Schmidt bats away the criticism, but I detect the public mood is shifting, especially on privacy. For once, Europe is ahead of the US.

FRIDAY, 11 JUNE

The *Guardian, New York Times* and other international news organisations have published leaks from 250,000 classified US diplomatic cables, part of a data dump obtained by WikiLeaks, the whistleblowers' website. There are embarrassing disclosures about official views on Pakistan's nuclear weapons programme, US commanders' withering criticism of the UK's military effort in Afghanistan and allegations that Russia's intelligence agencies are using mafia bosses to carry out criminal operations. We'll have to follow up, however painful.

> *Matching the story turned out to be trickier than I imagined. For a while afterwards, every other* FT *foreign news story was peppered with 'according to WikiLeaks'. Finally, I imposed a temporary WikiLeaks ban. It was time our reporters did some original reporting rather than parroting or feeding off selectively leaked documents.*

WEDNESDAY, 16 JUNE

To the News International summer party at the Orangery in Kensington Gardens. Rupert Murdoch's pulling power is extraordinary. David Cameron has turned up with his wife,

Samantha, complemented by Nick Clegg. Both Miliband brothers, David and Ed, are present, no doubt eyeing Murdoch newspaper support for their campaign for the Labour leadership following Gordon Brown's decision to step down. Mark Thompson, head of the BBC, has joined other usual summer party suspects such as Martin Gilbert, the gregarious Scottish boss of Aberdeen Asset Management and BSkyB director; Sir Philip Green, the billionaire Topshop retailer; and James Corden, the actor and comedian. I say hello to Rebekah Brooks, the flame-haired editor of the *Sun*. We're now on first-name terms after our pre-Christmas lunch at San Lorenzo, Princess Di's favourite celebrity hangout. Then I spot Rupert standing on the lawn, well apart from the crowd. Politicians are lining up to kiss the patriarch's ring.

The summer party was peak Murdoch in Britain. Within weeks, the tabloid phone-hacking scandal would break, ending the spell which he had cast over Britain's political class for three decades.

THURSDAY, 1 JULY

Guy Dinmore, our Rome correspondent, has a strong story from a private dinner with Jeffrey Immelt, CEO of GE, the American jet-engines-to-healthcare giant. Immelt, sitting alongside top Italian business executives, blasted Barack Obama and said the national mood in America was 'terrible'. Business does not like the president and the president does not like business, he said. Immelt also has some choice words about China, saying resource-rich countries risk being 'colonised' and Beijing is becoming increasingly protectionist. 'I am not sure that in the end they [China] want any of us to win, or any of us to be successful.'

Our story is ready to go until GE puts on the squeeze. A top Italian executive, who I happen to be friendly with, calls to protest that the session was off the record. Guy insists the ground rules were not clear and what Immelt said is a matter of great public interest. I've been hearing for weeks the same complaints about Obama's lukewarm attitude to business. GE will be furious but they'll get over it. *We have to publish.*

MONDAY, 26 JULY

Tony Hayward is out. His biggest mistake was to lead from the front line. A baby-faced, diminutive Englishman from Slough striding the Louisiana beaches was never going to convince Americans he was the right man for the job of clearing up the oil spill. Hayward ended up being branded 'the most hated man in America'. His successor is Bob Dudley, the tall, quietly spoken oil executive from Mississippi. He will go down well with the Houston oil-industry fraternity, the people who really matter. Dudley's previous job was in charge of the BP joint venture with TNK in Russia, a perilous assignment which ended up with him fleeing the country. I make a note to get in touch. It's important I have the same relationship that I had with John Browne and Tony Hayward.

TUESDAY, 24 AUGUST

Breakfast with David Miliband at the Cinnamon Club, favourite watering hole for MPs. The ex-foreign secretary is favourite to win the Labour leadership. He's 45, a highly intelligent, confident public performer from the Blairite wing of the party, but there's something missing. David can't resist showing he's the smartest guy in the room. He learnt his craft under Tony Blair, but there the comparison ends. Blair connects naturally with people. You know you're being seduced but you don't really mind. David is a lecturer, just like his academic father. He doesn't really listen to people.

I ask David how his campaign is going. Good, but he's put on weight over the summer holidays because he's not eating properly. I want to ask him about how it feels to be running against younger brother, Ed, an unreconstructed Brownite. David won't bite. So I ask him how his campaign is going down with the trade unions. Unite, the country's largest, has just backed Ed.

David says he's not worried about the union vote. He cannot afford to be too close to the unions, because he needs to occupy the centre ground in a future general election.

LB: 'David, this isn't a general election. You're still running in the primaries.'

David Miliband missed his chance. Ed Miliband scraped to victory, thanks to trade union backing. We will never know how David M. might have fared against Cameron. He moved to New York with his family and reinvented himself as a highly successful head of the International Rescue Committee, the refugee charity. The two brothers are said to be back on speaking terms.

WEDNESDAY, I SEPTEMBER

The *New York Times* has produced a stunning piece of reporting showing that phone-hacking at News International was common practice and went way beyond a couple of rogue operators. The *Times* also says, based on court records and interviews, that the Metropolitan Police failed to pursue leads suggesting that the *News of the World* was routinely listening in to people's mobile phones. This comes on top of earlier *Guardian* revelations. I'm envious and slightly ashamed that it took a foreign newspaper to nail the story.

TUESDAY, 7 SEPTEMBER

Baroness Buscombe is in my office pleading the case for the Press Complaints Commission, the voluntary regulatory body for printed newspapers and magazines. She's accompanied by Stig Abell,* her (able) deputy director. My enthusiasm for the PCC vanished after it agreed to look into a complaint from a retired Thai police officer in Bangkok who had taken umbrage at a column by David Pilling, our Asia editor. David criticised the Thai military for 'mowing down' protestors. *That's exactly what they were doing. Killing people. Why is the PCC investigating complaints from people in faraway countries who are apologists for violent regimes?*

---

* Stig Abell, a journalist who rose through the ranks at the Press Complaints Commission, later became its director. In 2013, he joined the *Sun* as managing editor, making the improbable but successful transition to editor of the *Times Literary Supplement* in 2016. Helped to launch Times Radio in 2020.

When Buscombe pushes back, I lose my rag. If this happens again, I warn her, the *FT* will pull out of the PCC.

In fact, the PCC was not long for this world. The phone-hacking scandal was primarily a matter for the police, but the impression took hold that the PCC had simply looked the other way. Pressure for a public inquiry grew.

FRIDAY, 1 OCTOBER

Lloyd Blankfein, chairman and chief executive of Goldman Sachs, makes a rare phone call. He says the *FT* has caused 'real damage' to Goldman because we've misreported a speech he gave to European regulators and falsely claimed Goldman is threatening to move or cut back on its European operations. What he said was indeed more nuanced, but our banking editor Patrick Jenkins has not exactly committed a capital offence and anyway we've since tweaked the story. Blankfein won't let go, arguing the fault goes beyond accuracy or fair interpretation. It is symptomatic of an 'endemic weakness' in newspapers and of news exaggeration, and the pressure to push the story beyond its 'natural life' in order to sell. There is a built-in incentive to exaggerate, distort and 'hype' headlines. *That's a little rich coming from the banking profession which is never knowingly undersold, but I'll leave it there.*

Lloyd and I both know that our relationship goes beyond this story. Goldman sponsors the annual *FT* Business Book of the Year award. He's way too smart to mention this and I'm certainly not going there. I like and respect Lloyd. Hell, against most colleagues' wishes, I decided the *FT* should vote him Person of the Year last year, even after his flippant remark that banks were doing 'God's work'. I realised it was an offhand remark but others failed to get the joke. Bankers these days are more unpopular than journalists and estate agents. Now he's having a sense-of-humour failure.

Lloyd B: 'All the power is at your end.'

LB: 'I am no Solomon.'

Lloyd B: 'No, because you do not possess Solomonic wisdom but you do have Solomonic power.'

Goldman continued to believe that the FT *had a built-in bias. Several years later, a top executive told me repeatedly that our Goldman stories were 'clickbait' to attract attention and readers to our website. He was right that Goldman stories scored highly, but that was because Goldman was one of the most powerful banks in the world. It was also a source of news because of questionable clients, like Sir Philip Green and 1MDB, the Malaysian state investment fund from where several billion dollars was stolen. Goldman, for better or worse, was always going to be a subject of interest to the* FT — *and all forms of media. Despite those occasional bumps, I still regarded Blankfein as one of the most original minds on Wall Street.*

In the evening, bang on 6pm, Bob Diamond, the American boss of Barclays, arrives to see me one-on-one in my office. The time for remorse is over, he says, ignoring the fact that a bit of remorse would probably go a long way. The City establishment and the Bank of England haven't forgiven him (or Barclays) for dodging the UK government bailout. Diamond says the banker bashing has to stop. We need banks willing to take risks and work with the private sector to create jobs and boost economic growth, he says. The *FT* should help.

Diamond wants to go back to business as usual and is appealing to my better capitalist half. But a campaign defending bankers is premature. Multiple investigations are still under way in London and New York about banker misconduct, like the rigging of the Libor rate. I agree that we need banks to make the modern economy work, but this thing ain't over.

In the new year, Diamond appeared before a Parliamentary committee and declared that the time for 'remorse and apology' was over. He declined to say if he would waive his bonus, as he had done for the previous two years. He was pilloried and later forced out.

9–23 OCTOBER, INDIA–PAKISTAN TRIP

An elderly gentleman takes his seat near me on the flight from Dubai to Calcutta, the starting point for my ten-day trip to India and Pakistan. Victoria points out that it's Rowan Williams, archbishop of Canterbury, engrossed in an ancient, threadbare tome.

How to address the archbishop? Your Holiness sounds too papal. Maybe 'Your Grace' or 'Father'. I'll settle for 'Archbishop'. We discover we are both visiting Calcutta and New Delhi. The plane lands and his Grace is whisked away in a mini motorcade. The *FT* commoners are greeted by James Lamont, our South Asia bureau chief, a veteran foreign correspondent with a patrician gait.

Victoria would like to go sightseeing, starting with the Victoria Memorial Hall and the Indian Museum (Jadu Ghar). After a couple of hours, jet lag is kicking in hard. We return to the Oberoi Grand hotel. My room key won't work. I summon a bellboy and demand a new key. Entering the room, everything looks slightly unfamiliar. Suddenly, an elderly white man emerges from the shower, wrapped in a white towel. It's the archbishop. What a relief he's not wearing his spectacles!

Next day, it's late-morning Assam tea with the governor of West Bengal, M.K. Narayanan, formerly India's chief spook, in Raj Bhavan, former residence of viceroys, when Calcutta was the capital, and a copy of the Curzon family's Kedleston Hall in Derbyshire. We talk about terror, Pakistan and China. The dapper, silver-haired governor says Chinese influence is spreading in Burma, Pakistan and Sri Lanka. The Indo-Chinese border dispute – rooted in Beijing's claims over all of historical Tibet – remains unresolved. 'But a war would be disastrous for China.' *And surely India, too, governor.*

MK turns to America. George W. Bush was an underrated president. He faced down critics to push through a landmark nuclear cooperation deal with India. He quotes Dubya on India approvingly: a billion people, a million problems and still a democracy.

After visits to Mumbai, Delhi and the walled fort town of Gwalior, we fly to Amritsar, site of the Golden Temple and the British massacre of Sikhs in 1919. From there to the Wagah border crossing, an Asian Checkpoint Charlie where armed guards lower their national flags and strut their stuff at sunset. Soon we are racing in a convoy to Lahore, one of the power centres of the Raj and an ancient city of learning.

Salman Taseer, governor of the Punjab, receives us in his official residence with stunning gardens, spacious rundown rooms with faded colours and high ceilings, including one containing a sprung ballroom floor. The governor is a slightly louche individual with slick black hair and an imperious tone. A former political prisoner, he is a long-time ally of Benazir Bhutto and her widowed husband, President Asif Ali Zardari. His central message is reminiscent of Richard Holbrooke's: Pakistan is not Afghanistan.

Nevertheless the recent Taliban offensive in the Swat valley – which threatened to seize the Punjab – is an existential threat to the Pakistani state. Taseer brands the insurgents a mixture of foreign fighters, smugglers and bandits with no links to Islam; in his words 'brainwashed, illiterate tribes'.

Within eleven weeks, Taseer was dead, assassinated by one of his bodyguards for tolerating blasphemy.

Final stop: Islamabad, where we begin aboard a Russian-built Mi-171 helicopter for a two-hour tour of the flood zones to the north of Islamabad, courtesy of the Pakistani air force. This is followed by a weaving drive past potholes and buffalo to the hilltop home of Imran Khan, one of the finest cricketers of his generation and now an opposition politician. Time for an interview – and a round of cricket in his magnificent garden overlooking Rawalpindi and Islamabad.

Tall, sinewy and at 57 still strikingly handsome, Imran greets me in his airy, stylish home. He is wearing a white shalwar and cream kameez, matched by brown Peshawari sandals. I have brought a new cricket bat, new pads and new batting gloves, courtesy of Farhan Bokhari, the *FT*'s long-time correspondent in Pakistan. *(Presumably, all on* FT *expenses.)* Imran and I warm up with talk about his philanthropy – he's raising money for flood victims and for a cancer hospital in memory of his mother – and the ugly state of Pakistani politics. Then a smart walk to a makeshift wicket in his garden and six balls delivered at reduced speed by the maestro, the last dispatched with an impressively straight bat to the edge of the garden and down the hill into the underbrush. 'Good shot,' says Imran, 'but we will not find the ball now.'

On to dinner with President Zardari, Imran's political foe. After numerous checkpoints, we enter an underground car park filled with black Mercedes and Range Rovers. Ten heavily armed security guards escort us upstairs to a large room with no natural light and two heavy electric sliding doors which open and shut for no apparent reason. The private quarters are littered with portrait pictures of Benazir Bhutto, his murdered wife and former president of Pakistan. This place is half-bunker, half-shrine.

Our bespectacled, black-haired host – known as Mr Ten Per Cent for his business proclivities – speaks in halting English. When dinner is served, I notice that Zardari employs a food taster. Victoria and I look at each other, not daring to say: 'We'd like to have some of that too, if you don't mind.'

During the meal, Zardari either deflects or ignores questions until I press him about Pakistan's use of Islamist militants in neighbouring Afghanistan as leverage in a future peace settlement. 'When you wear gold earrings and they are too heavy,' he says, 'you take them off.'

Zardari never remotely had that margin of manoeuvre, especially with Pakistan's armed forces and fearsome intelligence services in the background. He completed his term in 2013 but continued to be dogged by charges of money laundering. He continued to campaign for justice in the case of his wife's murder.

TUESDAY, 26 OCTOBER

To the John F. Kennedy School at Harvard to deliver a lecture 'Can the euro survive?' My host is Nick Burns, the dean and veteran State Department diplomat. I'm fortunate to be able to draw on colleagues such as Martin Wolf, our in-house German commentator Wolfgang Münchau and a new recruit, Martin Sandbu, a Norwegian economist who has taught in the US. These lectures help me organise my views on big subjects. They're also good for establishing the *FT*'s brand (and my own) as a 'thought leader'.

The American elite have always had doubts about Europe's single currency. Bob Rubin once likened Europe to a museum. (I imagine the French room devoted to social solidarity, the German room to industry and the Italian room to the Renaissance spirit.) Plenty of people in Washington still view the EU as a marginal player when it comes to the exercise of power.

My job is to present the case for guarded optimism. It's true the original euro construction was flawed. The enforcement procedures for budgetary discipline don't work. There's no bailout mechanism. But the EU is slowly getting its act together. I set out four scenarios from here:

Scenario A: France and Germany agree the status quo is unsustainable. The EU eurozone agrees to fiscal transfers to make the monetary union work, along the lines of the US model of transfers between states. Conclusion: Greece does not default.

Scenario B: The euro survives but the present eurozone does not. Greece defaults, abandons the euro and introduces

172

a flexible exchange rate. A smaller, more tightly formed euro-zone survives which is built around the Franco-German core. Mervyn King leans this way.

Scenario C: The euro collapses. Germany says it will no longer accommodate the majority of eurozone members. It is strong enough to go it alone. Conclusion: very unlikely. There's too much at stake politically and Germany's currency would go through the roof.

A Greek default is by no means inconceivable but countries will fight hard to prevent it. I would put some money on Scenario A; but muddling through – Scenario D – may be a better bet.

The lecture drew polite applause from the students and Nick was happy. I would award myself a B++. I was right to argue that politics was the strongest factor keeping the eurozone together. But progress on eurozone reform was agonisingly slow and Grexit came close in 2014–15.

MONDAY, I NOVEMBER

Gordon Brown wants to see me in his Parliamentary office in Portcullis House. After the election, Brown sent me a spidery note thanking me and the *FT* for our (mostly) responsible coverage of his premiership and leadership during the financial crisis, and wishing me well for the future. Otherwise radio silence.

On arrival, Brown's aide greets me nervously. Something feels wrong. Brown greets me and inquires twice after my daughter, remembering she spent her gap year in Africa. Then he gets to the point.

GB: 'How could you do it?'

LB: 'Do what?'

GB: 'You know what I mean ... support the Conservatives ...'

When I suggest that the *FT*'s endorsement of Cameron was somewhat nuanced, Brown flies into a rage. Cameron and Osborne will drive the economy into a deep recession. They don't understand the importance of international cooperation to tackle the next phase of the financial crisis. They're a bunch of Little Englanders. By backing the Tories, the *FT* (and me) are parochial Little Englanders too.

GB has half a point on the Tories and their Europhobic tendencies, but I've worked in Washington, Brussels and New York. My children were educated overseas. How dare he call me parochial!

Brown apologises. A brief period of calm ensues. Then he repeats the question: 'How could you do it?' Another tirade follows.

Finally, I tell Brown I have to get back to the office. A grumpy goodbye. On the way out, Brown's aide apologises. 'That was quite something,' I reply, 'but by Gordon's standards I would say: pretty mild.'

SUNDAY, 5 DECEMBER

Julian Assange, founder of WikiLeaks, has been arrested this morning by officers from Scotland Yard. He is facing extradition to Sweden where he faces charges of sexual molestation and a single count of rape. Tonight, he is spending the night in Wandsworth prison.

Jane Owen, editor of *House and Home*, the *Weekend FT* supplement, knows Mark Stephens, Assange's lawyer. She's an old friend who is never short of a madcap idea. Today she's suggesting that I do a Lunch with the *FT* with Assange in Wandsworth prison. I've heard Assange is an egomaniac and a nightmare to deal with. *Thanks, Jane, but I'll pass on this one. So, I suspect, will Wandsworth prison.*

MONDAY, 13 DECEMBER

Amanda Thirsk from Prince Andrew's office has been in touch. The Duke of York would like to see me at 3pm at Buckingham Palace. Our earlier Dubai conversation is fresh in my mind. What is Andrew up to now? Never having been inside the Palace, I'm up for an adventure.

It's a splendid early-winter's day. The sun is shining. I take a stroll down Pall Mall and take a left at the main gates in search of a royal entrance. On the corner, at Palace Gate, I ask a security guard to let me in. 'Wrong entrance, Sir. You have to proceed to the main gates.' I sprint back to the bearskin-hatted grenadiers guarding the main entrance and make a breathless entry into the Palace. Thirsk greets me and we ascend by lift to what appears to be the first floor. A long walk on an even longer carpet to the Duke of York's office. He's on the phone in another room. I've made him wait for a few minutes, now it's payback.

Prince Andrew greets me, sits down and stares intently. 'Do you have an interesting job?'

LB: 'I certainly do.'

HRH: 'What *do* you do?'

Rather than talking in grand statements, I retreat into details. I recite my routine: rise at 6.26am; car pick-up at 7am; arrive at office 7.35/40, having digested the *FT* newspaper and online stories. Working breakfast or more reading.

9.30am news conference, 10.30 leader conference, maybe lunch out of the office . . .

And so the surreal exchange goes on until I ask: what can I do for you, Sir?

HRH says his public role is misunderstood. He is delivering real value for the nation in his role as trade envoy. How can he get across the value of what he's doing? Would I consider sending an *FT* journalist on a trip with him? How about the editor?

I decline, politely. As for coverage, we've already done a Lunch with the *FT*. The prince looks disappointed. What advice might the editor of the *FT* have?

LB: 'I'm a journalist. I'm not in the advice business. But I could make an observation.'

The Duke of York perks up.

LB: 'It might be a good idea to stop doing real-estate business with Kazakhs.'*

Soon afterwards, I make my royal excuses and leave.

---

* Timur Kulibayev, son-in-law of Nursultan Nazarbayev, president of Kazakhstan (1990–2019), purchased the prince's Sunninghill Park house for £3m more than the £12m asking price.

TSUNAMI

The recurring theme in 2011 was upheaval: in the Middle East, where the Arab Spring brought millions on to the streets of Cairo, Damascus and Tripoli; in the eurozone where the debt crisis concentrated in Greece; and in my own industry where the phone-hacking scandal blew up in spectacular fashion, forcing Rupert Murdoch to close the News of the World *tabloid newspaper.*

I was fortunate that Roula Khalaf was in place to manage the Arab Spring coverage. She had covered the region for 15 years, building a strong network of correspondents. The Arab Spring encapsulated a dilemma for America and the west: whether to support the nascent democratic movement with more than rhetoric or whether to prop up the old autocratic order in the name of stability. In Libya, the US helped the UK and France to topple Colonel Gaddafi's brutal regime, letting loose anarchy in the country. Egypt's size, culture and history made the country central to the Middle East. Here the foreign policy choices were even less clear-cut.

The stakes were much lower in the UK where Cameron responded to the tabloid phone-hacking scandal by ordering a public inquiry led by Lord Justice Leveson. This was to consume my attention and time for two years as I struggled, along with fellow Fleet Street editors, to devise a new system of self-regulation to

*replace the discredited Press Complaints Commission. My
frustration only grew as I watched the digital giants led by Apple,
Facebook and Google consolidate their hold on the distribution
channels for media and increase their share of digital advertising.*

*The tabloids had broken the law and abused public trust. But
newspapers in general had lost their role as the gatekeepers between
elected politicians and the public. Their best hope was to use the
internet to their advantage, building a loyal audience unlimited by
geography. The FT's mission was to be the most trusted source of
news, commentary and analysis on the stories that mattered. The
most immediate was the eurozone crisis. In early 2011, I had a
lucky break.*

WEDNESDAY, 16 FEBRUARY

Victoria and I have escaped London to spend a brief winter
vacation in the Virgin Islands. This morning, as I lay sun-
bathing on the beach, my mobile phone rings. It is Mario
Draghi, governor of the Bank of Italy.

I first met Mario in 1996 when he was a senior official at
the Italian treasury and I was on sabbatical as a visiting fellow at the European University Institute in Fiesole, outside
Florence. Mario was one of the key negotiators on the single
currency and Italy's entry into the eurozone in 1999. We hit
it off and have kept in touch ever since, even while he left
public service briefly to join Goldman Sachs before returning as Italy's central bank governor.

Mario apologises for disturbing me – 'You are in the Car-
ibbean, really?' – and then works his way round to the
pressing question: how do I assess his chances of becoming
the next president of the European Central Bank? Axel

Weber, head of the German Bundesbank and the front-runner, has just dropped out* of the race. Mario wants to know whether being an Italian is an obstacle to becoming ECB president, especially in the eyes of the Germans.

We both know the Italian caricature: fast cars, frivolous spenders. *Essentially unserious.* The Germans are of course *very* serious, especially when it comes to saving money and sticking to the rules. But Mario is the mirror opposite of the Italian caricature, a Roman by birth whose father was a central banker. He is one of the co-architects of the euro, a truly international central banker. And his stint at Goldman has reinforced his intuitive feel for financial markets.

I remind Mario that all appointees to top European jobs – like president of the European Commission and president of the European Central Bank – are supposed to leave nationality at the door. He is a strong candidate and I reassure him of that.

Mario sounds less than convinced.

LB: 'Mario, you never know what might happen. You definitely have a chance.'

Mario's call felt like a subtle overture to obtain the FT's *support for his candidacy. He always had my vote because he was simply the best person for the job. In June, EU leaders appointed Mario as ECB president. From that moment, our relationship grew even closer. We were in this crisis together.*

---

* Weber pulled out of the ECB race on the grounds that he opposed the ECB's activist bond-buying programme. He was nominated in July 2011 as chairman of UBS, the Swiss bank.

TUESDAY, 8 MARCH

To Downing Street to see David Cameron for a 'catch-up'. The prime minister doesn't want to talk about the recent botched SAS mission to Libya – apparently a plan to insert British diplomats accompanied by armed SAS and MI6 officers into rebel-held territory in Libya. When their helicopter landed, the party was immediately surrounded by young rebels and held captive for four days. The mission looked like a good-faith effort to open a dialogue with the Gaddafi opposition; maybe something more sinister. We are supposed to be good at this stuff, I say. Cameron shrugs: 'These things happen.'

The prime minister is more interested in exchanging thoughts about the eurozone crisis. He likes our economics commentator Wolfgang Münchau, finding it highly amusing that a pro-European newspaper like the *FT* has a German sceptic writing about the euro. Wolfgang doesn't parrot the standard Brussels line, says Cameron.

The PM seems to think that the only salvation for the euro is via a great leap forward on economic integration. He's worried about the City of London being exposed to new regulations, with the UK on the sidelines. *I'm not sure the Germans are ready for the big leap.* Nothing much else to take away from the meeting, except my earlier exchange with Craig Oliver, Cameron's new press secretary. He says – without prompting – that Andrew Lansley's proposed reforms of the National Health Service are a mess.*

---

* Andrew Lansley, Conservative MP and health secretary, had pushed through controversial reforms of the NHS, once described as so big they could be seen from space. Later awarded a peerage.

Cameron always wanted to talk to me about Europe, or maybe it was the other way round. I knew Europe was his party's Achilles heel; he knew the FT *was the best-informed and most influential newspaper on matters European. I rarely got much else out of him.*

FRIDAY, 11 MARCH

A magnitude-9 earthquake has shaken north-east Japan, sending a 39m tsunami hurtling onshore, killing thousands of people and rendering many more homeless. The tidal wave damaged the cooling system of the Fukushima nuclear reactor. My first thought is whether our Tokyo bureau and commercial staff are safe. They're OK, but this is an epic natural disaster requiring extra reporting power and fine judgements about how close our journalists venture to the fall-out zone around Fukushima. I'm soon heading for a long-planned trip to South Korea, China and the Philippines, where the *FT* has established an office handling finance and some basic editing functions, part of the trend to outsourcing. Tokyo is now a must stopover.

The FT *was fortunate to have fluent Japanese-speakers like Demetri Sevastopulo and Robin Harding who wrote moving dispatches on the human suffering after Fukushima. Later, Kana Inagaki and Leo Lewis wrote incisively about the corporate disaster of Tokyo Electric Power (Tepco) which operated the Fukushima plant, and the wider failures of a cosy regulatory regime. Our Japanese coverage was top notch, which, as it turned out, was fortunate for me and the* FT.

18 MARCH–1 APRIL

First stop on my tour of North Asia is South Korea and the border post of Panmunjom in the Demilitarised Zone demarcating North and South. Back in Seoul, I meet Lee Jae-yong (J.Y. Lee),* heir apparent in the family that controls Samsung, one of the great South Korea conglomerates (*chaebol*). Samsung makes TV sets, refrigerators and washing machines, smartphones and, crucially, semiconductor chips. He says the internet revolution has led to an explosion of demand in tablets and mobile phones, along with a huge increase in data services.

J.Y. Lee was passionate about Samsung products, regularly bringing his high-tech gadgets to the Sun Valley media conference for display to delegates invited to his room. In August 2017, he was found guilty of bribery, embezzlement, capital flight and perjury charges and sentenced to five years in prison. His sentence was cut in half on appeal and he was released in February 2018 on a four-year probation. His case led to the impeachment of then-President Park Geun-hye and inflamed popular anger over the power of Korean conglomerates. In 2019, J.Y. Lee faced a second trial on corruption charges, but continued as de facto head of the company.

MONDAY, 28 MARCH

A lightning trip to Shenzhen to visit Huawei, the fast-growing Chinese telecoms equipment supplier and – just

---

* J.Y. Lee was long viewed as the dauphin to head Samsung, which was founded by his grandfather as a grocery trader and in 2012 would account for a fifth of South Korea's exports.

maybe – secure a first ever interview with its charismatic founder CEO Ren Zhengfei. I'm accompanied by Kathrin Hille, our Beijing technology correspondent who happens to be German but is also a fluent Mandarin-speaker. Shenzhen looks like a replica of Silicon Valley circa 1989 – trim lawns, university-style campuses and lots of young software engineers milling around.

We are greeted by senior Huawei executives, including Ken Hu, vice president, who informs me he spent 160 days on the road last year. After a group photograph, we tour the facility to inspect the Wi-Fi masts, phones and other sophisticated telecoms equipment which has made Huawei number two in the world with $28bn in annual sales.

I want to hear directly from 'Chairman Ren' the story of how he left his job in the People's Liberation Army to build Huawei. But he is reportedly unwell. This sounds like a diplomatic excuse for avoiding a western journalist. Over lunch with Ken Hu, I take copious notes. Then, without warning, I am summoned to a room, from where I spot a distinguished elderly man being escorted along a campus path by two nurses.

Ren enters, spluttering with what appears to be flu. One nurse places a silver spittoon near my left foot, while another prepares acupuncture in case the patient begins to feel poorly. I introduce myself and Kathrin – with no handshakes.

Ren says he owes everything to Deng Xiaoping, the reformist leader who succeeded Mao and abandoned the command economy in favour of a controlled market economy. Deng wanted to restructure a bloated PLA. Ren, a regiment commander, lost his job but went into making packet-switching equipment for phone operators. Slowly,

Huawei grew. First in neglected rural markets, then in the cities and later overseas, defying efforts from state operators to shut down the fledgling start-up.

In 1992, Ren visited Silicon Valley. 'When I went to the USA, I took $80,000 in cash because I didn't know what things would cost.' Where did he put the money? Ren laughs and points to his breast pocket, saying he had the rest of the cash sewn into his jacket.

Ren says he continues to study American technology companies, especially semiconductor makers like AMD, Intel and (then) IBM. After the dotcom bubble burst in the early part of the century, Huawei grew too fast and came close to bankruptcy, he says. But now it has recovered. 'We have been very successful in the Chinese market but we have suffered political difficulties because the government did not believe we would be so successful.'

This fits the company narrative that Huawei is independent of the state. Ren and his executives deny they have benefited and continue to benefit from massive subsidies, as alleged by the Americans. Ren knows Huawei has started to attract interest from US regulators, adding ominously, 'We are determined to crack the US market . . . My personal belief is that the Americans are afraid that Huawei is too strong.'

Ren's interview – deemed off the record at the time – provided a fascinating insight into the company's global ambitions later reflected at length in an FT feature. It foreshadowed Huawei's emergence as the leading force in 5G technology, triggering opposition in Europe and the US where President Trump imposed wide-ranging sanctions. By the time the west woke up to the competitive threat, Huawei had either gobbled up or smashed the competition.

WEDNESDAY–THURSDAY, 30–31 MARCH

The streets of Tokyo are semi-deserted. Under leaden skies, an eerie calm. I've just completed half a mile in an empty pool at the Park Hyatt hotel, where Bill Murray played an ageing actor in *Lost in Translation*. Mure Dickie, our Tokyo bureau chief, has arranged an interview with Yukio Edano, the Japanese prime minister's chief cabinet secretary who is the government's public face in the crisis.

Half a dozen Japanese aides greet us with bows and smiles. Several thank me for coming to Japan. I thank the officials for arranging the interview with Edano who has been appearing every night on television in a signature blue-collar jacket usually worn by janitors and production workers. The jacket has become a sign of solidarity with emergency workers and engineers trying to help the tsunami victims and fix the nuclear plant at Fukushima.

Edano's aides say he's barely slept since the crisis broke, usually staying overnight in his office. Today he is about to receive President Sarkozy of France, but he's pleased to meet the editor of the *FT*. My first words are sympathy for the victims of the tsunami/nuclear disaster. We discuss how progress at Fukushima is faring (slow) and rehousing the homeless (not bad).

I ask Edano how long he will continue to wear his blue jacket. Unless things get back to normal, I say, Japanese people will continue to embrace *jishuku*, or 'self-restraint', a term which I picked up from our local correspondent, Gwen Robinson. Of course I'm showing off with my schoolboy Japanese, but I'm also trying to establish a connection with Edano. *Jishuku* is a typically subtle Japanese concept: the notion that consumers will avoid spending money in order to express regret and a feeling of responsibility at a time of grief and suffering.

One word in Japanese. Twenty-five words in English. There would come a time when these language lessons would come in useful.

A flicker of a smile appears on Edano's face. 'I'm thinking of changing into the regular sort of business suit.' Then he retreats into Japanese ambiguity. 'If needed, I would immediately change back into this jacket.'

The very next day, Edano dropped his blue jacket.

TUESDAY, 12 APRIL

Tea at Bill Berkley's midtown apartment in New York. The billionaire investor, a New Jersey native, first started trading when he was 12. He's super-smart, if hard to follow on complex matters like insurance and credit derivatives. Bill makes a very simple but important point: the speed and scale of financial transactions is near incomprehensible. Even ordinary people appear able to lay their hands on sums of money and make astounding bets. Hey, there was even someone in his building who made millions, he says.

I forget to ask Bill the tenant-trader's name, but I leave with a better understanding of how technology had upended traditional power structures on Wall Street. Well before the Great Crash and Thatcher–Reagan deregulation, the heads of the banks knew what was going on inside their houses. They also counted for something in New York society. Now, as Henry Kaufman, the legendary bond-market supremo, once told me one sunny afternoon on a walk after lunch down Sixth Avenue: no one knows what's going on in the banks and no one speaks for Wall Street any more. The traders had taken over. It was an ominous if poignant moment.

After the crash, algorithmic trading increased exponentially. The new power-players are the 'quants'. If the unit of trade is 100 shares, and you can buy and sell those shares for a profit of 1 per cent, and you can do it in a hundredth of a second, eight hours a day, something fundamental has changed. The quants have left the traders in the dust.

WEDNESDAY, 13 APRIL

To Washington to take the political temperature after Obama's stinging reverse in the midterm elections, thanks to the impressive showing of the Tea party, the low-tax, fiscally conservative movement inside the Republican party. Newly radicalised, the Republicans are holding the president to ransom over government spending, refusing to support an extension of the debt ceiling. Technically, the US government could go into default. Where is the bipartisan support for a compromise? Where is the president?

One politician trying to bridge the yawning divide is Senator Mark Warner, a Democrat from Virginia who's eyeing a future run for the White House. He's a member of the 'Gang of Eight' senators trying to forge a comprehensive deal on the debt ceiling and tackle the federal budget deficit. Warner says recent events have been 'an embarrassment to the country'. The Tea party is drinking to the prospects of a prolonged stalemate.

The budget stand-off is one more sign that Republicans and Democrats have forgotten the art of deal-making. In the

Reagan and Bush years, Jim Baker was around to bridge the partisan divide; now he's sitting in the offices of his law firm in Houston watching in frustration. *Memo to self: another reason to fix that Lunch with the FT with James A. Baker III in his Texan lair.*

Towards dusk we visit Ken Duberstein, Reagan's former chief of staff, now a corporate lobbyist and Washington insider. There's a loss of public confidence in institutions and a breakdown of trust in DC, he tells us. Obama's style has not helped. 'He's very good with big crowds but how much did he reach out to Republicans early on? There's a point in the president socialising with Congress.'

Obama doesn't care much for a cigar on the porch with Republicans. Hell, he's barely reached out to Congressional Democrats. Maybe he's a little too cool, too cerebral for grubby Washington politics. Sometimes I think he would be better on the bench of the US Supreme Court.

THURSDAY, 5 MAY

A fast turnaround to Dublin to speak to top businessmen and industrialists about the eurozone crisis. Danny McCoy, the garrulous head of the Irish business federation, has been pressing me for months to come over. He's desperate for an *FT* vote of confidence in Ireland which is still recovering from a spectacular real-estate bust. I'm sympathetic because the Irish have been the most loyal Europeans, and they've been screwed by the Germans and Trichet's ECB. My speech predicts a rescheduling of European debt and a slow recovery in Ireland. On the evening news, I'm later informed, my speech has eclipsed coverage of Taoiseach Enda Kenny's arrival in Washington.

The taoiseach's trip to the US passed without incident except for a memorable correction in the *New York Times*: 'An earlier version of this article incorrectly referred to the new Irish prime minister Enda Kenny as a woman. Enda Kenny is a male.'

FRIDAY, 10 JUNE

John Makinson, chief executive of Penguin, has dropped in for breakfast. An old *FT* hand, he's been running Penguin for a decade. I suspect he's still interested in succeeding Sir David Bell in the nebulous role of chairman of the *FT*. It could be a useful bridge between the *FT* and Pearson but I'm wary. John does not make a direct request but he does raise a more interesting story: Amazon threatens Penguin's books business but is also a substantial beneficiary of favourable tax arrangements in Luxembourg. John claims these tax avoidance schemes give Amazon founder Jeff Bezos a huge advantage and suggests we look into it.

A missed opportunity. I should have pressed harder for a follow-up. We were slow to understand and report on the level of tax arbitrage among footloose multinationals, especially the tech giants.

MONDAY, 13 JUNE

Alec Russell, who's made a fine start as comment and analysis editor, has come up with a new idea to strengthen our online offering: a roster of top-class, regular outside contributors ready to comment in a timely manner on the big subjects of the day. Larry Summers, who has just stepped down as Obama's chief economic adviser, will lead a group including Anne-Marie Slaughter, Sir Howard Davies, Peter Mandelson and George Soros. With my approval, Alec has branded the group the 'A List'.

Philip Stephens, the *FT*'s long-time chief political commentator and unofficial trade union leader for the in-house columnists, asks to see me. He is grumpy about the 'A List'. He tells me Martin Wolf, Gillian Tett, John Gapper and, naturally, himself are now effectively the 'B List'. *Oh please!*

FT colleagues have always been sensitive about A and B classifications. Back in 1999, when I told Ed Luce that he had failed to land the economics editor job, he was baffled and upset. I had to explain that the successful candidate (Ed Crooks) was an A, while Ed was still a B. Ed took a few years to recover but later became one of the FT*'s best writers and columnists. Literally, an A+.*

MONDAY, 4 JULY

An Independence Day bombshell. The *Guardian* is reporting that the phone of Milly Dowler, the 13-year-old murdered schoolgirl, was hacked by journalists from the *News of the World* and a private investigator, Glenn Mulcaire. The *Guardian* also reported that some messages on her phone had been deliberately deleted in order to free up space for new messages, giving the impression she was still alive.

This source of the deletions turned out to be unprovable, but the fact that the phone of a murdered schoolgirl had been hacked shocked the public conscience, forcing the government to call for a judicial inquiry.

WEDNESDAY, 6 JULY

I'm in Sun Valley attending the Allen & Co. media conference. Sir Martin Sorrell tips me off that Rupert Murdoch is flying home early to London. We stand up the tip and the story appears on page one, accompanied by a picture of an ancient-looking Murdoch in Sun Valley. He won't like the shot and nor will his image-conscious wife Wendi Deng, but this is one helluva story. Back in London, Murdoch announces he's closing the *News of the World*, the scandal sheet he bought in 1969. The last edition will be on Sunday.

FRIDAY–SATURDAY, 8–9 JULY

More explosive *Guardian* phone-hacking revelations. Murdoch's News International has paid off dozens of prominent victims. If suppressed evidence were to become public, the number would be far higher, exposing Murdoch to huge damages claims. Andy Coulson, former editor of the *News of the World* and until January 2011 Cameron's spokesman, knew about the practice and encouraged it, the *Guardian* claims. Cameron's decision to hire Coulson as a tabloid guard dog looks even more reckless. The *Guardian* has exposed evidence of a criminal conspiracy at one of the world's top media organisations.

MONDAY, 18 JULY

Alan Rusbridger has invited me to a crunchy 'muesli breakfast' at the *Guardian* to talk about the upcoming Leveson inquiry into the culture, practice and ethics of the British press. Cameron has set the widest possible terms for the inquiry which will look at journalists' relations with politicians, the police and the public. Witnesses, including editors, will give testimony under oath.

Last week, Leveson asked an awkward question about journalists operating in the public realm: 'Who guards the guardians?' I've always seen our role as watchdogs but, for all their often good work at exposing cant and injustice, the tabloids are also peeping toms, trampling over privacy and holding celebrities and politicians to ransom over sexual indiscretions. That's part of their business model as well as the price of free speech.

In the coming months, Alan would try to bring other editors on board to have an honest debate about press regulation, privacy and public accountability. Tony Danker, a smart Ulsterman and management consultant, facilitated the discussions, which I attended as often as possible, along with Chris Blackhurst of the Independent. *James Harding at* The Times *and Tony Gallagher of the* Daily Telegraph *made a couple of guest appearances. John Witherow of the* Sunday Times *and Paul Dacre of the* Daily Mail *steered well clear. They thought Alan was a misguided liberal intent on upsetting a comfortable status quo where the major news organisations sat in judgement on themselves via a (relatively) toothless PCC. I assumed Dacre and Witherow preferred porridge for breakfast too.*

THURSDAY, 1 SEPTEMBER

To the Old Vic to see Kevin Spacey play Richard III. My first experience of Shakespeare's hunchback villain was at the Edinburgh Festival in 1980 when the Georgian National Theatre Company came to town. I did not understand a word but the performance was mesmerising. Spacey's strong if a tad hammy.

An astonishing story out of UBS, the giant Swiss bank. A rogue trader by the name of Kweku Adoboli has run up losses of more than $2bn. What were the bets? Where was the supervision? I am due to see the head of UBS's investment bank in London, a craggy blond German by the name of Carsten Kengeter. To my amazement he turns up on time. Not much light on the affair, but at least he didn't cancel. That's classy from Carsten K. – a gesture that in my book buys a lot of goodwill.

Meeting with Ed Miliband in his office in Norman Shaw South building in the House of Commons. One of those sessions which begin with the politician saying with a straight face: 'I'd love to know the *FT*'s views on . . .' One of today's topics is income tax. Miliband still wants to raise the highest band to 50 per cent (from 45 per cent). My response is that it won't raise much money, if any. Besides, it sends a poor signal to middle-class voters. I want to hear Labour talk about 'aspiration', not inequality. Ed has the same big brain as his elder brother David, and a little more charm. But he's not much of a salesman. Besides, the *FT*'s not going to ditch Cameron–Osborne now. We're barely 16 months into the coalition.

Ed Miliband was on to something with his concern about inequality in modern Britain but higher income taxes were not the right prescription.

WEDNESDAY, 19 OCTOBER

The lord chief justice, Igor Judge, has delivered a remarkable speech on the independence of the press, describing it as 'a constitutional necessity'. He's even quoted John Wilkes:* 'The liberty of the press is the birthright of a Briton, and is justly esteemed the firmest bulwark of the liberties of this country.'

I've only met Judge once, at a 'get to know the senior judiciary' dinner for a select group of editors at a London restaurant. The lord chief justice looked a little out of place without his robes that night, but he projected a quiet authority which commanded respect. *Must have him round for dinner. Well, I tried twice and the same message came back both times: dinner was sadly not possible but Lady Judge hugely enjoys reading the* Weekend FT.

Judge says he has no desire to interfere in the Leveson inquiry. *Of course not.* But his 'remarks' come just after the official opening of the inquiry, with great fanfare in the Queen Elizabeth Conference Centre opposite Westminster Abbey. Judge is sending a not-so-discreet warning to the government and Lord Justice Leveson: when it comes to press regulation, be careful what you wish for. I've copied and pasted a passage in Judge's speech which must rank as one of the best summaries of why an independent press matters.

'An independent press, or one or other of its constituents, will also from time to time behave, if not criminally, then with scandalous cruelty and unfairness, leaving victims

---

* John Wilkes (1725–97), a brilliant, dissolute journalist and politician, was expelled from Parliament for his incendiary publications, and became an early champion of the right to a free press.

stranded in a welter of public contempt and hatred or uncovenanted distress. But on the very same day one of the other constituent parts of the independent press may reveal a public scandal.'

Judge's warning was prescient. Leveson's attempt to devise a new system of press regulation would meet with fierce resistance from editors and proprietors. Dacre's Daily Mail *frequently quoted John Wilkes – no doubt a coincidence. My view was equally robust: I did not want the state involved in press regulation, and phone-hacking was a criminal matter for the police (who admittedly failed to do their job). Leveson barely covered the elephant in the room: the internet's impact on newspapers' business model. In this respect, it was flawed.*

SATURDAY, 29 OCTOBER

Dinner with Nick Clegg at Chevening, the early 17th-century country retreat in Kent, usually the grace-and-favour mansion of the foreign secretary. Clegg, deputy PM, has pulled rank. He is in good form, ranging effortlessly across domestic and foreign affairs. I'm placed next to Miriam, who is definitely down on the Tories. Nick pulls me aside after dinner to share his own reservations. The coalition is working at the top, his relationship with Cameron good. But he's still sore about the way the Tories ditched support for electoral reform. The Alternative Vote (AV)* referendum in May was

---

* The Alternative Vote proposal would have seen voters rank their preferred candidates in order and required the winner to gain 50 per cent support. Second and third choices would count if no candidate won 50 per cent in the initial rounds.

the best chance in a generation to introduce a form of proportional representation, the only path for the Lib Dems to secure power as a majority party. The Tories torpedoed it during the campaign. I suspect Cameron's behaviour does not bode well for the coalition.

SUNDAY, 13 NOVEMBER

Mario Monti, my old friend and source when he was EU single market and competition commissioner in Brussels, has been appointed the head of a new technocratic government in Italy. And so ends Silvio Berlusconi's bread-and-circuses act. His allies are casting the president of Italy's intervention on behalf of Monti as a coup from Frankfurt/Brussels. They're half right. There has been no election; but Italy has been paralysed for months, unnerving financial markets and driving up bond yields. Something had to give.

Monti is a world apart from the fun-loving *Cavaliere*. He is a deeply serious, decent man, an academic economist by training who approaches every problem methodically in a rich baritone from his native Varese in northern Italy. He's also a huge fan of the *FT*. Monti will steady Italy's listing ship. But he's not a politician. I give him two years in office, at best.

TUESDAY, 29 NOVEMBER

Paul Dacre has called a meeting of select Fleet Street editors and press bosses in the Silhouette private dining room at the Chancery Court hotel in High Holborn. The room feels like a Speakeasy with Dacre doing a passing imitation of Marlon Brando in *The Godfather*. He goes around the table introducing attendees, like Lord Black of the *Daily Telegraph*, Paul Vickers of the Mirror Group and Peter Wright of the *Mail on Sunday* as if they were crime bosses. I can (almost) hear Dacre saying: 'I'd like to thank my good friends from New Jersey, Chicago, Las Vegas . . .'

Alan Rusbridger of the *Guardian* arrives late and is on guard throughout. Dacre's message is that Fleet Street must stick together in the face of Leveson. Alan questions the role of the Press Standards Board of Finance (Pressbof), the shadowy group which represents newspapers and magazine proprietors alongside the discredited Press Complaints Commission. Alan argues it is untransparent and unaccountable – a direct shot at Dacre and Black who effectively run Pressbof. Dacre declines to rise to the liberal bait – for now. *For the first time in my editorship, I am being drawn into an industry fight where I may have to choose sides.*

FRIDAY, 9 DECEMBER

Breakfast with Ian Davis, former head of McKinsey, at our usual rendezvous at the Wolseley restaurant next to the Ritz. Ian has been a mentor of sorts, offering advice on leadership and change in a big organisation. He's grappling with both challenges in his roles as chairman of Rolls-Royce and a director of BP, still embroiled in the Deepwater Horizon disaster. 'What's on your mind,' asks Ian, his standard opener. Well, I've done six years as editor. This year has been good, but not outstanding. How do I convey a fresh sense of urgency to my top team and to *FT* journalism?

Ian pauses: 'I've always thought it useful to talk about "a second term" . . .'

A second term. This is exactly the phrase I need to give a sense of purpose and renewal to my editorship. I will try it on with colleagues in the new year.

SATURDAY, 10 DECEMBER

A calamitous European summit in Brussels for David Cameron. Through the night, the prime minister held out against a proposal for a 'fiscal compact' among eurozone countries led by France and Germany. They pointed out, correctly, that the UK was not a member of the single currency and therefore had no standing. When Cameron threatened a veto in the early hours, they ignored him and agreed among themselves. Tonight, in the grounds of Fort Belvedere, Edward VIII's home, at a gigantic dinner and fireworks party celebrating Galen Weston's* birthday, I spot a shattered Cameron beside his wife, Samantha.

LB: 'How are you, Prime Minister?'

DC: 'I've had better days.'

LB: 'I'm sorry to hear that.'

DC: 'Don't be too hard on me.'

WEDNESDAY, 14 DECEMBER

An eye-opening interview in Frankfurt with Mario Draghi, newly installed as president of the European Central Bank. He's flagging that the ECB will soon take on a bigger role, alongside the European Financial Stability Facility (EFSF),

---

* Galen Weston (1940–), British-Canadian businessman with global retail and food distribution interests, including a majority stake in Associated British Foods which owns Primark, the discount clothing chain.

otherwise known as a 'firewall' or 'big bazooka' capable of intervening to stabilise markets.

Ideally, he says, governments would have built a firewall, then recapitalised the banks and then asked the private sector to take losses on their marked-down assets on banks' balance sheets. In fact, the reverse took place. 'It was like letting a bank fail without having a proper mechanism for managing this failure, as it had happened with Lehman.'

Draghi is too diplomatic to point out that private sector involvement (PSI) took place after pressure from the German government. He knows he will need Merkel's support for a more active ECB role. That's why he's talking up the need for fiscal discipline and restoring trust between northern and southern states. Managing public deficits and pushing necessary structural reforms to boost growth, he says, must be part of the remedy, alongside monetary policy. *It's the unspoken (and unfulfilled) bargain in the eurozone.*

I ask Draghi whether he would be prepared to go further, in effect putting the ECB's entire credibility behind intervention such as US-style quantitative easing or something else?

'People have to accept that we have to and always will act in accordance with our mandate and within our legal foundations,' he replies.

Mario has left the door open to dramatic intervention, Fed-style. But he's used such careful wording that the FT cannot – and will not – hype the story. The most valuable takeaway is that I now know his mind. Mario Draghi is ready to act.

NEW MEDIA, OLD MEDIA

The Leveson inquiry into the culture, practices and ethics of the British press took up a huge amount of time and energy in 2011 – and 2012. Apart from my own appearance at the public inquiry in January, I gave several speeches and lectures. I was also being lobbied incessantly by fellow editors and politicians to take a stand on future regulation, a concept entirely alien to American journalists who could rely on their rights to free expression under the First Amendment.

    Leveson was a sideshow compared to the threat from the digital giants of Silicon Valley which were transforming the media landscape. Facebook, which had just gobbled up Instagram, went public in May with a value of $104bn. Closer to home, the eurozone debt crisis continued to roil financial markets until Mario Draghi made a dramatic summer intervention. The FT *was able to draw on an extensive network of correspondents led by Peter Spiegel in Brussels. Peter's Spanish was passable and his French sounded as bad as Boris Johnson's, but he dominated the eurozone story.*

TUESDAY, 10 JANUARY

A nervous debut in front of the Leveson inquiry at the Royal Courts of Justice. Nigel Hanson, our in-house lawyer, has prepped me on the finer points of libel law, data protection and the operation of the Press Complaints Commission. Emma Gilpin Jacobs, the *FT*'s communications chief, is standing by in the courtroom, ready to critique my performance on the stand. Emma told me the other day that the only 'narrative' that mattered was Lionel Barber going down – naturally not in the legal sense – as the editor who presided over the digital transformation of the *FT*.

Carine Patry Hoskins, counsel to the inquiry, opens with a few gentle questions about the *FT*'s standards and ethics. I cite the *FT*'s code of conduct and our rule that all stories are supported by two independent sources. The bigger point, I insist, is that any new system of regulation requires a level playing field between the printed press and the internet. The private life of a football star cannot be fair game for digital publishers and off bounds for newspapers, for example. The problem is not new. Back in 1936, the US press had a field day with Edward VIII's affair with American divorcee Wallis Simpson, but the popular press in the UK could not touch it.

Leveson intervenes with a succinct summary of my reasoning. By way of a compliment, I say his lordship has cut to the heart of the matter.

LJL (a light scold, in a light Mancunian accent): 'You don't need to be polite.'

LB: 'I wasn't being polite, I was being flattering.'

Leveson probes my idea of a new regulatory body to replace the PCC, with more diverse, outside membership and tougher powers of investigation. I talk about the prohibitive costs of libel and the imbalance of power between plaintiff and publisher, mindful of the *FT*'s expensive run-in with Terry Smith. Leveson is considering independent arbitration as a means of reducing costs to publishers and obtaining a quicker remedy for reader complaints.

> *Leveson was right to ask: who guards the guardians? The* FT *opined that Britain's system of self-regulation could give the impression of a magic circle of editors sitting in judgement on themselves. We were open to reforming the PCC or creating a new body. But I was firmly against state involvement.*
>
> *I would have liked to spend more time with Lord Justice Leveson, debating the balance between the right to privacy and the public's right to know. This appeared to be the biggest question of the day for the media. In fact, as the Snowden affair would soon show, the debate over privacy had shifted to a far bigger and more important battleground involving national security and the (complicit) role of the tech giants who were also gathering vast troves of their own personal data.*

SATURDAY, 14 JANUARY

I've casually raised the idea of a 'second term' as editor to convey a sense of renewal at today's strategy 'Here Day'.* No objections, just a few wry smiles. My concern is how to drive change in the face of opposition from the National Union of Journalists. The chapel — *there's barely a churchgoer among them but that's the old collective noun for the in-house union members* — hate my idea of introducing more flexibility into the annual pay round. I'm trying to reward people according to merit rather than length of tenure, all within a tight editorial budget. We're at a stand-off.

---

* A highfalutin term obscuring the fact that we were working at home rather than playing 'away' at an expensive hotel venue.

I need more support and that means a change of managing editor. It's tough on Lisa MacLeod but the NUJ think they've got her number. My choice as her replacement is James Lamont, whom I watched close-up on my trip to India and Pakistan in 2010. James is low-key but robust. He's constantly thinking about the next year or so, my weakness to date because I am so often at the mercy of daily news events. I also need someone to tell me where I'm going wrong, someone who's going to remove me from danger in a conflict.

When I was 17, my school rugby coach moved me from scrum half to fly half. When I asked him why, he replied: 'Because you're always getting into fights with the forwards.' My move to playmaker worked brilliantly but I failed to appreciate that avoiding unnecessary fights also applied off the rugby pitch, especially in management. The role of editor as playmaker suited me better too.

WEDNESDAY, 18 JANUARY

Mario Monti, Italy's prime minister, pays a state visit to the *FT*. He's also seeing David Cameron in Downing Street. The silver-haired Monti has been in Berlin and Paris delivering the same reasonable message, with a hint of frustration: he will pursue economic reform but his technocratic government needs help. Italians are restless as a result of austerity, he tells us. There's a backlash building in Italy against the EU, Germany and the European Central Bank.

Monti's warning about anti-EU sentiment in Italy was prescient. The Five Star Movement and the anti-immigrant Liga would gain ground steadily, eclipsing the mainstream centre-right and centre-left parties. Italy, a founder member of the EU, was turning

Eurosceptic. The failure of the eurozone to produce steady economic growth was key.

THURSDAY, 9 FEBRUARY

Tony Blair has come to lunch and there's not a space left around the table. His discourse on world politics and global trends is a tour de force. The fifth anniversary of TB's departure from Downing Street comes up in June. How about an interview with me, any time, any place in the world? I set one condition: Blair has to talk about his lucrative business activities. TB looks interested. We agree to talk further.

TUESDAY, 13 MARCH

White House state dinner. Victoria and I are guests of President Obama, courtesy of Ambassador Susman in London. In the reception line, Obama and the First Lady Michelle greet myself and Victoria warmly. Cameron looks at me and exclaims: 'What are you doing here?' Well, I say, we're guests of the White House.

Over pre-dinner drinks, I survey the other guests: Harvey Weinstein, the Hollywood mogul; Sir Richard Branson, the Virgin billionaire; *Vogue* editor Anna Wintour; *Downton Abbey* actors Hugh Bonneville and Elizabeth McGovern; actors Idris Elba and Carey Mulligan; Apple's super-designer Sir Jonathan Ive; and, last but not least, George Clooney.

Clooney and I met in New York at a private showing of his movie *Good Night, and Good Luck* based on the life and work of Ed Murrow, the CBS news anchor. Somehow we end up tonight talking about Silvio Berlusconi. I recount *il*

Cavaliere's boast about his magnificent four-poster bed in Palazzo Grazioli, his private residence in the heart of Rome. I heard the story from François Fillon, then French prime minister. He said Berlusconi insisted on showing him the bed in question and asking him to guess why he had never slept in the bed with a woman. When the Frenchman said he had no idea, Berlusconi replied: 'Because I would never know whether the woman wanted to sleep with me or just sleep in the bed.'

Clooney laughs and then tells me that Berlusconi apparently told the same story to Vladimir Putin.

Dinner is crisped halibut with potato crust, served on baby kale from the White House garden. Main course is Bison Wellington aka dressed-up buffalo from North Dakota. Not my taste. Nor for that matter Cameron's choice for the after-dinner band: Mumford & Sons.

FRIDAY, 20 APRIL

To the Cooper Union in New York to attend a packed hall paying tribute to Christopher Hitchens, the heathen's heathen, in the words of Janan Ganesh, our newly recruited columnist from *The Economist*. Hitch threw the best parties and engaged in the best conversations, preferably after midnight. Fifteen or so years ago, I remember Hitch coming to dinner at our art deco home in Brussels. He asked several questions about its heritage, about which I was scandalously ignorant. He was on a trip to visit war graves in Flanders and spoke vividly about the suffering in the trenches, until the port ran dry.

I always envied Hitch's ability to write such beautifully crafted sentences; always logical, reasonable, with an undercurrent of moral outrage. In my review of *No One Left to Lie To*, his polemic against Bill Clinton, I was less than generous. Hitch never took it personally – more than can be said for his feuds with one-time friends like Sidney Blumenthal and his later battles with liberals over his support for the war in Iraq. Victoria and I read every word he published in *Vanity Fair* about his final battle with cancer. Like everyone else in Cooper Union, where Abraham Lincoln delivered his anti-slavery speech in 1860, we will miss Hitch dreadfully.

FRIDAY, 8 JUNE

Bo Xilai, one of the most powerful politicians in China, has been detained, along with his wife Gu Kailai. They are suspected of being involved in the murder of British businessman Neil Heywood who was either her lover or complicit in corruption – or both.

This is a sulphurous tale of intrigue, as told by our Beijing bureau chief Jamil Anderlini, a fluent Mandarin-speaker born in Kuwait with an Italian-American father and a mother from New Zealand where he grew up. Jamil is one of our most valuable foreign correspondents, infinitely adaptable, teak-hard and wise in the ways of China (thanks, in part, to his Chinese wife, Sophia).

Today, I'm heading an *FT* delegation to lunch at the Chinese embassy. We are all braced for a dressing down about our Bo coverage. Ambassador Liu does not disappoint, urging the *FT* to ignore 'rumours' and focus on the 'big picture'. Fairly soon, I lose my patience.

LB: 'Does the ambassador happen to know Bo Xilai and could he possibly tell us what sort of man he is?'

Ambassador: 'I knew Bo Xilai when he was mayor of Dalian and I was deputy chief of mission in Washington.'

LB (mildly intrigued)

Ambassador: 'One day, we received an important message in Washington from Bo Xilai in Dalian. He wants to meet important Americans.'

LB (intrigued)

Ambassador: 'So I draw up a list of important Americans: Brzezinski, Carter . . . Kissinger . . .'

LB (more intrigued)

Ambassador: 'Next day, we received a message from Dalian. Bo Xilai does not want to meet Brzezinski, Carter, Kissinger . . . he wants to meet Stalin.'

LB (stunned): 'But, Mr Ambassador, Stalin is dead.'

Ambassador: 'I'm sorry . . . my English pronunciation. I mean Bo wants to meet [Sylvester] Stallone.'

Bo was not the only Communist to share a fascination with Hollywood. When I was on sabbatical at Berkeley in 1992, I met an academic called Frank Li who once acted as an English translator for Madame Mao. During the Cultural Revolution, Li was sentenced to hard labour in the countryside. Later, he was taken one night to the party leadership compound in Beijing and escorted into a dark room where he could dimly make out a woman sitting in front of a large film screen. It was Madame Mao. The film was Midnight Cowboy, *one of several he interpreted for the improbable film buff and member of the Gang of Four.*

SATURDAY, 9 JUNE

I'm sitting with Tony Blair on the rooftop terrace of the Office of the Quartet Representative in Jerusalem, his part-time job mediating between Israelis and Palestinians in between raking in millions of dollars as an adviser to banks and governments around the world. The sun is going down over the golden Dome of the Rock, completed in AD 691/2 by Caliph Abdul Malik ibn Marwan on top of the Second Jewish Temple. Trim and tanned, Blair is wearing his third shirt of the day, a white twill with a middle button unaccountably absent.

Two hours before, the man known to his colleagues simply as the Boss was sitting in a room inside posing for his picture to be taken by Jillian Edelstein, one of the world's great portrait photographers. Everything was going smoothly until Jillian happened to remark on the size of TB's hands. Britain's ex-prime minister demurs but she persists. The Boss is offended. 'Darling, I don't have big hands. Do I, Lionel?'

Momentarily lost for words, I say that TB's hands are larger than mine, but smaller than Bill Clinton's. Victoria, I tell TB, always admired Clinton's hands because they were like marble and blessed with especially long fingers.

Blair sighs, almost wistfully. 'Yes. Bill has pianist fingers.' For a moment Jillian and I both thought we had misheard.

My rooftop interview with Blair, later published in the *FT*'s weekend *Magazine*, lasts almost two hours. We range across his multiple roles since stepping down from power, aged 54: philanthropist, statesman, mediator, financial fixer. By the *FT*'s estimates, he's made tens of millions of dollars since leaving office, thanks to his advisory roles to governments like Kazakhstan and Kuwait, speaking fees (up to $300,000 a session) and commissions on deals. He employs more than 150 people in his advisory business and foundations.

On the Iraq war, the blunder that cost him so dearly, Blair won't apologise but he sounds semi-repentant. 'In the

Middle East, I have a far deeper understanding of what the issues are . . . that its politics is profoundly affected – in a way that I kind of superficially understood but didn't understand profoundly enough – by religion.' In someone other than Blair, the admission would come across as glib but his charm is oddly disarming.

I ask him if he misses being prime minister. 'Some days. Probably because I forget what it was like.' Then he realises his answer is phoney. 'When there are big issues you want to be there.'

Whatever one may think of Tony Blair, he was never afraid to engage with the big issues. He remains one of the most substantial politicians of his generation.

WEDNESDAY, 13 JUNE

The *FT*'s editorial leader conference is still almost exclusively male, and retains an atmosphere akin to a senior common room.

Heavyweight columnists like Martin Wolf, Philip Stephens and John Gapper are comfortable talking – and interrupting. Roula Khalaf and our feisty business editor Sarah Gordon find the mansplainers mildly amusing but often frustrating. *One day I will deal with the alpha-male problem, just not today.*

I've called a special meeting to discuss the coalition government's austerity policy because public opposition is rising steadily and it may not be doing the economy any favours. Several heavyweight commentators argue fiscal policy is too tight and constraining growth. I'm inclined to give Cameron–Osborne the benefit of the doubt. Chris

Giles, our economics editor, makes the decisive intervention with a clear steer that the UK economy appears to be turning. To shift our stance now would look odd. This chimes with my recent conversation with Ana Botín,* CEO of Santander UK bank. She thinks unemployment will fall faster than expected in the next year, better than the Bank of England forecasts.

Botín's prognosis was correct. The UK economy was turning, though the green shoots were not visible for another few months. With hindsight, we should have debated more thoroughly the costs of austerity, especially within the criminal justice system and local government where the provision of services suffered lasting damage.

TUESDAY, 26 JUNE

Dick Costolo, CEO of Twitter, has dropped by for an editorial round table. Twitter is 'still in its infancy', he says in his understated way. He and the board are grappling with how best to scale the business: how to 'monetise' 150 million users addicted to conversation in 140 characters. Twitter is a great source for breaking news but Costolo does not want to assume the responsibility of being a de facto publisher running a news organisation with journalists. *No kidding.*

Twitter has become all the rage in the Middle East. The Arab Spring has helped, though something called Whats-App may have even greater convening power, through encrypted messaging. Twitter promises anonymity but that

---

* Ana Botín took over as chairman of the Spanish bank in 2014, following in the line of her father, grandfather and great-grandfather, all named Emilio.

carries a price in abuse, vitriol and the posting of violent images because basically the company does not employ a filter. The mainstream media like newspapers and TV are often criticised as 'gatekeepers' but at least we are committed to general standards of accuracy and providing some context to our reporting.

Twitter's influence in media and politics would only grow, not always for the good. The company's decision in 2017 to double the number of permitted characters to 280 hardly improved the quality of discourse. More importantly, politicians increasingly turned the medium against the press. There would be no greater exponent than the tweeter-in-chief, Donald Trump, who, at the latest count in 2020, had more than 80m followers.

THURSDAY–FRIDAY, 28–29 JUNE

A lightning trip to Brussels to watch one of the most important EU summits in years unfold in the giant Justus Lipsius building. Most of the action is behind closed doors in a room almost the size of a football pitch to accommodate 27 EU leaders, their key advisers and a gaggle of interpreters. Peter Spiegel's verdict: Merkel has moved just enough to put a new eurozone architecture in place. Greece remains in peril but there's no apocalypse – for now.

MONDAY, 2 JULY

To the Royal Box at Wimbledon to watch the quarter finals on centre court with Victoria. During the tea interval, my mobile phone rings. It's Marcus Agius, outgoing chairman of Barclays. Marcus has taken the fall for Barclays' involvement in the Libor rate-rigging scandal. Now he's trying to persuade me that his departure protects Bob Diamond, Barclays CEO. This strikes me as improbable. The City establishment have had Diamond in their gunsights ever since Barclays rejected the government bailout and took money from Qatar. Bob's a goner, I tell Agius. We agree to disagree.

Hours after our call, Agius was summoned along with senior Barclays director Sir Michael Rake to the Bank of England for a meeting with Mervyn King. The governor made clear how unhappy the regulators were with the gung-ho culture at Barclays. Agius's departure would not solve the problem. Within 24 hours, Diamond was gone.

THURSDAY, 26 JULY

A seminal moment in the eurozone crisis. Mario Draghi has declared the ECB will do 'whatever it takes' to save the euro. In case anyone isn't listening, he adds: 'And believe me, it will be enough.' The ECB has made it unequivocally clear that it is standing behind the single currency.

'Super Mario', as he would soon become known, called the markets' bluff. Within days, the bond yield 'spreads' between creditor and debtor countries began to narrow, giving Ireland, Italy, Spain and Portugal desperately needed breathing space. The end of the eurozone crisis was in sight, if not for Greece.

THURSDAY, 9 AUGUST

A visit from Peter Grauer, chairman of Bloomberg. No specific agenda, he says. This seems unlikely. Grauer has spent years on Wall Street before entering the news business. It feels like he's checking us/me out. I'm hearing that Marjorie may step down at the end of the year as Pearson CEO. Marjorie once said that the sale of the *FT* would only happen 'over my dead body'. *Once she goes, Grauer must sense, like me, that the* FT *will be in play.*

FRIDAY, 7 SEPTEMBER

To California – for business and pleasure. My plan is a whistle-stop tour of Los Angeles with our well-connected correspondent Matthew Garrahan; spend the weekend with family and friends, followed by three days doing interviews in Silicon Valley, catching up on the tech scene.

First stop is breakfast with Jeffrey Katzenberg, co-founder of DreamWorks, the film production company he set up after leaving Disney. Katzenberg, who produced box office hits such as *The Little Mermaid* and *The Lion King*, is pleasant if a little guarded. As we sip coffee in the morning sun, Katzenberg talks about DreamWorks' collaboration with China, where he's set up an animation studio in Shanghai. The Chinese are spending millions on developing entertainment to feed to the urban masses. It's an antidote to alienation. I ask Katzenberg whether he knows Wang Jianlin, the Chinese billionaire, whose company Dalian Wanda has just bought the AMC cinema chain in the US.

Indeed he does. Someone rang up the other week to say Mr Wang was in town. Would Jeffrey care to throw a dinner party in his honour? *Sure, no problem.* Mr Wang, who does not speak a word of English, turned up with his entourage and proceeded to slag off every American studio in Hollywood, says Katzenberg.

Disney? Shit. Paramount? Shit. Fox? Shit. Universal? Shit.

Barely after the main course has been served, Mr Wang announces he's leaving. He has to get back to China on his private plane.

Where might Mr Wang have parked his plane, asks Katzenberg.

Long Beach.

Well, Mr Wang, let me tell you something . . . The next time you come to Hollywood, I suggest you don't park your plane in Long Beach. You park your PLANE in Burbank. . . . . . next to my PLANES!

MONDAY, 10 SEPTEMBER

A morning at Google to learn more about artificial intelligence (AI). This is terra incognita. Amit Singhal, a top executive in Google Search, says the AI dream has been around since the 1950s. In those days, AI was concentrated on statistical language like word count. Now the world has become exponentially more AI-friendly: data centres have become cheaper, billions of documents are on the web, computing is ubiquitous.

These changes have transformed what Singhal calls 'social information'. Who people trust, what people want, where people would like to go. Google has its Android device, the calendar and email, all of which is 'predictive' technology. The other X factor is the app, the software application to perform specific tasks which can be downloaded in a flash on a mobile phone (as opposed to a desktop computer). 'The web is dead,' says Singhal, 'it is now the app world.'

To reinforce the AI point, Google has arranged for me and my colleague Richard Waters to take a trip down the highway in a self-driving car, a fat white vehicle with a large piece of navigation kit on the roof. We strap ourselves in, a human driver guides us down a few streets and then the machines take over. As we fly down the highway, I catch a glimpse of the future. A real car draws up in the outside lane. So fascinated by our autonomous vehicle is the driver that he briefly swerves into another lane.

TUESDAY, 11 SEPTEMBER

Super-early breakfast with John Doerr of Silver Lake, one of the Valley's best-known venture capitalists. Our meeting gives me further confirmation that the worlds of tech and media are changing faster than I've realised. 'Facebook owns identity in the network. Google has delivered another identity system,' says Doerr, 'Apple has 400 million users with credit cards.' The only Big Data company he does not mention is Jeff Bezos's Amazon. Doerr says the Facebook IPO earlier this year may have disappointed initially *($104bn valuation is not exactly chump change but whatever)*; the reality is that Apple, Facebook and Google are the new power hierarchy in Silicon Valley.

> *Memo to the editor: the* FT *needs to forge a convincing strategy for mobile platforms or we risk being crushed. We did a good job launching our HTML5 web app last year but the awesome distribution power of Apple, Facebook and Google will always tempt them to dictate commercial terms. That's mainly for John Ridding to decide, but as editor and board member I want my say.*

SATURDAY, 15 SEPTEMBER

Serious training for my upcoming cycling weekend in the Pyrenees. I'm doing a 25-mile ride in Pennyhill Park in the grounds of Windsor with Team Sky, the British cycling team which dominates world cycling. The pace is testing for a Mamil (translation: middle-aged man in lycra). After the ride, all cyclists are invited to meet Derbyshire-born David Brailsford, manager and trainer of Team Sky, who specialises in something called 'the aggregation of "marginal gains"'. This is about technological improvement, but also diet, mental resilience and power-to-weight ratios.

Brailsford's presentation was compelling. So was his winning record. But his record was later tarnished by revelations about Team Sky's use of a questionable antihistamine drug, triamcinolone, leading to strong criticism in a Parliamentary report.*

TUESDAY, 18 SEPTEMBER

Farewell party at Broadcasting House for Mark Thompson, director general of the BBC.† He's done a very good job in the circumstances. Everyone and their auntie has an opinion of what's wrong and what's right for the nation's public

---

* House of Commons, Digital, Culture, Media and Sport Committee, *Combatting Doping in Sport*, 5 March 2018: https://publications.parlia ment.uk/pa/cm201719/cmselect/cmcumeds/366/36606.htm.

† Mark Thompson: BBC director general 2004–12 who moved to become CEO of the New York Times Company, one of a number of British journalists to make a successful switch across the Atlantic. He stepped down in 2020.

broadcaster. I remember Mark as a thick-skinned co-editor of *Isis* magazine when we were at Oxford together. He once rejected an article of mine, an early indication of suspect editorial judgement at the BBC.

My impression is that Mark would have liked to stay on a little longer, but Lord Patten,* chairman of the BBC Trust,† wanted to settle the succession. The new director general, George Entwistle, seems perfectly pleasant. On my way out, a BBC Trust member buttonholes me. She was *very* surprised to see my name appear several times as a possible DG in newspaper gossip columns. What was my explanation?

I'm way too tipsy to be offended.

George Entwistle lasted 54 days. He was forced to resign after failing to deal effectively with the fall-out from the Jimmy Savile sex-abuse scandal. His successor was Tony Hall, chief executive of the Royal Opera House, a long-time BBC executive and the safe choice.

TUESDAY, 9 OCTOBER

Michael Bloomberg, mayor of New York, arrives in a black motorcade for a quasi-presidential visit to the *FT* for midmorning coffee.

---

* Chris Patten: Conservative MP and grandee under Margaret Thatcher and John Major. He was the last British governor of Hong Kong and is chancellor of the University of Oxford.

† The BBC Trust was the governing body of the BBC between 2007 and 2017, later replaced by a board of directors, with oversight powers transferred to the broadcasting and telecoms regulator Ofcom.

Bloomberg recently turned 70 but looks a little younger: a small, trim, nattily dressed alpha male who's made billions and carries it lightly. The mayor gets the VIP treatment with a cordoned-off lift to the first-floor newsroom, where I give him a potted history of the digital transformation of the *FT*. He looks vaguely interested. In the riverside news conference room, senior journalists have gathered to hear whether Bloomberg is interested in acquiring the newspaper. For 40 minutes and more, we dance round the question until one veteran commentator asks the $1 billion question (assuming the *FT* could fetch a billion). Would the mayor consider buying the *FT*?

Bloomberg offers a theatrical pause. 'What do you mean? I buy the *FT* on the newsstand every day . . .'

Mayor Bloomberg's visit came just after Pearson had announced that Marjorie was stepping down as CEO at the end of the year. He knew his appearance at the FT *would generate a buzz. Whether he really was interested in buying the* FT *was never entirely clear. He may simply have wanted a better view of his new, state-of-the-art, carbon-neutral headquarters directly across the river.*

12–15 OCTOBER

To Tarascon with Team Terry Smith for two consecutive daily rides through the Pyrenees, 75 miles each, including a stretch from the Tour de France. First day is gruelling – more than 2,700m ascent. Next morning I can barely move. Soon I'm ready to throw in the towel. A younger rider offers encouragement and I keep going. By late afternoon, I am cantilevered off my bike. Completing that second 75

miles ranks as one of my greatest achievements, later captured in an *FT Weekend* feature entitled 'Mud, Sweat and
Gears'.

MONDAY–TUESDAY, 22–23 OCTOBER

A rapid-fire visit to Barcelona to deliver a lecture on 'Lessons from the eurozone crisis' at the IESE Business School.
Javier Solana, formerly Spanish foreign minister, made me
an invitation I could not refuse. The Catalan independence
movement is gathering momentum and Javier wants to bend
my ear about the new centre-right government's intransi-
gence. My lecture – which shows sympathy with Spain's
efforts to clean up its banking sector – goes down well. Spain
needs more support from its European allies, especially
Germany, I argue.

*My diagnosis was good, my prescription less so. I was fairly
confident that Spain would need financial assistance from
the EU and the IMF as part of its reform package. I
underestimated the political courage of the new Rajoy
government.*

31 OCTOBER–7 NOVEMBER

A week-long trip to New York and Washington culminating
in Obama's election-night victory. No surprise. Mitt Romney
was too wooden and too wealthy to appeal to a majority of
Americans. But there's little sense of history-in-the-making
compared to 2008. The best I can offer is a post-midnight
video interview in front of the White House.

TUESDAY, 13 NOVEMBER

Maria Miller, the secretary of state for culture, media and sport, has again asked to see me ahead of the Leveson report publication. Miller is a former advertising executive with the air of a school headmistress. She's pressing for a commitment that newspapers will 'implement' Leveson. I'm politely non-committal.

THURSDAY, 15 NOVEMBER

An early-evening 'courtesy' phone call from Peter Wright, former editor of the *Mail on Sunday* and Paul Dacre's batman. He's tipping me off that the *Daily Mail* is publishing an article – well, a series of articles – about Sir David Bell. *Nothing too much to worry about. Paul just wanted you to know.* How many articles, I ask? Quite a few, it transpires. I call David to pass on the message. He is outraged at the *Mail*'s attempt to blacken his name ahead of the official report of the Leveson inquiry where he acted as an adviser. I have no idea what's in the *Mail* coverage and little useful advice to offer.

FRIDAY, 16 NOVEMBER

The *Mail* 'exposé' of Sir David Bell contains eleven pages of vitriol dressed up as investigative journalism, including a large front-page photo of David wearing a garish red and purple tie and grinning smugly. David – obviously a proxy for Leveson – is accused of being part of a 'coup by the Left's old boy network'. The *Mail* describes the Media Standards Trust – which David sponsored as a rival body to the discredited Press Complaints Commission – as 'a quasi-masonic nexus of the "people who know best"'. Dacre appears to be goading David to sue. On my reading, the *Mail* has ventured right up to the libel line but not crossed it.

> *This was standard operating procedure for the* Daily Mail, *which had its own formidable army of lawyers and was always willing to spend serious money to fight its cause in court.*

In the afternoon, a visit from Elon Musk who has parked his red Tesla at the back entrance to the *FT*, part of a London tour to show why he is one of the most exciting entrepreneurs in the world. Right now he's juggling not just one world-class innovative venture but three: the Tesla electric car; a new Gigafactory battery manufacturing plan; and SpaceX, the space rocket maker whose ultimate goal is to foster space transportation and help us to colonise Mars.*

Musk makes light of our sceptical questioning. How to achieve scale in electric car manufacturing to compete against the likes of GM and Ford? How to ensure there are enough electric chargers available for mass travel by electric car? How to get to Mars? *Well, let's start with how to get to Pall Mall.* He summons John Gapper to join him for a joy ride to his next destination: *The Economist* in St James's. On arrival, Musk hands the keys to John, who may or may not be insured, and asks him to drive the car back to the *FT*, where the Tesla

---

* In 2020, Tesla overtook Toyota as the most valuable car company in the world based on its stock-market price – a dramatic shift in power.

team is waiting nervously. *Rarely has a Tesla been driven so slowly, John later told me.*

Then on to Lou Susman's 75th birthday-party dinner at Bellamy's restaurant in Bruton Place. Senator John Kerry has come. Lou raised tens of millions of dollars for Kerry when he ran for president in 2004. Tall and craggily handsome, Kerry is placed next to Victoria but soon disappears to take a series of calls from Washington. Lou informs me that Obama has lined him up to be the next secretary of state.

THURSDAY, 29 NOVEMBER

The Leveson inquiry has finally published its report, an epic with more pages than Tolstoy's *War and Peace*. It documents the incestuous relationship between the tabloids, politicians and some senior police officers, but clears Cameron of being too close to the Murdoch empire. The judge is calling for a new media watchdog with statutory underpinning, 'free of influence from the industry or government'. New powers include fines based on turnover for 'suspected or systemic breaches' of the code. There's also a proposal for a new libel-resolution unit, with arbitration on the menu.

Leveson is fighting yesterday's war. The balance of power has shifted decisively in modern media. Newspapers have lost their influence as gatekeepers between the public and the politicians. Facebook and the digital giants — not mass-circulation tabloids — are the new Powers That Be.*

---

* *The Powers That Be* was Pulitzer Prize-winner David Halberstam's book on the rise of America's mass media as a political force, from FDR's fireside chats to Watergate.

TUESDAY, 4 DECEMBER

Cameron has summoned Fleet Street's editors to Downing Street to discuss how to implement Leveson. What is the collective noun for a group of editors: a cluster, a herd or maybe just a hack, as in a hack of smokers? All told, there must be 20 of us in the room, many unfamiliar faces. The PM claims with a straight face he's just here to support Maria Miller. He calls for meaningful change, *whatever that means*. This is the man who hired Andy Coulson as his press secretary, the ex-*News of the World* editor at the epicentre of the phone-hacking scandal.* Cameron is also text-best friends with Rebekah Brooks, long-time editor of the *Sun*. He may be prime minister but at this moment, in this room, I cannot take him seriously.

TUESDAY, 11 DECEMBER

To Frankfurt, to interview Mario Draghi at the European Central Bank. Draghi's 'whatever it takes' declaration in the summer has calmed markets. He confesses that he had been preparing for a fortnight to make a forthright statement to the financial markets, but none of his advisers had been apprised of the precise wording. I ask him if he had rehearsed the now famous line and he laughs: 'No, I'm not really that theatrical.'

The *FT* has made Draghi Person of the Year. If he pulls off this juggling act, the Jesuit from Rome will go down in history as the man who saved the euro.

---

* Andy Coulson, editor of the *News of the World* 2003–7, Conservative party director of communications and Downing Street press secretary 2007–11. Found guilty at the Old Bailey in 2014 on one count of phone-hacking and sentenced to 18 months in prison.

2013

HAPPY ANNIVERSARY

The Financial Times *celebrated its 125th anniversary in 2013. We had come a long way since the four-page City of London newspaper pledged in 1888 to be the friend of the 'Honest Financier and the Respectable Stockbroker'. One hundred and twenty-five years later, we had a newsroom of 600 journalists: half the size of the* New York Times, *but still capable of packing a punch. In 2013, I was determined to drive digital transformation further, faster. This would require politics and theatre on my part.*

TUESDAY, 1 JANUARY

I'm joining Twitter, maybe the most significant conversion since Saul of Tarsus. I have ranted at times about the futility of saying anything serious in fewer than 140 characters; but I want to make a statement. In 2013, we will shift to 'digital first' journalism. In practice, this means that the newspaper will be derived from our online content – not the other way round. We need a change of mindset as well as a change in workflow. Encouraged by James Lamont, my new managing editor, I have drafted my first-ever New Year note to staff, calling for 'imagination and a good dose of courage' and setting out editorial strategy, including the launch of FastFT, our new online breaking-news service.

Arthur Sulzberger, the New York Times *proprietor, congratulated me on my New Year message when we met in Davos. He wondered aloud why the* New York Times *newsroom had yet to produce a similar strategy note. Why indeed? In May 2014, the* NYT *published their own* Innovation Report, *a weighty tome which charted a new (and highly successful) digital course for the Grey Lady.*

Tweeting became a mild addiction which drove Victoria to distraction but provided a useful platform for promoting FT *journalism. Journalists using the medium were either trigger-happy or too inclined to blur lines between their own views and* FT *reporting. We would issue the odd reprimand, but it remained difficult to control. Journalists had a duty to their employer who paid their bills, but they increasingly wanted to be their own 'brands'. The problem only got worse.*

MONDAY, 14 JANUARY

Mariano Rajoy is the fourth and least charismatic Spanish prime minister I have interviewed. He lacks the feline charm of Felipe González, the handsome socialist who presided over Spain's democratic transformation. He (thankfully) does not suffer from the hauteur of José María Aznar, González's centre-right successor. José Luis Rodríguez Zapatero was a socialist show horse, as I discovered in 2010. Rajoy, by contrast, is a grey character with spectacles and a wispy beard, a Galician from Spain's north-west. As the Spanish say, if you meet a Galician on the staircase, you can never be sure whether they are going up or down. After sitting with Rajoy for two hours in his office in the Moncloa, I have made up my mind: he is the man of the hour, a credible reformer set on restoring Spain to Europe's premier economic league.

'It is the old cliché that Rajoy never takes decisions,' Rajoy tells the *FT*. 'They say about the Gallegos [Galicians] that they like to wait and see – and they say the same thing about me. But in the year since I took over the government I reduced the public deficit in a situation where we were in recession. I pushed through structural reforms and a reform of the banking sector. I would like to know: how many non-Gallegos would have taken those decisions?'

Bankers in Madrid have told me, and our new Madrid correspondent Tobias Buck, they're convinced Rajoy is going to seek assistance from the European Central Bank. The PM has calculated that the promise of support from the ECB will lower borrowing costs in the bond market, thus rendering an actual request for assistance redundant. He's also adamant that the eurozone will remain intact.

Rajoy's judgement was correct. Spain had no need to apply for ECB assistance, because Draghi's pledge of support was sufficient insurance policy. The prime minister's remarks on Catalonian independence were ominous. He described Spain as the 'oldest country in Europe' going back five centuries. No Spanish prime minister could give up on his own country. He was legally correct but politically inflexible. Tensions rose steadily before the Catalan separatist party staged a flawed referendum in 2017 which led to a botched declaration of independence and the biggest political crisis in Spain in 40 years. Rajoy stepped down in 2018.

WEDNESDAY, 23 JANUARY

Cameron has taken the biggest gamble of his political career, pledging an in–out referendum on Europe. He wants a 'new settlement' with the EU, whatever that means. Back in 1975, Harold Wilson held a referendum on renegotiated terms of UK membership of the then European Economic Community and won handsomely. Forty years on, the Conservative party has turned increasingly Eurosceptic, in some quarters outright Europhobic. Cameron fears a rupture in his party akin to the Corn Laws in the 19th century.* Philip Stephens says Britain's departure from the EU is a possibility rather than a probability, adding: 'The danger is that, in bowing to the populist clamour, Mr Cameron has created a political dynamic that leads to departure, while Europe is being made a scapegoat for Britain's self-inflicted economic ills.'

MONDAY, 11 FEBRUARY

Lord Black has invited me to join him in a meeting at Downing Street to talk to David Cameron about Leveson. It's a small group only, with Paul Vickers of the Mirror Group and Peter Wright of the *Mail on Sunday*. The meeting is inconclusive but I feel privileged to be present as the 'swing vote'. On the way out, I bump into Paul Dacre who has clearly been invited to his own meeting with the PM. *Maybe I'm not so important after all. When will Cameron learn that Dacre is not his best buddy?*

---

* The Corn Laws created the dividing line in the Conservative party in the 19th century, pitting landowners against the rising manufacturing interest. Prime Minister Sir Robert Peel's 1846 decision to repeal the Corn Laws – which regulated the trade and price of grain – split his party for decades.

TUESDAY, 12 FEBRUARY

Prodded by colleagues, I've composed an anniversary tribute to the *FT*, doing my level best to avoid self-congratulation. There's a few references to awkward moments (the half-hearted Labour party endorsement in 1992; our flirtation with UK membership of the euro) but also a recognition that on issues like the Iraq war, which we opposed, our judgements proved right.

Big international stories have played to the *FT*'s strengths: the collapse of the Soviet Union and the unification of Germany; the creation of Europe's single currency; globalisation and the quadrupling of the world's labour market between 1999 and 2009 as China, India, Russia and large parts of Latin America became market economies; the birth of the internet and the dotcom bubble; and finally the 2007–9 global financial crisis. 'Robert Rubin, who served as treasury secretary and Citigroup chairman, once told me that the *FT* was invariably more useful than his daily CIA news digest,' I write. 'The celebrated investor Warren Buffett described the *FT* as an essential guide to currency and trade stories.'

Sometimes I wish we were regarded as less of a niche publication in the UK and more of a national treasure, but our international standing is what matters. That is what drives our business and our news agenda. After working 16 years overseas, it is also where I am (marginally) more comfortable.

FT veterans have passed on several anecdotes for my article. The best one, hopefully not apocryphal, features a Chinese ambassador in Africa who was asked why he always carried a copy of the pink paper. 'We always read the *FT* in the embassy,' he explained, 'because capitalists never lie.'

TUESDAY, 5 MARCH

We've dispatched to favoured parties and contributors a special anniversary book collection featuring 52 classic Lunch with the *FT* interviews. F.W. de Klerk, who presided over the end of apartheid in South Africa, has written a note of thanks. So has Anatoly Chubais, Mr Privatisation in post-Soviet Russia. Nigel Lawson, 80, is less impressed.

'I am surprised that you were unable to agree to my suggestion of a complimentary subscription to FT online, as it would have been a friendly gesture which would have cost the FT absolutely nothing – zilch,' he says in a handwritten note to me. 'I read the FT, at no charge, in the library of the House of Lords, so there is no way that it would make sense for me to pay for a subscription to FT online. That is why I have never done so, nor will I ever do so. But there you go, as Willie Whitelaw used to say.'

I had expected more from Lord Lawson, a former *FT* journalist. As a Thatcherite and a reforming chancellor of the exchequer, he was surely familiar with Milton Friedman's book *There's No Such Thing as a Free Lunch*.

28 MARCH–3 APRIL

A maiden five-day visit to Myanmar to witness a political transformation as momentous as the post-apartheid transition in South Africa. The military dictatorship is over, press censorship has been lifted and hundreds of political prisoners released. The fearsome generals have returned to barracks or reappeared wearing *longyis*, the 2m-long sheets of cloth sewn into a cylindrical shape and worn round the waist. A gesture to civilian rule.

Gwen Robinson, the garrulous Australian who never sleeps, is our south-east Asia correspondent and resident Myanmar expert. She has set up a fabulous itinerary starting in the capital, Yangon, where we have our own night tour of the magnificent British colonial architecture, with the golden Shwedagon pagoda glowing in the background. Onward the next morning to Bagan, the ancient capital south-west of Mandalay and once home to more than 10,000 temples. We then drive 170 miles south-east to the capital, Naypyidaw, via a diversion to the town of Meiktila. Gwen has heard reports of a massacre of 50 Muslims, amid ransacking of homes and shops. She wants to see evidence first hand. A local MP takes us to where he said he watched a Buddhist mob beat and burn at least 15 schoolchildren to death as police stood by. A lone sandal lies on the ashes.

Naypyidaw, the capital, feels like a leap forward ten centuries. As we tootle along the city's 20-lane highways, little is visible beyond the odd car or sentry in olive-green uniform wilting in 40 degrees heat. The architecture is a combination of Sun King grandeur and Legoland. The Burmese parliament is a 31-building complex surrounded by a giant moat, apparently designed to deter would-be invaders.

Our interview with President Thein Sein takes place in a palatial residence inherited from his predecessor, General Than Shwe. We ascend to the first floor via an elevator marked VIP, to be greeted by five aides, each of whom tenders a military salute (a first in 35 years of journalism). The president is polite but firm: it's time for the west to lift sanctions permanently as a reward for Myanmar breaking with the past. Gwen cautions that sanctions have created a class of crony businessmen acting as agents of the dictatorship. Human rights groups are holding out against relaxation, because of misplaced loyalty to Aung San Suu Kyi, the opposition leader and Nobel Peace Laureate known simply as the Lady.

Unfortunately, the Lady is too busy to see the *FT* but we do visit her party's headquarters in Yangon, where loyal footsoldiers are not entirely enamoured with the woman feted in the west for spending 15 years under house arrest. One veteran talks of a cult of personality and intolerance towards dissent. George Soros, the philanthro-capitalist, is inclined to err on the side of generosity. But then he is a member of a consortium bidding for a Burmese telecoms licence. Over dinner we are all agreed: the forthcoming election will determine whether Myanmar will become a sham democracy or a beacon for the region.

Aung San Suu Kyi was installed as state counsellor, a position akin to prime minister, in 2016. But she remained beholden to the military and drew severe international criticism for her inaction in response to the genocide of the Rohingya people in Rakhine State in 2017. Her reputation never recovered.

MONDAY, 8 APRIL

Margaret Thatcher has died, aged 87. The *FT*'s position on Mrs T is, well, complicated. We opposed the Falklands war and we disliked the hectoring, confrontational style which proved her undoing in the end. But the *FT* was generally supportive of her reforms, particularly privatisation and restoring a proper balance between the state and the economy.

I grew up in the 1970s when militant trade unionism and incompetent management created the 'British disease' which paralysed the country. Mrs T's treatment was at times worse than the cure, but on balance she was a tremendous force for good. I commission Martin Wolf to write a personal assessment of the Iron Lady.

'Margaret Thatcher was the most important peacetime prime minister of the UK since the late 19th century. She transformed the Conservative party and British politics, overturning the ruling assumptions about the relationship between the state and the market,' he writes. 'Thatcher was also a towering figure on the global stage. Her close ideological connection with US president Ronald Reagan gave her a global role unlikely ever again to be occupied by a British politician.'

Martin says Thatcher was never the 'Saint Joan of free markets' as championed by true believers, more a pragmatic politician who 'showed little interest in embarking on suicidal attempts to demolish pillars of the welfare state, like the National Health Service'. In the end, he says, Mrs Thatcher made a significant contribution 'in her time', but her legacy looks less transformative in the aftermath of the financial crisis. It's a fine piece to grace page one. I would have been marginally more generous.

WEDNESDAY, 17 APRIL

I am sitting in St Paul's Cathedral with several hundred mourners at Mrs Thatcher's funeral service, staged with solemn pageantry. Britain's ruling class is out in force, including

Fleet Street's editors. Paul Dacre takes his seat a few rows in front of me. The American delegation looks thin in the aisles. VIPs include former vice president Dick Cheney, former secretaries of state Baker and Schulz, but no Clintons, Bushes or top officials from the Obama administration. This feels churlish. Richard Chartres, bishop of London, presiding at the funeral, said Mrs Thatcher was a symbolic figure, 'even an ism', alongside capitalism, Communism and socialism.

Thatcher was indeed an 'ism'. Like most 'isms', she was divisive. But she transformed modern Britain and helped end the Cold War. Not a bad legacy.

19—25 APRIL, CHINA

An interesting invitation via David Giampaolo, an American private equity entrepreneur, to join the annual meeting of the China Entrepreneur Club in Kunming, China, near the borders of Vietnam and Myanmar. The club features the cream of Chinese capitalism, billionaires like Jack Ma of Alibaba and Wang Jianlin, the property developer who has his eye on a Hollywood studio. These trips are always tricky to judge: time out of the office versus time spent in the field. On balance, I'm going. It's a chance to network and stop over in Beijing where our bureau chief Jamil Anderlini invariably sets up interesting interviews. Kunming offers some sit-down time with Wang and other capitalists, all of whom are gung-ho about overseas expansion. More fascinating is a two-hour visit in Beijing to the home of Ai Weiwei, the controversial Chinese artist-dissident.

Jamil and I arrive at Ai Weiwei's compound to see 15

security cameras trained on his home. Ai Weiwei has draped them in red lanterns, an aesthetically pleasing means of obscuring their view. He is a thickset man with short hair, a large black beard and a face weathered by extralegal detention. (He's just spent 81 days in custody in a secret location subject to constant interrogation.) We sit down for a makeshift breakfast and a lesson in Chinese history. In the early days of Communism, he says, everything was sacrificed for the project and a nation beset by poverty. Today, the legitimacy of the party is in question. Weibo, the social network, offers a chance for citizens 'to put the state on trial every day'. If one sentence is deleted, 'they create their own enemy.' The artist pauses to sip his coffee. 'It's like an immune system which is collapsing.'

At the end of our conversation, Ai Weiwei takes us for a tour of his studio where several young women researchers, at least one from Europe, mill around. I see a collection of aluminium bicycle wheels piled up on the floor and inform Ai Weiwei that I am a cyclist. He smiles and asks me if I would like to take one of the wheels home to London, autographed of course. *Is my name Lionel Barber?*

TUESDAY, 30 APRIL

The New York Stock Exchange has invited the top team led by John Ridding to ring the closing bell to celebrate the *FT*'s 125th anniversary. Most people want to ring the opening bell because there's always a chance the closing bell will signal a decline in the market by the end of the trading day. Today, the S&P closes at 1597.57, up 0.25 per cent on the day. *Phew!*

THURSDAY, 9 MAY

Robert Swannell, chairman of Marks and Spencer, wants a quiet word about the *FT*'s reporting on Britain's faded national treasure. M&S has a strong food business but it's always one step behind on clothing (with the possible exception of male underwear, in my experience always reliable). Like other retailers, it's been slow to embrace the internet, relying instead on stores which are expensive to maintain. Swannell is ex-Schroders,* a City gent with a cut-glass accent. He would like me to shift our long-time retail reporter Andrea Felsted, admittedly a bit of a terrier. I am happy to take a look at our coverage but there's no way I'm moving Andrea.

My dealings with Britain's retailers were invariably colourful, no more so than with Sir Philip Green, the pugnacious billionaire owner of Topshop, Miss Selfridge and two superyachts parked off the coast of Monaco, his weekend retreat and home for wife, Tina, and two children.

In 2016, Green called me to complain about a story, effing and blinding as if I was one of his minions. We rapidly got into a shouting match which ended with an improbable overture from the one-time king of retail.

Green: 'Wotcha want?'

LB: 'I'm sorry. I don't understand.'

Green: 'Wotcha want? A cake?'

LB (flummoxed): 'OK, I'll have a cake.'

Green: 'What kinda cake?'

LB (guessing wildly): 'An almond cake.'

---

* Schroders, the FTSE 100-listed asset manager, was founded in 1804 by two brothers from Hamburg.

The following week, Green strode into the FT *newsroom bearing an almond cake. It was a peace offering of sorts. Hostilities resumed shortly thereafter.*

THURSDAY, 6 JUNE

A cascade of revelations in the *Guardian* about the National Security Agency's bulk collection of phone data from millions of US customers of Verizon, one of America's bigger telecom providers. The secret court order covers domestic and international calls. US news organisations reported in 2006 that the NSA was secretly collecting phone data to detect terrorist activity after 9/11. But until now there's been no indication that the programme was continuing under Obama. This story feels like it's going to get a lot bigger.

SUNDAY, 9 JUNE

Edward Snowden, 29, a contractor from Booz Allen Hamilton contracted to the NSA, has revealed himself to be the whistleblower behind the exposure of secret surveillance programmes. I'm torn about what to think about this story. In principle I support the *Guardian*'s decision to publish, laying bare the scale of data collection and holding the intelligence agencies (and their willing accomplices in Silicon Valley) to account. On the other hand, the security services already have a hard enough task tracking terrorists dedicated to destroying public confidence in the state.

The Snowden affair put the Leveson inquiry in perspective. The space between private and public in western democracies had become blurred, perhaps irretrievably. In the tabloid phone-hacking scandal, grubby journalists were the villains. Now the scoundrels were the data-mining companies and intelligence agencies. And they were operating on a scale unimaginable to the likes of the News of the World. *Leveson had his guns trained on the old enemy.*

SUNDAY, 16 JUNE

The Russian ambassador Alexander Yakovenko called yesterday to ask if I would join a small group for dinner with Vladimir Putin at the embassy. I assumed it was a hoax. Apparently not. Russia's strongman, back in office as president, is interested in meeting 'experts' ahead of this week's Group of Eight meeting in Northern Ireland.*

I am placed to Putin's right, next to Sergei Lavrov, the lugubrious long-time Russian foreign minister. Caviar and vodka are served. Putin opens with a bland statement in Russian before zeroing in approvingly on Stephen King, HSBC's chief economist, and his newly published book, *When the Money Runs Out: The End of Western Affluence.* Putin ignores everyone except King, who is purring loudly. After 15 frustrating minutes, Lavrov turns to me. 'Speak! This is a hard country . . .'

After catching Putin's eye, I intervene in German in a bid to impress the former KGB agent once stationed in Communist Dresden: 'Mr Prime Minister, what you must understand about Europe is that we are all German these days. All European countries are adjusting their economies

---

* Lough Erne was the last G-8 summit which Russia attended. The group shrank to seven after Russia was banished following its annexation of Crimea.

on German terms: Spain, Italy, Greece, Portugal – even the Baltic states . . .'

Putin: 'Why do you mention the Baltic states?'*

I start to reply but the conversation quickly moves on to the eurozone sovereign debt crisis and the transatlantic relationship and energy. Putin declares at one point that he is delighted to speak freely without journalists present. This could be a calculated insult to me and John Micklethwait, editor of *The Economist*; more likely a rare oversight. Mickle asks Putin about America's shale-gas revolution and its impact on world energy prices, especially Russia's oil and gas output.

Putin: 'Shale gas is temporary phenomenon.'

Guests nod approvingly.

Putin raises a glass of red wine. 'This is colour of water in North Dakota.'

Dinner ends after precisely two hours. Putin thanks his guests and rises from the table, only to spot a piano in the corner of the room. 'I've been practising playing the piano,' he says, casually. Would the guests like to hear him play? *Well, who's brave enough to say no?* Putin sits down and plays 'Chopsticks' in a high octave. 'St Petersburg!' he pronounces.

Then he plays 'Chopsticks' in a low octave. 'Moscow!' he explains. Putin rises to our clapping, marches to the exit

---

* Estonia, Latvia and Lithuania declared independence after the collapse of the Russian empire in 1918. The three states were annexed by Moscow in 1940, invaded by Nazi Germany and returned to Soviet control at the end of World War II. After the collapse of the Soviet Union, their absorption into the EU and NATO was neuralgic for Russian nationalists like Putin.

and then turns, ostentatiously summoning Bob Dudley, chief executive of BP, for a tête-à-tête in the foyer.

> *Putin's musical bagatelle remains a source of fascination. Was it a subtle way to destabilise a powerful audience or a signal that even the most ruthless ruler can succumb to moments of sentimentality? Putin's poker face gave nothing away. Eight months later, he gave the order for Russia to annex Crimea, the first change of borders in Europe by force since 1945.*

TUESDAY, 18 JUNE

An uncomfortable outing in front of the House of Commons select committee on media. MPs are frustrated by the failure to reach agreement on Leveson. My verdict is not exactly helpful: 'We are in no man's land.'

All proceeds vacuously until Labour MP Paul Farrelly, an ex-*Observer* journalist, invites me to comment on the *Daily Mail*'s evisceration of Sir David Bell for being a liberal do-gooder intent on undermining the freedom of the press. David is a man of integrity, a mentor going back many years, I tell MPs. Then again, no legal action has been taken in response to the *Mail* story. *I might have been more forthright in David's defence but I generally made a point of avoiding public criticism of other journalists. There were exceptions; Dacre was not one.*

WEDNESDAY, 17 JULY

Matteo Renzi, hot favourite to become Italy's next prime minister, is in London to woo investors – and the *FT*. He delivers a ponderous PowerPoint presentation on his proposed political and economic reforms. Never seen that before. I'm tempted to paraphrase Lord Acton: power corrupts, PowerPoint corrupts absolutely.*

FRIDAY, 16 AUGUST

My secret weapon in my campaign to transform the *FT* newsroom is Tony Major, the quiet man from Hull. (Tony is my man going back 15 years, a newspaperman to his fingertips, an expert on design and production and a useful backchannel to the National Union of Journalists.) I promoted him several years ago to help me think about the future of the newspaper. He went off to visit *Svenska Dagbladet*, the top Swedish daily in Stockholm, and returned with the concept of 'fast' and 'slow' news.

Svenska's Martin Jonsson, who pioneered the concept, has come to see me in my office. He says fast news describes events like accidents, emergencies, news conferences and other 'breaking news', all of which apply to the website. Slow news covers trends or stories which are less time sensitive. At *Svenska*, a higher proportion of the print newspaper is now pre-planned slow news, allowing editors and reporters to focus on 'feeding' the website first with breaking news.

This was a lightbulb moment. I suddenly began to see how the FT *could truly go digital first by inverting the production of news, making the newspaper essentially an outgrowth of the news and views published on ft.com.*

---

* John Dalberg-Acton, 1st Baron Acton (1834–1902), Victorian parliamentarian, staunch liberal and anti-nationalist, is the source of the aphorism 'Power tends to corrupt, and absolute power corrupts absolutely.'

23–27 AUGUST, CHINA

On arrival in Beijing, everyone is talking about President Xi's anti-corruption campaign. There are rumours that dozens of senior military and lowly bureaucrats are under arrest, the 'tigers' and 'flies' whom Xi has vowed to track down. A Chinese source says there is 'a new Emperor' in Beijing.

An audience with Xi was never on the cards, but my old contact, Ambassador Fu Ying, has arranged for a meeting with a senior official in Zhongnanhai in the Imperial City which serves as the headquarters of the Communist party. Jamil Anderlini, our Beijing bureau chief, is accompanying me, sharing the thrill of walking the same path in the leadership compound as Che Guevara and Richard Nixon. The names of buildings and gardens are wonderfully resonant: Water Clouds Pavilion, Benevolence Hall, Garden of Abundant Beneficence and our destination: the Hall of Martial Achievements.

This is no ordinary interview. The senior official takes my opening question on the state of the Chinese economy and expounds at length. He brooks no interruption. The message is unequivocal: Chinese growth will come in on target at 7 per cent in 2013. There will not be any room for slackening off in China, whatever the uncertainties in the world economy. Just a fortnight ago, US financial markets had a nervous fit after the Fed signalled it would start to 'taper' its special government bond and asset purchase programme known as quantitative easing (QE). Towards the end of the conversation, the official asks me for my own views on the 'taper tantrum' and what it might mean for the US and Europe. I'm cautiously optimistic, contrasting it with the 1998 Asian crisis when overextended sovereign borrowers got into trouble because of their dollar-denominated debt. This time, countries like Indonesia, South Korea and Thailand are in relatively better shape. The official listens intently. Fu Ying later thanks me, holding out the prospect of an on-the-record interview at a later date.

> *From Beijing's standpoint, the off-the-record exchange was a useful means of communicating the party's commitment to maintaining economic growth at all costs, whatever the global uncertainty. It was also an implicit reminder that, despite Xi's rapid accumulation of power, there were other senior officials who counted, especially on economic policy. And finally, as often in China, it was an opportunity for a member of the party leadership to listen to a candid assessment by a western observer — later described by Fu Ying as one more step on the ladder leading to a relationship of mutual respect and trust.*

FRIDAY, 13 SEPTEMBER

Georgette Mosbacher, businesswoman, philanthropist, New York socialite and Republican heavyweight, has asked me to put together a dinner with an 'interesting' British politician. My first choice is Boris Johnson. Thankfully, London's mayor is up for joining us at Scott's in Mayfair.

On arrival, I ask to be taken to Boris's table. The waiter escorts me to Boris Becker,* which provides an excellent

---

* Boris Becker, German tennis champion, won three Wimbledon titles in the 1980s. His personal life is almost as colourful as his namesake's.

opening anecdote for our own dinner. The real Boris has come with his barrister wife Marina Wheeler. After the triumph of the London Olympics, the mayor is on top form. He's even touting his improbable plan for a new airport in the Thames Estuary, known as 'Boris Island'. As the clock draws towards 10.30, Boris says he needs to get home, naturally on his bike, his contribution to curbing carbon emissions. Georgette, Victoria and I are detained briefly on exit by Charles Saatchi.* As we leave the restaurant, skirting the paparazzi, we spot the mayor folding his bike and disappearing into a gas-guzzling taxi.

SATURDAY, 14 SEPTEMBER

Broken collarbone after toppling over on my bike in the Surrey Hills, part of my training for the assault on Mont Ventoux with Team Terry Smith. The pain is hard to cope with, sleeping even harder. I take the plane to New York next day to chair the Business Books of the Year judging panel. Victoria thinks I'm insane. She may be right.

McKinsey have taken over from Goldman Sachs as co-sponsors of our £30,000 business book award, and I owe it to them to turn up. Besides, it is always fun trying to forge a consensus among seven strong-minded judges, including Vindi Banga of Clayton, Dubilier & Rice private equity and Marks & Spencer director; Rik Kirkland, the top Fortune editor now head of McKinsey Global Publishing; and

---

* Charles Saatchi, born in Iraq, is the legendary ad man who with his brother Maurice built Saatchi & Saatchi into the world's biggest agency. Also a leading art collector, he opened London's Saatchi gallery in 1985.

Baroness Shriti Vadera, former top adviser to Gordon Brown and board member at pharma giant AstraZeneca and BHP, the natural resources giant. All under the watchful eye of Andrew Hill, *FT* management editor. The 'biz books' are intellectually stimulating, occasionally hard going. My description of reading worthy shortlisted books is 'eating broccoli'. The judges usually get the hint.

9–16 NOVEMBER

Jo Johnson, Boris's younger brother, now Conservative MP for Orpington, has invited me to attend Prabodhan *(rough translation: Exhortation)*, a new Anglo-Indian business and political forum. I'm also planning high-level interviews, including Narendra Modi, the firebrand chief minister of Gujarat, whose conservative Bharatiya Janata Party (BJP) has built a strong lead ahead of the election. India has tired of the Gandhi dynasty and its hold on the Congress party. Modi is attracting millions to his rallies, using holograms and social media to build a cult-like following. 'Modi reminds me of Thatcher in 1979,' says Arun Jaitley, a lawyer and likely next finance minister, sitting in his booklined office in Delhi, 'he's like a typhoon. We just don't know when it will hit land.'

David Cameron has flown over to Delhi to speak at the Prabodhan conference in a bid to strengthen commercial ties with India, perhaps the next economic superpower but one. Other high-powered guests include Peter Mandelson, Richard Lambert, formerly CBI boss and Peter Sands, the irascible CEO of Standard Chartered Bank with the silver hair and Harry Potter glasses. Sands berates me in public over the *FT*'s coverage of his bank. He protests too much. Now I'm going to tell the banking team to take an even harder look at StanChart's numbers.*

After Prabodhan, I fly with India bureau chief Victor Mallet to Ahmedabad and take a short drive to Gandhinagar, the state capital, to meet Modi. The chief minister's office is cavernous: a giant wooden map of the western trading state hangs over an equally gigantic oblong wooden desk. A portrait of a proud Gujarati lion hangs in the north-west corner of the room.

Modi is a hard-edged, ambitious man blamed for tolerating, if not inciting, anti-Muslim violence in his home state in 2002. Thousands of people were killed. There's no point in raising directly the mass killings because he will just turn off. So I opt for the beguiling style of David Frost, declaring that the world is waiting – *waiting* – to see what the self-styled man of action will do once in office.

Modi: 'It is not about me – it is about the party and the team.' *The voice is confident, the English almost perfect, the modesty improbable.*

LB: 'How about economic reform?'

Modi: 'Everyone agrees on 90 per cent of what is needed to be done in India.'

LB: 'How about liberalisation of the retail sector to help bring down food prices – and opening up the market for foreign companies to compete against entrenched city merchants?'

---

* Sands, ex-McKinsey, presided over rapid growth at StanChart, which outstripped rivals after the financial crisis. By the end of his nine-year tenure, performance slipped and the bank was fined by US authorities for breaching sanctions against Iran. He resisted pressure to quit but announced his resignation in February 2015, alongside the chairman Sir John Peace.

Modi (guffawing): 'Ah, that falls into the 10 per cent.'

The chief minister talks a great deal about farm reform and raising living standards. He rejects any notion of anti-Muslim sentiment. 'The government religion is the nation first. The Holy Bible is the constitution.'

Modi is a lot sharper than Rahul Gandhi, who has granted me a private conversation – no interview, I'm afraid, with the scion of the Nehru–Gandhi dynasty – in his modest home in Delhi. Rahul, dressed in a simple white kurta pyjama and sandals, talks vaguely about Congress's mission to alleviate India's terrible poverty and his recent campaign trip to Bihar, one of India's poorest states. He seems either shy or diffident, almost overwhelmed by the burden of leading his party in the shadow of his grandmother Indira and his father Rajiv, both murdered. *Compared to Modi, definitely low-energy.*

In Mumbai, we are treated to a two-hour tutorial from the central bank governor, Raghuram Rajan, a brilliant academic from the University of Chicago.* He pledges a 'dramatic remaking' of the country's banking sector to bolster competition, liberalising rules to allow new entrants and foreign banks. He also wants to prod state-owned banks into owning up to bad corporate loans. Laudable, but risky because these companies have deep political ties. Next stop is Mukesh Ambani, India's richest and most powerful businessman. He tells me about his next big move: offering broadband to the masses via cheap phones. The project will be called Jio.

---

* Raghuram Rajan, former chief economist of the International Monetary Fund, served one three-year term only as RBI governor, stepping down in 2016.

The launch of Jio signalled a revolution in the telecoms sector. Mukesh drove down prices, squeezing rivals and pushing his brother Anil's highly indebted company, Reliance Communications, into bankruptcy. As the dominant force, Mukesh in 2020 invited outside US investors led by Facebook to take equity stakes in Jio. Brilliant strategy from a ruthless operator.

Final stop in Mumbai: James Crabtree, our talented local correspondent, has arranged seats to watch Sachin Tendulkar, India's greatest ever batsman, in his 200th and final Test match. Everyone in the ground and the millions of Indians watching on television want the Little Master, now 40, to make a century against the West Indies. Alas, it was not to be. Tendulkar fell at 74 to a sharp slip catch. The groans turned into a standing ovation as he made his way off the pitch – a memorable end to a memorable trip to the subcontinent.

TUESDAY, 19 NOVEMBER

Sir Alex Ferguson, veteran manager of Manchester United, leaves nothing to chance on or off the football field. He's written a new book on his life as the winningest manager in English football and he has selected me to interview him on stage at the Barbican in front of 500 devoted fans. His charmingly pugnacious son, Jason, has choreographed every step from my entry to mild applause, followed by his father's entry to a thunderous standing ovation, accompanied by his own Mao-style self-handclaps. I have no problem with Sir Alex's personality cult. He is a brilliant motivator of men who brought sackloads of trophies back to Old Trafford. Does he realise he's being interviewed by a Spurs fan of 52 years' standing? 'No problem,' retorts the Boss. 'That was the last time [1961] that Spurs won the League, right?'

Our conversation over, Sir Alex invites me back to the dressing room to chat over a glass of vintage red wine – a post-match ritual he used to share with Arsène Wenger of Arsenal and José Mourinho of Chelsea. The no-nonsense Glaswegian famous for giving his players the 'hairdryer', shouting at them inches from their faces, is a lot milder in person, if still a little wary of journalists. On that night, and in two later conversations, we discover a mutual interest in American history, especially the Civil War period. To my surprise, Ferguson's sympathies lie with the underdog. 'The romance was always with the Confederates. They were never going to win.'

I loved talking to super-managers and leaders like Sir Alex Ferguson. He was a role model in helping me think about nurturing and retaining talent but also about rotating and renewing the top team. He had a sixth sense in knowing when it was time to bring in fresh blood.

22–30 NOVEMBER

Our Turkish Airlines flight touches down shortly after 2am in Tehran, the start of an eight-day 'proconsular' visit with Roula and Victoria to Iran. Within hours, world powers in Geneva announce an interim deal to curb the Iranian nuclear programme. The timing of our trip could not be better.

I've long been fascinated by Iran, a country of ancient culture and tradition held in the grip of Islamic fundamentalism since the 1979 revolution which toppled the Shah. Roula, newly promoted to foreign editor, working with Najmeh Bozorgmehr, our long-time Tehran correspondent, has set up a host of interviews including, we hope, President Hassan

Rouhani, the self-styled pragmatic reformer who triumphed in the presidential election.

Our first meeting is with Hossein Shariatmadari, the hard-boiled editor and commentator at *Kayhan*, mouthpiece of Islamic fundamentalists. Inside his office in scruffy downtown Tehran, the walls are lined with books, alongside framed, coloured scrolls from the Koran and two portrait photographs of Ayatollahs Khomeini and Khamenei and a photo-portrait of Hassan Nasrallah, the firebrand cleric and Hizbollah leader. Shariatmadari preaches radicalism at home and abroad. The Arab revolutions are not an Arab awakening. 'It is an Islamic awakening.'

A more nuanced picture emerges from an hour-long conversation with Akbar Hashemi Rafsanjani, one of the founding fathers of the Islamic revolution, veteran kingmaker and a multimillionaire in his own right thanks to dubious business activities.* We meet in the stunning Marble Palace museum, scene of a failed assassination attempt on the Shah in 1965 (aides proudly show us the bullet holes in the entrance walls), which is surrounded by a vast garden filled with giant plane trees. Parrots squawk in the autumnal sun, dimmed by urban pollution.

At 79, Rafsanjani is in the twilight of his political career but I am thrilled to meet a historic figure, the man known as the Shark who bamboozled the Reagan administration during the Iran–Contra affair and has pulled strings in Iran politics for three decades. Rafsanjani is optimistic that a comprehensive nuclear deal can be done in a year's time now

---

* Akbar Hashemi Rafsanjani was president of Iran between 1989 and 1997, and previously speaker of the Iranian parliament between 1980–89. He died in 2017.

that talking to the Americans is no longer taboo ('It was breaking the ice, the second stage will be more routine'). He insists that Iran had no interest in developing nuclear missiles and dismissed Israeli threats of a retaliatory missile strike. 'Israel is so small; no small fish can eat big fish.'

While Roula and I are interviewing movers and shakers in Tehran, Victoria has driven with an old Iranian friend to Shiraz, the ancient city known for its literary history and many gardens. She reports back that the mosques are magnificent but the waterway has run dry, one more sign of environmental pollution. We're still waiting for confirmation of our interview with President Rouhani, the subject of intense haggling. I agree to extend my visit by 24 hours.

Finally, the official summons to a pink-marbled palace downtown to meet Iran's president, impeccably dressed in clerical black robe and white turban. As we shake hands in front of the TV cameras, I take a diplomatic gamble and whisper in his right ear in a heavy Scottish accent: 'Thank you for seeing us, Mr President. I bring special greetings from Scotland!' Rouhani recognises that I'm not carrying a bottle of whisky – *Allah forbid since alcohol is officially banned in Iran*. I am in fact referring to Rouhani's postgraduate studies at Glasgow Caledonian university. He gives a broad smile. We've connected, I believe.

Rouhani wants reform but he is no Gorbachev. He alludes several times to 'other centres of power', an oblique reference to the Revolutionary Guards.* What's most

---

* The Revolutionary Guards are the dominant wing of Iran's armed forces tasked with guarding the political system. Centre of hardliner power and an independent economic force within the regime.

striking is his denunciation of the mismanagement and corruption under his populist predecessor Mahmoud Ahmadinejad. Western sanctions have wrecked the economy and stoked inflation. He needs to boost living standards, no doubt aware that the hardliners are waiting in the wings. Sanctions relief is critical but he will not bow to demands in Israel and Congress that Iran completely dismantle its nuclear facilities. On that point, he is unyielding: '100 per cent, no!'

The FT *visit to Tehran coincided with a moment of hope. But the nuclear deal eventually disappointed both sides. The Iranians wanted more sanctions relief as a reward for compliance with the nuclear accord, while the Americans wanted an end to radical Islamist subversion overseas. Rouhani was caught in the middle. President Trump repudiated the deal in 2019, but Europe stayed aboard.*

FRIDAY, 13 DECEMBER

Lunch with John Fallon at Pearson headquarters at 80 Strand. Same old salad with a little bit of cold chicken, followed by fruit. Fallon asks about my interview with Sir Alex Ferguson, not his favourite person (he must be a Manchester City supporter). Unlike Marjorie, he has no natural feel for journalism, even if his heart is in the right place when it comes to editorial independence. Today, as usual, he wants an update on progress of potential candidates to replace me as editor, and general succession planning. But this time he's more specific, saying he is looking at a 'transition' in a year or two. I know that ten years is a fairly common standard for leaders of organisations. My own predecessors, Geoffrey Owen and Richard Lambert, left after ten years. If that's what Fallon has decided, then I have a couple of years to go in the best job in journalism. *There's plenty to do — and I've got plenty of gas in the tank.*

THE CROWN PLANNER

Dramatic political events would dominate 2014: the Orange Revolution in Ukraine; a bitterly fought independence referendum in Scotland; and the rise of UKIP, the English nationalist-populist party led by Nigel Farage. The eurozone crisis continued to fester but the central question remained whether Greece could survive inside the single currency area. Chancellor Merkel kept her options open. The future of the FT was also a matter of speculation. Was Pearson ready to sell? And how long did I have left as editor?

TUESDAY, 7 JANUARY

The two-man North Korean diplomatic delegation led by Ambassador Hyon Hak-bong arrives on time from its embassy in Ealing, west London. I'm hopeful the ambassador might help to secure a visa for an *FT* correspondent to visit Pyongyang. No easy task at the best of times and these are, in some respects, the worst of times in the Hermit Kingdom.

Last month, the North Koreans announced the execution of Dear Leader Kim Jong-un's uncle, Jang Song-thaek, nominally second-in-command in the regime. He was accused of being 'an anti-party, counter-revolutionary factional element' and 'despicable human scum'. News accounts later claimed Jang had been stripped naked and fed to ravenous Manchurian hunting dogs.

I've ordered colleagues to steer clear of starving dogs until after the main course. Hyon confirms that Kim's uncle was executed by firing squad. Apparently he was involved in smuggling, but the ambassador is evasive when pressed for details. His colleague/minder barely speaks. He's just digesting our views on North Korea ahead of the visa application. At the end of lunch, I escort Ambassador Hyon to the front entrance and thank him for his visit.

Ambassador: 'Thank you, Mr Barber. I have a question. How old are your computers here at the *Financial Times*?'

LB: 'Well, the desktops are around seven years old. The tablets are newer.'

Ambassador: 'What do you do with the desktops when you've finished with them?'

LB: 'I don't really know. I suppose we throw them away.'

Ambassador: 'If I want to buy one, how much would it cost?'

Our diplomatic exchange did not lead to a business transaction. Ambassador Hyon's deputy defected to the west a year later. The FT *did eventually secure its visa and a memorable video dispatch from Pyongyang by Jamil Anderlini.*

SATURDAY, 11 JANUARY

A productive editorial strategy day. We are on track to redesign the newspaper with a classy new font to be called Financier. I am worried about cost but Tony Major and our chief designer Kevin Wilson (a steal from the *Guardian*) assure me that the introduction of page templates will make the production of the newspaper much simpler. This is a revolution: many Fleet Street news organisations, with the exception of *The Times*, are running down their newspapers and doubling down on digital. But newspapers are still a valuable source of advertising revenue. I reckon we can give our 'slow news' newspaper a new look *and* go digital first. When colleagues (occasionally) challenge me, I quote the old American saying: 'We can walk and chew gum at the same time.'

17–19 JANUARY

Every year since becoming editor I have been invited to spend two days at an elite Anglo-French forum called the Colloque. It takes place in alternating venues: the Trianon in the Palace of Versailles and the Four Seasons Hotel in Fleet, Hampshire. Sponsors include top British and French companies with an interest in European affairs, agreeable company and fine wine. The French delegation is almost exclusively old white male establishment; the British somewhat more diverse, drawn from politics, media and business, with several members of the Cabinet led by George Osborne and Michael Gove.

The corridor gossip this year is about President François Hollande, spotted last week on the back of a scooter en route to the apartment of his mistress, Julie Gayet, an actress. A magazine – *Closer* – took pictures of the French president entering and leaving the apartment. In private Hollande is said to be a hoot, a gifted raconteur and mimic with raw sex appeal; in public he comes across as a backroom bureaucrat who does not know his own mind. A French delegate tells me that the tittle-tattle over the scooter story has obscured its greater political significance. *Le Président, il avait* une *femme mais* deux *politiques. Maintenant il a* deux *femmes mais* une *politique.* The President had one wife but two political strategies. Now he has two women but (only) one political strategy. Entendu, *as they say in Paris.*

SUNDAY, FEBRUARY 23

Violent protests in Kiev have toppled the pro-Moscow government in Ukraine, ousting the elected president Viktor Yanukovich who has fled to Russia. Martin Wolf suggests we write an editorial defending 'The Orange Revolution' and calling on the US, Europe and Russia to recognise Ukraine's right to take its place among western democracies.

'This is a moment of immense opportunity – and immense danger for Ukraine, for the EU and for Russia,' we write. More than any single moment since the collapse of the Soviet bloc, the revolution that began in Kiev heralds 'the hour of Europe'. Sitting in the editor's office on my Sunday shift, I add a line addressed directly to Vladimir Putin in Moscow. 'This is not 1956 in Hungary or 1968 in Czechoslovakia when the Kremlin crushed popular uprisings with brutal force. Permanently destabilising the country is a tactic, not a policy.'

In the event, Mr Putin chose the path of destabilisation, stoking a proxy war in largely Russian-speaking eastern Ukraine which triggered economic sanctions by the US and EU. Ukraine's position on a geo-political fault line in Europe, perched precariously between the European Union and Russia, remains contested and is likely to stay that way.

MONDAY, 24 FEBRUARY

Paul Dacre was disconcertingly pleasant the other day on the phone, but I told him I could not commit the *FT* to join IPSO, the newspaper industry's new body for self-regulation of the press. John Fallon at Pearson and John Ridding are against, and I'm embarrassed about admitting to Dacre that, on this matter, it's not my (sole) call. Like Dacre, I believe the government's alternative of a Royal Charter is a backdoor to state regulation of the press.* The other way to go is to create the *FT*'s own system of self-regulation. I've written a draft proposal with one central premise: 'We are a genuinely different news organisation with a global footprint and an expanding digital model, all of which sets us apart from our British competitors.'

In new media, the barriers to entry have fallen and information is communicated instantly to mass audiences. Of course, news organisations must comply with the law, criminal and civil. But national regulation based around print media is meaningless. None of our direct established

---

* The idea of a Royal Charter, widely credited to Sir Oliver Letwin, set a legal basis for a post-Leveson oversight regime. It was a ruse to avoid the government passing legislation to regulate the press, but most news organisations refused to sign up and formed their own body, the Independent Press Standards Organisation (IPSO). The FT's refusal to sign up to the Royal Charter or IPSO was a permanent source of irritation to the two opposing camps.

competitors – Bloomberg, the *New York Times*, Reuters and the *Wall Street Journal* – is ready to join a UK regulatory body. None of the aggregators – *BuzzFeed*, *Business Insider* or the *Huffington Post* – will be caught in the net either. My challenge is to devise a system for the *FT* which is credible, robust and immune to the charge that we are 'marking our own homework'.

One option is to appoint a US-style 'readers' editor', an independent figure who can deal with complaints and hold editors accountable. The *Guardian* has a readers' editor, but later conversations with senior editors at the *Washington Post* and *New York Times* convince me that this is a recipe for trouble, especially if the appointee is given a column to sound off every week in the newspaper. John Micklethwait provides a riposte. '*The Economist* already has a readers' editor,' he tells me over one of our regular breakfast pow-wows; 'he's called the editor.' Mickle's right. All serious reader complaints come to me as editor and I will respond personally or via our in-house lawyer, Nigel Hanson.*

FRIDAY, 28 FEBRUARY

Breakfast with Sir Jeremy Heywood at the Cinnamon Club. The Cabinet secretary is relatively relaxed about the upcoming referendum in Scotland. A majority vote against

---

* I vetoed the idea of a readers' editor and proposed instead an 'editorial complaints commissioner' with an appellate function only. John Ridding said it sounded too negative. I pointed out that complaints are by their nature negative. We agreed to appoint a tough-minded barrister, Greg Callus, who reported to a three-person board composed of two former Fleet Street editors (Patience Wheatcroft and Ian Hargreaves) and Ridding himself. It was rigorous and it worked.

independence looks assured, bolstered by the Scottish Labour party which should be solidly No. ('They're tribal on the Clyde.') We turn to Europe, where Cameron is under increasing pressure from UKIP led by Nigel Farage and from malcontents in his own party.

Heywood insists people are too negative about Britain's standing in the EU. We've chalked up wins on the proposed European banking union which will protect the City of London. There's a reasonable deal on the EU budget as well as agreement on carbon emission limits by 2030. Heywood is more worried about the erosion in Britain's 'political/military' position. Libya was reasonably stable after the allied intervention led by Cameron and Sarkozy toppled Gaddafi; now 'it's a mess.' The House of Commons vote last year against military action in Syria was 'a blow'. The UK is absent from negotiations on the Iran nuclear deal, absent from international oversight of Syria's pledge to destroy its chemical-weapons stockpile, and missing in action in diplomacy to end Russian aggression in eastern Ukraine.

This is a comprehensive indictment of Cameron's foreign policy. Heywood, who is usually guarded, confides that he is also worried about developments at home, especially the impact of George Osborne's austerity programme. The squeeze on public spending under way since 2010 will be 'very hard to maintain' as the economy improves. Welfare cuts – £20 billion is apparently under discussion – are 'just not possible on this scale'. The problem lies partly in Cameron's commitment to protect the education, foreign aid and health services from spending cuts. This so-called ring-fencing means that choices are limited and other spending departments bear a disproportionate level of cuts. Heywood says the impact on the criminal justice system and legal aid is a 'huge worry'.

As for the Conservative party, Heywood is dismissive. 'They're out of control. They've got no discipline.'

During my editorship, I conversed with Sir Jeremy Heywood roughly once a year over lunch and we chatted privately at social occasions. These were candid exchanges. He used me as a sounding board. I gained a (fairly) neutral insight into the affairs of government. Aside from our last lunch, a few months before he succumbed to cancer, this was the frankest, at times most damning assessment of the Cameron-led coalition government.

2–16 MARCH, SOUTHERN AFRICA

The commander-in-chief of the Economic Freedom Fighters finally appears, dressed in black. Black hood, black tracksuit, black air pump trainers. The trademark Breitling wristwatch is conspicuously absent. An aide wearing a Che Guevara hat sits in the background. Julius Malema, firebrand populist and scourge of the African National Congress, is running 45 minutes late but is still keen to present the acceptable face of the revolution.

We are sitting on a balcony in something akin to a safe house, a remote lodge in the four-star 500-plus-room Kruger Park Lodge near Hazyview, a rundown town near the border of South Africa and Mozambique. A sign on the lawn warns: 'Beware hippos'.

I owe this remote encounter to Andrew England, our Johannesburg bureau chief. Initially, the message from the Malema camp was less friendly: JuJu does not speak to white capitalists. Then Andrew pointed out that the *FT* had endorsed Neil Kinnock in 1992. That apparently clinched the interview.

I ask Malema whether things have improved after 20 years of ANC rule in South Africa. 'No! We are worse off than we were under apartheid,' says Malema, eyes flashing. 'Before we did not have electricity or running water. Democracy has given us [blacks] the vote but there is still no clean water or electricity. We are in more pain than ever.'

Malema calls President Zuma 'a monster' and describes black empowerment entrepreneurs as 'parasites'. His political heroes are Fidel Castro of Cuba, Hugo Chávez of Venezuela and Robert Mugabe in neighbouring Zimbabwe, 'despite all his mistakes'. Malema's own political programme fits the same revolutionary tradition: state expropriation of land and natural resources; launching a state mining company with 45 per cent offered to private investors; and a change in the constitution to allow control of the means of production.

The interview with Julius Malema – the Marxist theoretician from the township – was a high point on a 14-day tour of Southern Africa, including South Africa, neighbouring Namibia and Angola, front-line states in the war against apartheid. I wanted to write a long feature on South Africa's second great struggle: the transition from the bush to government and the heavy expectations which come with black majority rule.

A brief interview with President Zuma on the election trail was hardly encouraging. Engaging, raffish and indelibly corrupt, Zuma, 71, came across as the great survivor. He insisted the ANC had 'a good story to tell' about social and economic progress. In fact, the Zuma presidency added up to lost years for South Africa. His

successor, Cyril Ramaphosa, estimated that the looting of the state
under Zuma had cost the country more than $30bn.

Once again, I've been asked to find a good speaker at one of
the numerous conferences and dinners which the *FT* holds
in partnership with sponsors – a vital revenue stream for the
FT and one I have pledged to support as editor even if it can
occasionally lead to sticky situations.

This year, I've caused a kerfuffle among judges of the *FT*'s
annual Boldness in Business awards, sponsored by ArcelorMit-
tal, the giant steel group. I've proposed Nigel Farage to deliver
the keynote speech at the gala dinner at the Royal Institute of
British Architects near Regent's Park, where we recognise bold
businesses, large and small, from around the world. At least
two judges are threatening to boycott the event on the grounds
that Farage is a racist. I have little in common with Farage apart
from the fact that we attended the same school, Dulwich College, in south-east London. We did not overlap, and we have no
social history. My sole criterion is that he is a force in British
politics and our audience of businessmen and -women will find
him interesting and entertaining. At any rate, the award is about
boldness and this is a bold choice as speaker.

The argument over Farage pertained to my own editorial judgement
but it also foreshadowed the debate about 'de-platforming' speakers
because of their controversial views. Farage was not a proto-fascist,
even if some UKIP members were unsavoury, swivel-eyed loons.
That night Farage connected to his audience, sticking it to pro-
Europeans like me who, he said, were on the wrong side of history.
I was slow to grasp Farage's everyman appeal.

MONDAY, 28 APRIL

Pfizer, the US pharmaceutical giant, has launched a hostile bid for AstraZeneca, one of a tiny handful of world-class British pharma companies and a crucial part of the UK science base. Pfizer is an acquisition machine which has spotted that the proposed deal would allow it to avoid significant tax liability on the huge cash pile it holds overseas, as many US large corporations do. The *FT* is generally supportive of takeovers and reluctant to interfere in free markets. We ridiculed, for example, the French government's decision to protect the foodmaker Danone on the grounds it was a strategic asset. The Pfizer bid feels different because AstraZeneca is a vital British asset in a high-value sector. 'Tax arbitrage cannot be allowed to drive this deal alone,' the *FT* thunders. 'Broader national interests are at stake.'

Next morning, Ian Read, Pfizer's Scottish-born CEO, arrives at the *FT* with his top team, on his way to Downing Street to see Cameron. Read, who's dropped his native accent for the occasion, is visibly miffed. He complains that the *FT* editorial has failed to understand the benefits and synergies of the proposed combination. When he's finished, I lay out a copy of the *FT* and theatrically open it on the page of our editorial. 'Let me reassure you,' I say, referring to the Danone defence, 'the *Financial Times* is *not* a French newspaper.'

Kraft's earlier takeover of Cadbury, the storied chocolate maker, had soured attitudes to hostile bids. The US confectionary and food giant had backtracked on commitments to preserve jobs. Kraft later merged with Heinz and then tried to gobble up Unilever, the Anglo-Dutch consumer industries giant. This was a super-sized meal too far.

THURSDAY, I MAY

To Hughes Hall, Cambridge university, to make good on my promise to deliver the prestigious City Lecture. Sarah Squire, Victoria's cousin, is president of Hughes and has been nudging me to speak. Not a problem. It's a chance for me to organise my thoughts on a subject close to my heart: 'Can banking clean up its act?'

My answer, delivered to a politely receptive audience of students, practitioners and town elders, is: probably not. But the industry should make a bigger effort to restore public confidence. 'We cannot turn bankers into saints. Nor should we do so,' I conclude. 'Bankers have begun to clean up their act. But more must be done. The alternative may not be a living hell, but it will be a prolonged period in purgatory.'

FRIDAY, 2 MAY

Jane Owen, editor of *House and Home*, the *FT* weekend section, has come up with another madcap idea. She wants me to interview Prince Charles. *Yes, you heard that correctly.* I've known Jane for more than 30 years, when she was the royal correspondent of the *Sunday People* tabloid, later joining *The Times* and turning herself into a top editor and gardening correspondent. She is not someone you say 'No' to easily.

At 4.30am, hung-over from last night's wine-heavy dinner, I'm having second thoughts about this royal escapade. On the car ride to Luton airport to catch the early-morning flight to Glasgow, I plan the day ahead. I'm headed to the estate of Dumfries House, a grand mansion in the Palladian style, exquisitely restored as part of Charles's experiment in 'heritage-led' regeneration. Our meeting is intended to establish chemistry between the editor and the prince, part of a courtship which will go on for several more weeks.

A chatty Scottish chauffeur picks me up at Glasgow airport but is soon lost for words as we drive aimlessly around the 2,000 acres of grounds around Dumfries House. He ends up dumping me at the wrong door of the mansion, where I am greeted by a friendly Scottish woman servant: 'Good morning, Sir, are you here for the squirrel symposium?' 'No, I am not here for the squirrels,' I reply, 'I'm here to see Prince Charles.'

Upon entering the correct front door, I bump into Lynn Forester de Rothschild* and Carlos Slim, the Mexican telecoms billionaire, both apparently royal buddies. We exchange small talk before they depart by helicopter. Then an unexpected arrival: Geordie Greig, editor of the *Mail on Sunday*. He's suspicious about my presence, as I am about his. Each of us senses the other has an exclusive interview with Charles. I have a sinking feeling that I've been played by Buckingham Palace.

In fact, there's no *Mail* interview on the cards, just a chance for Geordie to inspect the royal estate and keep tabloid ties warm with His Royal Highness. As we walk through the grounds, Charles peppers staff with questions about the placement of trees and the correct pruning of the rhododendrons, maintaining 'social distancing' with his newspaper visitors. I'm a little frustrated but an aide says the prince will engage properly later in the evening, over drinks and dinner.

At dinner, where I am placed at one remove from the

---

* Born in New Jersey, Lynn Forester de Rothschild graduated from Columbia Law School and made a fortune in telecommunications before marrying Sir Evelyn de Rothschild, scion of the banking dynasty.

prince, I mention I started my journalistic career in Scotland and once shook his hand outside Holyrood. Anything to establish a personal connection. By the end of the meal, I start to get a sense of the man. Unfailingly polite, passionate about regeneration, hostile to the consumer society and intensely wary of the press. He's definitely interested in pursuing the *FT* connection, but royalty will not be rushed.

FRIDAY, 9 MAY

I have commissioned Simon Schama, the historian and wordsmith, to compose an essay in defence of the United Kingdom and against Scottish independence. It is a powerful riposte to the Scottish nationalists but also a lesson in patriotism which English nationalists like Farage have too long appropriated for themselves.

Scottish independence, Simon argues, would create a shrunken country divided by borders, barriers, perhaps passports, opening a psychological wound which would take an age to heal. 'Something precious will have been irreparably destroyed: a nation state based not on some imagined romance of tribal singularity but one made up of many peoples, languages, customs, all jumbled together within the expansive, inclusive British home.'

Simon reminds readers that Great Britain was originally a Scottish enterprise. It was a Scottish king – James Stuart – who once on the throne insisted that the two kingdoms be called Magna Britannia. En route south to assume power in 1603, James issued coinage bearing the new designation of Great Britain. Thereafter numerous Scots contributed to 'the great British enterprise', whether in architecture (John Adam), philosophy (David Hume, Adam Smith) or business (the great Scottish merchants like William Jardine and James Matheson). Never more so than in the Victorian era, when Scots made outsized contributions to government, the military and the colonial service.

Simon Schama's essay demonstrated that the Scottish independence referendum was about more than economics and money. It was about culture, history and politics. If only David Cameron had made the same case in the Brexit referendum.

WEDNESDAY, 7 MAY

To Clarence House for a second 'get to know you' meeting with Prince Charles. As we sip tea, I mention my recent visit to Tehran and the *FT* interview with President Rouhani. Charles says, casually, that he remembers meeting the Shah on one of his visits to the UK. I talk about my time as an *FT* correspondent in Washington. He mentions his time with Richard Nixon in the White House. (Nixon advised the young prince to 'be a presence' and not to shy away from controversy altogether. *On the matter of modern architecture, Charles certainly took Tricky Dicky's advice.*) Charles is polite and engaging but always on guard. *No guarantees but, on balance, I believe the interview is in the bag.*

THURSDAY, 29 MAY

Breakfast with Jeremy Darroch, the long-serving, successful CEO of British Sky Broadcasting, the satellite TV company. Darroch is a straight-talking Northumbrian, born in Alnwick, the son of a tax inspector and grandson of a miner. I want to know what he makes of Rupert Murdoch's ambitions to take full control of Sky. Back in 2011, News Corp, Murdoch's media conglomerate, tried to build on its minority stake but backed away because of the phone-hacking scandal. Three years on, Murdoch is reported to be interested in renewing his bid for control. Darroch acknowledges Murdoch's contribution as founder to BSkyB's success, but the phone-hacking affair has soured him on News Corp these days: 'It's a Death Star,' he tells me, grimly.*

In 2018, News Corp finally launched a bid for the remaining 61 per cent of BSkyB, but the UK competition authorities ruled that the bid was not in the public interest due to concerns about media plurality. A bidding war followed in which Comcast, which owns NBCUniversal, triumphed over a rival offer from the Walt Disney Company. Wisely, they stuck with Jeremy Darroch as CEO.

Murdoch later sold his film and television assets in 21st Century Fox to Disney. The perpetual buyer had turned into the tactical seller, cashing out at the moment that prices for content providers were at an all-time high. On one matter, he remained true to form: he kept his beloved newspapers.

TUESDAY, 3 JUNE

I greet Prince Charles in the Yellow Drawing Room on the first floor of Clarence House. His guard dog Kristina Kyriacou nestles next to me on a dark cream sofa, a little too close for comfort. A manservant arrives with a tray of coffee and tea, directing me to place the bone-china cup of char on a nearby table, well away from the prince.

---

* The Death Star: a moon-sized space station, featured in Star Wars, reputedly capable of destroying an entire planet.

Charles, 65, is wearing a double-breasted suit and City black shoes. We begin with Dumfries House, where Charles came to the rescue in 2007 using a £20m loan from his charities. The money has since been repaid and Charles believes the original ambitions are becoming reality: the restoration of the house and its gardens; the creation of an outdoor centre; a cookery school; and cottages soon to be converted into guest rooms for weddings. These form part of the regeneration of impoverished former mining communities in East Ayrshire.

What about the walled garden shaped in the form of a Union Jack? Was this a subtle hint about the royal family's views on Scottish independence, I ask?

HRH: 'No, I just think it looked rather fun. It's fun the way you look at it like that.'

LB (after an awkward silence): 'I had to ask . . .'

HRH (adapting the catchphrase from Francis Urquhart in *House of Cards*): 'Naughty, naughty. You might very well think so. I couldn't possibly comment.'

We turn to modern architecture and urban development, rattling through his experiments like Poundbury in Dorset, rising house prices in London and the importance of 'grammatical rules' in architecture. I sense a world-weariness and frustration on the part of the future king. 'All that's been going on for the last 100 years is that people have just chucked nature out the door, which is coming back to bite us and kick us in the teeth, big time.'

As I prepare to leave, Charles, unprompted, asks me what I make of journalists using the Freedom of Information Act to make public his 'black spider' letters and memos. These are the prince's handwritten notes to ministers over the years on farming, global warming, social deprivation and modern architecture. Charles insists he wrote the letters on the understanding they were private. Just as I am about to reply, Kristina Kyriacou, his hands-on press secretary, ushers me out, eager to stop more headlines about 'The Meddling Prince'.

Shakespeare's words come to mind: uneasy lies the head that wears a crown. The Bard was right that with great power comes great responsibility. But it also sometimes comes with great vulnerability, especially if you have spent so long as the crown-in-waiting.

The 'black spider' memos were released after a Supreme Court ruling against the government in 2015. They were entertaining, if somewhat underwhelming. My interview with Charles appeared in House and Home *under a headline composed by Jane Owen:* 'The Crown Planner'. *You can take the journalist out of a tabloid, but you can't take the tabloid out of a journalist.*

FRIDAY, 6 JUNE

Richard Waters, our west coast editor, has written an eye-opening column on the anniversary of the Snowden revelations about mass surveillance. He says the debate has extended to the role of Big Tech companies and their collection of limitless amounts of data. Until Snowden, conventional wisdom included a free pass to Big Tech operating alongside a borderless internet free of regulation. This argument now sounds complacent, he writes.

'In reality the ground had already been shifting, as politicians and regulators took a keener interest in the expanding digital realm. Any hopes of retaining the light-touch regulation of the internet's earlier days, when governments were grappling with its implications, already looked like wishful thinking. But the shock from the Snowden disclosures has greatly accelerated the shift.'

FRIDAY, 5 SEPTEMBER

Martin Wolf has delivered a fresh broadside against Scottish independence. Last year, Martin torpedoed the idea of the Scots abandoning the pound and creating their own currency in a newly independent Scotland. Today, he argues that independence and retention of the British pound together do not make sense. Scotland's borrowing and its fiscal deficit would be controlled by binding agreements, as would regulation of its financial sector. This hardly amounts to sovereign equality for a newly independent nation. QED.

THURSDAY, 11 SEPTEMBER

Lunch at Buckingham Palace with Chinese vice premier Ma Kai, courtesy of an invitation from Prince Andrew. The Chinese also want to know whether the Scots are going to vote for independence. A poll suggests the referendum race has suddenly and unexpectedly tightened. Pulses are racing in Whitehall. There's chatter about the queen making an intervention this weekend. Prince Andrew gives me a nod and a wink, wink, but he cannot possibly say more. We adjourn to lunch where Ma Kai offers a few generalities about China's growth prospects and the world economy. When I turn to my right, Prince Andrew tries to engage me in small talk.

HRH: 'Do you shoot?'
LB: 'No, Sir.'

HRH: 'Do you fish?'
LB: 'No.'
HRH: 'Do you ride?'
LB: 'Well, I do like to go cycling . . .'

MONDAY, 15 SEPTEMBER

Everything was going swimmingly after the first copies of the redesigned *FT* newspaper hit the streets last night. This morning the first complaints about the new Financier font are arriving in my inbox. At least 20 readers, many of them elderly, complain that the type appears to float in the newspaper. Others complain about the amount of blank space. By tea time, I'm starting to wobble. Has this redesign been a ghastly unforced error? I call in Kevin and Tony and pretend to be calm. Their message is: hold your ground. Readers will get used to the new paper. They just hate change.

And we did stick with Financier. Some readers left and a few new ones joined. Growth remained on the digital side. But our redesigned newspaper won several awards for its modern look. It had a new lease of life.

FRIDAY, 19 SEPTEMBER

Scotland has voted 55–45 in favour of preserving the Union. The queen's intervention on Sunday – she told a well-wisher, 'Well, I hope people will think very carefully about the future' – may have tipped the balance. My sense is that the Scots were too canny to take a leap into the unknown. After this defeat, Alex Salmond, the SNP leader, is surely a spent force. Nicola Sturgeon, his feisty deputy, is set to take over what feels like a one-party state north of the border.

MONDAY, 22 SEPTEMBER, MANCHESTER

Ed Miliband has delivered a party conference speech promising a '10-point plan to build a world-class Britain'. Who comes up with these platitudes? Miliband's diagnosis is not so wide of the mark — austerity's impact on public services, the marginalised, the rise of inequality — but his prescriptions still feel skimpy.

Dinner with Alistair Darling is a treat. He is the unsung hero of the Better Together campaign against Scottish independence. Darling says he feels mentally and physically shattered. He was always confident he would carry the day until that last poll which was 'deeply misleading'. The media played it up because they wanted to make the referendum a real contest. Gordon Brown delivered 'the best speech ever' in defence of the Union. Darling is contemptuous of the SNP 'thugs' intimidating voters and a pliant press, particularly in Scotland. Alan Cochrane of the *Daily Telegraph* was a notable exception. 'He was brilliant and brave.'

Darling's account of the campaign raised a delicate question: were the press, including the FT, *too soft on Alex Salmond? I heard stories about voter intimidation and pressure on academics to support Scottish independence or keep quiet. I resolved to strengthen our Scotland coverage because the independence question was bound to come back, in one way or another.*

28–30 SEPTEMBER

My chance to run a slide rule over the Cabinet at this year's Conservative party conference in Birmingham. After the win in Scotland, George Osborne is breezily confident about prospects for the Brexit referendum. He's predicting a poll in 2017, assuming (which he does) the Conservatives will win the election. He also says the implosion of the Liberal Democrats in the European Parliament elections this year offers opportunities for Conservative candidates, even in Lib Dem strongholds in the west country.

The rest of the Tory high command are a mixed bunch. Liam Fox, former defence secretary, is an ebullient empty vessel. Jeremy Hunt, health secretary, has a good bedside manner. Theresa May, home secretary, is the vicar's daughter turned spectre of the deep state. Chris Grayling, justice secretary, has few answers about the terrible state of prisons and the criminal justice system. He's more exercised by the European Court of Human Rights which he claims impinges on the sovereignty of Parliament. Reluctantly, I agree to publish a Grayling op-ed on the subject, on the grounds that we rarely give space to Tory Eurosceptics. On reading the piece post-publication, I remember why.

William Hague is a good deal more agreeable. He made his reputation aged 16 at the 1977 Conservative party conference when he declared, memorably, 'Half of you won't be here in 30 or 40 years' time . . . but I will be, and I want to be free.'

Now foreign secretary, Hague is the party's elder statesman, adamant that Britain needs a referendum on Europe. Without the prospect of one, UKIP would be even higher in the polls. 'There's no way back.'

Germany, he says, will be key to a 'new settlement' between Britain and the EU. Merkel has only let the UK down once, allowing Jean-Claude Juncker, the Luxembourger, to become president of the European Commission. Remaining in the

EU is a 'strategic imperative' for the UK, 'but not at all costs', he says.

Back in 2010, Hague was a key Conservative negotiator on the terms of a coalition deal with the Liberal Democrats. The Lib Dems desperately wanted to secure a commitment to House of Lords reform in return for electoral boundary changes. Hague says this was a 'strategic mistake' on their part because the boundary changes greatly advantaged the Conservatives.

At the end of seven days of negotiations, Hague says he returned home and collapsed in a chair.

'What have you done?' his wife Ffion asked.

'I think I've just destroyed the Liberals,' replied Hague, who claims he promptly fell asleep.*

WEDNESDAY, 1 OCTOBER

Lunch at the Chelsea Arts Club with Petr Aven and Mikhail Fridman, two Russian oligarchs trapped between east and west. Both Aven and Fridman have extensive business interests outside Russia and they both enjoy their bases in London. US-led sanctions over Crimea and Ukraine have put them on the spot. Is their loyalty primarily to Mother Russia or are they citizens of nowhere who prefer to put most of their money in the west? *Sooner or later, Putin will force them to choose.*

---

* The 2010 Conservative–Lib Dem coalition pact included a promise to bring forward proposals for a wholly or mainly elected House of Lords. But in 2012 Nick Clegg was forced to abandon a bill to that effect, in the face of Tory opposition. Hague's original judgement was correct on all counts.

WEDNESDAY, 29 OCTOBER

To Ben Bradlee's funeral at Washington's National Cathedral, the last warrior king of modern newspaper journalism. Bob Woodward says Ben's passing marks the end of the 20th century. More like the end of post-war print journalism. Ben's days as editor were the golden years when newspapers made money hand over fist, and reporters like Woodward and Bernstein were treated like gods.

Bradlee died aged 93, and the *Post* has passed from the Graham family to a new owner, Jeff Bezos, founder of Amazon, the online retail leviathan. Bezos, the shaven-headed billionaire, is sitting directly in front of me. He never met Bradlee. He got to know him a whole lot better during the service. David Ignatius, a *Post* veteran, rehashes the story about the secretary who took down a dictated Bradlee note to an aggrieved reader. 'Is dickhead one word or two?' she inquired.

At the end, two sailors delivered a tautly wrapped flag to Sally Quinn, a widow bereft, and a bugler sounded taps from high in the neo-Gothic rafters. Bradlee was a navy man who witnessed the horrors of war in the Pacific, the last Good War America fought. He was a patriot, an unfamiliar word these days. He loved his country and he loved life. And I loved him dearly too.

WEDNESDAY, 5 NOVEMBER

Vladimir Yakunin, the former KGB agent who runs Russian railways, arrives with a retinue of bodyguards. Several have sausage fingers and no visible sign of a neck. I'm suitably impressed. But I do insist that only one 'aide' accompanies

Yakunin in my office. Yakunin has been on a US sanctions list since Russia annexed Crimea. He's charming, polite and uninformative. My sense is that this is a reconnaissance mission. Yakunin knows Putin well. They're said to own neighbouring dachas on the Karelian Isthmus. We agree to keep in touch, in London or in Moscow.

Yakunin proved a useful source in the coming five years – more 'market colour' than scoop provider. He invariably came with a thoughtful gift such as a vividly illustrated book on Russian art, culture or history. His conversation was occasionally less highbrow. He once asked: 'Why is it, Lionel, that all the women in London look like men?'

THURSDAY, 18 DECEMBER

My annual turn at the *FT* pensioners' lunch which invariably ends mid-afternoon with well-oiled veterans recounting war stories in a corner of the newsroom. After lunch, Sir David Bell asks whether he might drop by my office for a coffee. No specific agenda, naturally.

There was plenty in the air about the future of the FT*, but no sense of what might happen or what it would mean if it did. None of which I felt entirely comfortable in sharing with my old friend and mentor. This was a moving story, one certain to develop further in 2015.*

SECTION FOUR

———

BREXIT AND THE RISE OF
NATIONAL POPULISM

2015

ENTER NIKKEI

The new year opened with an act of terror in Paris. Two masked gunmen burst into the offices of Charlie Hebdo, *the satirical weekly magazine, killing 12 and wounding 11 people. Radical Islamists would commit other acts of mass violence in Europe. Every editor wrestled with how to present the image and the story without making the perpetrators look like martyrs to a cause.*

On a personal level, there was only one story which mattered in 2015: the sale of the FT *to Nikkei, the Japanese publishing giant. John Fallon compared stewardship of the* FT *and a prospective sale to carrying a porcelain vase across a marble floor. To his credit, he did not let it slip. There was trepidation about what would come next, but also excitement about new opportunities. I would enjoy an unexpected fresh start as editor, supported by new owners with global ambitions.*

WEDNESDAY, 18 FEBRUARY

John Fallon told me over one of our regular lunches that he did not want to go down in history as the man who sold the *Financial Times.* Now he appears to have changed his mind. He has come to realise that owning a media company is an expensive proposition. The *FT* needs capital to grow, I tell him, but instead we are living from hand to mouth to meet annual profits targets set by Pearson. Inevitably, this raises the question: is Pearson still the best owner of the *FT*? John Ridding is of the same view.

Nevertheless, until fairly recently, such a question would have been considered sacrilegious. Pearson has owned the *FT* since 1957. For many years, it was an unwieldy conglomerate with disparate interests such as fine wine (Château Latour), waxworks (Madame Tussauds), bone china (Wedgwood), North Sea oil and Penguin Books. In the late 1990s, under CEO Marjorie Scardino and CFO John Makinson, it sold off the big brand assets and made a multi-billion-pound bet on the education business. But it retained control of Penguin, a near 50 per cent stake in *The Economist* and full ownership of the *FT*. Even when times were hard, after the dotcom bust, Marjorie stayed loyal to publishing, print and editorial independence.

But media properties have been put up for sale recently, at fancy prices. In 2007, the Bancroft family sold Dow Jones and the *Wall Street Journal* to Rupert Murdoch, and the Graham family sold the *Washington Post* to Jeff Bezos of Amazon in 2013. Soon, the *Los Angeles Times*, *Time* and *Fortune* magazines would go under the hammer. The *FT* under Pearson ownership looks like an anomaly, even though engineering a sale (which would include selling its stake in *The Economist*) is fraught with risk.

As we pick at our chicken-and-salad main course, John hints that he's had several informal approaches but will not reveal much detail. *We're both treading fine lines here. If John tells me too much he risks compromising my role as a journalist. On the other hand, I am the editor with a direct interest in the future of the* FT. Somewhat gingerly, he sounds me out about possible suitable buyers starting with American publishers like Bloomberg and Hearst. Then he mentions Axel Springer, the German newspaper and publishing powerhouse, and a new name: Nikkei, the Japanese publishing giant.

My view is that a trade buyer like Bloomberg would spell the end of the *Financial Times* brand. Axel Springer is a dynamic company, I say. Mathias Döpfner, the CEO, counts as a friend; but Springer owns *Bild*, the racy German tabloid, which would sit uneasily with the august *FT*. Nikkei is a bit of a mystery to me. I've bumped into their correspondents from time to time, but they seem very far away in Tokyo, quite aside from the differences in language and culture.

My lunch with Fallon marked the point of no return. It was clear to me that it was not a question of whether we would be sold, more a question of when and to whom. I made a mental note to brush up on my German and read up on Nikkei.

FRIDAY, 20 MARCH

I've been cultivating Lynton Crosby for months, knowing he is first choice to run Cameron's re-election campaign. The silver-haired, razorblade-chewing South Australian helped John Howard's centre-right party to win four straight elections Down Under. His contempt for journalists has transferred effortlessly from Adelaide to London. We meet at the Great Gallery restaurant at the RAC Club in Pall Mall which must rank as the best-furbished London club, with a full-size marble swimming pool and Turkish baths.

Crosby begins by telling me that voters are 'fucked off'. All the old assumptions about working hard and keeping a job are gone. Immigration is a serious problem. Conservatives have to hammer a single message: trust us with the economy, Labour are 'way too risky and incompetent'. Execution is the challenge: this means a targeted 'ground campaign' in multiple constituencies.

I ask Crosby how he proposes to deal with UKIP and the coming man, Nigel Farage, who is standing in South Thanet. Will the Tories be targeting his seat? Crosby looks incredulous: 'If you want to win the Vietnam war, you don't just bomb the paddyfields. You kill Ho Chi Minh.'

In that one lunch, Crosby laid out the future Tory campaign: attack Labour as irresponsible lefties, target vulnerable Lib Dem seats, neutralise UKIP on immigration and stop Farage from winning a Parliamentary seat. I wish I had paid more attention.

21 MARCH—4 APRIL, JAPAN, CHINA

My annual trip this year is to Japan, a chance to revisit Tokyo but also to explore the hinterland with Victoria. We take the train to Hiroshima, where a few skeletal buildings still protrude from a former atomic wasteland. Then on to the beautiful island of Miyajima, Kanazawa's magnificent fortress and the town of Takayama in the Japanese mountains famous for its gilded floats and parades.

Then I receive a message from Angela Mackay, the head of the *FT*'s Asia commercial operation, that Nikkei senior management would like to invite us to lunch. Intrigued, I proceed with Angela and Robin Harding, our Tokyo bureau chief, to Nikkei's skyscraper headquarters near the Imperial Palace, and a delightful meal attended by several top Japanese executives, led by Naotoshi Okada, soon to be elevated to Nikkei CEO and president. Soon I find myself the target of polite but intense interrogation about the *FT*'s journalism and its editorial strategy.

Nikkei has serious financial power based around its business newspaper with a circulation of 2.7m and related media interests, including market indices; but executives frankly admit they are too reliant on print and need to increase their 430,000 digital subscribers. As usual, I talk too much, occasionally dropping in English jokes – a dangerous habit soon to be discontinued. After lunch, as I descend in the Nikkei elevator, I realise that the joke is in fact on me. I have been metaphorically undressed, stripped of all the information my hosts need (for now) about the *FT* and its transformation from print to digital.

MONDAY, 13 APRIL

From the day he was appointed CEO of Barclays Bank, Antony Jenkins has talked about remoulding its gung-ho culture into something more ethical and public-spirited. He has won an unlikely endorsement from the archbishop of Canterbury and the sobriquet 'St Antony'. How much that matters to his own restive board is another question, as I'm dying to tell him over our one-on-one lunch at his office in Canary Wharf.

I am reliably informed that a rump of Barclays directors are unhappy with Jenkins, a mild-mannered man from the Potteries whose strength is in retail banking. Jenkins seems oblivious to the threat and talks enthusiastically, maybe a little too enthusiastically, about progress on cultural change at Barclays under the TRANSFORM programme which has three elements: Turnaround, Return Acceptable Numbers, Sustain Forward Momentum.

Over dessert, a mixed lemon, raspberry and vanilla sorbet, I cannot resist mentioning my own tip on imminent management change at Barclays. 'Antony, I'm not sure you enjoy majority support of the board.' Jenkins looks startled and probes me on my sources. This is awkward. I cannot possibly reveal where I got my information but the sources are rock-solid. I make my excuses and leave.

Three months later, Jenkins called me very early one morning Rocky Mountain time and said he was stepping down as Barclays CEO. He was polite as usual but sounded rueful. What he could not say – but which I knew – was that a faction of the board yearned for a return to the days when Barclays was a global player in investment banking. Hence their choice of Jes Staley, (another) American investment banker, as his successor.

MONDAY, 20 APRIL

The general election campaign is a curiously low-key affair. Ed Miliband is Blair/Brown-lite; David Cameron is still too smug; Nick Clegg has lost his fizz. In these circumstances, I'm happy to escape for a couple of nights at the five-star Beau-Rivage Palace hotel in Lausanne on the edge of Lake Geneva, in my capacity as host of the *FT*'s annual Commodities Summit. This is one of our most important revenue generators, originally conceived by Javier Blas, a garrulous Spaniard who was our chief natural resources reporter before defecting to Bloomberg. Javier's idea was to bring the world's top commodity traders – Glencore, Gunvor, Trafigura, Vitol, many of them still privately owned – and stick them in the same room as bankers and publicly owned mining companies, like Anglo American, BHP, Rio Tinto. They could talk to each other and the *FT* could get to know the big movers and shakers, like Glencore's Ivan Glasenberg who's still playing rugby aged nearly 60 and the inscrutable Norwegian Torbjörn Törnqvist of Gunvor.

The commodities summit worked a treat until environmentalists got wind of the conference. Tonight they're out in force, chanting slogans about capitalist conspiracies and the degradation of the planet. Our conference staff are fretting about a Green assault on the building and the cost of the police operation which is going to cut our profit margin.

FT conferences contained in-built conflicts between our duties as inquiring journalists and our responsibilities as event organisers, but on balance I believe they were manageable, even if they required constant monitoring to ensure things did not become too cosy. It was a push-me, pull-you relationship.

WEDNESDAY, 22 APRIL

Back in London, I report to colleagues that several businessmen, including Ian Taylor, CEO of Vitol, the giant oil trader and a big Tory donor, have told me they are disappointed with the Conservative election campaign which is 'lucklustre' and 'very negative'. Sarah Gordon, business editor, makes calls around the main business lobby groups. Lynton Crosby is soon on the phone. What's going on? Where did this story come from? Who's been blabbing? The *FT* does not speak for business or the City. *Your Westminster correspondents are all Marxists or Labour sympathisers.*

Crosby is relentless: 'This election is not being fought in Kensington and Chelsea where the rich don't even pay taxes . . . It's being fought in Solihull, St Austell and Preston.'

Crosby suggests that if we delay publication he will deliver campaign literature proving his strategy will deliver a Tory majority. My judgement is that our story needs more sourcing. Twenty-four hours later, we publish a front-page story quoting many (unnamed) top businessmen complaining about irresponsible Tory spending pledges and worrying about the threat of a Labour government. 'The negative campaign has been disastrous,' says an anonymous donor.

The real story was that Crosby and Cameron were targeting Liberal Democrat seats in their supposed strongholds in the southwest of England. Their campaign could be summed up as 'kill the coalition' to win an overall majority.

FRIDAY, 24 APRIL

I'm hearing second-hand that Pearson is in serious talks with Axel Springer which might lead to a full sale of the *FT*. John Ridding is heavily involved in the secret talks, dubbed Project Falstaff. I draw up a note on editorial independence, partly as an insurance in future negotiations with a new owner. My starting point is the separation of editorial from advertising and the commercial operation – a principle well understood by Pearson, the *FT* CEO and the *FT* editor over five decades and more. The editor enjoys the sole power of appointment and dismissal within *FT* editorial, though he/she may elect to discuss senior appointments with the CEO or the proprietor. Similarly, the editor bears the ultimate responsibility for editorial quality and standards, and can be dismissed only by the proprietor.

'The principle of editorial independence at the FT is a tribute to the restraint of Pearson, our owners, and to the culture of our journalists,' I write; 'its power does not derive from a written guarantee, rather from daily practice and the accumulated power of precedent in the newsroom.'

My document put down a marker. Whether it would be a serious insurance policy was another matter. I was mindful that Marcus Brauchli had been forced out as WSJ *editor, despite all the friendly words and assurances from Rupert Murdoch.*

WEDNESDAY, 29 APRIL

George Osborne has invited me to Downing Street for a pre-election-day conversation, a reprise of our encounter in 2010 when he hinted about going into coalition should the Conservatives fail to win a majority. This time, he's railing about failing to 'cut through'. Media coverage, especially the BBC, is relentlessly negative. You can't go anywhere without someone sticking a microphone in your face, asking about austerity, cuts to the National Health Service and food banks, he complains.

It all sounds grim until a chipper Cameron swings by. 'I've been visiting places [in England] like St Austell,' he says, noting that the weather in Cornwall this time of year has been rather pleasant. He then proceeds to offer a gracious thank-you for sticking with the Tories through austerity, but there's no appeal for an *FT* endorsement this time round. *Maybe he already knows where we stand.*

THURSDAY, 30 APRIL

The *FT* has come out in favour of a Conservative-led government ahead of next week's election. We're holding our

noses over Cameron's Europe policy and his planned referendum. On balance, the case for continuity rests on the
economic record of the coalition government. We advocate
tactical voting in favour of Lib Dems in seats where they
are the incumbent or main challenger. 'There are risks in re-
electing Mr Cameron's party, especially on Europe,' we
conclude, 'but there are greater risks in not doing so.'

FRIDAY, 8 MAY

Against the odds, Cameron has won a slim majority. The Lib
Dems have been crushed, slumping from 57 seats to 8. Ed
Miliband, who faltered badly at the end, is to step down as
Labour leader. As I compose my 6am commentary in the editor's office, in time for a special election-morning tabloid, I
reflect that the polls and the pundits got this election wrong –
with the exception of Scotland, where the SNP won a
landslide. 'Nationalism played a winning hand. England in
effect voted against the SNP and the Tories were the chief
beneficiaries.' The clarity of the Tory victory is therefore misleading. 'The UK is heading into a period of considerable
political uncertainty. Shades of John Major in 1992?'

*A few days after the election, I called Lynton Crosby who
was celebrating with a bottle of fine wine somewhere in the
Mediterranean. I told him he had been right about the campaign
and I was wrong. He might have gloated; in fact, he was gracious.*

WEDNESDAY, 10 JUNE

To the *Guardian* HQ near King's Cross for a farewell party for
Alan Rusbridger, editor for the past 20 years and a chance to

meet his successor Kath Viner, the first female editor of the Guardian and an acclaimed playwright. I will miss Alan. So will all the reporters and editors he backed when the chips were down. Alan exercised power lightly. I never heard him raise his voice. He remained unflappable in the face of threats, writs and mounting losses, the result of heavy investment in new printing presses and digital expansion aimed at making the *Guardian* the number-one liberal brand in media. Alan presided over breathtaking investigative reporting like WikiLeaks, Snowden and the Murdoch phone-hacking scandal. He took on British institutions. He was, as several *Guardian* colleagues remind me tonight, fearless. As I listen to the tributes and his own speech (a tad too long), I find myself admiring his guts and his appetite for risk and make a personal vow: before I step down at the *FT*, I want one, maybe two massive scoops which will make a difference too. And that means changing the head of the *FT* investigations team and appointing Paul Murphy, who just happens to be an ex-*Guardian* man.

WEDNESDAY, 8 JULY

Mathias Döpfner stands 6 feet 7 inches tall, a dashing figure who in an earlier age might have sported a duelling scar on his left cheek. At 52, he is perhaps the most powerful man in German media, a former newspaper editor who crossed over to become Axel Springer CEO. His ambition is to make Springer a global media company, which is why he is desperate to buy the *FT*.

We meet in his chalet in the margins of the Allen & Co. conference in Sun Valley, Idaho, where Hollywood moguls and Silicon Valley titans gather every year for four days of conversation mixed with biking, golf, skeet shooting, tennis and whitewater rafting. Victoria and I have been invited every year since 2010 and it is our favourite conference, a chance to make new friends and mix with old ones.

I've cleared my Döpfner meeting in advance with John Fallon and John Ridding. Neither was comfortable, fearing I might trespass into talk about valuations. That's a misunderstanding. I'm not interested in money. I want to hear from the prospective proprietor on editorial independence and his plans for the newsroom. Mathias is charming and persuasive, speaking English fluently with a slight American intonation. Our friendship goes back more than a decade when we met over lunch in Manhattan. He knows I am a fluent German-speaker, familiar with German culture and German media. Our future relationship, he says, will be fine. This is not about me, I reply, it's about the next editor and the one after that. What are the ground rules on editorial independence?

Döpfner says the division between editorial and commercial at Axel Springer is an established fact. He mentions a *Bild* newspaper story exposing Volkswagen management's use of prostitutes for the pleasure of union bosses. (The tabloid used an image of a hooker astride the VW motif – an amusing if expensive joke.) VW ordered an advertising boycott, but Mathias held firm and the car giant backed down. Almost as an afterthought, Mathias mentions he might like occasionally to write for the *FT*. Well, OK, he used to be a music critic. I also know he is a fierce defender of Israel. Does the prospective proprietor have any particular topic in mind?

MD: 'No. Nothing special. Just an occasional piece.'

LB: 'Really? That's never happened under Pearson.'

MD: 'Well, naturally, only with your permission.'

LB: 'What happens if we disagree?'

MD: 'Then it is a matter for the editor. But I'm sure we won't. We understand each other, Lionel.'

LB: 'But we might disagree. And when an editor and proprietor disagree once, that's OK. Twice, that's not a good idea. Three times, then we have a problem.'

Pearson's talks with Axel Springer were well advanced by this stage. My conversation with Döpfner suggested Springer was lukewarm about our business operation and strategy. He wanted faster growth, especially in the US. I returned to London convinced that he had set his heart on the FT and would not take 'Nein' for an answer.

WEDNESDAY, 22 JULY

I've been wearing my Texan cowboy boots this week, all burgundy leather and stacked heels purchased on a road trip to Amarillo, Texas, in the spring of 1992. These boots were my little statement: whatever the outcome, editorial will walk tall as the sale of the *FT* draws closer.

Nothing has so far leaked about the Springer talks. *Amazing*. Martin Sorrell phoned yesterday but I was politely evasive. I have begun to speak confidentially to half a dozen of my top team, on the principle of no surprises. I want a group of trusted colleagues around me after the shock news of the *FT* sale, likely to be announced tomorrow. Several colleagues have voiced unease about Springer. I have my own doubts, especially about job losses in the newsroom. The other day, John Ridding asked me: 'Are you up for change?'

Wtf. I've been up for change from the day I took over as editor.

We're talking about the sale of the *FT*: 125 years of history, 600 journalists, one of the last independent media brands in the world. OK, I found Pearson a frustrating owner at times. Increasingly, it felt like the *FT* was a misfit. None of us felt inspired by John Fallon's new company slogan: efficacy. We all knew that he didn't have the desire or the money to invest in the *FT* to help us compete with deep-pocketed rivals. But Pearson and Fallon understood the importance of editorial independence. How could this be guaranteed under new ownership?

The topic often came up in conversation with Marjorie and David Bell. Both were attracted by the idea of an independent trust which could defend the editor against a capricious owner, a bit like the arrangement at The Economist. *The theory was fine, but how it would work in practice was tricky. Any new owner, having paid a handsome price for the* FT, *would not wish to have their hands tied. Glen Moreno, Pearson chairman, argued that it would diminish the sale value of the* FT, *to the detriment of Pearson shareholders. David countered that editorial independence, complemented by journalistic excellence, was in fact intrinsic to the value of the* FT. *David had a point, but Glen wasn't interested.*

Last week, nudged by David and other friends of the *FT*, I updated my earlier memo on editorial independence: 'The principle of editorial independence is intrinsic to our journalistic culture. It does not derive from a written guarantee from our owners. We live and breathe it every day in the newsroom. In nearly ten years as editor, I have never once felt under obligation to publish an article in response to pressure from Pearson. Our owners have invariably refrained from interference even in sensitive matters such as general elections, the global banking crisis and in cases where friends or allies of the senior management would have dearly liked to influence the news coverage or opinions of the newspaper.'*

THURSDAY, 23 JULY

The board of Pearson meets today to make a final decision on the sale of the *FT.* Anshu Jain, outgoing co-chief executive of Deutsche Bank, informed me earlier this week that he had advised Döpfner to put pressure on Pearson by insisting on an early deadline. A corporate jet is on the tarmac in Berlin, ready to take off for London in the event of a successful Springer offer. This morning I've spoken to Ridding and Fallon who say an announcement will come in the afternoon. Then the extraordinary occurs: a Reuters report that Pearson is in 'advanced talks' with Axel Springer on a sale of the *FT.* It's like a bomb has gone off in the newsroom. Frantic calls, emails and people lined up outside my office. I call Fallon who explains there has been a 'cock-up', with someone – *who?* – sending Reuters a draft press release by mistake.

'In that case, the gloves are off,' I respond, charging off to the news desk to order them to write an immediate follow-up to the Reuters story. Fallon has, however, also informed me that a late entrant, Nikkei, has come to the bidding table – a fact I am obliged not to share with colleagues. I simmer in my office for two minutes and immediately return to the news desk to spot our chief M&A reporter Arash Massoudi. 'Just to be clear,' I tell Arash, 'do not assume there is a sole bidder.' *Let me repeat: no sole bidder.*

In our haste to match the Reuters story, we publish a main

---

* This memo was later shared with Nikkei.

headline which leans too heavily towards Springer as winner in the *FT* auction (a lapse eagerly picked up later by our competitors). But Arash and the team soon verify – independently – the Nikkei interest. Within an hour, the Japanese media group, advised by Rothschild, emerges as the winner, thanks to an all-cash £844m bid. This audacious, eleventh-hour gatecrash – so out of character with the normally slow-motion Japanese – took everyone by surprise, including Pearson and certainly Springer.

Without much ado, the Pearson board approves the superior bid, leaving Springer – which has spent months examining every part of our business – as the jilted suitor. Fallon calls, notifying me that he will speak late afternoon to all *FT* staff. Ridding and I will join him in the sixth-floor conference room of the *FT* which I later access via the canteen kitchens, escorted by Isaac, our Spanish head of catering. *Amid high drama, a touch of comic farce.*

I read out a crisp statement that the Pearson era has passed and it is now time to embrace a new owner from across the globe. Nikkei executives are listening in from Tokyo, local time almost midnight. History is being made but it's passing me by. I am drained, too exhausted to take it all in, let alone think about my own future. The burden of carrying a secret for the past year has taken a toll. Then again, I have a sense of relief that from today we at least have certainty. It is time to mark the moment and look to the future.

By 7.30pm, I am heading home, ready to share the day's drama with Victoria, when I remember that tonight, of all nights, we are hosting 30 *FT* team leaders with their wives and husbands. This is a regular summer event which takes place in our back garden, a way of saying thank-you to colleagues. Tonight no one is quite sure whether the *FT* sale is a matter of celebration or sorrow. My phone rings and it is John Fallon.

JF: 'Have you read the coverage?'

LB: 'Yes, I have read the coverage.'

JF: 'Have you read the "inside story" about the sale?'

LB: 'Well, I saw an early draft but I can assure you others will have . . .'

JF: 'Well, you're the fucking editor. You're supposed to have read it.'

John had half a point. But everyone was irritated and exhausted, including John Ridding. He complained about our suggestion he was happy about separating from Pearson. In fact, he was a driving force behind the FT *sale.*

FRIDAY, 24 JULY

On the suggestion of Richard Lambert, I have written an editorial on the sale of the *FT* to Nikkei under the headline: 'A new future for the FT, without fear or favour'. My favourite passage: 'Our owners have understood that [editorial independence] means the right to investigate and the liberty to voice uncomfortable opinions. We report deeply on the City of London and Brussels but we are not a house organ. We adhere to the liberal market tradition of Adam Smith, but also to the robust irreverence of Smollett and Swift.'* And then a concluding note of optimism. 'In the spirit of adventure and mutual trust, the FT joins the Nikkei family

---

* Tobias Smollett (1721–71) and Jonathan Swift (1667–1745): two great British satirical writers, respectively Scottish and Anglo-Irish. Swift is best known for his novel *Gulliver's Travels*.

and looks forward to writing the next chapter in our distinguished histories.'

WEDNESDAY, 29 JULY

My one-on-one with the new proprietor, Tsuneo Kita, chairman of Nikkei and the driving force behind the *FT*
acquisition, will be the most important meeting of my career. What do I say? I've spent five days preparing. Sir Howard
Stringer, the ex-Sony chief executive, emphasises the importance of etiquette and understated language in Japanese
culture. We rehearse together Howard's wording.

'My goal is to bring out the best for both companies.
(*Pause.*) We will be stronger together. (*Pause.*) My colleagues
and I in the newsroom are honoured that you have chosen us
as your partners.'

Just as I am feeling comfortable, Mike Skapinker, a veteran writer on management and acting letters editor, knocks
on my door. He hands me a ticking time bomb in the shape
of a letter to the editor from Michael Woodford, the former
president and CEO of Olympus Corporation, the Japanese
optics and camera-maker. Woodford, who turned whistleblower on his own company in 2011 and exposed an
accounting fraud, claims Nikkei journalism is 'self-censoring
and deferential' and not independent of corporate Japan: 'If
the FT had been owned by Nikkei at the time of the Olympus scandal,' he writes, 'I would have unquestionably gone to
The New York Times, Wall Street Journal, Bloomberg or
Reuters [rather than the *FT*].' Worse still, the letter singles
out Kita-san, head of Nikkei, and his number two Naotoshi
Okada for criticism, claiming they are unqualified to choose
the next editor of the *FT*.

I called a meeting of my top team. Most argue the letter is unfit for publication in its present form. A lone voice disagrees. I call up Woodford to see if he is amenable to removing the personal attacks and shortening the letter. At first, he sounds reasonable but within 24 hours he's threatening to go public with accusations that the *FT* is censoring his letter ahead of passing into Japanese ownership. I call Woodford and tell him: don't try muscling me. I request more time to consider publication, given the imminent arrival of the Nikkei delegation. Woodford agrees to a deadline of next Monday.

FRIDAY, 31 JULY

Kita-san, accompanied by his eight-strong entourage, arrives on foot shortly before the appointed time of 12.45pm. John Ridding greets the new owners of the *FT*. Kita-san, a tallish sexagenarian with thinning black hair, steps forward in his dark suit, white shirt and tie, accompanied by the shorter, silver-haired Okada-san. The four (new) amigos pose in the *FT* foyer for an official photograph. Then the Japanese delegation heads to the sixth floor with Ridding. At 2.07, seven minutes after the appointed time, JR knocks on my door and I welcome not a one-on-one but a four-man delegation and female interpreter led by Kita-san.

The new proprietor listens to the Howard Stringer intro approvingly before delivering an unambiguous guarantee of editorial independence, backed up by a commitment to invest in the long-term success of the *FT*, a world-class brand. I thank him for his pledge on editorial independence and emphasise how the value of the *FT* is intricately tied to its integrity and journalistic excellence. Then I make three points.

First, the *FT* is like a Meiji-era house: stylish elegance and flowing design on the outside but inside the kitchen plumbing does not work, the curtains are getting ragged and one of the bedrooms is distinctly tatty. *(I almost mention the crazy aunt in the attic but as every word is being written down, I wisely pass on the joke.)* Second, we need to get to know one another better. We need young journalists from Nikkei with good English to come to the *FT* and vice versa. I pledge to come to Tokyo at least three times a year. Finally, I emphasise the need for ambition and growth, especially in the US.

At the end of the speech, Kita leans forward saying he has heard that *FT* editors step down after ten years. Would I be prepared to stay on?

I would be honoured.

Honoured? Behind that formal answer, I was elated. Nikkei had given me an early, unequivocal vote of confidence. Here was a new lease of life as editor of the FT, *but also a chance to make history with new owners on the other side of the world with a different language and culture. There were plenty of people, including 'friends of the* FT', *who were convinced the sale was a mistake and the alliance with Nikkei would never work. The history of Japanese companies making acquisitions overseas was at best undistinguished. I was determined to prove them wrong – and to produce even better journalism during my 'third term' as editor.*

WEEKEND, 1–2 AUGUST

Victoria and I are spending the weekend in Dorset with Tom Stoppard and Sabrina Guinness. I ask Tom what he would do about the Woodford letter. He agrees it is a tricky issue but says the editor of the *FT* cannot be bullied into publishing. My heart agrees, but my head says there will be trouble if I don't print the letter. I call Shriti Vadera, one of the savviest people I know. 'You have to publish. Every word,' she says. 'That's the only way to make it go away.'

The penny finally drops. I will indeed publish every god-damned word. But on the principle of no surprises, perhaps the most valuable principle in the relationship between editor and proprietor, I also inform Kita-san of my decision. I make clear that I do not agree with the content of the letter, I also predict this will be the end of the matter. He takes my advice – another big vote of confidence. And so it plays out, without a squeak of controversy. Woodford writes to thank me and asks if I might be available for a coffee some time.

Pass.

2–6 SEPTEMBER

In line with my original promises, I'm making the first of my regular visits to Tokyo and, as usual, I am suffering mind-numbing jet lag on day two. Despite completing half a mile in the swimming pool at the Palace hotel and jogging round the Imperial Palace gardens, I've still found myself wide awake at 3am. The next day or two are all about fighting through mental fog, mindful that I am about to embark on meetings critical for building trust between myself as editor and Nikkei as owners.

Unlike John Ridding, I have decided against learning basic Japanese. The language is too hard and I don't have the time. Howard Stringer has advised me to listen and watch, a valuable tip because every intonation and gesture in Japan carries greater weight than in the less formal Anglo-Saxon world.

I've also spent time with James Lamont, my key partner in the Nikkei relationship, plotting my messaging to Kita-san and his top team. And I've reshuffled my top team. Roula Khalaf, foreign editor, will become my new deputy, replacing John Thornhill who will take a new role as innovation editor writing on technology in all its aspects. John has done a fine job, but several colleagues have reinforced my view that we must signal there's a new chapter about to begin under new owners. Alec Russell, news editor, will take over *Weekend FT*, a big opportunity for expanding readership and developing leadership credentials. Peter Spiegel will move from Brussels to become news editor.

After several days, I take the train to Kyoto, accompanied by Toru Yoshida, a top Nikkei executive and former Paris correspondent. After a day's sightseeing, including a specially arranged tour of the Golden Temple, I sit down to dinner with Kita-san at Wakuden, one of the finest restaurants in Japan. He is still visibly excited that he has pulled off the purchase of the *FT*. He tells the story of how he had long coveted the *FT*, writing a letter to Pearson several years ago that if the newspaper was ever up for sale, Nikkei would be interested. Then, in July 2015, the moment he heard Pearson was indeed open to buyers, he jumped on a plane and met John Fallon, a key first encounter when the two bonded.

Kita-san, who is still suffering from a heavy cold after an exhaustive travel schedule, is a great storyteller. He loves talking about his time as a reporter and how as a manager to pick and nurture talent. But he's also sharing these details, I sense, because he thinks he can trust me. This is part of our own bonding process, a gradual getting to know each other which must rest not on a common language but on our own experience as working journalists and our joint commitment to independent public service journalism. I leave Tokyo confident that our relationship is going to work just fine.

FRIDAY, 9 OCTOBER

The Chinese ambassador has invited me to the embassy to prepare the ground ahead of President Xi Jinping's state visit to London. I bring James Kynge, our resident China expert, who tells me Xi has demanded – and will receive – treatment worthy of an emperor, including a ride with the queen in her state carriage embellished with diamonds and sapphires and fashioned from fragments of Sir Isaac Newton's apple tree and King Henry VIII's *Mary Rose* warship.

The ambassador knows the British government is desperate for closer economic ties. He asks how China should describe the new relationship. Where does Mr Barber stand on 'golden moment', 'golden age' or 'golden era'? *I don't like any of them.* On balance, *golden era* is the best of an overhyped bunch. Just do not assume, I tell the Chinese delegation, that the next government will feel bound by the phrase. Who knows, it might be led by newly elected Labour leader Jeremy Corbyn.

TUESDAY, 20 OCTOBER

The queen is shorter close-up than I imagined, President Xi nowhere near the towering presence projected on camera. I'm standing in the reception line at Buckingham Palace, a commoner in pressed white tie relatively low in the international pecking order.

'Lionel Barber, editor of the *Financial Times*,' bellows the royal flunkey.

A slight bow before Her Majesty and a brief handshake with President Xi, the most powerful leader since Mao. Xi offers a cursory 'Nihao'. Peng Liyuan, China's glamorous First Lady and ex-People's Liberation Army pin-up singer, offers a warm smile and what sounds like 'Good evening'.

The Duke of Edinburgh, a cadaverous 94-year-old with a liverish complexion and fierce staring eyes, shakes my hand. As I depart for the dining room, a royal voice echoes in the background.

Duke of Edinburgh: 'Haven't you just been taken over by the Chinese?'

LB: 'Yes, Sir. But not by the Chinese. The Japanese!'

Victoria and I arrived early at the Palace, two of 167 guests selected for the state dinner to honour Xi. Security was friendly but rigorous: requests for ID, checks for bombs under the car bonnet but nothing as vulgar as metal detectors or personal frisks. Ascending a winding staircase with a red carpet, we pass several enormous royal portraits and a giant crystal chandelier hanging from a ceiling somewhere in the sky. A member of the royal household directs all guests to the reception room where ancient, China-related artefacts are on display.

David Cameron enters with Samantha and makes straight for Sir Henry Keswick,* head of Jardine Matheson, one of Hong Kong's oldest trading houses. I shoehorn my way into the conversation about China rather than the perennial topic of Europe and the coming referendum. Cameron says he wants a word next month because the *FT* is being 'beastly'.

---

* Sir Henry Keswick (1938–), born in Shanghai, educated at Eton College and Trinity College, Cambridge, long-time chairman of Jardine Matheson, has often described himself as a 'humble Scottish merchant'.

The PM says the UK needs to go 'the extra 20 per cent' with the Chinese, convincing them that we are serious about building a long-term economic relationship and allying ourselves with *the* rising power. He comes across as defensive, mindful that media coverage has focused on the extravagant welcome for Xi. In fact, Xi does not just want pomp and pageantry. He is demanding atonement for the sins of the colonial past. As the *People's Daily* noted this week: 'The national humiliation that China suffered in modern times began with the rumble of cannon from British warships.'

In her dinner remarks, the queen pays homage to modern China's economic miracle. Xi has the good grace not to repeat his earlier comment that Chinese tea is older than the British version. But he is still relatively abrasive, making several references to the 'anti-fascist war' against the Japanese in World War II, knowing that the Japanese ambassador to London is present in the room.

As Scottish bagpipers in kilts play a wailing lament, I lean over to my Australian neighbour, a senior executive of Arup, the professional services company, who is chomping his way through Balmoral venison. What did he make of Xi's speech? He too had felt uncomfortable. He also knows *(how?)* about my request to interview President Xi in Beijing. (We rejected Beijing's offer of a pre-state-visit interview by fax, later accepted by the *Wall Street Journal*. We want an interview with Xi, not a press release.) 'I know about your request,' says the Aussie exec, 'but of course the *FT* is now under Japanese masters.'

The Chinese authorities would constantly raise the issue of Japanese ownership of the FT. *It was a not-so-subtle effort to influence our coverage and correct anti-China bias, real or imagined. I remained vigilant because China was such an important story for the* FT. *I also insisted at every opportunity that Nikkei had no say over editorial decisions or stories. This had the additional merit of being true.*

31 OCTOBER–7 NOVEMBER

As dusk falls in Riyadh, a black Lexus arrives to whisk us to the Royal Palace, a maze of courtyards and sandstone buildings which are the working quarters of King Salman and his favourite son and deputy crown prince, Mohammed bin Salman, known by his acronym: MBS. The *FT* interview is the highlight of a seven-day trip with Roula to Saudi Arabia, taking in Riyadh, the coastal resort of Jeddah and Taif, in Mecca province.

The soon-to-be most powerful man in the Saudi government bar the ailing monarch is a tall, thickset man with bulging arms, a large beak and receding jet-black hair. Two elderly royal aides sit behind me, one serving as an interpreter. As I prepare to speak, a servant plants a small glass of Arabic coffee in my right hand. I set it down on the table in front of me and remark that this is my first visit to the desert kingdom. A princely gesture halts me mid-sentence. 'You cannot continue until you make your request.' An aide explains to the baffled English editor that failure to drink proffered coffee is interpreted as harbouring a business request.

'OK, I would like a second interview,' I say. A mild royal guffaw.

MBS talks in machine-gun bursts, firing out economic data and statistics. He is part McKinsey man, part modern desert warrior determined to project Saudi power in the region against Iranian influence, notably in the proxy war of attrition against Tehran-backed Shia Houthis in neighbouring Yemen. He's already looking to his place in history, the man who forged a new future for Saudi Arabia beyond oil, weaning the middle class off oil and gas subsidies and establishing a new relationship between state and citizens.

MBS also signals frustration with the Obama administration's nuclear deal with Iran. 'There is no doubt that America is the number-one power in the world. But if the Americans are number one, then they must act like number one,' says the prince, adding pointedly that he wants good relations with Vladimir Putin. 'We see the US as our number-one ally but we do not see Russia as our enemy.'

Putin, he boasts, has contacted him nine times. The deputy crown prince – who also doubles as defence minister and chairman of Saudi Aramco, the state oil company – has visited Russia twice; Putin has even invited him to go skiing. My response: 'In that case, I would advise your majesty to wear a helmet.'

The royal aides turn nervous as MBS is becoming increasingly outspoken. When I ask him what his favourite book is (a clumsy attempt to probe his education), the prince digresses with a tale of how King Salman tutored him at an early age, handing him successive jobs in government including a stint in Riyadh with a mandate to tackle the crime rate.

Time is pressing. One silver-haired aide indicates enough. As we are ushered out, I marvel aloud at how his progress has been seamlessly upward at such a tender age. Ah, yes, the age being 31?

'Thirty,' MBS corrects me – useful official confirmation of what appeared to be a state secret.

The MBS conversation confirmed his status as a coming man in Saudi Arabia. The scale of his ambition to modernise the oil-dependent state was breathtaking, but at this point it was hard to gauge how much was rhetoric and how much an achievable plan for action. He told us he had spent $1bn on management consultants alone, a foretaste of the extraordinary sums he was willing to spend on high-technology investments through his Japanese partner, the SoftBank Vision Fund. We skirted his plans for the partial privatisation of Saudi Aramco, having been given a steer that it was on the cards in a private conversation with the veteran Saudi oil minister Ali al-Naimi.

More disturbing were dark hints about opposition to his modernisation plans within Saudi Arabia. The prince appeared to display a ruthlessness worthy of a young Bashar al-Assad, another moderniser in his early years. This vindictive streak would become ever more apparent in the coming 18 months. Even as he lifted the ban on women driving and moved to reduce the power of Wahabi clerics, he also cracked down on political opposition and rivals in the royal family. Crown Prince Mohammed bin Nayef, a long-time intelligence ally of the US, was put under house arrest; dozens of businessmen were detained on corruption charges at the Ritz-Carlton hotel and only released after handing over billions of dollars in ransom repayments. Most seriously, two of his closest aides were implicated in the assassination of Jamal Khashoggi, the writer and dissident, whom Roula and I met over lunch in Jeddah.

FRIDAY, 13 NOVEMBER

David Cameron sweeps in half an hour late, blaming the delay on a spending review which overran. George Osborne is in tow, alongside Ed Llewellyn, the PM's chief of staff – a full court press to persuade the *FT* to get onside ahead of the Brexit referendum. The prime minister is jacketless, his midriff visible under a blue and white striped shirt. He begins not with Europe but with the visit of Indian prime minister Narendra Modi. Cameron says he can't quite make him out: Modi talks passionately about economic reform but has spent 41 days out of the country since he was elected 18 months ago in a landslide. Cameron wants a better economic relationship with India. I say the Indians are still chippy about their colonial past and obsessed with China's rise. Cameron says they're more interested in their nuclear neighbour Pakistan, a subject about which the UK knows plenty. When I suggest the UK could improve relations by easing visa restrictions, Cameron pushes back, referring to bogus higher education colleges or job seekers who stay on. 'We don't need more taxi drivers,' he tells me.

Cameron was no racist. But his off-hand remarks reflected abiding concerns in the Tory party about immigration levels. The irony was that Brexit addressed immigration from central and eastern Europe, not India or Pakistan.

We turn to Europe. Cameron is optimistic about the Brexit referendum campaign which will be well funded. He is betting on a 'decent deal' from EU partners because they recognise him to be 'a reasonable reformer'. The hardest bit will be tackling generous welfare payments to EU immigrants in the UK. He is hopeful of German support. I refer to the backlash against Merkel for letting nearly a million migrants into Germany these past ten weeks, including criticism from within her own CDU party. Can she survive?

'It's hard to see her being forced out,' says Cameron. 'Her biggest ally is General Winter.'

And the campaign. How does he forge a majority for Remain (the somewhat uninspiring slogan for the pro-EU camp)?

'Well, there's 30 per cent who want out and 30 per cent who defend EU membership with a passion and 40 per cent undecided. We'll work on them . . . We don't want too much emotion in the campaign. Business will be important but only one voice. We need to talk about the practical benefits of membership.'

And how about his own Conservative party? Will 100 MPs vote Leave?

PM: 'Maybe. But it's not a question of how many but who.'

LB: 'Theresa May?'

PM: 'She is a committed pro-European.'

LB: 'And Boris Johnson? Is he on a tight leash?'

PM: 'Boris will be Boris but he's never given an "Out" speech. I expect he'll give a few Churchillian speeches with some criticism of me. But that's to be expected because I'm leaving before the end of my full term.'

This was the most revealing conversation I ever had with David Cameron. He saw the Remain argument in practical terms, which ceded the emotional argument to the Leave campaign which produced simple slogans like 'Take Back Control'. In the end, as one friend pointed out, Remain was a boring verb while Leave was at least exciting. Dangerously so, just like Cameron's original decision to go for a Brexit referendum.

TUESDAY, 1 DECEMBER

From Tokyo, a Nikkei delegation led by Kita-san has arrived in London to mark the formal closure of their deal to buy

the *FT* from Pearson. I want Kita-san to address the newsroom but the *FT* minders are having, well, kittens. They fear
the NUJ will hijack the event and embarrass our new proprietor. *Oh please!*

On my own initiative, I issue an invitation to Kita-san,
saying that reporters and editors want to hear from him. The
message comes back that he would be delighted. And this
morning he's standing next to me by the main news desk,
reminding *FT* journalists that he once was once the news
editor at Nikkei and reassuring everyone that the *FT* is in
safe hands.

*Kita-san's appearance in the newsroom was a huge symbolic
moment, captured in a photograph later hung on a wall in the staff
canteen. He pledged to uphold editorial independence for the* FT
and he was a man of his word.

BREXIT

Nikkei's acquisition ended the uncertainty over the FT's future and my own as editor. In January, Kita-san offered me a generous contract which gave me the freedom and the certainty to focus on cementing the relationship with Tokyo, producing the best journalism in the world and managing my own succession. I also pressed John Ridding to set a bold target of 1 million paying readers by 2020 at the latest. This 'march to a million' created a unifying mission for editorial and business colleagues. We were all set.

Yet 2016 would also mark the moment that my world – and the FT's – turned upside down. Against expectations, the British people voted in a referendum to leave the European Union. The decision was a personal blow because I believed in EU membership passionately and the FT actively campaigned for Remain in its opinion pages.

Five months later, the American people voted for Donald Trump as president, again confounding expectations and predictions at the FT. Brexit and Trump challenged our judgements and our journalism. Together they pointed to a crisis of globalisation and liberal democracy.

MONDAY, 14 MARCH

The Vote Leave campaign is coming to lunch, at last. They've been holding out, arguing there was no point talking to the

Remain establishment over a fancy meal. I instruct Sebastian Payne, a new recruit from the *Spectator* magazine, to deliver a message: the *FT* is happy to serve shitty sandwiches from our canteen. That does the trick.

Dominic Cummings arrives unshaven in a scruffy green pullover, dark chinos and sneakers. He takes his seat – my usual seat – at the top of the table. The Leave campaign's head of strategy is accompanied by his clean-shaven, bespectacled partner Matthew Elliott, CEO of Vote Leave, and Paul Stephenson, communications head. Cummings immediately takes command, declaring that the two issues voters care about are immigration and money.

Brexit, he says, will save the UK £350m a week to be spent on the National Health Service. We all know this figure is misleading but Cummings says that as long as Leave and Remain are arguing how much it costs to be a member of the EU, Leave is winning. The precise figure does not matter. If the debate turns to trade and the economy, then Remain is winning. He refuses to discuss what comes after the UK leaves the EU.

Surely, I say, £350m a week 'savings' is a drop in the ocean compared to the cost of a Brexit-related shock to the economy? Cummings says he has no idea what damage such a shock might do. The figure is unknowable and the ordinary person in the street would have little understanding anyway.

The enormity of the faux pas sinks in. Cummings, momentarily flummoxed, says: 'This conversation is off the record, right?'

I could throw him overboard but offer a lifeline of sorts. 'That's OK, Dominic, we have lots of people come to the FT and show contempt for ordinary people.'

Cummings cut a shambolic figure that day but he was a master campaigner who combined cynicism with seductive slogans and modern polling techniques. The great British establishment, including the FT, fatally underestimated him.

WEDNESDAY, 25 MAY

Donald Trump, the billionaire New York real estate developer, has demolished all rivals for the Republican nomination for US president. His victory has stunned the political and media establishment who wrote him off as a narcissistic demagogue. Now, after delicate negotiations through several intermediaries, I am sitting down for lunch at the Coronado Club in Houston, Texas, to interview James A. Baker III, the only American to have served as White House chief of staff, treasury secretary and secretary of state.

At 86, Baker belongs to the elite group of Americans known as the Wise Men whose advice is still sought in matters of state at home and abroad. During my time in Washington, I watched him masterfully managing the end of the Cold War with President George H.W. Bush. In 1991, I interviewed him as the *FT*'s Person of the Year when America stood at the pinnacle of power. Now I am in the offices of Baker Botts, the Houston firm whose roots go back to 1840. Baker initially declared Trump off limits for the conversation. Now that's just one of those little ole misunderstandings.

The Coronado Club, founded in 1956 and named after the mid-16th-century Spanish conquistador, is part *Mad Men* set, part English gentleman's club. The smell of stale cigar smoke hangs in the air, alongside rustic paintings, elegant fireplaces and a bust of Winston Churchill. Our conversation over crab, jumbo shrimp, Tabasco (and cottage cheese!) begins with Brexit. Will the UK leave?

My response is that Remain is winning the economic argument. Leave has just admitted that Britain outside the EU would no longer enjoy access to the Single Market and would therefore enjoy a bilateral trade deal on the lines of Albania, Bosnia, Serbia and Ukraine.

'Albania? You're kiddin' me,' Baker exclaims. 'Boris Johnston [sic] said that. Really?' Actually it was Michael Gove, the pro-Brexit justice secretary. Baker looks flummoxed. The name 'Gove' clearly never made it to Texas. Baker declined to sign a Downing Street-inspired pro-Remain letter from former US treasury secretaries and secretaries of state. He thought – *rightly as it transpired* – that the gesture would look like interference and backfire. 'Deep down, I hope you stay in,' he concludes.

We turn to Trump. 'Like many people, I was surprised by the size of Trump's victory. It rang a bell the way Reagan came up in 1976 . . . I remember all the establishment Republicans thought that Reagan was a grade-B movie actor who would get us into a nuclear war and who was extraordinarily dangerous. You are seeing some of the same phenomenon.' Baker looks me firmly in the eye. 'But I am not comparing Reagan with Trump. I am not suggesting the two are the same.'

Baker says Washington no longer works; compromise has become a dirty word. 'What people don't understand is that Ronald Reagan was a pragmatist. We judge our presidents by what they get accomplished. Reagan used to say: "Jim, I'd rather get 80 per cent of what I want than go over the cliff with my flag flying."'

Baker is dismissive of Hillary Clinton who 'was never given anything to do. She was just there [at the State

Department] to run for president.' While the Texan won't admit as much, it seems he will hold his nose and vote for Trump. Is America strong enough to survive any shock, even a President Trump?

'Yes,' declares Baker, emphatically. 'I won't get my panties in a wedge because of what I am hearing from the political candidates. What they say in the campaign and what they do once they are in the White House are not the same thing . . . We are a country of laws, limited by bureaucracy and the power structure in Washington. Presidents are not unilateral rulers. If they do not know that, they will find out soon enough.'

Like many Republicans, Baker could not bring himself to back Hillary Clinton and instead put party loyalty first. One of the smartest politicians of his generation, he underestimated Trump and the coming assault on US institutions.

FRIDAY, 3 JUNE

The first Brexit debate at Sky studios in Osterley, near Heathrow airport. David Cameron v Michael Gove in front of a live audience. I've been invited as a pro-European commentator to counter Sir Tim Bell, Margaret Thatcher's PR guru, and Isabel Oakeshott, a *Daily Mail* columnist. Bell says there is an outside chance of an upset. People are fed up with being taken for granted by metropolitan elites. Tony Blair was too successful for his own good, occupying so much of the centre ground that fringe groups felt excluded. Now these same disaffected voters are turning to Brexit.

Until tonight, I had casually assumed that rational economic calculation would triumph over visceral emotion. But when Sky political editor Faisal Islam asks Gove to name any economists who back Brexit, the former education secretary declares: 'This country has had enough of experts . . .' *Gove's anti-elitist comment would become notorious. In fact, the audience applause drowned out the rest of the sentence: 'from organisations with acronyms.'*

SUNDAY, 5 JUNE

To lunch in Chelsea at the elegant home of John Studzinski, banker-philanthropist-socialite, in honour of Peggy Noonan, the conservative wordsmith who wrote Ronald Reagan's finest speeches, from the *Challenger* disaster to the 40th anniversary of the Normandy landings. Rupert Murdoch is the second guest of honour, accompanied by his new wife Jerry Hall. Murdoch is wearing summer casual, with no tie. At 85, he's once again discovered true love to complement his passion for newspapers. Ever since I watched him as a young reporter at the *Sunday Times*, I have marvelled at Murdoch's ability to be an Oxford-educated billionaire and at the same time a man of the people. Maybe it's his inner Australian that makes him want to poke what he once described to me as 'the jumped-up British establishment'. Or maybe he can sniff out political winners, from Margaret Thatcher to Tony Blair. Now he seems gung-ho for Brexit and favourable to Donald Trump. *Maybe he knows something we don't.*

Before we sit down for lunch, I corner Murdoch and complain that I cannot get on prime-time BBC to talk about the dangers of Brexit. Murdoch, who has long dismissed the BBC as a smug liberal establishment institution, perks up. I explain that BBC producers have made clear they're not interested in me because they have enough talking heads who are 'white, male and stale'.

'Oh no,' Murdoch shoots back, 'it's because you are white, male and straight.'

THURSDAY, 16 JUNE

One week to go before the decision that will shape Britain and Europe for a generation. The *FT*'s editorial's working headline is 'Vote Great Britain, not Little England' and I have secured an early morning slot on the *Today* programme. Nick Robinson, co-anchor, quotes Gove's quip about experts. 'You and your readers have done very well out of the EU.'

Mistakenly I assume he's talking about me personally and my six years in Brussels as a correspondent. Then again, there's a lot wrong with the BBC's Brexit coverage. The panjandrums are so worried about being accused of bias that everything has been reduced to claim and counterclaim, with little room for judgement on the respective weight of the argument. Tim Garton Ash, the (Europhile) historian, calls it 'fairness bias'.

Leave is still running rings round the media with its bogus £350m-a-week savings claim. Remain's scare stories are almost as bad. Today, the *Guardian* reports that Osborne's treasury is planning an emergency budget with massive public spending cuts and tax increases to combat the economic shock of a Leave vote. Already the papers are branding it a 'punishment budget'.

I call Osborne. What the hell is going on? The chancellor pours on the charm, praising my (poor) *Today* programme appearance. Leave's emotional appeal is drowning out the facts, especially on immigration, he admits. He's doubling down on 'Project Fear', the official warnings about the economic cost of withdrawing from the EU. Osborne has a reputation for being a born-again Machiavelli, but bludgeoning the British public sounds daft to me. How about something more positive and uplifting? 'That ship has sailed,' says the chancellor, grimly.

This was a turning point in the Brexit referendum. The Remain campaign had left it too late to make a political argument in favour of UK membership of the EU which could connect with voters resentful of metropolitan elites, immigration and years of austerity. No British government had ever made a serious political argument for EU membership. So Osborne and Cameron were reduced to the Project Fear economics argument which had proved effective in the Scottish referendum.

Terrible news: a Labour MP and Remainer campaigner Jo Cox has been shot and stabbed by a right-wing fanatic in Birstall, West Yorkshire. TV and radio want to know what it means for the Brexit referendum campaign, now suspended. This time, I have no appetite to be a Brexit talking head. Anyway, this evening is (finally!) the opening of Tate Modern II, the £270m extension to the old South Bank power station converted at the turn of the century into one of the world's top contemporary art museums.

Lord Browne, chairman of the Tate trustees (and arch Remainer), speaks of a new cultural cathedral in the heart of London. Guests include the elite non-dom community led by lead donor Len Blavatnik, the oil-to-music baron, Eyal Ofer, Israeli shipping billionaire (who has upped sticks to Monaco), and Lars Windhorst, the Gatsby-like German financier. I bump into Sir Simon Fraser, former top Foreign Office mandarin, who laments the appalling state of the campaign and

Cameron's decision to call a referendum. One of the nation's top spooks is more circumspect: if the decision turns out to be Leave, he tells me, we will spend several years disengaging from Europe. It will be a huge distraction. *How right he was!*

TUESDAY, 21 JUNE

To Downing Street with George Parker for an interview with David Cameron. The PM is glowing. Maybe it's his mood; more likely the breakfast-TV make-up. He won't predict the result, but is breezily confident. That's 'Dave's' strength and his biggest weakness. He thinks – *he knows* – he's good at being prime minister. But he's really a PR merchant, with no hard political core. I think back to Obama's early verdict on Cameron: sizzle. This is the third referendum he's called in five years; the last one on Scottish independence was a little too close for comfort. Cameron is no different from Thatcher and Major who ended up being destroyed by Europe. But there's a big difference: neither was insouciant enough to call a referendum.

FRIDAY, 24 JUNE

I've gone to bed with a bourbon on the rocks, relatively relaxed about the referendum result. Last night, I spoke to Ana Botín and Mario Draghi and assured them on balance that the vote would break for Remain, though it would likely be close. At 3.10am, I wake up with a jolt and check my iPhone. Sunderland has voted overwhelmingly for Leave. Twitter has a storm of comments declaring that Remain is in serious trouble. By 5am, when I arrive at the *FT*, the networks have called it for Leave. This is a political earthquake.

My first stop is the main news desk where exhausted editors are in a state of shock. Our Nikkei colleagues look stunned and slightly embarrassed. I check on the main news lines – future of Cameron, reaction from Brussels, financial markets, sterling – and then go to my office to edit our Brexit leader. Roula suggests I speak to staff. *Good idea.* But first, on the principle of no surprises, I need to speak to Kita-san in Tokyo. The proprietor, via interpreters, listens to my breathless take on events. Then, speaking rapidly, he says it will take time for the direction to be clear but the *FT* must be 'the essential guide'. Brexit, in other words, is undoubtedly a crisis, but also an opportunity.

Wise words but that's not how it feels right now. My job today is to rally spirits with a speech to the newsroom. 'This is not the vote we would have expected nor one which we would have wanted,' I say to staff as Tokyo listens in by speakerphone, 'but now we must do our job: to produce a great newspaper and website.'

Nick Clegg rings up, offering an opinion piece which arrives a few hours later. Nick asks if it comes across as too angry. 'No way,' I lie. And so the day speeds on, one big news decision after another, all taken at speed in the middle of what most of the *FT*, including me, views as a calamity. All I can do is focus on the *FT*'s journalism.

In the early evening, we debate the layout of a historic front page. We've dug up a photograph of a deflated David Cameron looking like he's put his foot through an Old Master. One snag: the photograph is a few weeks old, rather than taken on the day. Kevin Wilson, our top designer, argues persuasively in favour of publication, using a dramatic tinted black backdrop. Hugh Carnegy, executive editor, is unhappy. Alec Russell, weekend editor, who has done a superb job sharpening the inside pages, is minded to go with the picture. Today, of all days, I want impact. Publish and risk being damned!

SATURDAY, 25 JUNE

Shattered by the Brexit result, Victoria and I have sought refuge in the mud and rain of Glastonbury Festival. We are house guests of Roland Rudd, the ex-*FT* man who founded Finsbury, the City PR firm. Roland helped raise millions for Remain. He's beyond consolation and already talking up the idea of a second referendum. Feels premature. Anyway, why are we so sure Remain would win a second time round?

In the evening, as I watch Art Garfunkel croon his way through 'Bridge over Troubled Water', I go over the *FT*'s – *my* – mistakes. We did not lose the referendum. The politicians did. But we could have done a better job reporting on the depth of disaffection, especially among older voters and the 'angry white males' who have seen their incomes either cut or stagnate. Earlier, Roula had the great idea of dispatching *FT* foreign correspondents to the four corners of the UK to test voter sentiment. Three returned to London with the same message: Vote Leave. We missed the signal amid all the noise.

After the referendum, I faced a challenge as editor as to where my duty lay: to my own views as a Remainer, to the country or to the reader? The answer had to be: the reader. But our readership was split between international subscribers largely favouring Remain and a vocal rump in the UK favouring Leave. Managing this balance would preoccupy me for the next three years.

My guiding principle was that the FT *should be the most authoritative source of information about the mechanics of Brexit and the economic risks involved, a task ably led by George Parker, political editor, and Alex Barker, Brussels bureau chief. We also had a duty to contribute positively to the debate about the future of the UK. I did not share colleagues' enthusiasm for a 'People's Vote' or a second referendum.*

THURSDAY, 30 JUNE

British politics has been half Shakespeare, half Marx Brothers since the referendum. Boris Johnson, the face of Vote Leave and hot favourite in the race to succeed David Cameron, has withdrawn today. Boris turned out to be more Falstaff than Prince Hal: ill prepared, incoherent and undone by his own running mate Michael Gove, the Scottish libertarian. Gove says he no longer believes Johnson is right for the top job and has put himself forward. An act of betrayal, right up there. It's now Theresa May's race to lose.

FRIDAY, 1 JULY

Mark Carney, governor of the Bank of England, agrees to a catch-up phone call. He is a cool head to have in a crisis. The Bank of England has already acted decisively, cutting interest rates by a quarter point, purchasing assets by the bucketload and 'backstopping' the markets with £100bn of liquidity. Sterling has fallen 20 per cent but that's not necessarily negative, given the economy's need to adjust to external shocks. Carney wants the government to come up with a post-referendum plan as fast as possible. Merkel's intervention – allowing the UK time to invoke Article 50* – will help.

---

* Article 50 of the Treaty on European Union, which many assumed would never be triggered, gives a departing member state two years from

Carney says the UK needs to decide whether it wants a 'hard Brexit' (a shift to World Trade Organisation rules and bilateral deals with selective partners, including the EU) or a 'soft Brexit' which offers access to the Single Market, perhaps linked to UK concessions on free movement of people. This is the basic trade-off between market access and divergence which was, of course, never mentioned in the referendum: if the UK wants to maintain its favoured status, it will have to align with EU rules. But then what was the point of Brexit? *Some people are going to be very disappointed.*

WEDNESDAY, 13 JULY

Theresa May, sworn in as the new PM, unveils her new Cabinet. Osborne is out. Philip Hammond moves from foreign office to chancellor. Andrea Leadsom is the new environment secretary. May's circle is a world apart from the Chipping Norton set, the fun-loving group of media, political and show-business personalities – sometimes known as 'Chipping Snorton'.* Cameron's chums wear cashmere pullovers and green wellington boots and drive around in Range Rovers. May's lot are more austere, more serious, more uptight. Some seem to think a joint is another name for a night club.

---

when it gives notice of its intention to leave the union to negotiate an exit deal.

* Collective noun for Conservative media and political figures who live – or have country homes – around the Cotswold town of Chipping Norton in Oxfordshire. Leading members of the social circle include David Cameron, former *News of the World* editor and News UK executive Rebekah Brooks and *Top Gear* host Jeremy Clarkson.

WEDNESDAY, 20 JULY

A rare text from Boris Johnson, our new foreign secretary: 'When is your side going to admit that you lost the argument and stop treating Brexit as the new cancer? I have never seen such a load of miserable weedy liberal confirmation bias.'

Text was our favoured means of communication when Johnson was mayor of London. The Brexit referendum has chilled a relationship never that close in the first place. My reply: 'Boris, read the goddamn newspaper. We accept the result. PS We are also delighted to help you agree on what comes next — something you failed to discuss properly in the campaign.'

FRIDAY, 22 JULY

Breakfast with Masayoshi Son, the Korean-Japanese venture capitalist and founder of SoftBank, the Japanese technology powerhouse. Son is a short, balding man in his late fifties who speaks in an understated manner which gives no clue to his awesome financial power, largely based on a stake in Alibaba, the fast-growing Chinese tech giant. Son talks in vague terms about an epochal change coming with 'the internet of things', which explains why SoftBank has just snapped up Arm, one of Britain's few remaining world-class technology companies. Arm, which makes advanced semiconductor chips, will play a central role in the next wave of technological changes, says Son.* Memo to the editor: the *FT* must fix a Lunch with the *FT* with this man.

---

* In September 2020, heavily indebted SoftBank agreed to sell Arm to Nvidia, the US chip maker, for $40bn — a remarkable turnaround in strategy for Son.

Masa Son's $100bn SoftBank Vision Fund, backed by Mohammed bin Salman, soon turned the venture capital market upside down. Despite repeated promises, and a handshake in the presence of Google CEO Larry Page, Masa Son evaded Lunch with the FT. He understood that his power – or at least a good portion – lay in his mystique. Hence no formal interviews.

MONDAY, 25 JULY

A lightning trip to Brussels for talks with Eurocrats, capped by dinner with Sir Ivan Rogers, the UK's ambassador to the EU. Alex Barker, Brussels bureau chief, has brought me along to the ambassador's residence on Rue Ducale, where the Empress Josephine, spouse of Napoleon, once overnighted. I've known Ivan for 20 years, ever since he was an economics adviser in Sir Leon Brittan's cabinet. He's ferociously intelligent, expert in EU matters, but inclined to the melodramatic. Alex notes down two takeaways: Cameron relied far too much in his pre-referendum negotiations on Merkel's goodwill which in the end was not forthcoming. Second, May's team in Downing Street aren't great listeners. Rogers says 'he's willing to help but he won't hang around.' Alex and I both agree: Ivan is too forthright, *too expert*, to last very long in the May team.

MONDAY, 8 AUGUST

Damn Twitter! This morning, I accidentally posted a copy of a letter from the French embassy notifying me that I have been awarded the Légion d'Honneur for services to journalism. It was a private message to a friend, one of several I wanted to tip off about my award. Despite deleting the tweet, the Twittersphere has exploded and now the *Mail* has got hold of the story. The *Mail* says that I have been recognised for the *FT*'s 'relentlessly pro-European coverage' and quotes Jacob Rees-Mogg saying I should refuse the award for 'furthering the interests of a foreign government'.

The Légion d'Honneur was established in 1802 by Napoleon Bonaparte, the *Mail* notes. In addition to mentioning past recipients such as Sir Paul McCartney, Bob Dylan and Arnold Schwarzenegger, the *Mail* has produced a pen portrait of me as editor. Apparently, I am 'a weapons-grade social climber and name-dropper extraordinaire, with a statesmanlike aura'.

Powerful maybe; damned by own actions, most certainly.

TUESDAY–WEDNESDAY, 4–5 OCTOBER

Conservative party conference in Birmingham. Theresa May delivers a hardline defence of Brexit and an assault on cosmopolitan elites: 'If you believe you are a citizen of the world, you're a citizen of nowhere. You don't understand what the very word "citizenship" means.' What on earth will Mark Carney, our Canadian head of the Bank of England, make of this?

MONDAY, 10 OCTOBER

A sobering overnight trip to Brussels. Eurocrats are shocked by the anti-business, Britain-first rhetoric from the Tory conference. Everyone has picked up the 'citizens of nowhere' line. Whatever happened to English pragmatism? The conclusion: the UK is headed for a 'hard Brexit' outside the

Single Market and Customs Union. The direction of travel is set, says one EU veteran, 'we just don't know the destination.'

People in London do not understand how Brexit is viewed in Brussels as an existential threat to the EU. A special deal for the Brits is off the table because it would invite copycat Brexits.

Cecilia Malmström, the Swedish EU commissioner for trade, offers another view of Theresa May (they both sat on the justice and home affairs council). May is 'non-spontaneous', disciplined and always thinks things through. But she does keep her word. I ask about Mrs M's weakness for leopard-skin shoes. Is that a decoy?

A Scandinavian frown: it's more simple than that. She is just very shy.

MONDAY, 17 OCTOBER, MOSCOW

The dimly lit office of Russia's most famous political opponent of Vladimir Putin is located on the third floor of a shopping mall in central Moscow. Alexei Navalny is a tall, burly man with a spiky cowlick fringe, piercing pale-blue eyes and the hint of a paunch. He speaks good English, with a heavy accent. Friendly but watchful, he is dedicated to a twin mission: to expose state corruption and mount a serious bid for the Russian presidency in the 2018 election. 'Please, do not describe me as a dissident,' he tells his *FT* visitors. 'A dissident does not take part in the political system. I want to take part in the presidential election.'

Navalny has been arrested, beaten and jailed. His brother, he notes with a shrug of broad shoulders, has been stuck in a prison psychiatric ward in the latest official bid to shut him up. Navalny's courage is not at issue, even if his political company is sometimes less than savoury. Apart from attracting a cult status among Russia's youth following, he has also won support from ultra-nationalists, a charge met with another shrug of the shoulders. The goal, he insists, must be to use every inch of political space which Putin has afforded the opposition, from the nationalists to the liberals.

To that end, Navalny and his team are using social media and data analytics to build a serious campaign. A video exposé of Prime Minister Dmitry Medvedev's secret property empire near the Black Sea, along with vineyards and yachts, has attracted 24 million views. As we exit past a row of young workers head-down over laptop computers, Navalny points to a tabulated list of all his supporting groups around Russia. He has 130,000 dedicated campaign volunteers, tens of thousands of activists who have shown up for protests, and more than 1.7 million subscribers to his online video channels. Proud and defiant, Navalny is the last (visible) man standing in opposition to Vladimir Putin.*

TUESDAY, 18 OCTOBER

Sergei Ivanov, long-time chief of staff to Vladimir Putin, greets me in his Kremlin office. If he is smarting over his recent demotion – his portfolio now covers roads, railways and saving rare animal species such as the Siberian

---

* In August 2020, Navalny was poisoned on a campaign trip to Siberia. After a delay, he was evacuated to Berlin to receive treatment where doctors said they had found traces of Novichok, the deadly nerve agent.

snow leopard – his poker face gives nothing away. His English is fluent and almost accent free. 'It was much better when I was a spy,' he says in response to my compliment.

We are meeting in the wake of stunning revelations in America. Russian agents have hacked into the Democratic National Committee, according to the US government, a blatant, unprecedented interference in the US presidential election. Who could have thought this served the interests of Moscow, I ask, with mock credulity?

Ivanov's stares at his English interlocutor in icy silence, and then bursts into (equally mock) laughter at suggestions of state espionage. 'If the US has specific proof then they can show it to us . . . but I remember discussing special services with Donald Rumsfeld and Condoleezza Rice. Sources and methods are not disclosed.'

Perhaps, I suggest, Russia wants to show it can infiltrate and cause mischief in an election campaign. After all, Moscow has long accused Washington of interfering in its own 2011 presidential elections, stirring up liberal opposition to President Putin. Ivanov agrees that Russia has plenty of cause for retaliation and launches into a long list of grievances: American meddling in Ukraine which helped to trigger the downfall of Moscow's protégé Viktor Yanukovich; US efforts to exploit the collapse of the Soviet Union to try to convert a weakened Russia to liberal democracy; American naivety in trying to democratise the Middle East; the Iraq fiasco with Colin Powell ('a good man who was a good general'); the Libya debacle.

Ivanov's watery eyes narrow and he spits out his words under cigarette-tainted breath. 'It may be that someone should prosecute the US and UK for war crimes.' And for good measure: 'Can you imagine what would have happened with the democratisation of Egypt?'

We plough on through more misunderstandings, wilful or not, until I ask what chance of a fresh start with the new administration, Trump or Hillary. 'There's a lot of baggage. Heavy baggage. Smelly baggage. But yes, I hope that the anti-Russian rhetoric will stop after the election. We are ready for Realpolitik.'

There was little hint that Ivanov had an inside track on the US presidential election, though the Kremlin clearly favoured Trump over Clinton. Hacking was a finger-in-the-eye power play. After Obama, Moscow wanted to resume business, with a Republican or if necessary a Democrat.

FRIDAY, 4 NOVEMBER

The High Court has ruled that the UK government would require the consent of Parliament to give notice of Brexit through the Article 50 procedure. The *Daily Mail*'s front page has photographs of the three judges in ermine with the headline 'Enemies of the People'. I wonder whether Paul Dacre knows that the term 'Enemies of the People' was regularly employed in Nazi propaganda in Hitler's Germany and Stalin's Soviet Union.*

---

* *An Enemy of the People* was also the title of an 1882 play by Norwegian playwright Henrik Ibsen. It is doubtful that Dacre was aware of that fact either.

To New York for the US presidential election. I arrive late Sunday afternoon and switch on the TV. Donald Trump is addressing packed crowds in Minnesota. What's he doing in the Land of 10,000 Lakes? If he thinks Minnesota is in play, then he must think he has a chance of winning. My hunch is swiftly dismissed the following day. Jared Cohen, a super-smart ex-State Department official now at Jigsaw, a unit at Google, predicts Hillary Clinton will win. So does Bob Dilenschneider, the New York PR fixer. Bob Kaiser, the astute *Washington Post* news executive, now retired, declares flatly over tea at the Algonquin that the Democrats will take the White House.

I felt reassured, forgetting that we were in cosmopolitan New York rather than in battleground states like Michigan, Ohio and Pennsylvania where the election would be decided. I forgot, too, that Hillary Clinton had more baggage than a Boeing 747, as I wrote in a recent FT *editorial. Above all, I forgot the hard lesson of Brexit which had made a nonsense of conventional wisdom.*

On election night, I visit the *New York Times* to watch its CEO Mark Thompson talking on stage about the election. The former BBC boss is fluent and well informed. The questions assume Hillary Clinton will come out on top. Later, walking through the newsroom, I spot Dean Baquet, editor, his deputy Joe Kahn and Matt Purdy, a top news executive whom I first met during my summer at the *Washington Post* in 1985. 'It's going to be a long night,' says Matt.

I race to the *FT* office. 'A long night' means Clinton is no shoo-in. Trump, the ex-reality-TV host who has never held public office, must have a real chance of winning. Just before midnight, it looks over. Robert Shrimsley and I agree it's safe to declare victory for Trump. On television, the Trump dynasty is triumphant.

After three hours of sleep, I'm back in the *FT* office. Our coverage is fine but we need more on the Trump team and plans for government. Georgette Mosbacher, my old Republican friend, is helpful. She predicts Mike Pence will be a key figure in the administration. Steve Schwarzman, Blackstone boss, goes one better: Trump will confound everyone, especially with his brinkmanship. After eight years of Obama, America will have a pro-business president who will be great for the economy and for the stock market. He cites tax reform and a major infrastructure programme. *On almost every count, Schwarzman was right.*

THURSDAY, 17 NOVEMBER

The PM greets me with a slightly forced smile and by my first name. We take our places two seats apart around a large wooden table – a contrast with Blair who preferred sofa talk and Cameron who liked to banter with chums sitting in a circle of chairs.

Mrs May orders English tea. She is running late and apologises for failing to make time for me at the Tory party conference. I ask the PM about her speech attacking globalisation for rewarding 'the privileged few' at the expense of the 'just about managing' and questioning Bank of England monetary policy. Did she give any thought to how the outside world and financial markets would react? *A quizzical look.*

Well, I continue, the prime minister is virtually unknown

outside the UK. On my travels to Moscow, New York and Tokyo people ask what to make of Mrs May. *Another quizzical look. The prime minister clearly has not thought much about how her words would resonate outside the UK.*

We talk briefly about her commitment to an industrial strategy, immigration, Global Britain. The PM says we have to give British people a chance to take the skilled jobs rather than simply handing them out to foreign workers. I ask her if the problem is immigration from the EU? Has she put immigration ahead of, say, the interests of the City of London?

'It's not a binary choice,' the PM replies. *('Not binary' will become the two most overused words in the May and later Johnson governments on Brexit.)*

I ask why the government took so long to come to the defence of the judiciary after the *Mail*'s 'Enemies of the People' assault on the High Court judges.

'A democracy has two pillars: an independent judiciary and freedom of the press.'

May's answer was both correct and disingenuous. Freedom of the press did not preclude the government speaking up on behalf of the judiciary. As a journalist, it was hardly my job to remind the prime minister that there is a time and a place for defending institutions in a liberal democracy.

MONDAY, 5 DECEMBER

Somehow, I must try to make sense of an extraordinary year, when the unthinkable became possible, when Britain voted to leave the EU and a property tycoon and television host was elevated to US commander-in-chief. These events, I write, 'mark a revolutionary moment. Not quite 1789 or 1989, but certainly a thundering repudiation of the status quo. Some detect echoes of the 1930s, with Trump cast as an incipient fascist.'

Power in 2016 flowed to strongmen like Putin in Russia, Erdoğan in Turkey, Duterte in the Philippines and Xi in China. But the analogy with the 1930s is surely misplaced. We are nowhere near a Great Depression. Two million new jobs have been created in the UK since 2010. Something else is going on.

Brexit and the Trump victory can be explained in terms of a crisis of globalisation, where swathes of western voters have seen stagnant wages and an outsized share of wealth going to the rich 1 per cent. Immigration and technology have disrupted politics, deepening and accelerating the sense of dislocation. Power and legitimacy are being redefined in established liberal democracies, epitomised by Trump's 'winner takes all' approach and the 'will of the people' rhetoric in Britain.

After talking things over with Alice Fishburn, magazine editor, I propose the title for my end of the year essay: 'The Year of the Demagogue'.

SECTION FIVE

FINAL ACT

THE CENTRE HOLDS

In early January, Theresa May set out her terms for the UK's withdrawal from the European Union. She envisaged a clean break: no membership of the European Single Market, no membership of the Customs Union. It was a bold, even reckless move. Voters had approved the act of leaving the EU but not the terms of divorce or the future relationship with Europe. Tony Blair compared Brexit to selling one's home and buying an alternative residence without having bothered to take a look. May struggled and took the fateful decision to call a snap election.

Brexit and Trump caught the FT off-guard in 2016 (even as subscriptions continued to rise to almost 850,000 paying readers). We had to explain in greater depth the rise of populism and report on liberal democracy's fightback in the election battlegrounds of France, Germany and the Netherlands. Overall, we needed to understand our ideological opponents better. At the end of March, the opportunity arrived with an interview in the Oval Office with President Trump.

There was also much work to be done inside the FT, using our embryonic relationship with Nikkei as a catalyst for change. The nature of our conversation about diversity started to change, extending beyond personnel to the selection and sourcing of FT news stories and opinion. Working with Roula and the FT board,

I set out plans for gender balance at the top of the FT *by 2022–3, reinforced by a pipeline of younger female talent. And I began thinking about succession, a subject covered in a memorable three-and-a-half-hour interview with President Paul Kagame in Rwanda.*

FRIDAY, 20 JANUARY

As the sun goes down over Bourton-on-the-Water near Cheltenham, I sit in amazement watching television clips of Donald Trump's inaugural speech, with his pledge to stop the 'American carnage' of crime, shuttered factories and an abandoned middle class. 'The time for empty talk is over,' Trump declares. 'Now arrives the hour of action.' He sounds like Batman descending on Gotham City.

I'm at Cotswold School Academy Trust prepping for a live performance of BBC's *Any Questions?* hosted by Jonathan Dimbleby. Star guest is Jacob Rees-Mogg, the pinstriped Brexiter from Somerset. Jacob informs me that his father William was an ex-*FT* man before becoming editor of *The Times*. I can go one better: in the winter of 1977, over a drink at the Oxford Union bar, Rees-Mogg snr persuaded me that journalism was my vocation. On hearing my (mildly embellished) tale, Jacob, no fan of the modern *FT*, starts purring.

The live audience finds Rees-Mogg's fogey manner quaint, if not exactly endearing. My line about Trump as Batman is half serious but still gets a lot of laughs. On the drive back to London, I asked fellow guest Diane Abbott, Labour's Cambridge-educated left-wing firebrand, about the 'reverse takeover' of the Labour party by the Corbynites. The shadow home secretary is guardedly loyal towards 'Jeremy'. Then I ask her why Labour failed to mobilise against Brexit.

Abbott says the unions were broadly pro-European in the 1980s and 1990s when a liberalised Single Market also included a strong dose of protective social policy. This was Jacques Delors' bargain. But by the 2000s, the Single Market had come to look like a capitalist plot. Then came the eurozone crisis which devastated southern Europe. The appalling suffering in Greece was the final straw.

My conversation with Abbott made me even more sceptical about a second referendum. Labour was deeply divided and Corbyn had no appetite for a 'People's Vote'. Besides, the option was not on the table.

TUESDAY, 21 FEBRUARY

Sylvie Bermann, French ambassador, has put on a reception for me to receive my Légion d'Honneur at the ambassador's residence on 'Billionaires' Row' in Notting Hill Gate. Mark Carney has come, but the biggest surprise is Mario Draghi who initially declined but flew in quietly from Frankfurt. I pay tribute to my European mentors, many French. Pascal Lamy, Élisabeth Guigou, Jean-Claude Piris and, though we had our differences, Jacques Delors. Journalists are not in the business of collecting gongs, but I've spent nearly three decades living and breathing the European story. *Pace* Rees-Mogg, this honour may have come from a foreign government but it means a lot to me.

TUESDAY, 28 FEBRUARY

Breakfast at the Hay-Adams hotel near the White House with Gary Cohn, former second-in-command at Goldman Sachs, now head of President Trump's National Economic

Council. Cohn is a savvy operator, a Wall Street trader by temperament. He beat dyslexia as a kid but he's never experienced anything quite like the Trump White House. Especially former campaign strategist Steve Bannon, 'the wildest of the wild cards'. Many of the staffers are barely 30, they all have an opinion and there's next to no process. Cohn's job is to instil discipline and set priorities. The president's agenda is staggeringly ambitious: tax reform, a bonfire of regulations, a $1 trillion infrastructure programme and the repeal of Obamacare. Cohn lost out in the Goldman succession. His new job has visibly energised him. How long will he last?

The answer was a little over a year before he finally resigned. Bob Woodward's book Fear *later alleged that while in office Cohn had removed a draft letter – cancelling a trade agreement with South Korea – from Trump's desk so the president could not sign it.*

WEDNESDAY, 15 MARCH

Weapons-grade intelligence from Jonathan Hill, former EU commissioner.* Downing Street under Theresa May is 'a totally closed circle'. The PM relies on two advisers only: Fiona Hill and Nick Timothy, loyalists who served under her at the Home Office. Sir Jeremy Heywood, Cabinet secretary, has lost influence and no longer sits directly outside the PM's office. Ministers are routinely abused. Philip Hammond has

---

* Jonathan Hill, Baron Hill of Oareford: political adviser to John Major during the 1992 Maastricht treaty negotiations, EU commissioner for financial stability, financial services and capital markets union (2014–16)

been 'shredded'. With next to no access to the prime minister, business has been 'whacked'.

May's prospects are bleak, her priorities riddled with contradictions, says Hill. More social policy, but more tax competition. Immigration controls, but a commitment to 'Global Britain'. On Brexit, she doesn't command a majority in the House of Commons. Tory hardliners want out of the EU at all costs. A compromise deal won't cut it. There is a case for a general election. It will be the most important in 50 years.

FRIDAY, 17 MARCH

Jean-Claude Juncker, president of the European Commission and British bogeyman, has agreed to lunch with the *FT* in his private dining room in Brussels. He arrives on time at 12.30, all smiles behind a sober dark suit, white shirt and dashing pink tie. 'How come it's been so long?' he says in French, embracing me warmly, with a hint of a kiss on my left cheek. I first met Juncker 20 years ago when he was prime minister of Luxembourg and a mini-power broker between France and Germany. He's routinely dismissed in Britain as a federalist drunk, a tone-deaf bureaucrat and a German toady. In fact, he's been elected 14 times in his life, 9 times to the Grand Duchy's parliament and 4 to the European Parliament. In his passion for unity between the nations of Europe, he's the last Eurocrat standing.

What went wrong with Europe, I ask Juncker, as we tuck into our Carpaccio de Saint-Jacques, followed by veal cutlets, washed down with a glass of Mas Champart followed by Château l'Hospitalet de Gazin? *(The answer is not the cuisine, obviously.)* Juncker says the message of war and peace no longer resonates with the younger generation. EU enlargement to central and eastern Europe was inevitable after the fall of Communism, but extra numbers made the original club less cohesive. Now Europe, caught between the US and China, is losing weight economically and demographically. Brexit, says Juncker, is a 'tragedy' which will have negative economic consequences for the UK.

'I have met two destroyers,' Juncker tells me, 'Gorbachev who destroyed the Soviet Union and Cameron who destroyed the United Kingdom to some extent, even if there is no wave in Scotland to become independent.' Helmut Kohl, by contrast, was 'a modest giant, a little saint in a great church', who made the smaller European countries feel they mattered.

As we sip coffee, I remind Juncker that he once said power had an erotic quality. Is that still the case? Juncker replies that power these days is 'more and more exciting and less and less erotic'. How so?

'Eroticism is irrational; explicable but irrational. Why are you in love with a person? The day you know means the day you have stopped being in love.'

But surely, I say, there is always room for intuition, whether in love or politics?

'Yes,' says Juncker, 'these are the fucking moments.'

Whether Juncker was referring to a Euro-summit or something else was left unsaid. Two years later, his last act as Commission president was to broker a deal in the Brexit negotiations, a big favour to Boris Johnson who never had any time for him. The Luxembourger was a deal-maker from a bygone era. Even if he liked a tipple, preferably two, he did not deserve to be damned in the public eye.

THURSDAY, 30 MARCH

Sir Lynton Crosby arrives marginally late for our lunch at Rules, noting that I was late last time round. He's wearing a grey suit, silver tie and a big smile, the memory of last year's election triumph still fresh. You delivered a great victory, I say, smarmily. 'The people did,' he corrects me in that light Australian accent which invariably has a tinge of menace.

I'm on my way to Washington to interview President Trump. Crosby notes casually that Trump is still doing business from his new seat in the White House, working on deals in the Middle East. 'He cannot stop himself,' Crosby tells me, adding: 'He's not a populist, he's an opportunist.'

Crosby's verdict on May is that she's very cautious, over-reliant on a small circle, and impossible to penetrate. She owes her leadership victory to the Cameron political machine. As for the rest of the Tory contenders, Boris Johnson is 'well placed', Philip Hammond is 'not trusted' and George Osborne will find it hard being simultaneously editor of the *Evening Standard*, an MP and a highly paid adviser to Black-Rock. Crosby has got less time for ex-Cameron adviser Steve Hilton. 'He's got his head up his arse,' adding almost as an afterthought, 'quite a long way actually.'

I've heard May recently invited Crosby to Chequers to sound him out on a snap election. No way it will happen, he says. The PM has decided against. He might have called an election because of the importance of the Brexit decision. (Crosby backed Leave but says he stayed out of the campaign out of loyalty to Cameron. *Understandable, after he was rewarded with a post-election knighthood.*) The worst reason to call an election would be because the Tories think they can smash Corbyn and win an increased majority. 'Politicians should never take voters for granted,' he says, 'the people won't buy it.'

Crosby indicated that May had decided against a snap election but he still made the case for calling a poll to win a new mandate to push through Brexit. My feeling was that an early election was still on the table.

FRIDAY, 31 MARCH

Donald J. Trump is seated behind the Resolute Desk where his Democrat predecessor Harry S. Truman planted the sign 'The buck stops here!'. The newly elected president does not rise or extend a handshake. I thank him for receiving the *FT* delegation which includes Gillian Tett from New York, and Demetri Sevastopulo, our Greek-Irish Washington bureau chief, and thank him for subscribing to the *Financial Times*.

'That's OK,' says the president, 'you lost, I won.'

Trump cannot resist reminding people that his election victory, like Brexit, made chumps out of the mainstream media. 'You folks want a little something to drink?' he asks as an aide brings a Coca-Cola. I order the same, with ice. The president presses a red button on his desk. Demetri jokes he hopes it was not the nuclear button. Laughs – and relief – all round.

The Trump interview poses any number of pitfalls for the journalist. He is a master manipulator, a shameless propagandist and a narcissist who brands anything he does not like as fake news. Then again, he is president of the United States, a political figure who demands a measure of respect. How to balance all these considerations in the sanctum of the Oval Office will test us all to our limit.

The first thing that strikes the visitor about Trump is his physical presence. He is a very big man, even when sitting down. He's wearing a white shirt and a long ruby red tie which hangs well below his considerable waist. He speaks in a heavy New York accent in short bursts, punctuated with the word 'OK?' which either means are you following me or, more likely, this is the way it is and there's really no point in further debate.

Trump is visibly disappointed when he asks me if I have been here before and I answer in the affirmative. The president has turned the Oval Office, a place of decorum normally reserved for the most intimate conversations, into the equivalent of a medieval court. He is surrounded by a melee of aides, some sitting, some standing, each ready to answer his every demand.

When Gillian asks the president whether he regrets any of his tweets, Trump says 'Every once in a while there is a clinker [sic]),' before bellowing across the Oval Office: 'Where is Dan? Where is Dan Scavino, please?' Within seconds, Scavino, a former golf caddie who has been running Trump's social media since the 2016 campaign, walks over with a laptop to report that, at the latest count, Trump's combined following is 101 million.

'Without the tweets, I wouldn't be here . . . I have over 100 million followers between Facebook, Twitter and Instagram,' the president says proudly. 'Over 100 million. I don't have to go to the fake media.'

Trump is defiant about his support for Brexit (very good for the UK, OK?); unrepentant about his criticism of alliances (I believe in relationships . . . alliances have not worked out very well for us, OK?); and eager to play the statesman as he is about to host President Xi at his home in Mar-a-Lago

347

in Florida. He wants China's help in curbing North Korea's nuclear weapons programme, adding: 'If China is not going to solve North Korea, we will' – a threat of unilateral action which gives us our news story.

After nearly half an hour, we pose for photographs. I ask for a shot with the president next to a portrait of Andrew Jackson, the populist insurgent who served from 1829 to 1837. Trump obliges. Then he takes me to an adjoining room, 'a complete mess' he inherited from Obama. I assumed he was talking about the economy, but Trump, the real-estate developer, is in fact referring to the decor.

'Do you know who that is,' says the president, pointing to a portrait.

LB: 'Yes. Sir, it's Teddy Roosevelt.'

Trump (deflated)

LB: 'And, Mr President, you know that Teddy Roosevelt carried a big stick but he also spoke softly.'

Our conversation with Steve Bannon, Trump's consigliere, is illuminating but in a very different way. Dishevelled with longish, curly grey hair, he cuts a charismatic figure. His sentences are dotted with references to martial history, especially the Civil War. On opposite walls: a whiteboard chock-a-block with policies and a six-column list of campaign pledges under the words 'Make America Great Again'. Among the most eye-catching: repeal of Obamacare, branding China a currency manipulator, hiring Americans and changing the accounting rules for US companies. Bannon wants to overturn the global economic system which has benefited Wall Street, Hollywood and Silicon Valley as well as Milan and Chelsea. Globalisation has 'gutted' the American economy, he bellows. A new succession of strongmen – Modi of India, Xi of China, Duterte in the Philippines, Putin of Russia – and populists like Marine Le Pen and Nigel Farage are on the rise. Trump is the American prototype.*

The Trump interview was pure Sopranos on the Potomac. At times, I felt I was a prop on a film set with the anti-hero centre stage barking orders to underlings. Trump was mostly on his best behaviour. We came away with a big news story on North Korea but I regretted not asking Trump to talk about the difference between being CEO running a business and being president running a country. Overall, my judgement was that there were tentative signs that there was a 'little more method to the madness' of the Trump administration. Some colleagues disagreed. They turned out to be more right than wrong.

MONDAY, 3 APRIL

Discreet feelers to 10 Downing Street have finally paid off. Nick Timothy, the prime minister's enforcer-strategist, has agreed to see me. Tall, balding and with a full brown beard, Timothy enters the small Cabinet Office room where I have been waiting. Timothy has a reputation for being arrogant so I open with the Trump interview and my tentative verdict that things were not quite as crazy as the cartoon images of the presidency suggest. Timothy concurs. We turn to Theresa May's challenge of 'delivering' Brexit.

Consistency must be the watchword. The Parliamentary arithmetic is difficult. The House of Lords will be a problem. The system will polarise. May has to keep her word on taking the UK out of the EU. Business may be unhappy, but

---

* Fiona Hill, the Russia specialist in the White House, described Bannon as Trotsky trying to be Lenin.

'we're not running a business and business is not running politics.' The government has to avoid being pushed around. The SNP 'need challenging' in Scotland. May must make good on the pledges she made on the steps of Number 10 after her leadership win, to make Britain a country 'that works not for a privileged few, but for every one of us'.

Timothy is a self-styled radical thinker with a vision of a new working-class conservatism; but he comes across as very defensive compared to Steve Bannon, his White House counterpart. Bannon only plays offence.

I ask Timothy about the prime minister. How is she faring? What about President Trump grabbing her hand and leading her through the Rose Garden to a joint press conference inside the White House. A friendly gesture or the moment of subjugation? Timothy brushes the incident aside. May is not strong on personal contact. He's urged her 'to get on the phone'. As the clock ticks towards noon, I ask why May was unable in our last conversation to name any historical figure she admired. 'Politicians are not defined by labels,' he says, 'there are no heroes for Theresa May.'

For someone in a historic role, I found this lack of historic awareness telling.

4–14 APRIL, HONG KONG, JAPAN, CHINA

Thanks to Jamil Anderlini, newly promoted to Asia editor, my first appointment in Hong Kong is with the incoming chief executive, Carrie Lam, a steely, smart civil servant who grew up in the island's housing projects. Lam has an impossible job because she serves two masters: the people in Hong Kong and the Communist leadership in Beijing. Every chief executive since the British handover in 1997 has tried to please Beijing and ended up being deeply unpopular in Hong Kong. And matters are getting worse because economic growth has slowed, sky-high house prices are squeezing the middle class and a pro-democracy 'umbrella movement' is gathering force.

Lam describes Hong Kong as a 'super-connector' between the Chinese mainland and the rest of the world. She talks enthusiastically about new infrastructure projects and claims she will deal with the housing problem. Lam is definitely on top of her brief but her robotic style suggests to me she has no political sixth sense. The chasm between the older and younger generation comes home to me when a young man called Joshua Wong, 20, drops by the *FT* office.

Wong is the baby-faced radical in spectacles, recently released after spending 100 days in jail for 'unauthorised assembly'. His goal is free elections to select the chief executive, a message he is intent on spreading via social media to the younger generation. 'We have 7.5 million citizens but only 1,200 electors. Universal suffrage is logical'. And the necessary response, he believes.

Yet it is also logical that Hong Kong's democracy movement would likely spread to the mainland – which is why Beijing is desperate to stamp it out. Wong remains unrepentant. 'We absolutely support democratisation in China. If Hong Kong gets democracy then China needs to be democratic too.' While he draws the line against independence for Hong Kong, he makes clear that his ultimate goal is democracy and 'genuine autonomy'.

My conversations in Hong Kong suggested the island was heading for trouble. The pro-democracy movement fed off popular disaffection with the government. The declining quality of life was important, but so too was fear about a heavy-handed Beijing. The prospect of a full handover to China in 2047 suddenly felt a lot closer for a large proportion of the population.

FRIDAY, 28 APRIL

Paul Polman wanted to be a priest, then a doctor. Then the Dutchman turned to business, except he still likes to preach and his bedside manner still leaves much to be desired, as I discover over lunch at the Thameside headquarters of Unilever. Polman, 60, the long-time CEO of the Anglo-Dutch consumer goods giant, has just fought off a $143bn hostile bid from Kraft Heinz of the US. He feels he – and his company – deserve more recognition compared to the chainsaw capitalists – my phrase – that tried to take control of Unilever. Polman cannot hide his disdain for 3G, the giant private equity firm, which teamed up with Warren Buffett to mount its hostile bid, since abandoned. The takeover battle, he says, was a clash between a long-term sustainable model for multiple stakeholders and a model entirely focused on shareholder primacy. Polman pulled out all the stops, even ringing Buffett at five o'clock on a Sunday morning to ask him why he was teaming up with such people. It's a case study in leadership and managing a crisis, I say. Will he please talk to the *FT*? Polman plays hard to get. He doesn't want to relive the past. *Like hell, he doesn't. I'm going straight back to the* FT *and talking to our consumer industries editor Shari Daneshkhu to line up an interview. On the record this time.*

The Polman interview took place, offering many insights into a businessman who believed fervently that capitalism should have a moral compass. His successful defence of Unilever marked a turning point in the markets as a heavily indebted Kraft Heinz was forced to restructure and 3G drew breath. Sustainable capitalism had won a notable victory. Polman retired a year later.

SUNDAY, 7 MAY

Emmanuel Macron, 39, the political meteor who launched an independent movement En Marche from nothing, has won the presidential election in France. The former Rothschild banker beat the far-right candidate Marine Le Pen decisively, winning two-thirds of the vote. Tony Barber, veteran *FT* foreign correspondent who also happens to be my younger brother, writes that liberal democracy across Europe will breathe a mighty sigh of relief. 'Openness, tolerance and internationalism carried the day, but Macron's challenges during his five-year term will be severe. The French public is disillusioned with the ruling elite. Macron cleverly positioned himself as an outsider and a force for change, but he too is a member of the technocratic elite.'

All true. But my view is that, after Brexit and Trump, many assumed the populist virus would spread across the European continent. Whisper it softly: Brexit may well have been an antidote.

WEDNESDAY, 31 MAY

The *FT* faces a wretched choice in the UK election. Theresa May has been a massive disappointment, robotic on the campaign trail and curiously brittle. The Conservative manifesto is an unreadable hodge-podge where pledges on better conditions in slaughterhouses vie with improved living standards for the 'just about managing'. Labour under Jeremy Corbyn's leadership is even worse. Corbyn is a pacifist relic from the 1970s, in hock to the unions. He's spent his entire life in opposition – to his own party leadership – and he's been wrong on most of the important issues, starting with the Cold War.

On Brexit, both parties have engaged in a conspiracy of silence. Voters have no idea what life outside the Single Market and Customs Union will look like, let alone the economic trade-offs involved. May's talk about Global Britain does not square with her harsh rhetoric on immigration. Philip Stephens says the slogan should be: Open for Business, Closed for Foreigners. I have difficulty editing our final editorial which extends conditional backing to May. 'Her resolve on Brexit is not in doubt; but her ability to deliver the best deal for Britain in terms of the closest possible relationship with the EU is worryingly unclear.'

The FT *could have copied* The Economist *and endorsed the Liberal Democrats, but it would have been a futile gesture. There was no majority support for a second referendum – a key plank in the Lib Dem manifesto. In truth, we favoured a continuation of the Conservative–Lib Dem coalition, but Labour's revival made that option unrealistic. May squandered her majority and found herself weakened beyond repair.*

11–22 AUGUST, RWANDA AND CONGO

Paul Kagame, Rwanda's warrior-president, runs the most orderly country in Africa. The streets are spotless, villagers wear shoes (by decree), but the memory of violence is never far away. Kagame seized power in Rwanda after the Hutu majority attempted to wipe out the Tutsi minority, hacking and shooting as many as 1 million people to death in a six-week killing spree in 1994. Now, having just been re-elected to his third term as president with a reported 98.7 per cent of the vote, Kagame is waiting to receive me with our Africa editor David Pilling in his presidential mansion.

The father of the nation is tall and reed-thin, speaking in a hushed voice. I've always found that truly powerful people rarely raise their voices, preferring to force the listener to crane forward and hang on their every word.

Kagame is a chilling presence, not surprising for a man who has witnessed death and deprivation on a scale where human life must have appeared cheap. His story nevertheless is one of a single-minded will to power, to create a new nation in which Hutu and Tutsi could live together in peace. 'It is not that we developed or grew up under normal conditions,' he says. 'Now there is stability, there's a sense of security, there is hope.'

Kagame's critics claim he has created a police state. Certainly his political opponents have a habit of mysteriously disappearing, while others live in fear. Kagame, a former intelligence agent whose heroes were Che Guevara and James Bond, says those who call for liberal democracy in Rwanda 'can go hang'. Eyes flashing in anger, he adds that he – an African and a Rwandese – has no need to take lessons from the British, French or Americans who turned a blind eye to the genocide in 1994. Besides, he says, with some justification, western attempts to impose democracy in countries like Afghanistan, Libya and Syria have backfired disastrously. 'You think these countries will be countries again? Not maybe in our lifetime.'

I've prepared extensively for the Kagame interview by reading up and talking to those who know him well, like Tony Blair. Several have advised me to nudge Kagame on the question of his succession. Is he willing, or able, to give up power? Kagame says he only ran for president again because it was the will of the party and the people, a familiar refrain of autocrats going back to Julius Caesar. Rwanda is, of course, a special case – more fragile, more precarious than most states. Kagame says the problem is preventing someone 'bringing down what we have built'.

We have been sitting down for more than three hours. One last time, I try to press him to spell out the process of succession. 'It's doable, it's feasible, it's risky,' he says. 'I will be part of that process, inevitably.'

And, finally, the intimation of (political) mortality. 'There is always the reality that point comes, either naturally or otherwise . . . There is no way of avoiding it, but you can avoid leaving behind a mess.'

David wrote the full-length interview feature. On the flight home, Kagame's words about succession kept coming back to me. Of course I'm no president, but I need to start planning for the future of the FT *without me.*

THURSDAY, 14 SEPTEMBER

Heart-rending overnight news from Sri Lanka. Paul McClean, one of our most outstanding young journalists, has gone missing. Initial reports – later confirmed – said he had been snatched by a crocodile while washing his hands in a saltwater lagoon. Paul had just finished a surfing lesson. The entire newsroom is in shock, many colleagues in tears.

In the morning, I call Peter and Irene, Paul's parents. One of the hardest conversations I've ever had. Paul was only 24, a young man who had already made his mark as a reporter in Brussels. His memory will live on, I promise Peter and Irene. Late in the afternoon, a colleague alerts me that *MailOnline* is running a distressing photograph of Paul's body. This is too much. I leave a message for Paul Dacre who calls back an hour later. He listens sympathetically, while making clear he is responsible for the newspaper not *MailOnline*. I appeal to common decency. Dacre makes no commitments. Within minutes, the image is removed. Whatever else is said about Paul Dacre, I will not forget that simple gesture of humanity.

FRIDAY—SATURDAY, 15—16 SEPTEMBER

Since the Harvey Weinstein sex scandal broke, I've been looking for a way to take the #MeToo story forward. Peter Spiegel, news editor, has suggested we take a hard look at non-disclosure agreements gagging victims of sexual harassment, drawn up by (usually male) super-lawyers. Matt Garrahan, our media editor, acting on a tip, has flown to Los Angeles and hit the jackpot. Zelda Perkins, Weinstein's long-time personal assistant, is ready to break her NDA and reveal her own sexual abuse at the hands of her boss, as well as the suspected rape of a friend of hers. Weinstein's lawyers have threatened us but we've seen them off. The only issue is whether Perkins is legally exposed. My bet is they won't dare touch her. And I'm right.

At the end of 2019, the FT *named Susan Fowler, the software engineer who lifted the lid on sexual harassment at Uber, as Person of the Year. Her revelations helped to topple Uber's founder, Travis Kalanick. The choice of Fowler broke with an unspoken tradition of selecting establishment figures and reflected a new balance of power in the workplace and in Silicon Valley. Previously untouchable bosses would soon come under the spotlight. As in the Weinstein case, even the most high-powered, expensive lawyers would no longer be able to keep stories of abuse and sexual harassment out of the public domain.*

SATURDAY, 16 SEPTEMBER

Boris Johnson has published a 4,000-word manifesto in the *Daily Telegraph*, a naked power grab for leadership of the Conservative party. I got wind of it at a private dinner hosted last night by Georgette Mosbacher, who has heard privately she has been nominated as US ambassador to Poland. Aidan Barclay* was gloating about a big *Telegraph* scoop and clearly feels May is not up to the job. Boris claims he's merely 'rolling the pitch' ahead of May's keynote speech at the Tory party conference in a fortnight. If so, it's the biggest act of sabotage since environmental vandals dug holes and poured oil over the wicket at Headingley cricket ground, ahead of the Ashes Test against Australia in 1975.

MONDAY, 25 SEPTEMBER

Angela Merkel has won a fourth term as chancellor, but it's a pyrrhic victory. Her conservative Christian Democrat-led alliance enjoyed its worst election result since 1949. The

---

* Aidan Barclay, chairman of the *Telegraph*, runs the family business of his father and uncle, Sir David and Sir Frederick Barclay. The feud between the secretive billionaire Barclay twins and their family members went public in 2019.

far-right party Alternative for Germany is the third biggest party in parliament, having capitalised on Germany's refugee crisis. Gideon Rachman's sobering verdict: 'Germany has lost its immunity to angry, anti-establishment populism. That has serious implications for the German chancellor's ability to play the role of "leader of the western world", a title many bestowed on her after the election of Mr Trump.'

MONDAY, 2 OCTOBER

To Manchester for the Conservative party conference, including a session with the PM. I'm too late to meet Boris Johnson which is probably a relief to both of us. I'm still mightily jet-lagged from my trip to Tokyo; he's still mighty suspicious of the *FT*. Tory reaction to the Boris manifesto in the *Telegraph* veers from shoulder shrugs ('He cannot bear to be out of the limelight') to pungent putdowns. Asked what the rebellious ex-mayor of London brings to the Cabinet, David Lidington, the new justice secretary and staunch Europhile, says: 'Well, he does offer experience of local government.'

The PM is cold-ridden when George Parker and I are ushered into the hotel suite just after 3pm. Robbie Gibb, her new press supremo, asks what the continental Europeans think about the government's negotiating position on Brexit. I offer a tour d'horizon before asking, point-blank, why the PM does not simply sack Boris Johnson or 'dump him in the East River', a strained reference to my favourite Marlon Brando movie *On the Waterfront*.*

---

* *On the Waterfront*, which focuses on violence and corruption among long-shoremen, was in fact set in Hoboken, New Jersey, on the Hudson River. The film won eight Oscars.

May, staring blankly, says that there are different styles of leadership. My response is: I am only a little leader and you are the prime minister. My rule as editor is that people can say what they like behind closed doors, but once they go public with criticism, then it's over.

Long pause.

PM: 'Well there have been moments when collective Cabinet responsibility . . .'

A croaky voice begins to trail off

LB: '. . . has not been fully observed, prime minister?'

An official nod, of sorts. Through coughs and pauses, we meander to the end of the conversation. On departure, I wish the PM *'bonne récupération'* – a needless Euro-provocation which I regret the moment I leave the room.

Manchester was the moment I gave up on Theresa May. She was not a leader. Two days later, the PM went on stage for her keynote comeback speech, lost her voice and the stage set fell apart. A metaphor for her government.

TUESDAY, 24 OCTOBER

Melodramatic scenes in BA's business lounge at Heathrow airport. My lower back has gone into spasms in the middle of a phone call to Victoria. I scream out for help, while drawing a mental line against mouth-to-mouth resuscitation. It's obvious I cannot fly to Riyadh, where I am moderating a Saudi sovereign wealth fund (PIF) panel to showcase modern Saudi Arabia. The conference, inevitably billed as 'Davos in the Desert', is the inspiration of Mohammed bin Salman (MBS). The guest list must be worth a trillion dollars – perhaps more. I am half sorry to miss the schmoozing, but there's a nagging suspicion that the *FT* – and me – would be better keeping our distance. Maybe my back was trying to tell me something.

FRIDAY, 3 NOVEMBER

Alex Salmond, once the most powerful politician in Scotland, is in meltdown over a Lex column making fun of him as a would-be rescuer of the *Scotsman* newspaper, where I started my career almost 40 years ago. A Norwegian activist investor, Christen Ager-Hanssen, wants to parachute Salmond on to the board, possibly as chairman. When Salmond was SNP leader, he was regularly lampooned in the *Scotsman*; now he says he wants the newspaper to be pro-Scotland. 'That presumably means pro-SNP. His party dominates the Scottish parliament. Scotland does not need a *McPravda*,' Lex writes.

In response, Salmond has screamed at Jonathan Guthrie, Lex editor and author of the note. At Jonathan's request, I phone him and he screams at me.

Salmond: *'McPravda. McPravda.* What do you mean, *McPravda*?'

LB (after listening to a torrent of abuse): 'You can't take it.'

Salmond: 'What?'

LB: 'You can't take criticism. You never get any criticism in Scotland because the Scottish press is supine.'

Salmond: 'Supine? You're calling Scottish journalists supine?'

I have overreached, appallingly. I apologise to Salmond unreservedly and to all Scottish journalists, north and south of the border. We agree to forget the matter. *Well, not exactly. How could I ever erase McPravda from memory?*

SUNDAY, 5 NOVEMBER

Chilling story overnight from Riyadh, Saudi Arabia. Around 30 of the richest people in the Kingdom, several blood royals, have been detained at the five-star Ritz-Carlton hotel. The detention order ostensibly comes from King Salman but everyone is pointing the finger at Mohammed bin Salman. This marks a further consolidation of power. He is the coming man in the Desert Kingdom and the region.

Reports soon emerged of widescale torture and intimidation. When I mentioned these allegations at a private dinner in London, one of the Saudi guests, a prominent businessman, said the reports of torture were untrue. 'Unless, of course, you are the owner of the Four Seasons hotel and you find yourself detained for weeks in the Ritz-Carlton.'

THURSDAY, 9 NOVEMBER

Lunch with David Davis and his minder at Roux Brothers. The Brexit minister has cancelled on me three times but it's worth the wait. Boris Johnson is 'out for himself', Philip Hammond 'antsy', Michael Gove 'a freelancer'. How about the future of Damian Green, de facto deputy prime minister, who's been accused of making inappropriate advances to a young female journalist in addition to being embroiled in a row with the police over whether he had pornography

362

on his Parliamentary office computer? Does he think Green should resign? 'If Damian goes, it's all over,' says Davis.*

Davis predicts Northern Ireland will be very tricky to resolve in the Brexit negotiations. The European Commission are instinctively pro-Republican and they don't understand the Unionist predicament. The UK needs a pragmatic solution. Fisheries will be 'very complicated', especially with the Spanish. Parliament cannot stop Brexit. If the House of Lords tries to block, it will face a '1911 moment'† and the Commons would go for abolition. Remainer MPs don't want an election and the risk of a Corbyn government. They want to hold their seats. Davis boasts he was tough enough to defy the Cameron government on torture and human rights. These people are nowhere near as tough. So, I ask him, how did you succeed?

Let's start with the *Daily Mail*, says Davis. The way to get Paul Dacre on side is to say: 'It's not English.' When the UK handed over a suspected Al-Qaeda operative to Pakistan's fearsome ISI intelligence service, the *Mail* applauded. In response, Davis protested at the violation of human rights. Dacre was dismissive, saying the man was a terrorist. 'Yes, he's a terrorist,' Davis countered, 'but pulling someone's finger nails out is not English . . .'

At the end of the meal, the minister for Brexit leaves me

---

* Davis's judgement was premature. Green was forced to resign the following month. May staggered on for another 18 months.

† The 1911 Parliament Act ended the House of Lords' right to veto bills democratically approved in the House of Commons. This followed a constitutional power struggle between the lower and upper houses when the Liberal majority was thwarted in efforts to pass new taxes in the so-called People's Budget championed by David Lloyd George.

with a thought. 'There's something I want to tell you,' says Davis, pointing to the rise of populism after the financial crisis: 'you people are responsible for Brexit and Trump!'

This is a ridiculous argument. The Financial Times *is not the government. But we are part of the establishment. Maybe Davis does have half a point.*

WEDNESDAY, 22 NOVEMBER

Woody Johnson, the new US ambassador in London and close friend of Trump, has asked to see me once I've sorted out a new US visa at the embassy in Grosvenor Square. We greet each other. He stares at me. I stare at him. Britain faces one of the most testing times in its history, I declare, gravely. Johnson agrees, adding: 'Maybe since 1066.' The Norman invasion was not quite what I had in mind, but we can pass on that. Woody declares that Trump signals the end of the old order. The new president represents change on a grand scale. Johnson says people in Britain, including the *FT*, need to be more positive: 'Leadership appears at the darkest hour' – which may, or may not, be a reference to the portrait of Winston Churchill looking on.

TUESDAY, 28 NOVEMBER

Lunch with Sir Jeremy Heywood at Osteria dell'Angolo, the unassuming Italian restaurant opposite the Home Office. The Cabinet secretary is under extraordinary strain. He had a cancer scare over the summer and was plainly mortified when there were suggestions in the press that he was too ill to do his job. Now, visibly pale, he is trying to reconcile irreconcilable positions on Brexit within the Cabinet, the ruling Conservative party and Parliament and between the UK and the EU. Even for a master bridge-builder like Heywood, the task is proving impossible.

Heywood asks me how I assess the Brexit negotiations. Not good, I reply. May says she wants a 'bespoke deal' with Brussels but in reality she's trying to have her cake and eat it. There is an unavoidable trade-off between access to the European market and alignment with its rules. Heywood grunts, a frequent means of communication. Then he perks up. The big victory for common sense this year was Cabinet agreement on a transition period before the UK finally withdraws from the EU. May was 'resistant until the end' before Philip Hammond finally carried the day. Heywood does not believe that Britain will crash out of the EU on 31 March next year without a deal. There's too much at stake for all parties, he says, neatly wrapping up his napkin. As he slips on an overcoat and we step out of the restaurant, I wish him and the family a happy Christmas. Then he trudges off towards Whitehall, a lone figure fighting a losing battle for common sense.

TUESDAY, 5 DECEMBER

Breakfast with Mark Carney at the Bank of England. We talk about Brexit and the City. There's £40bn of EU-related revenue at risk. It breaks down roughly as one third low margin, cross border commercial lending; one third asset management and one third high risk derivatives business which relies on the City's sophisticated 'plumbing'. Crucially, we bear the risk for clearing transactions, sums amounting to trillions of dollars. Does the EU want it and can it do it? EU banking regulators are not up to much. Insurance can go, but fund management (coveted by the French) must stay in the Square Mile. Equivalence of outcome is the new buzz term, which falls short of the certainty provided by the mutual recognition of regulation. Everyone is trying to find a way to maintain access to the Single Market while allowing for some regulatory divergence. *This is one vicious circle which I don't see being squared, even in the Square Mile.*

By evening, I am in New York, hopping off to Georgette Mosbacher's annual Christmas party, the last in her magnificent Fifth Avenue apartment opposite the Metropolitan Museum of Art. Over drinks, I have a 25-minute conversation with Ed Rollins, former Reagan campaign manager who knows Trump and Bannon well. Trump is chaotic, cannot read anything beyond a page. POTUS likes Mulvaney but feels McMaster talks down to him ('This is South Korea, Mr President, a divided country next to China . . .').*

Rollins tells me that a war plan is ready to attack North Korea with low-level nukes. He's nervous that the US might really launch a pre-emptive strike. Trump is adamant that the US cannot live with a nuclear Korea. Ed is a crusty old operator, who won the 1984 presidential election hands down, took part in the Korean presidential election for Roh Tae-woo† and likes Koreans ('they are much more interest-

---

* Mick Mulvaney, a Republican congressman, was appointed by Trump to head the Office of Management and Budget before replacing General John Kelly as acting White House chief of staff. Lieutenant General H.R. McMaster (US Army), soldier and military historian, was appointed national security advisor in place of Michael Flynn.

† Roh Tae-woo, president of South Korea from 1988 to 1993, rose to the rank of general during the Korean war before supporting the military

ing and friendly than the Chinese and Japanese'). Bannon tried to win too many battles, he says. The first months of Trump were chaos. General Kelly has restored order.* But Jared Kushner is 'wildly arrogant and out of his depth'. Moving the US embassy to Jerusalem is irresponsible and dangerous. Putting Kushner in charge of delivering a peace plan for the Middle East is laughable.

FRIDAY, 8 DECEMBER

Mario Draghi is sipping English tea in a booth near the entrance of the Dorchester. Now 70, he is remarkably preserved. A few lines on the Roman face, a full head of black hair flecked with grey. Sympathetic but probing eyes, with an easy smile. We exchange thoughts about our respective jobs, rushing around the world. He has exercised power discreetly, working his relationship with Angela Merkel, managing his majority on the European Central Bank board, and steering mercifully clear of Italian politics. And, all the time, maintaining a back channel to the editor of the *FT*, both as a sounding board and as a second vehicle of communication to the world. It's been a mutually rewarding, often fascinating experience, even if I have occasionally had to remind Mario that I cannot – and will not – intervene every time he raises a question about coverage. The reporters must do their job, I insist. The commentators serve at the pleasure of the editor

coup led by his schoolfriend Chun Doo-hwan. Roh later led democratic constitutional reforms after Chun's repressive rule.

* US Marine Corps General John F. Kelly, who served President Trump first as secretary of homeland security and then as chief of staff, tried to impose a measure of discipline on the chaotic White House.

but otherwise they have free rein. I preside over a broad church, maintaining accuracy, authority and quality.

Mario's job is almost done. Now the question of succession is in the air – another parallel with my own career trajectory. We run through ECB candidates and tiptoe round the inevitable question: can a German get the top job? Jens Weidmann, head of the Bundesbank and former top adviser to Merkel, is pushing his candidacy behind the scenes. But he's been the *Neinsager* during the eurozone crisis, voting against all of the extraordinary measures proposed by Draghi. He is the epitome of German economic orthodoxy. A German cannot be ruled out of the running per se, we agree. But this German has surely ruled himself out by his own actions and words. Mario won't say as much but I know him well enough by now to know what he thinks. We agree to speak again in the new year.

MONDAY, 18 DECEMBER

People often ask me: is Madison Marriage a real person? My answer is: you bet. Her byline may not match earlier memorable *FT* bylines such as Guy de Jonquières or Friederike von Tiesenhausen. But Madison Marriage is box office: she has already made her mark as the *FT*'s tax and accountancy correspondent with a string of hard-hitting scoops.

Madison, working with Paul Murphy, my newly appointed head of investigations has come up with a compelling story. A charity with the portentous name of the Presidents Club holds an annual men-only dinner at the Dorchester hotel which has raised hundreds of thousands of pounds for charitable causes like Great Ormond Street hospital. Three hundred male attendees, many high-rollers from London's property sector, are entertained by 130 hostesses clad in skimpy black dresses, black tights and high heels. Paul claims women have been manhandled and propositioned during the dinner while a raucous after-party has featured women deemed to be prostitutes. In the age of #MeToo this story is ripe for exposure. Paul says he knows how best to pull it off.

Madison wants to pose as a hostess and provide a first-hand account, corroborated by a friend who worked as a waitress-hostess last year. This raises numerous questions, starting with the ethics of going undercover. In more than three decades working at the *FT*, a cardinal (if unwritten) rule was that journalists could never misrepresent themselves. Could the end justify the means in this case? And, anyway, was this story of everyday sexism really an *FT* story?

I've been sitting on a decision for more than a week. Today, having made up my mind, I invite Madison to drop by my office. Is she aware of the risks, to herself and the reputation of the *FT*? What will she do if exposed? Her answers are measured but I detect an undercurrent of outrage that could interfere with her journalistic judgement. She is absolutely right that this behaviour should not be tolerated and she wants it exposed. Fine, I say. But stick to the facts and steer clear of the emotion.

Then I take a look at Madison (and myself), pause theatrically and say: 'Go for it.'

2018

PRESIDENTS CLUB

The #MeToo movement claimed several scalps in 2018, notably Harvey Weinstein, the Hollywood film mogul. It also exerted a powerful influence on media coverage. A separate FT *story, several months in preparation, was the definitive account of why Sir Martin Sorrell was ousted at WPP, the company he founded and built into an advertising and marketing colossus.*

FRIDAY, 19 JANUARY

Madison Marriage returned safely after midnight with an eyewitness account of young women hostesses being groped and propositioned at the Presidents Club dinner. Wired up with recording equipment beneath a short black dress, she suffered her share of harassment and abuse. We have a cracking scoop but we must be able to defend publication. Was the subterfuge justified? Do we risk putting out of business a worthy charity without due cause? Is the Presidents Club an *FT* story or tabloid mutton dressed as lamb?

The threat of an injunction is real. Rich, powerful supporters of the Presidents Club, many in banking and property, will use every means to protect their identities and reputations.

The charity has raised more than £20m over the past 33 years; Thursday night alone raised £2m. Auction items included lunch with Boris Johnson and tea with the governor of the Bank of England Mark Carney (who later denied any knowledge). But we have eyewitnesses to ritual humiliation of young women, many of them students. The girls were asked to sign a suspiciously long non-disclosure agreement which our lawyers initially suggested could prevent publication. Then Madison said she was given no time to read the document, rendering the NDA redundant.

I still want every last detail checked and double-checked. We have Excel sheets of VIP guests and patrons going back several years: Martin Sorrell; retail billionaire Philip Green; high-end property developer Nick Candy; and Formula One boss Bernie Ecclestone. One wrong fact and the costs will be punitive. I'll take a look at early drafts, but I'm off to Tokyo on Sunday and Roula is headed for Davos. Robert Shrimsley, Mr Cool in a crisis, will put the story to bed.

21—22 JANUARY

I am reliably informed that 'sexual harassment' began appearing as a term in Japan around 1990. It was adopted, Japanised and instantly shortened to 'sekhuhara', combining the first half of both words. So far, so good. The problem for Nikkei colleagues is the name 'Presidents Club'. Why no apostrophe? *(An* FT *reader later offered an explanation: 'The lack of a possessive apostrophe in the Presidents Club tells every potential attendee all they needed to know.')*

Back at the Palace hotel, my mind scrambled by jet lag, I make two last calls to London as snow falls on the streets of Tokyo. At 3.15am, close to the newspaper deadline in

London, I instinctively wake up and call the main news desk. Robert is making final tweaks and edits. No comeback from the lawyers. We're ready to publish. A couple of hours later I wake up again to read the opening paragraph: 'At 10pm last Thursday night, Jonny Gould* took to the stage in the ballroom at London's Dorchester Hotel. "Welcome to the most un-PC event of the year," he roared.' A few paragraphs later: 'Over the course of six hours, many of the hostesses were subjected to groping, lewd comments and repeated requests to join diners in bedrooms elsewhere in the Dorchester.'

By early afternoon, Tokyo time, no one thinks any more that Madison Marriage is a made-up name. Tens of thousands of people have watched her video, filmed as she was preparing to go undercover. Our story has gone viral. Within hours, the Presidents Club announces it is shutting down.

This was a moment to savour, a rare occasion when journalism holds power to account and generates an instant result. The Presidents Club supported worthy causes but the organisers were guilty of condoning behaviour unacceptable in modern Britain. Our scoop reminded readers and our journalists that the FT was not afraid of taking on the corporate establishment. The Terry Smith debacle I inherited as editor in 2005, where we had agreed sheepishly to a costly settlement, was a distant memory. From now on, FT investigative journalism would be a force to be reckoned with. I felt we'd come full circle.

---

* Jonny Gould, presenter of Channel Five's Major League Baseball show – not the radio and TV presenter who has worked for Smooth Radio, Talk Radio and Sky News.

FRIDAY, 2 FEBRUARY

The *FT*'s coming home. We're moving headquarters from One Southwark Bridge, where mice roam and the lifts creak, to Bracken House, where printing presses once thundered through the night. There are only a handful of us left with memories of the old BH newsroom, nicknamed the Blue Lagoon because of its sea-blue-painted walls. The Nikkei leadership has a feel for tradition and architectural style. Our new building will have a roof-terrace view of St Paul's, a great place for a summer party. Less fun will be breaking the news to colleagues: no more individual offices; the new *FT* newsroom will be open plan.

MONDAY, 12 FEBRUARY

Philip Hammond is the self-appointed leader of the grown-ups in the May Cabinet. People poke fun at 'Spreadsheet Phil' but these days someone has to mind the shop. Over a lukewarm coffee at the treasury, the chancellor explains how he intends to preserve as close a relationship as possible between the UK and EU in the interests of business and economic growth. Hammond is the voice of reason, surrounded by Brexit ultras like Jacob Rees-Mogg and Steve Baker determined to leave the EU at all costs. Jo Johnson, Boris's younger Europhile brother, told me the other day that all the Brexiters want to do is 'ride into Valhalla'.

FRIDAY, 16 FEBRUARY

Since Presidents Club, Madison Marriage has become the go-to journalist for women claiming they have been mistreated in the workplace. Now someone who has worked for Martin Sorrell has made a tentative contact. It's a tantalising lead. My advice: keep the person warm, see if they will speak off the record, and report back to me.

TUESDAY, 20 FEBRUARY

Chinese New Year lunch at the embassy. Ambassador Liu wants my assessment of the Mueller investigation* and the odds on Trump being impeached. Several Chinese notetakers, pens poised, are waiting for my response. *Time for English waffle because I'm not inclined to reveal what I really think: impeachment is a high bar to mount.*

First course is sushi, no doubt a little joke at Nikkei's expense. We turn to the subject of North Korea and the stand-off with Washington, where Donald Trump has called Kim Jong-un 'little rocket man'. Ambassador Liu served in Pyongyang in his last posting and had several meals with Kim, who is apparently a big fan of video games. Liu brands the Japanese as 'troublemakers' pushing the US to extreme positions on North Korea's nuclear programme. Chinese influence over Kim and the NK leadership is limited. Only a diplomatic solution will work. 'We are making the suggestions,' says Liu, 'no one else is.'

We turn to UK–China relations and Brexit. The ambassador chides us for failing to report that the PM's meeting with President Xi was a great success which showed a golden era in Sino-British relations. My retort: it feels more like the

---

* Robert Mueller, Republican former federal prosecutor and FBI director, was investigating Russian interference in the 2016 US presidential election.

bronze age under Theresa May who's gone slow on Chinese investment in our nuclear industry and is under pressure over Huawei, the telecoms equipment supplier eager to invest in Britain's 5G technology roll-out. Liu argues that, after Brexit, a new diplomatic calculation will apply. The degree to which the UK shows independence from America will determine how close the future relationship will be with China.

This was the first hint of China's 'wedge strategy', an attempt to prise the UK away from the US through the lure of economic rewards. UK foreign policy had long balanced the US 'special relationship' with membership of the EU and an open door to Chinese investment. After Brexit, Beijing was effectively saying that the British would have to pick sides. In 2020, the UK sided with the US and banned Huawei from participation in 5G.

WEDNESDAY, 21 FEBRUARY

Sergio Marchionne must surely be the most dynamic, visionary and impossible-to-work-for boss in the global car business. Back for his regular *FT* lunch, Marchionne is cussing like a tinker and calling for consolidation in the motor industry. The Italian-Canadian head of Fiat-Chrysler makes the Brazilian-Lebanese turnaround king Carlos Ghosn look robotic by comparison.* Last summer, Marchionne made an

---

* Carlos Ghosn: Brazilian-born architect of the global auto alliance between Nissan and Renault. A famously flamboyant chief executive, who also held French and Lebanese nationality; he staged a daring escape from Tokyo after being detained under house arrest on criminal charges of financial misconduct.

unsolicited approach to General Motors and was swatted aside. Mega-mergers must happen, he insists, if the car industry is to cope with the cost of new environmental rules and the transition to electric vehicles. Sergio is the dynamo who won't stop spinning. But there's a hint of humility. For the first time, he mentions the word succession.

Five months later, Marchionne was dead. He was only 66. He had stepped down from all his positions after complications from surgery. We are all poorer without his company.

FRIDAY, 9 MARCH

Red and fallow deer roam the grounds of Stud House, the early 18th-century manor set in the parkland of Hampton Court, where Evgeny Lebedev is hosting a dinner for Mohammed bin Salman, de facto ruler of Saudi Arabia. My driver is hopelessly lost but – minus GPS – we eventually find a way to the front door. A butler-bodyguard escorts me into the drawing room where Tony Blair and Richard Branson are sipping lemonade ('I'm sorry, Sir, but I'm afraid it's a dry evening tonight'). Blair offers me a valuable update on world politics: Trump's nuclear summit with North Korea ('risky but worthwhile, if properly planned'); the prospects of a trade war with China, and his own overview of the Middle East and Africa. I spot Russian ambassador Alexander Yakovenko and ask him about the attempted assassination of former GRU* double agent Sergei Skripal in Salisbury. The Kremlin could not possibly have authorised such an

---

* Glavnoye Razvedyvatel'noye Upravleniye (GRU): the main military foreign-intelligence service in Russia.

operation, says Yakovenko. Perhaps other forces are involved. *A classic diversion.*

Other VIP guests arrive: Princesses Beatrice and Eugenie; Len Blavatnik,* Damien Hirst, Jonathan Rothermere, Tristram Hunt† and Hartwig Fischer;‡ Jacob Rothschild, George Osborne and Steve Schwarzman, the Blackstone boss and trusted Saudi interlocutor and investor. Finally, the crown prince enters. He is still only 32, visibly larger than I remember: a huge domed head with receding black hairline; an exquisitely cut, extra-extra-large suit jacket, calf-leather shoes and a protruding belly. Osborne glides into his orbit, joined by Schwarzman. After what seems an eternity, we are ushered into the banquet room, a vast table seating at least 30 people. Evgeny, impeccably attired, guides a question-and-answer session over dinner.

I ask MBS about his vision for the region after the convulsions of the Arab Spring and the invasion of Iraq. The crown prince says Iran must be challenged on all fronts, from East Africa to Lebanon, Qatar and Yemen. Iran 'is not a proper country'. It is based on extremist ideology, not the nation state. Iran will never change as long as it is run by a theocracy and its economy controlled by the Revolutionary Guards. Saudi Arabia is preparing for the worst possible

---

* The British-American philanthro-capitalist Len Blavatnik had made a fortune in natural resources in post-Soviet Russia. He was knighted in 2017 for his philanthropy which includes multimillion-pound donations to the Tate and to Oxford university to create the Blavatnik School of Government.

† Tristram Hunt, historian, broadcaster and former Labour MP, was director of the Victoria and Albert Museum.

‡ The German art historian Hartwig Fischer was the first non-British national appointed director of the British Museum, in April 2016.

outcomes, including war. *I sip my water and wish it was something stronger.*

A guest inquires about Trump's impact. 'Trump is great, that is to say 99 per cent great,' says MBS. 'God Save America.' What's the 1 per cent? The US decision to move the embassy from Tel Aviv to Jerusalem. This makes things harder with the Palestinians (though ordinary Saudis don't have much time for them). After Obama's vacillations, MBS says, Trump is Saudi Arabia's new best friend intent on defeating Isis and terrorism. Trump is making America great again. The US will be the focus of Saudi investment (1 trillion dollars at home, 1 trillion abroad) with the SoftBank Vision Fund being a prime vehicle.

Osborne asks about MBS's personal security. The crown prince reveals he has been the target of two assassination attempts. His anti-corruption purge has made enemies. He's unapologetic about the mass arrests of Saudi's business elite. They were required by law. The economic reform programme will continue as part of his modernisation of Saudi Arabia. He talks at length about the reform of the education system and better treatment of women. Every second MBS sentence is punctuated with 'super'. As in 'super-dangerous' or 'super-great'. The crown prince is a force of nature, serenaded by the high and mighty in English society. Some guests will have departed fearful about the future. By my reckoning, the majority, transfixed by the prospect of mega-deals in a modernising Saudi Arabia, will give him the benefit of the doubt.

The Stud House soirée with MBS removed any lingering doubt that the crown prince was calling the shots in Saudi Arabia. I was struck by how much more confident he had become,

in his command of the English language and his overall
demeanour. His commitment to modernising his country was
impressive, but I was shocked by the casual way he talked about
the risk of war in the region. Overall, this was a young man on
a tear.

TUESDAY, 13 MARCH

A triumph at the British Press Awards. The *FT* has won newspaper of the year, the first time since 2008. Our march towards
1 million paying readers, now well beyond 900,000, must have
been a big selling point to the judges. But so was our journalism. Matt Garrahan scooped business journalist of the year,
Pilita Clark took her third straight prize in environmental
journalism; and we won news team of the year for a series on
the Europopulists, conceived and executed by Roula. I am
beyond proud. This vindicates my bet on 'long form' journalism, deep and original reporting with high impact and value.
Journalism is not about winning prizes. But when you take the
top award in British journalism for the second time, there's
no alternative but to sit back and celebrate.

THURSDAY, 22 MARCH

A snow storm has delayed my flight to New York where I
am due to interview Steve Bannon on stage. Several *FT*
colleagues think it is a very bad idea to give a platform to
America's foremost nationalist-populist.

'I do understand the free-speech argument, and the
strength of opinion against the idea of "no platforming"
anyone,' says one editor. 'However, I wonder, would we ever
invite, say, a Muslim preacher who used hate speech to speak

at an *FT* conference (even if he had created a very popular website)?'*

I'm uneasy with the suggestion that I am guilty of moral equivalence. As a journalist, I have a duty to understand all sides of the political debate, even more so in these polarised times. I've interviewed world leaders with blood on their hands: Uribe in Bogotá, Kagame in Kigali, Putin in Davos. I don't do moral litmus tests. Bannon is not being given a platform as such. He is being invited to sit down for an interview with the editor of the *FT* at our inaugural Future of News conference in the Time Warner building in Manhattan. And I have no intention of giving him an easy ride.

On arrival, I find Bannon characteristically friendly offstage and pugnacious onstage in front of the cameras. He talks up the prospects of a populist breakthrough in Europe, particularly in Italy where two-thirds of the electorate voted for anti-establishment parties led by Matteo Salvini's proto-fascists and the Five Star movement. When I ask why he chose to stand alongside Marine Le Pen, the French far-right leader, Bannon bristles:

SB: 'Why are you describing Marine Le Pen as controversial when she almost won the French presidency?'

LB (prepared): 'Because she's rewritten French history, starting with the deportation of the Jews in 1940.'

Turning to America, Bannon says Donald Trump has his 'sea legs' and will soon revert to a John F. Kennedy presidency which relied on six or seven advisers and dispensed with a White House chief of staff. The analogy with Camelot

---

* Breitbart News, founded by American conservative Andrew Breitbart who conceived it as 'The Huffington Post' of the right. Bannon stepped down as executive chairman in January 2018.

is seductive, but not for the reason Bannon imagines.* It fits my view that President Trump is like a medieval king presiding over a submissive court.

At the invitation of Alec Russell, I wrote an essay in defence of the interview as a journalistic form in the Weekend FT.† *In early September, the editor of the* New Yorker *David Remnick bowed to pressure and abandoned an interview with Bannon onstage. Zanny Minton Beddoes of* The Economist *went ahead.*

THURSDAY, 29 MARCH

Exactly one year has passed since Theresa May made the fateful decision to trigger Article 50 of the Lisbon treaty, setting in motion the UK's withdrawal from the EU. There's been plenty of commotion in the Tory party, but little progress beyond last December's skeletal deal. My explanation: May's government spends 1 per cent of its time negotiating with Brussels and 99 per cent negotiating with itself.

WEDNESDAY, 4 APRIL

The *Wall Street Journal* is reporting that Sir Martin Sorrell, 73, has been suspended pending an investigation into an allegation of improper personal behaviour and possible misuse of company funds at WPP global advertising agency. No detail. This is beyond infuriating. The *FT*'s investigations team has been assembling a comprehensive picture of Sorrell's conduct

---

* Camelot was Jackie Kennedy's description of John F. Kennedy's presidency, based on a 1960 Lerner and Loewe musical inspired in turn by King Arthur's castle and court in English myth.
† 'Was it right to interview Steve Bannon?', *Financial Times*, 30 March 2018.

in the workplace for weeks. We have employees claiming verbal abuse, high-handedness as well as questions about his expenses claims. The *WSJ* story looks like a 'backfire', a PR industry term for starting a small fire to distract attention from a potential conflagration or simply a pre-emptive leak to embarrass Sorrell (no easy task). Madison Marriage and Paul Murphy are deflated. My job is to pick them up, fast. This feels like a far bigger story than I had imagined.

SATURDAY, 14 APRIL

Yet another leak to the *Wall Street Journal* designed to spoil our own investigation into Martin Sorrell. The *Journal* is quoting anonymous sources saying he has stepped down from WPP, the company he founded 33 years ago and built into a world leader. Martin once declared he would 'carry on until they carry me out of the glue factory'. From the American Colony hotel in Jerusalem, where I am on a family cycling holiday in Israel, I send a message to a frustrated Paul Murphy. *We will get to the bottom of the Sorrell saga. Whatever it takes.*

TUESDAY, 17 APRIL

David Cameron has been almost invisible since the debacle of the Brexit referendum, a sensible decision in the circumstances. For the past year or more, he's been self-isolating in a designer shed at his home in Oxfordshire writing his memoirs. He's keeping busy with part-time jobs: chairman of Alzheimer's UK and heading the LSE–Oxford Commission on State Fragility, Growth and Development. Now that the commission's report is complete, he wants some coverage, and maybe a little company, over lunch at the *FT*.

Cameron opens the conversation with an overview of fragile states in Africa, elections, power-sharing and constitutions. It's all very worthy and no doubt important but somewhat secondary to Brexit. Sarah Gordon addresses the proverbial elephant in the room: 'Do you ever wake up at three o'clock in the morning and ask yourself: what have I done?'

'I sleep very soundly,' Cameron replies. Not entirely convincingly.

MONDAY, 23 APRIL

Rajeev Misra arrives with his team from the Softbank Vision Fund, bearing slides and sales pitches. Misra is a former Deutsche Bank trader and top executive who would make P.T. Barnum blush. Among the Vision Fund's top investments are WeWork, the office-space leasing company; Flipkart, India's answer to Amazon; and a dog-walking start-up called Wag into which the Vision Fund has pumped an agreed $300m.

SoftBank's Vision Fund reportedly raised $100bn, thanks in part to Saudi money and the personal backing of MBS. They were the new power in the world's venture capital market, able to amass and deploy funds so colossal that they ended up distorting the whole VC market. But investments like WeWork gradually turned sour and SoftBank itself was forced to dispose of assets – a trend exacerbated by the coronavirus pandemic.

MONDAY, 11 JUNE

Finally, we've nailed the story of Martin Sorrell's downfall. For the past week, I've been editing more than ten drafts of the 4,500-word story co-written by Madison Marriage and Matt Garrahan, a dramatic narrative of how Britain's most famous advertising tycoon was toppled by hubris, allegations of personal misconduct and a sharp decline in his business. Paul Murphy has played an invaluable reporting role too.

This has been one of the most challenging stories of my editorship. I resolved weeks ago that the *FT* would find out why Martin Sorrell was first suspended and later quit the company he built from nothing. The answer is more explosive than I ever imagined, especially inside the cosy London media-business community where allegations of misconduct are magnified tenfold.

Over the past four months, Madison and Paul have interviewed more than 25 people who worked closely with Sorrell, including women who complained of routine verbal abuse in the workplace. (Sorrell has accepted he can be difficult at times, especially in cases of poor performance, but denies abusing or bullying staff.) During the course of interviews with WPP employees past and present, a picture has emerged which includes an alleged visit to a Mayfair brothel a year ago – said to have been witnessed by two employees, one of whom later reported it to the company. This alleged incident, which prompted the board investigation, raised questions about the possible use of company funds and appeared to fit a pattern where personal and company expenses were hard to separate.

The journalistic question is how far we can go into detail about personal conduct, especially since there was no proven use of company funds and the board later described the sums involved as 'wholly immaterial'. This is not merely a matter of legal risk but also a matter of taste. Is it justified to mention the alleged visit to the brothel? Are the witnesses reliable?

Will they testify on our behalf in court if Sorrell sues? And, finally, how can we establish the reliability of sources when many have signed non-disclosure agreements?

Then there is the personal question: I've known Martin for 20 years, swapped regular gossip and socialised with him (and his wife Lady Sorrell, an accomplished businesswoman in her own right and a long-time media contact at the World Economic Forum in Davos). Hell, I've even done him the odd favour, seeing a client or appearing at a conference as a guest speaker. How bad do I feel about exposing his alleged indiscretions?

Not too bad. After all, Sorrell's pay package was £70m in 2015 and £48m in 2016 based on a long-term incentive plan related to five-year share price performance.* Investors are entitled to know exactly why he resigned. We must report the story, but I insist that we give Sorrell credit for what he built at WPP, until recently a great British success story in which he played an indispensable role.

Shortly before the expiry of our deadline on answering questions about his treatment of staff and the Shepherd Market incident, Sorrell calls me on my mobile phone. He won't talk, citing confidentiality clauses in his severance agreement with WPP. But he does say he will 'go nuclear' if the *FT* publishes anything which damages his family. I have some sympathy but I tell him we are going to publish a full story based on four months of solid reporting. We won't back down and he would be best advised to cooperate. Several tense off-the-record phone calls follow. Sorrell denies all charges of impropriety and is adamant that he will say nothing

---

* Sorrell defended his high compensation in an *FT* op-ed headlined 'Mea Culpa – I act like the owner I am', 5 June 2012.

which could breach his NDA or put at risk his severance package worth £20m.

Sorrell appeared to be a victim of 'Founder's Syndrome' where the boss is so synonymous with the company that they forget their accountability to the board and shareholders. No doubt some members of the WPP board wanted Sorrell out, viewing him as overpaid and overstaying his welcome. But one of the great managers of reputations failed to manage his own. Soon after stepping aside, Sorrell launched a new venture, S4Capital. He has always denied any wrongdoing in relation to his departure from WPP and never forgave me for publishing the story.

THURSDAY, 28 JUNE

The Melbourne Mining Conference dinner is a raucous gathering of 500 or so drunken alpha males which takes place every summer at Lord's Cricket Ground. A couple of years ago, John Murray, a grizzled Aussie headhunter whom I met over lunch in Melbourne, asked me to help make the dinner a little more civilised. His suggestion is a one-on-one fireside chat with a top mining executive. Neat idea, I replied. How much are you going to pay me?

We settled on a decent fee which, as usual, goes to a charity of my choice. This year, my interviewee is Jean-Sébastien Jacques, the globe-trotting French CEO of Rio Tinto, the London-based mega-miner. I've had a pre-interview with JSJ, as he is known to colleagues. He came across as a little cocky, but we established something of a rapport talking about leadership, strategy and safety, a big issue given the number of industrial accidents. Tonight at Lord's, all goes smoothly until I ask how he manages his weight given his heavy travel schedule. The one-time rugby player takes umbrage and asks what other sneaky questions I have in mind. Then he demands to see my list. When I decline, JSJ snatches the papers off my lap and refuses to hand them back. The audience loves the stand-off. They laugh even louder when they realise that this whole scene has not been rehearsed.

I never got my question sheet back and I never shook hands on stage with JSJ. In dozens of one-on-one conversations with powerful people, I've never experienced such a display of corporate petulance in public.

FRIDAY, 29 JUNE

A long-delayed lunch with Ian Taylor, one of Britain's wealthiest and least-known businessmen who runs Vitol, the world's largest independent oil trader. Ian is recovering from two bouts of major throat-cancer surgery and finds it hard to eat and drink; even speaking is difficult. Sensing, perhaps, that time is precious, he wants to share his life story with *FT* readers.

We meet at the Goring hotel near Buckingham Palace. Taylor is seated at his usual far corner table, a gaunt figure in dark suit, white shirt and navy blue tie. When I joke about the great, the good and the Goring, he bursts into a fit of coughing-cum-laughter. 'It's a bit of a cheat,' he confesses, 'my office is around the corner.'

As I chew my way through Orkney scallops and Cornish cod, washed down with a glass of white wine, Ian talks about carousing in pre-Chávez Caracas to managing backchannel deals in Kazakhstan, Iraq, Libya and former Yugoslavia. He's had the odd scrape – who doesn't in the oil industry? – but he's kept his nose clean, generously funding the arts and the Conservative party. After the Brexit referendum, Taylor was on David Cameron's resignation honours list. Then news of the honours names leaked. Besieged by the press, he called me for advice.

LB: 'How much does the knighthood matter?'

IT (hesitating): 'Not that much.'

LB: 'Then why would you want to be on the losing team?'

Taylor withdrew his name from Cameron's resignation honours list before it was published. The document included the PM's closest aides and cronies and ranked in notoriety alongside Harold Wilson's in 1976. Ian Taylor died in June 2020.

MONDAY, 9 JULY

Boris Johnson has stepped down as foreign secretary. His resignation letter claims May's proposal for a common rule book with the EU would leave Britain with 'the status of a colony'. I assume that's marginally superior to vassalage, the term favoured by Jacob Rees-Mogg. Johnson is the third Cabinet minister to resign from May's Cabinet. A.J.P. Taylor's adage about the Austro-Hungarian empire comes to mind: the prime minister's position looks hopeless, but not serious. Johnson is biding his time before striking for the leadership. *I'll wager Sir Lynton Crosby will be in his corner.*

THURSDAY, 19 JULY

To the Spanish embassy to celebrate the 20th anniversary of the Centre for European Reform, the leading pro-European think tank in London. Charles Grant has been a rare voice of sanity, well informed and trusted by high-level sources in

Berlin, Brussels and Paris. Charles is also a dogged fighter, more prone to shrug his shoulders than shout. We worked as Brussels correspondents, him for *The Economist*, me for the *FT*. Many of our old Maastricht-era contacts are present tonight, a lot greyer and more depressed about the state of the nation. Lord Kerr, the old fox and Foreign Office mandarin, talks hopefully about a second Brexit referendum. Other ex-diplomats lament how Britain has turned inward. Nobody has a good word to say about Cameron. With Brexit drawing ever closer, it feels less like a celebration, more like a wake.

9–10 AUGUST

A delicate diplomatic mission to New York to see Gillian Tett, US managing editor. Gillian has been a fine reporter-columnist and a five-star ambassador for the *FT* in America. I want her to make the most of all these strengths, but I also want to retain Peter Spiegel, one of our top reporters and editors. He's had his ear bent by James Harding who's just launching a new online media venture called Tortoise. James says he wants Peter to run it and Peter's very attracted by the prospect. *Seriously?* But he would be interested in the US managing editor role in New York. Gillian will not want to move because she is a candidate to be my successor. Some-how, I have to accommodate Gillian and Peter. They are both stars and the *FT* needs both of them. Perhaps I should call Sir Alex Ferguson for advice.

In the event, no call was necessary. Peter took over as US managing editor in 2019, the first American to take the key post. Gillian stayed in New York as a global commentator and chair of the newly formed editorial board in the US.

Fascinating snippet in Tom Mitchell's profile of Wang Qishan, China's one-time anti-corruption tsar and now right-hand man to President Xi. Wang told a visiting VIP delegation from America that he had recently seen *Three Billboards Outside Ebbing, Missouri*, the Hollywood hit movie set in redneck America. Now, he declared, he really did understand Trump supporters. Wang has since become more circumspect, telling a recent Wall Street delegation that 'neither side has to prevail' in the bilateral trade war.

Back in the spring, Wang, 70, was effectively suggesting the Chinese knew the Americans better than they knew themselves. Beijing underestimated Trump, figuring he could be bought off with flattery and a few concessions. 'He [Wang] thought he had it all figured out,' said one executive.

There was less to Wang's burst of humility than met the eye. I later heard from a participant in the Beijing meeting that Wang's tone was in fact hectoring. After mentioning Three Billboards, *he asked the Americans how many Chinese movies or books they had watched or read. Did they not know the first lesson of Sun Tzu's* Art of War: *Know your enemy!*

A week in Tokyo to spend time with the Nikkei leadership, make a weekend diversion to Hong Kong and back to Tokyo for an interview with Prime Minister Shinzo Abe. As usual on my regular trips to Japan, I am bringing one of my potential successors, this time Roula Khalaf. In our customary one-on-one in his office, with just a note-taker and interpreter present, Kita-san says he wants me to be 'the first *FT* editor' in Bracken House where we return in spring next year. He also reveals that he would like to 'start deciding' my successor in 2019. This will be a joint decision.

The process of transition is under way. Stepping down some time in the next 12 months or so feels not only fair but right. I will have done 14 years as editor, longer than any editor since Sir Gordon Newton. My job now is to make the most of the final stretch and help Kita-san manage the succession.

The interview with Shinzo Abe has partly come about via Nikkei channels. If Abe can stay in place until November 2019, he will be the longest-serving leader in Japan's democratic history. An unthinkable proposition when, scandal ridden and sick, he stepped down as prime minister during his first term after one year in office.

As my colleague Robin Harding, a fluent Japanese-speaker, reminds me on the taxi ride to the official residence, Abe's second term has been marked by ruthless top-down control, a tale of progress but few enduring results. Unemployment is down, but the curse of deflation remains. Despite many summits, there is no sign of a deal with Russia over four disputed islands. And Donald Trump has been the 'unreliable boyfriend', withdrawing from the Trans-Pacific Partnership (TPP) trade pact and running down alliances, much to Japan's discomfort.

Abe, 64, is more assured than in our previous two interviews, even allowing himself a rare smile. 'I think it is time to face squarely the major structural issues of the Japanese economy, including the declining birth rate and the ageing society, and I am determined to do that.' On Brexit, Abe reveals that he would be happy to welcome the UK into the TPP deal 'with open arms' – a statement bound to create waves in London. Mindful of my own situation, I ask, diplomatically, about Abe's plans for succession.

'People do not necessarily have to continue in the same career, they can launch their own life,' he says. 'I'm looking forward to enjoying my second life.'

Maybe Abe's sending me a message. If only I spoke Japanese.

TUESDAY, 2 OCTOBER

On our trip to Saudi Arabia, barely three years ago, Roula and I had a quiet lunch with Jamal Khashoggi in Jeddah. He was mildly critical of MBS, but in recent months grew more strident in his regular columns in the *Washington Post*. Now he's gone missing in Istanbul after paying a visit to the Saudi consulate in order to renew his visa.

Jamal Khashoggi was killed in the most brutal manner imaginable, first drugged and then asphyxiated and later dismembered by a Saudi hit squad. The official explanation in Riyadh was that he had been killed in a 'rogue operation' by a team of agents sent to persuade him to return home. The CIA concluded that MBS had ordered the operation, according to multiple US news reports.

THURSDAY, 4 OCTOBER

Victor Mallet, our veteran Asia news editor, has had his application for his Hong Kong visa renewal rejected. This is unprecedented for any foreign correspondent working in HK and bodes ill for press freedom. The sanction has

Beijing's fingerprints all over it, but Carrie Lam gave no clue when I saw her a few days ago over breakfast at her official residence in Hong Kong. Victor had earlier hosted an event at the Foreign Correspondents' Club for Andy Chan, leader of the pro-independence HK National Party which was later banned. China requested that the event be cancelled. The FCC refused. Victor, I later discovered, defended the decision to go ahead in his role as deputy head of the FCC. He appears to have been punished as a result.

Naturally, I deplore Beijing's blatant attempt to muzzle free speech and to deny our application for a visa renewal. But Victor was not acting in his capacity as an *FT* journalist and, so far, there have been no further reprisals against the *FT*. My judgement, after sounding out the *FT*'s China experts James Kynge and Asia editor Jamil Anderlini, is to avoid escalation. We will write a strong editorial, I will lodge a diplomatic protest and appeal with Carrie Lam, but we will not go to court in Hong Kong. My focus is on protecting the integrity of our coverage of China, where we also have an important Chinese-language version of the *FT*. If the Beijing authorities escalate the matter, then we enter different territory.

Victor's visa was not renewed, our diplomatic protests were ignored by the Chinese and Hong Kong authorities. The matter was closed, though the crackdown on free speech and assembly in Hong Kong continued unabated.

FRIDAY, 12 OCTOBER

A dozen *FT* retirees have invited me to lunch at Sticky Mango near Waterloo station. This feels like an appearance before a House of Lords select committee. I talk about our reporting, the digital transformation of the *FT* and editorial independence under Nikkei. Nods of approval. Polite congratulations. What the nosey-parkers really want to know is how long I intend to stay on as editor. *No worries. They will be the last to know.*

18–23 OCTOBER

Nick Clegg calls me from London as I'm in the middle of a Californian breakfast, full of fruit and muesli, talking to a tall man who knows all about artificial intelligence and its impact on journalism. 'What's up, Nick?' To my amazement, he says he's joining Facebook as a senior adviser to Mark Zuckerburg. My first question is how much influence he will really have in a company where 'Zuck' and Sheryl Sandberg run the show. The company's reputation is in the basement after the Cambridge Analytica affair.* I've watched Zuck on stage and he's tone deaf. I've dealt off and on with Sheryl for almost 20 years and she's worse than tone deaf. She doesn't give a flying fig about what other people think, because she assumes, sometimes correctly, that she's ten times smarter than everyone else in the building. *Nick, I fear, will be eaten alive.*

And yet. Facebook must know they're about the most hated tech company in Silicon Valley. They have nearly 3

---

* Cambridge Analytica was the UK political consultancy that powered its voter analysis with unauthorised access to private Facebook data on 50 million people. The group, which worked for the Trump and Vote Leave campaigns, was backed by the American hedge fund billionaire and conservative activist Robert Mercer.

billion users around the world and they have paid next to nothing for two game-changing acquisitions – Instagram and WhatsApp. But they're smart enough, maybe even humble enough, to know they cannot continue on their present path. They need someone who can speak on their behalf without the usual Facebook arrogance and condescension. Nick Clegg, decent, incorruptible and out of luck in Brexit Britain, may just be their man.

TUESDAY, 30 OCTOBER

To Lady Margaret Hall, Oxford, to attend a panel on journalism in honour of Paul McClean. Irene and Peter, his still-grieving parents, are present. Alan Rusbridger, now LMH principal, has organised the event. He has invited his former protégée Janine Gibson, editor in chief at *BuzzFeed* UK who led the *Guardian*'s Pulitzer Prize-winning Snowden coverage. Janine is entertaining, gossipy and well informed about digital media. She would add something special to the *FT*.

This was our first meeting. Others followed. In the spring of 2019, I invited Janine to play a bigger role in the digital transformation of the FT. *This was part of the broader succession plan and transition from my editorship.*

5–9 NOVEMBER

I'm spending a week in New York and Washington with one question in mind: is the US heading into a new Cold War with China? After a dozen meetings with senior officials, intelligence sources and businessmen, mostly organised by my Mandarin-speaking Washington bureau chief Demetri Sevastopulo, I draw up a memo on US–China relations to share with senior colleagues in London.

Trump's America First policy has changed the terms of debate over China. He has won over large sections of the business establishment which is now saying in public what they have long said in private about Chinese protectionism, the lack of a level playing field and intellectual property theft. The Democrats, worried about being outflanked, are even more hardline on China.

Senior US officials are visibly thrilled at the display of power against China on multiple fronts. These include trade tariffs as well as law enforcement at home and abroad against suspected spies and Beijing's attempts to 'turn' Chinese academics working in the US. Measures also include a more robust posture in the (contested) South China Sea; cyber counter-measures against Chinese infractions; and the modernisation of the US nuclear arsenal. This is Cold War-style mobilisation.

There is nervousness in some quarters about Trump's aggressive approach. Some worry about the danger of sidelining allies; others fret about 'recklessness'. But in the political-military complex there is relief that the passivity of the Obama era is over (his failure to challenge China's incursion in the Scarborough Shoal* was described as a 'historic error' where Beijing achieved more in one year than it could normally manage in a decade). Another perspective is that the US missed China's rise because it was so focused on the

---

* The Scarborough Shoal, located in the South China Sea close to the Philippines, is among China's most ambitious claims to date in its drive to fortify remote islands and boost its territorial claims in strategic waters.

war on terror and radical Islam. 'We fell asleep,' one senior US official tells us.

Nobody seems to know what the president thinks or wants in the US–China trade relationship. Some fear he will 'do a Singapore', emerging with a one-and-a-half-page agreement with President Xi, just as he did with Kim Jong-un of North Korea, which ultimately means nothing. Others say at best he will agree not to escalate the tariffs against China, to give breathing space for a deal and avoid undue damage to the economy. Or he may do nothing – and make Xi sweat.

We do know, however, that there is a titanic battle for Trump's ear. Peter Navarro, the China hawk who criticised 'billionaires' and 'unpaid foreign agents of Wall Street' (and helped set up the *FT* interview with Trump) is in one camp; others like Robert Lighthizer, the inscrutable US trade representative, are playing a strategic game of 'decoupling' the US economy from China, starting with high-tech items such as semiconductors but extending to other parts of the US manufacturing supply chain. Still others want an early trade deal for fear of tipping the US economy into a recession.

Finally, Trump is definitely running for a second term, so the relationship between politics, the economic cycle and the stock market (Trump's key 'feel good' barometer) is critically important. If the economy slows down in the next 12 months, Trump's appetite for a trade war with China may diminish. On the other hand, he may believe, like Reagan confronting the Soviet threat, that America can face down its rival. Trump is nowhere near as stupid as he sometimes seems, but as one official said: 'We don't know how far the administration has thought through the second- and third-order consequences of what they are doing.'

Most of these judgements stood the test of time. US–China relations continued to deteriorate. While it was premature to talk of a new Cold War, I still stand by my memo's opening sentence: 'We have entered a new phase of world history similar to the Great Power rivalry of the late 19th century. The US–China relationship, where strategic competition threatens to become strategic conflict, stands centre stage.' The Covid-19 pandemic that broke in 2020 – frequently referred to by Trump as the 'Chinese virus' – became the latest staging post in the conflict.

TUESDAY, 20 NOVEMBER

Ken Hu, the top Huawei executive, has asked to see me. We first met in Davos a decade ago and later on my visit to Shenzhen. Hu wants advice on what Huawei should do now that it is in the cross hairs of the Americans. I tell him Huawei has a massive problem because it is viewed as an arm of the Chinese state. And I offer a prediction based on my visit to Washington: 'You guys are going to get whacked!'

TUESDAY, 27 NOVEMBER

Reed Hastings, the Netflix boss, drops by for lunch in the Bracken room. He's so laid back, he's almost horizontal. But he's a brilliant visionary who has built a business at scale, as impressively as Jeff Bezos at Amazon. For most of our lunch, the Netflix boss errs on the side of modesty. Then the killer quote when one of our reporters asks him to explain Netflix's business model: 'We actually compete with sleep,' replies Hastings, 'and we're winning.'

THURSDAY, 6 DECEMBER

Bombshell out of Canada. Meng Wanzhou, the daughter of Huawei's founder Ren Zhengfei, has been arrested at the request of the US government. Meng is a senior Huawei executive and was in transit. This marks a serious escalation in the Trump administration's efforts to sanction Huawei and pressure Beijing. *I told Ken Hu what was coming, but who would have thought it would have come to this? Certainly not me.*

FRIDAY, 7 DECEMBER

As Theresa May faces her darkest hour on Brexit, there's talk in Whitehall of 1914 and the Guns of August. War was not what people wanted or planned. It just happened. Almost by accident.

The prime minister faces an agonising choice. She can 'stick' with her Brexit withdrawal deal and, against all odds, secure a majority in the House of Commons. She can 'twist' in the hope of winning better terms from Brussels. Or she can 'fold' and arrange for the Brexit question to go back to the people in a second referendum. After the botched election, May's position is almost hopeless. She has to rely on the Democratic Unionist party in Ulster who resemble a group of Bible Belt preachers: literal, implacable, but maybe open to a bribe, electorally speaking of course. I can't see how May secures a majority in the House of Commons. Jeremy Corbyn is a closet Brexiter who won't lift a finger. May could pull her vote and plead with Brussels for concessions, but these will be minimal.

May did indeed pull the vote three days later. The Brexit hardliners declared a partial victory, invoking the spirit of Dunkirk. They conveniently forgot that Dunkirk in 1940 was a defeat leading to a humiliating retreat. An Italian diplomat summed up the May government's position to me: 'In 1940, Britain stood alone, surrounded by enemies. Thank God. In 2018, Britain stands alone, surrounded by friends. OMG.'

SUCCESSION

From my front-row seat, I had watched the world change dramatically during my years as editor. These were turbulent times, starting with the global financial crisis and ending with a crisis of liberal democracy. I had witnessed the rise of China and a concentration of power among the Big Tech companies whose presence in our daily lives was ubiquitous. And I had placed my chips on a few select areas: the Weekend FT, *original, long-form journalism adaptable for print and online, and digital transformation which would drive us past the milestone of 1 million paying readers in 2019.*

The timetable for my departure as editor at the end of the year was in place. The choice of my successor was finally a matter for Kita-san in Tokyo, supported by me. It would consume our attention for much of the year as we considered the separate internal candidates, all outstanding journalists. With 12 months to go as editor I was more determined than ever to make my last year count. Two investigative projects were in the works: one into Wirecard, a German digital payments company and stock market favourite; and the other into UKFast, *a private Manchester-based software company. Both were high risk, high reward. And then there was a long-sought interview with Vladimir Putin in the Kremlin.*

At home, Theresa May would step aside for Boris Johnson, the opportunist par excellence. He rammed a Brexit deal through Parliament after winning a thumping election victory against Corbyn's hard-left Labour party. By December, the UK had reached the point of departure, the first member ever to leave the European Union. In Europe, a more orderly changing of the guard took place. Mario Draghi stepped down as president of the European Central Bank, succeeded by Christine Lagarde, head of the International Monetary Fund. Ursula von der Leyen became the first ever woman president of the European Commission.

SATURDAY, 5 JANUARY

Sunrise over the western Sahara. A brilliant orange glow illuminating the night sky. Watching dawn break in mid-flight to South Africa feels like an epiphany of sorts: I will shortly see Kita-san in Tokyo to talk about the transition and my succession. I want to make my every word count.

Herbert Allen, host for our bike tour in the Cape wine country, has been involved in many of the big media deals for the past 50 years. He's counselled Hollywood moguls and counts Warren Buffett as one of his closest friends. Herb's advice is unvarnished, invariably delivered in a matter-of-fact manner.

HA: 'You remember what Ted Williams used to say?'

LB: 'I've heard of Hank Williams, the country and western singer. But Ted Williams?'

HA: 'Ted Williams always said he wanted to go out on a home run.'

Williams hit a home run for the Boston Red Sox on his last at-bat in 1960, aged 42. He refused to tip his hat to Fenway Park fans who he felt had failed to show sufficient respect for his achievements. I'm no Ted Williams, the best slugger baseball ever produced; but on one matter we stand united. There's no point in hobbling out to the plate with a dodgy back and rickety knees. I, too, want to go out on a home run.

27 JANUARY—3 FEBRUARY, TOKYO

Three years have passed since Nikkei completed the purchase of the *FT*. The honeymoon is over and that's no bad thing. Everything is a little more businesslike. As customary in the new-year visit to Tokyo, I have brought James Lamont, managing editor with a hatful of new editorial initiatives to grow our readership and revenues. And I will base myself in the Nikkei newsroom, where I will again guest-edit the English-language *Nikkei Asian Review*.

The *NAR* transformation from a print magazine to a digital-first operation is tangible evidence of a global media alliance in action. *FT* secondments, led by Michael Stott, a key hire from Reuters, and Chris Grimes, the quiet man from Georgia, have presided over changes which will serve as a beacon for the rest of the Nikkei newsroom.

My regular trips are exhausting but fascinating. Nikkei have a first-class intelligence operation in London, picking up every snippet of gossip about the *FT*. They want to know how we operate down to the most minute detail. I call their approach 'looking under the hood'. Of course, even when you understand how the engine works, you have to know which direction to drive the car. I believe I have helped to develop that narrative road map for Nikkei–*FT*.

Beyond all this detail what matters in Japan are the personal relationships, often forged over dinner where the cuisine is exquisite and the beer, saki and wine flow. These intimate gatherings, in private rooms where shoes are banned in deference to tatami mats and polished wooden floors, are where the real business is done. It has allowed me to bond not just with Kita-san but also with his expected successor, Okada-san, a quietly spoken but forceful character with a keen appreciation of art, culture and history.

My one-on-one meeting with Kita-san takes place as usual in his 30th-floor office, with Mount Fuji just about visible in the distance. A large TV set, permanently set to CNBC markets coverage, sits in the middle of the room, muted. Kita-san dispenses with his customary small talk and informs me that I will step down at the end of the year, six or so months after the move to Bracken House. I respond by quoting Ted Williams: I want to go out on a home run.

Kita-san and I have reached an agreement. I can be sure our conversation will remain confidential, and I know the timetable for my succession. I can now focus on my last months, at ease with the decision and with myself.

WEDNESDAY, 6 FEBRUARY

Dan McCrum is one of our most tenacious financial journalists, a former Citigroup equity research analyst with a grasp of numbers and spreadsheets. For more than three years he's been digging into Wirecard, a Munich-based payments-processing company recently valued at more than Deutsche Bank and regarded as one of Germany's rare high-tech successes. Doubts about Wirecard's accounting have long plagued the company, but Dan's probing and his stories have been met by legal threats, intimidation and orchestrated attacks on social media. Wirecard have never sought to engage with the *FT*, or indeed with me. Today, after hours of legal consultation, I approve a damning story showing how a top Wirecard executive based in Singapore inflated revenues and profits growth. Our story is based on whistleblower accounts and an unpublished interim report by a top Singapore law firm, Rajah & Tann. This has been a Herculean effort, with heavy legal risk, conducted by Dan and Paul Murphy in the investigations team and Nigel Hanson, in-house lawyer.

The FT story triggered a collapse in Wirecard's share price. German investors were outraged. Wirecard accused our reporters of colluding with short sellers and successfully lobbied BaFin, the German financial regulator, to impose an unprecedented ban on short selling. Wirecard also engaged Herbert Smith Freehills, the blue-chip London law firm. As a publicly traded company in the prestigious Dax index, they had no problem spending several million pounds trying to stifle a negative story. The FT did not have that kind of money. And so began a stand-off which would consume more of my time than any single story in 2019. As events would later show, it was worth every penny and every hour.

THURSDAY, 7 FEBRUARY

Lunch with the Russian ambassador at the embassy in Notting Hill. The borscht is tasty but the best dish is reserved for last. The Big Guy may be ready to see you in Moscow, says Ambassador Yakovenko with his teddy-bear smile. I try to hide my satisfaction. I've been trying to secure a sit-down interview with Vladimir Putin for five years. All requests have either been politely rejected or the terms have never been right. Putin must be ready to talk. *We'll figure out why later. For now, I'll start prepping. Pronto.*

TUESDAY, 12 MARCH

Many believe that Martin Selmayr is the most powerful man in Brussels. I suspect he does too. The German secretary general of the European Commission is a master manipulator, a backroom bureaucrat who was formerly Jean-Claude Juncker's chief of staff. Today, Selmayr has no need for overt displays of power as he delivers a damning verdict on Britain's handling of the Brexit negotiations to Alex Barker and me.

Theresa May, he says, is trapped by her own red lines which offer no room for the *compromis à la belge*, where no one understands what's been agreed but everyone emerges feeling they're a winner. *I saw that happen more than once in my days in Brussels.* Selmayr says the Commission has tried hard to accommodate the UK position but it's proven impossible. Everyone, including Juncker, has given up on the idea of a second referendum. Brexit will stand, he says, 'but the only people who applaud Brexit are Trump and Putin.'

Selmayr cannot resist a touch of condescension. 'Britain is a prisoner of its past. You believe that British exceptionalism will carry the day and that EU rules will somehow be waived. This will not happen.'

We heard the same message from every bureaucrat in Brussels. One official likened the May government's approach to being a member of a tennis club who suddenly wanted to play by golf-club rules. It was hard to disagree.

MONDAY, 1 APRIL

John Ridding announces that the *FT* has passed its milestone of 1 million paying readers. Finola McDonnell, head of PR and marketing, has arranged for miniature bottles of signature pink champagne to be dispatched to staff, with a tag attached: 'Thank you.' *The timing – April Fool's Day – is unfortunate.*

FRIDAY, 5 APRIL

A call to Mathias Döpfner about the Wirecard case. Mathias still hasn't quite got over the disappointment at losing out to Nikkei at the last minute in the bid to buy the *FT*, but we've remained good friends. I need advice because Wirecard has mobilised gullible sections of the German press against the *FT*. They have also lobbied BaFin, the German financial regulator, which has filed a criminal complaint against our reporters Dan McCrum and Stefania Palma and several short sellers accusing them of market manipulation. The company has also filed suit in Munich. Their claims are utter rubbish but my legal bills are mounting. Mathias says keep calm, avoid personal attacks, stick to the facts. Don't make this a battle between the Anglo-Saxon press and the German establishment. I make a vow to stay cool, but this story is becoming personal for Dan, Paul and, dare I say, me.

12–21 APRIL, LUCKNOW, DELHI, MUMBAI

Narendra Modi's face is everywhere in India, in newspapers, on television and on social media – a cult of personality in India not seen since Indira Gandhi. Now, thanks to persistent lobbying by our Delhi bureau chief, Amy Kazmin, the *FT* has been granted an hour with India's prime minister in his official residence at 7, Lok Kalyan Marg, formerly Race Course Road, in New Delhi. More than five years have passed since my last trip to India, and my last encounter with Modi, in his chief minister's office in Ahmedabad in his home state, Gujarat. The prime minister, immaculately attired with an orange kurta and grey trousers matched by a trim white beard, greets me like an old friend. We pose for photographs in his newly refurbished office overlooking a lawn with strutting peacocks.

Modi has a vision of an urbanised, industrialised and modernised India, but his economic record to date has been patchy. His hard-edged rhetoric on corruption has unnerved the strutting multimillionaires in Mumbai and dented business confidence. People are afraid, I tell Modi. He smiles grimly. 'If the sun rises over darkness and people are afraid, it is not the fault of the sun.'

Modi speaks Hindi rapidly, interspersed with English and piles of statistics such as the length of road and rail track, the number of gas cylinders and toilets delivered to rural areas. His answer to my first question about agricultural reform takes the best part of 15 minutes. Every now and then, he stares at me, checking whether I have absorbed his message. The earlier smiles have disappeared.

On foreign affairs, Modi wants a seat at the top table, alongside China, Russia, Japan and the US. This is the world's new permanent five, rather than the UN Security Council which includes the UK and France, he suggests ('That era has gone'). At the recent G-20 meeting, Modi tells me proudly, two separate meetings were held between India, Russia and China, and India, Japan and the US. 'India was the common factor in both meetings.'

Mahatma Gandhi once said that 'India lives in its villages.' Modi has shifted that narrative to an 'aspirational nationalism'. He has lit expectations among hundreds of millions, particularly the younger generation; but the transition to a market-based digital economy will inevitably produce winners and losers. That is not something which Indian political culture has ever really embraced.

On departure, Modi hands me an envelope and urges me to open it. I assume it's a copy of the official snapshot on arrival today. In fact, the envelope also contains official photographs of our first meeting in Ahmedabad. A touching memento, but also perhaps a gentle reminder: we have you on our files.

I departed not much the wiser about how Modi would bring about his vision of a modern India, but I had no doubt regarding his determination to make his country a front-rank power. He kept his Hindu nationalism pretty much under wraps, but there was still an edge of menace about the man who, lest we forget, had his finger on a nuclear button. While Modi would soon win a crushing election victory, his second term would be marked by a weaker economy and rising religious intolerance. Modi joined Trump and Xi in the ranks of the world's strongmen, albeit running the world's largest democracy.

TUESDAY, 23 APRIL

Carl-Henric Svanberg, the perpetually tanned Swedish head of the European Round Table of Industrialists, is one of the more thoughtful businessmen I know. He regularly comes to my office for a catch-up; Victoria and I often attend his Christmas 'Glogg' party at his home in Kensington. As chairman of BP, Carl-Henric, as he insists on being called, had to clean up the Deepwater Horizon mess, at a cost of tens of billions of dollars. Now he's trying to mobilise Europe's business and political establishment behind an enlightened 'stakeholder' capitalism, a third way between authoritarian China and protectionist America. Europe may have heavier taxation and suffer from more red tape than America, but he insists that the European tortoise will overtake the American hare. 'Over time, if inequality keeps on growing,' he says, 'it will come back and bite them.'

MONDAY, 29 APRIL

Sebastian Payne, our irrepressible political reporter, is hunting down Tory leadership candidates for me to meet. Michael Gove might be up for an evening drink. Jeremy Hunt is biddable. Boris Johnson is lying doggo. I will pass on Dominic Raab.*

First audition over dinner at the Cinnamon Club is Sajid Javid, appointed today as home secretary. The son of a bus driver, 'the Saj' grew up in Bristol, went to a comprehensive school, started reading the *FT* aged 14 (so he tells me) and made a few million as a trader at Deutsche Bank. May will be gone by autumn, he predicts. *Really, that long?* Only Sajid Javid can restore and expand the pool of black, Asian and multi-ethnic voters, he assures me. He is the man to see off Jeremy Corbyn who, on present trends, could win not just one election but two. *Surely a stretch?* By the end of our main course, the home secretary has blitzed through policing statistics, immigration, terrorism and Brexit. He's mastered his briefs, but there's not many laughs. Is there any *FT* advice at this stage? 'Try smiling,' I reply.

---

* Dominic Raab, Conservative MP for Esher and Walton, was a Brexiter hardliner who rose to be foreign secretary in the Johnson Cabinet.

FRIDAY, 17 MAY

A reception for the great, good and not so good on our return to Bracken House. We had planned a roof-terrace party but outside there's torrential rain. Turnout is a little disappointing but Richard Lambert, Geoff Owen and Marjorie Scardino are present, as are Kita-san and a small Japanese delegation looking proud and happy. Speeches are mercifully brief. Lots of nods, winks and the odd question about my likely tenure as editor. Victoria has helped me come up with a flattering rebuff: 'Your sources are obviously a lot better than mine.'

FRIDAY, 24 MAY

Theresa May has suffered cruel and unusual punishment at the hands of her party. Six months of pleading with European leaders for a better Brexit deal, alongside six months of humiliating defeats in Parliament. Watching her resignation speech outside 10 Downing Street, face etched with tears, I'm impressed by the stoicism. One sentence in her speech sticks in my craw, maybe hers too: 'Compromise is not a dirty word.' Just after 5.30pm, the draft *FT* editorial arrives on my computer screen for inspection. 'To coin a predecessor's phrase, Theresa May was the future once . . . She wanted to deliver Brexit, to do so via agreement with the EU, and to keep her party together. These three goals proved irreconcilable.'

WEDNESDAY, 29 MAY

Jeremy Hunt arrives for breakfast at the Corinthia hotel with a Union Jack badge in his left lapel and not a hair out of place. The ex-head boy at Charterhouse looks almost every inch like

THE POWERFUL AND THE DAMNED

Britain's foreign secretary. Whether he is Britain's next prime minister is another matter. Hunt is running as the 'sensible candidate' in the Tory leadership race, but not many of his arguments make much sense. He claims he could secure a better Brexit deal. But there's no wiggle room, I protest. On the contrary says Hunt, the EU would cut some slack for a new Tory leader, with the exception of Boris Johnson. 'He has no friends in Europe,' says Hunt, who succeeded Johnson as foreign secretary.

On that last point, we are in broad agreement. Johnson was the most undiplomatic diplomat in his brief stint at the Foreign and Commonwealth Office. I ask Hunt about political leadership in the age of populism. Are there lessons to be drawn from Nigel Farage's UKIP success? Hunt singles out Trump's tweets which reach a target audience every morning. Saying outrageous things is the fastest way to dominate the news and conversation. 'Being technocratic and boring does not work.'

Is the foreign secretary, the man in charge of Her Majesty's diplomatic service, suggesting we have reached the end of rational debate?

'No, no, no,' says Hunt, rapidly settling the bill.

I am not so convinced.

Mid-afternoon, I'm on the Eurostar to Paris to attend the Élysée palace ceremony where President Macron will award the Légion d'Honneur to Mario Draghi. The French establishment gathers in the early-evening sunshine, headed by former President Nicolas Sarkozy, Michel Camdessus, former head of the IMF, several ex-heads of the French treasury and Mark Carney as the Anglosphere's chief representative. Macron describes Draghi as the 'son' of Europe's founding fathers, Monnet, Schuman and Spinelli. 'Whatever it takes' will go down in history as the words which saved the European economy from drowning.

Draghi, visibly moved, notes that Sarkozy's support for an Italian for the top job at the ECB was critical. Twice, he acted in response to existential threats to the euro, first the sovereign debt crisis and then Greece, despite advice from some quarters to cut Athens loose. *We all know but cannot say the word: Germany.* Draghi makes a final political point: he always acted within the central bank's mandate, a judgement vindicated by the European Court of Justice.

THURSDAY, 6 JUNE

From his sun-bleached office on Queen Victoria Street, Matt Hancock, health secretary, has his eyes on Downing Street. The job of prime minister is something of a long shot, but he takes inspiration from Macron and Obama. 'If you don't try, you will never know.'

George Osborne's protégé hails from Chester not Charterhouse, which may be why he is taking shots at Jeremy Hunt ('terrible flip-flops'). Still only 40, Hancock oozes ambition, laced with a matey charm. He's rightly contemptuous of May's political skills, listing a litany of errors like the promise of a confirmatory vote that threatened a second referendum in Scotland which he considers a terrible outcome. 'The Union is much more important than Brexit.'

On my way out, I spot a copy of Pete Buttigieg's presidential campaign book, *Shortest Way Home: One Mayor's Challenge and a Model for America's Future*, strategically placed on the minister's desk. Like Buttigieg, Hancock is fluent and smart but now is not the year.

SUNDAY, 9 JUNE

One million people are marching in the streets in Hong Kong. The crowds are getting bigger by the day. Carrie Lam triggered the protests by pushing through a bill which allows for extradition of Hong Kongers to the mainland. She's now refusing to pull the bill and ruling out an amnesty to allow a debate about democracy in Hong Kong. The longer the stand-off endures, the greater the risk of intervention by China. *Lam is acting under orders from Beijing, but her lack of political skills, evident in my first meeting last year, has made a difficult situation impossible.*

THURSDAY, 20 JUNE

I have been invited to join mourners attending the funeral of Jeremy Heywood at Westminster Abbey. Five prime ministers – Major, Blair, Brown, Cameron and May – are in attendance, joined by Nick Clegg. A rare moment of political unity in a fractured nation. Heywood was just 56 when he succumbed to cancer. Every speaker, in person and on video-tape, pays tribute to the Cabinet secretary's intellect, industry and ability to manipulate the strings of power, irrespective of which party held them. Gordon Brown delivered the best line: 'In May 2010, I left a handwritten note to David Cameron saying something like "The country is in good hands, Jeremy is running it."'

Not even Heywood, the most powerful civil servant in the country for almost a decade, could resolve the divisions in the Cabinet, the Tory party and the country over Brexit. Many other gifted civil servants such as chief UK Brexit negotiator Ollie Robbins would

*find themselves blamed for supposedly selling out to Brussels or
simply crushed by the internal contradictions in the government's
position.*

TUESDAY, 25 JUNE

Mario Draghi has been maddeningly elusive these past few
weeks. I've been trying to coax him into an interview with
the *FT* which in my mind will be his last will and testament.
Mario has procrastinated, anxious to sit down but unsure
about the timing. The faltering European economic recovery has introduced an extra complication. Like me, Mario is
thinking about his legacy. Finally he agrees to a meeting in
his office on the 40th floor of the ECB's new skyscraper
tower overlooking Frankfurt and the Rhine.

Through towering glass windows, the view of the city is
magnificent despite the sweltering summer heat. To the north,
nestling in the hills, sits the Bundesbank, Germany's central
bank, a dour concrete monument to economic orthodoxy
based on controlling inflation and protecting savers. Draghi's
opening line, no doubt rehearsed, alludes to the difference in
architecture and philosophy. 'This [ECB building] embodies
our values,' he says, 'transparency and independence.'

Under Draghi, the ECB has turned from the German
Bundesbank into the Fed, an institution whose instruments
for crisis management extend far beyond taming inflation.
His loose monetary policies and bond-buying on a massive
scale reassured financial markets, even if low interest rates
punished savers. What he won't say, despite my pushing, is
that he's been in permanent warfare with the Bundesbank
hawks led by Jens Weidmann. They tried but failed to block
his every move in the eurozone crisis, mobilising the

German media who have caricatured him as a vampire sucking the blood from German savers. Yet, unlike his French predecessor Jean-Claude Trichet, Mario is not afraid of the Germans. He cut a deal with Berlin: criticise in public, go along in private.

We both know this. We've talked about these tensions privately for several years, but Mario won't go public. As a result, even after 90 minutes of conversation, there's no bite in the interview, nothing truly memorable. Mario seems to be holding back, perhaps uneasy about the presence of Claire Jones, our ECB correspondent. I agree, as is customary, to have all of his quotes approved before publication, a courtesy the *FT* accords central bank governors who rarely conduct on-the-record interviews because every word can influence financial markets. We therefore have no timetable for publication. Irritating but manageable. Anyway my mind is on Moscow and an even bigger interview with President Putin.

Mario came to my office for a second-round interview in September with no else present. It was not ideal because I risked 'bigfooting' my own correspondent. On the other hand I knew Mario better than anyone and we wanted the exit interview for the FT, *which appeared later that month.*

WEDNESDAY, 26 JUNE, MOSCOW

The choreography for an interview with Vladimir Putin is worthy of the Bolshoi Ballet; every step rehearsed, nothing left to chance. Our stage tonight is the Cabinet room in the Kremlin Senate building next to Red Square. It is an imposing chamber with statues of the four great imperial tsars: Nicholas I, Alexander II, Catherine the Great and Peter the

Great overlooking the president's working desk. The *FT* interview with Putin will take place at a small round table nearby, filmed by Russian television and broadcast the following evening. It is his first serious interview with a western publication in several years.

I have done more prepping for this interview than usual. Bill Burns, a former US ambassador in Moscow and one of the top career diplomats of his generation, has helped with tips on Putin's psychology. Bob Zoellick, a mentor for three decades and another Russia expert, has advised me to stay on the high ground and avoid the prosecutorial style. Tony Barber, a former Reuters correspondent in Moscow, has kindly responded to my request for help on the interview, including what would turn out to be the killer question.

Shortly after 6.30pm, our Russian interpreter Henrietta arrives in the foyer of the Metropol hotel. Henry Foy, *FT* Moscow bureau chief, says she is the best in town, selected to interpret for David Cameron on his maiden trip to Moscow in 2011. I intend to ask Putin about the attempted assassination of former GRU double agent Sergei Skripal. Is Henrietta familiar with the phrase 'fair game'? *She is, but she may not quite use those words with the president.*

Putin is running late, as usual. Then the official summons. Rain is lashing down outside as we take a four-minute taxi ride to the Kremlin. After my interviews with Dmitry Medvedev and Sergei Ivanov, I've become vaguely familiar with the vast long corridors with red carpets. We enter a large room with yellow-painted walls, white stucco ceilings and a table crammed with cakes, sweets, tea and coffee which I privately dub the Polonium Suite. From there, we take in the grandeur of the Cabinet room. Four fearsome security guards walk in, size up the foreign visitors and occupy four spare wooden chairs. For the next hour, Henry and I are left standing, making small talk with Kremlin flunkeys.

Three hours later, just after 11.30pm, Vladimir Putin makes his entrance. A short, compact figure with a touch of swagger. 'Welcome to the Kremlin, Mr Barber,' he says in barely discernible English. *(What is it with these softly-spoken strongmen?)*

'Thank you, Mr President,' I answer in English, before breaking into German.

LB: 'It's good to see you again, after our meeting over dinner in London in 2013.'

VVP (switching to German): 'Where did you learn German?'

LB: 'I was a student in Germany where I was a translator and interpreter. But I studied at Oxford: German and modern history.'

VVP: 'What is modern history?'

LB: 'At Oxford, modern history in my day began in AD 300.'

VVP (staring blankly): 'What do *you* think is modern history?'

LB (brief pause as I unscramble my mind): 'Everything after 1989.'

VVP: 'OK, let's begin.'

Over the next 90 minutes, the interview burns like a slow fuse. I ask whether Putin's risk appetite has grown the longer he has remained in power. Risk must always be well justified, he replies. 'But this is not the case when one can use the Russian phrase: "He who does not take risk never drinks champagne."' *The classic KGB double negative.*

When I ask Putin about Russian involvement in Venezuela, a flash of irritation appears on his otherwise deadpan face: 'It seemed we had started so well . . .' he says, seemingly more in sorrow than anger. I ask if Sergei Skripal is fair game.

Putin remains impassive, refusing to be provoked. He evades the questions, talks in generalities and then, almost as an afterthought, says: 'This spy story is not worth five kopecks . . .'

LB: 'Some people might say that a human life is worth more than five pennies.'

Putin stares straight through me and says grimly. 'Treason is the gravest crime possible and traitors must be punished. I am not saying the Salisbury incident is the way to do it. But traitors must be punished.'

When I pose the Tony Barber question the mask slips a notch further: there has been the populist backlash against elites and the establishment with Brexit, Trump's election, the rise of the AfD in Germany, but how long can Russia remain immune?

Putin replies that the purpose of government – never to be forgotten by those in power – is to create a 'stable, normal, safe and predictable life' for ordinary people. Western elites forgot this lesson and lost touch with their populations. 'So the liberal idea has become obsolete. It has come into conflict with the interests of the majority of the population.'

I cast a glance at Henry. We have our story: on the eve of the G-20 summit in Osaka, Putin has declared the end of the liberal idea. His words, at this moment in history when liberal democracy is under assault from nationalism and populism in Europe and America, will cause a firestorm.

Throughout the Kremlin interview, Putin played statesman, a model of self-discipline, never raising his voice, never banging the table, always composed. It was at times an unnerving experience, even though we had prepared for our private encounter with the master of destabilisation. My question about the populist threat in Russia somehow struck a nerve, a sign perhaps that Intel's Andy Grove was right when he said: only the paranoid survive.

Postscript: The Kremlin made no effort to doctor the transcript apart from a request to change Putin's intimate use of 'Donald' to 'President Trump', and a plea – which we rejected – to remove a direct criticism of Angela Merkel regarding her refugee policy. Russian TV carried the full interview. Our story was followed up around the world and was the talk of the G-20 summit in Japan.

TUESDAY, 2 JULY

Breakfast with Philip Hammond at the Corinthia hotel. The chancellor, accompanied by his special adviser Sonia Khan,* has abandoned all pretence. He wants revenge against the Brexit rebels led by Boris Johnson who have toppled Theresa May and are about to shunt him from office. Hammond has been defence minister, foreign secretary and chancellor of the exchequer. Once powerful, he now stands damned by the majority of his own party. As the waiter brings another pot of English tea, I sense Hammond's inner fury as he contemplates his fall. He stood by his Remainer principles, he stood by Theresa May, only to be sabotaged by the Brexiters in his own Cabinet. From his new position on the back-

---

* Sonia Khan, treasury political adviser, worked for Hammond and his successor Sajid Javid until she was abruptly and publicly fired by Dominic Cummings, Boris Johnson's top adviser, for disloyalty on Brexit. Escorted under armed guard from Downing Street, she became unwillingly the first example of the US-style 'perp walk' in British politics.

benches, he is determined to mete out the same treatment to the new government under Boris Johnson.

TUESDAY, 23 JULY

One of the most difficult decisions of my editorship. I have called in RPC, an independent law firm, to investigate Wirecard's accusations that our reporters have engaged in collusion with short sellers. My hand was forced after a secretly recorded tape emerged of one of our sources claiming he knew the content and timing of the *FT*'s stories. Paul Murphy insists it's a set-up. I am confident that the charges are rubbish and I stand fully by the lead reporter, Dan McCrum. Some colleagues think I have overreacted, but my commitment to gold-standard journalism means we have to show in public that the *FT* is above suspicion.

The RPC investigation lasted more than two months and found no evidence of collusion. The day I received the report, I gave the go-ahead to a devastating 2,000-word feature by Dan McCrum laying bare Wirecard's dodgy relationship with third parties in Dubai, Ireland and the Philippines. Internal documents suggested that sales and revenues at these key Wirecard units may have been invented. His revelations forced Wirecard to call in KPMG to conduct an independent audit, separate from EY, its long-time auditor. The 74-page report raised yet more questions about its accounting. In June 2020, Wirecard imploded after the company was forced to admit that nearly $2bn of cash, supposedly parked in two Philippine banks, had gone missing. After four years of investigation, the FT had uncovered a gigantic fraud, the equivalent of Germany's Enron. It was one of my proudest moments.

WEDNESDAY, 24 JULY

I still find it hard to believe that Boris Johnson has made it to Downing Street. He was an agreeable buffoon in Brussels as the *Daily Telegraph* correspondent, though adept at hiding his ambition. Maybe that's why we never took him seriously, even when he was mayor of London. *Big mistake.* The prime minister is rattling on today about higher wages, more spending on the police and NHS, and a new deal to 'level up' the regions. Most eye-catching is his 'no ifs or buts' commitment to leave the EU by 31 October. 'The doubters, the doomsters, the gloomsters – they are going to get it wrong again,' says the would-be Winston Churchill. 'The people who bet against Britain are going to lose their shirt because we are going to restore trust in our democracy.'

Betting against Britain? I assume he's talking (wrongly) about the FT.

WEDNESDAY, 31 JULY

Victoria and I are attending the Google Camp conference in Sicily with top-class speakers from every corner of the world. The British tabloids have gone to town over the number of private jets stacked up at Palermo airport and a bogus story about Prince Harry lecturing his audience in bare feet. They've missed the real story. HRH and his bride Meghan Markle, I hear reliably, are utterly disillusioned with public life in Britain and seriously contemplating leaving the country for a new life. *I doubt this story will move sterling but it will certainly rock the British establishment.*

Boris Johnson wants to prorogue Parliament for five weeks in order to curtail debate on the Brexit deal he hopes to strike with Brussels. Dominic Cummings is no doubt the architect of this plan to ram a deal through the House of Commons. It's time to fight back with a stiffer than usual *FT* editorial, reminding the prime minister how representative govern-ment works. Knowing that Johnson is a student of history, I insert a passage which draws from John Stuart Mill on the role of MPs.* 'Their part is to indicate wants, to be an organ for popular demands, and a place of adverse discussion for all opinions relating to public matters . . . and to check by criticism, and eventually by withdrawing their support, those high public officers who really conduct the public business.'

Johnson backed down on prorogation, no doubt in deference to J.S. Mill.

Conservative party conference in Manchester. Dominic Cummings wanders into the room wearing a grey tracksuit with trainer shoes. He cuts the same scruffy figure who strolled into the *FT* a few weeks before the Brexit referendum. Now he is the insurrectionary at the epicentre of power in Downing Street. His eyes are sunken, deprived of sleep due to the high political drama but also to an unspecified stomach problem. (He's said to have promised his wife to

---

* John Stuart Mill (1806–73), English philosopher, is best known as a proponent of utilitarianism.

have an operation after 31 October, the latest deadline which the government has imposed for completing a Brexit deal or simply leaving the EU, popularly but misleadingly known as 'crashing out'.)

My opening question – 'Robespierre or Rasputin?' – elicits a weak smile. Then I ask Cummings why he has encouraged incendiary language like 'Surrender Bill', 'capitulation' and 'constitutional coup'. (The latter he denies, though I happen to know it was used in Cabinet by Jacob Rees-Mogg.) Cummings defends the importance of powerful rallying cries, citing the '99' call practised by the Lions in the 1974 rugby series against the Springboks. (When one forward shouted '99', the pack led by the legendary Irish lock forward Willie John McBride would retaliate en masse against on-field violence, fists flying.)

Cummings seems indifferent to the prospect of violence, or maybe he's realistic like the lions in South Africa. He says the UK should have had two referenda, one on exit and the second on the terms of departure. Now, the UK must leave, 'no ifs and buts because the health of democracy depends on it'. Holding a second referendum would see people killed in the streets, he says. He also predicts that Leave would win anyway, probably by 65 to 35, a far bigger margin than in 2016. Then again everywhere would be 'a smoking ruin'.

Cummings speaks in a matter-of-fact, almost diffident way, with dull Durham intonations. It occurs to me that I am watching a modern-day Puritan, certain in his cause, severe in his judgement. He has correctly identified that Brexit has led to polarisation and deadlock, to the point where Parliament has all but ceased to function. But his anti-constitutional remedies like prorogation and his apocalyptic predictions of violence leave me shocked and depressed. The space for rational debate in British politics has vanished. *Maybe Jeremy Hunt was right after all.*

FRIDAY, 18 OCTOBER

Boris Johnson has struck his Brexit deal. He has antagonised and charmed the Europeans, stared down the Brexiters and sold the DUP down the river. The Irish backstop has been lost in a mist of claim and counterclaim. Under the deal, Northern Ireland will be subject to EU Single Market rules, at best legally semi-detached from the rest of the UK. An inevitable but (constitutionally) dangerous outcome to prevent a hard border between north and south.

Late in the afternoon, long after the dirty deal was struck, my mobile phone rings. It is Boris Johnson. He is courteous to a fault, abandoning the faux bonhomie usually reserved for me and fellow journalists. Do I have a few seconds to discuss his deal? Well, prime minister, I respond, it's going to take a bit longer than that.

After ten minutes of back and forth, it is time to talk about the world after Brexit. To govern is to choose. Will Britain stay close to the EU or consciously diverge?

'The choice is not a binary one,' he replies, aping the language of Theresa May. In his mind, everything is *sui generis* (Ancient Greek or Latin references are obligatory in any conversation with Johnson). The UK can support the EU on foreign policy like Iran, take a Singapore option on boosting pharmaceuticals and carve out bespoke trade deals with the rest of the world. This is the familiar story of pick-and-choose politics, exactly what European officials have long assured me is impossible. Johnson was once asked about his position on Europe: 'I'm pro-secco and anti-pasta,' he joked. *Nothing much has changed.*

SATURDAY, 19 OCTOBER

I'm listening to a rare Saturday sitting of Parliament to debate Johnson's Brexit deal. The prime minister repeats the old saw that the British have been half-hearted Europeans. There's so much more to the story of Britain's troubled membership of the EU, as I witnessed first hand in my time as the *FT*'s Brussels correspondent. The British had far more influence than the tabloid caricature of perpetual victim. Now, as I prepare to step down as editor, it's time to make one last trip to Brussels. I want to set the record straight.

THURSDAY, 24 OCTOBER

My trip to Brussels begins with a private dinner hosted by my old friend Jean-Claude Piris who served for 22 years as the top EU lawyer. A permanent presence at dozens of European summits, Jean-Claude has seen everyone – Thatcher, Kohl, Mitterrand, Blair, Chirac, Merkel – in action. He knows every nook and cranny of every EU treaty from Maastricht to Lisbon, via Amsterdam. 'Britain's departure is an act of self-harm, a strategic mistake,' he tells me. But he detects little appetite in Europe for a second referendum: 'Mentally, people have moved on.'

Next day, I do the rounds with Alex Barker. He's arranged meetings with half a dozen of the wisest Eurocrats, most of whom have dealt with the British first hand during the Brexit negotiations. The exchanges are invariably stimulating, often depressing.

'The most surreal aspect [of Brexit] is that your political class has gone rogue,' says one Belgian veteran, citing the breakdown of relationships between ministers and civil servants, once Britain's greatest strength. 'There is a complete disconnect with the politicians who don't want to hear things any more. You now have the worst possible opposition [Jeremy Corbyn] and a terrible government. Imagine if that happened to Germany.'

Another diplomat describes British ministers as 'empty suits' contributing nothing to debate, but several confess to being mildly seduced by Johnson's charm, especially after the Brexit deal when he spoke to EU leaders about his schoolboy days in Brussels and his daughter singing to Beethoven's 'Ode to Joy', the European anthem. 'It was a beautiful moment,' says one veteran.

It was mildly humiliating having to listen to Eurocrats denigrating Britain's ruling class. But Brexit had rent the UK asunder, leaving everyone diminished, if not immediately impoverished. Once again, I cursed David Cameron's decision to hold a referendum. On the flight to Tokyo, I wrote a long personal essay on Britain's troubled relationship with Europe, declaring that 'the UK desperately needs a new narrative, one that reunites the country and sets a course for whole- and half-hearted Europeans alike.'

26 OCTOBER–2 NOVEMBER

Touching down in Tokyo just after 7am, I realise that this will be my 14th trip to Japan since April 2015. I wonder if I will miss the routine: the old man in the arrivals lounge holding my name sign. Not a word of English, just a nod and a gesture to follow him to the car park. A brief wait before the modest car-cum-minibus pulls up. A chug-chug through minimal traffic to the Palace hotel, followed by impeccable service at the reception. The temptation to go to sleep, to be resisted at all costs. Instead, a half-mile swim in the hotel pool and an hour's walk or jog round the Imperial Palace, hopefully in spring or winter sunshine. On reflection, I am ready to move on, at peace with myself but on edge about how the final act in my editorship will play out: the choice of my successor.

The last time I suffered a bout of nerves like this was in the run-up to my first meeting with Kita-san in my office in the summer of 2015, one week after Nikkei's purchase of the *FT*. Fortunately, I have a distraction: England v New Zealand All Blacks in the Rugby World Cup semi-final. Eddie Jones's stars are battering the best team in the world. I'm watching in my hotel bar with JP Rathbone, my partner in travel in Latin America, both witnesses to one of the great English sporting achievements. I assume the final against South Africa ought to be a stroll, until I receive texts from two South African business pals, Johann Rupert and Ivan Glasenberg, both of whom know their rugby and appear quietly confident.*

The meeting with Kita-san goes smoothly. We are in agreement that Roula will be the next editor. She has been an outstanding deputy these past three years and more, universally respected in the newsroom and a fine journalist in her own right. She will be the first female editor of the *FT*. Now we must avoid loose lips and prepare for Kita-san's visit to

---

* Johann Rupert, chairman of the luxury group Richemont; Ivan Glasenberg, chief executive of Glencore, the world's largest commodities trader. Their hunch was right: South Africa whipped England 32–12 in the final.

London to anoint Roula, but the unenviable task of breaking the news to disappointed candidates falls to me.

My essay on Brexit and Europe has appeared on the front of the *Weekend FT*. Many favourable emails. Alec Russell has done a fine job with the edits. I wonder if he has spotted the hidden message in my headline: 'Point of Departure'. *This is, after all, a very personal contribution, an attempt to tie threads together: my departure as editor and journalist at the* FT*; Britain's departure from the EU. The end of an era? Not quite. But still a sense of a hinge point and a new beginning, whatever that may be.*

Breakfast with Richard Gnodde, the tall, languid South African who runs Goldman Sachs International from its London headquarters. We've had regular conversations since I became editor. He's invariably thoughtful and well informed. He liked my Brexit essay but makes an even more important point about life after our departure from the EU.

In the past 30 years, the City of London has never had it so good. Thatcher's Big Bang deregulation attracted well-capitalised American investment banks which swallowed up the UK houses. The launch of the euro gave a second fillip to the City, delivering a new pool of capital for investment and trading. The UK – outside the single-currency zone – enjoyed the best of both worlds. Gnodde cautions that 'Singapore-style' deregulation post-Brexit will only antagonise the Europeans. Dublin, Paris, Milan and Frankfurt will not compete with London any time soon. Let sleeping dogs lie. *Is anyone in the government listening?*

TUESDAY, 12 NOVEMBER

Late tonight, a text message from Roula: 'OMG. Thank you Lionel for believing in me.' She really did not know she was the next editor of the *FT* until Kita-san broke the news over dinner. We speak briefly but warmly, and I sense that she is experiencing the same thrill of landing the best job in journalism that I felt 14 years ago over lunch with Sir David Bell in Manhattan. And that same Robert Redford moment when the candidate learns he's won the race: *What do we do now?*

Early next morning, in separate meetings in separate rooms, I inform the disappointed candidates. John, Alec and Robert are all three outstanding journalists who could have easily taken the top job. I've had easier conversations in my time as editor. Afterwards I redraft my own statement on stepping down and send out an email announcement that I will speak to staff at 9.30am.

By now the news is spreading like a prairie fire. Roula and I walk together to the news desk and I deliver my own statement which might be summed up as *job done*. Towards the end, my voice cracks. Keeping a secret about my exit for almost a year has been a test of self-discipline. Managing the succession in tandem with Kita-san has also been a test of discretion. But we got there in the end, and I'm OK because it suddenly all makes sense. Roula, in her own speech, is more than generous in her tribute to my time as editor.

I have achieved what I set out to do: the restoration of the gold standard in the FT's *reporting and commentary, and the*

*establishment of a sustainably profitable business based on digital
transformation, to the point where we have more than 1 million
paying readers. And, after 2015, I have contributed to a third great
task: cementing a global media alliance with our new owners,
Nikkei.*

    *Besides this sense of accomplishment, I know there's been a toll:
the travel, the jet lag, the daily stress of leadership and management.
Keeping people motivated. Moving people. Maintaining an eye on
the next generation. The editor's job can be a lonely one. In the
early days, I had Martin Dickson as my daily confidant. More
recently, I was in and out of Roula's office, always before morning
news conference, recounting the previous night's gossip and checking
on stories to follow. Throughout my tenure as editor, I also had
Victoria as a sounding board, someone whose judgement was second
to none.*

Naturally, I will miss being in the mix, taking that late-
night call from someone who wants to bend my ear, share
gossip or make the occasional confession. And there's the
'proconsular' trips with Victoria to faraway places, from the
São Paulo favella to the Mumbai flea market and the volca-
noes of Congo as well as the setpieces with world leaders. As
Robert Shrimsley would later remark: sometimes one had
the feeling that Lionel Barber was starring in his own TV
show.

Then again, what I most enjoyed about my time as editor
was 'walking the floor'. I loved hearing what reporters were
working on, loved encouraging them to follow leads, often
offering them names or contacts. And I loved occasionally
inviting the younger journalists to drop by my office so I
could take a look at the copy, maybe even edit it myself to
make it that little bit better.

There's nothing to beat being in a newsroom, especially when something really big is happening. Brexit, Trump's election, the fall of Lehman Brothers, the sale of the *FT*. In these moments of crisis-cum-drama, when everyone else is losing their head, the editor is supposed to be detached from the immediate action but ready to be drafted when necessary. Being a reporter at heart, I found it hard to stay away from the news desk. I wanted to be in the thick of it, and most of the time I was.

Ben Bradlee warned that life after editorship would reveal who one's real friends are. Some of my *FT* circle will remain friends, on new terms which may be more comfortable for both of us. For Ted Williams going out on a high was one ball into the bleachers. For me, it was my relationship of trust with Kita-san, digital transformation and, finally, Putin, Brussels and Roula as my successor. As editors go, that's a home run.

Back in my office, the emails flow in, notes of commiseration, congratulations and thanks from *FT* journalists, young, old and departed. These personal notes, especially from the younger generation, mean so much more than words.

Mid-morning, there is a tap at the door. John Gapper pokes his head round. In his understated way, he says: 'You saved the *FT*.'

Then the door gently closed.

EPILOGUE

In late December 2019, a news item caught my eye about a mysterious virus spreading through the city of Wuhan in central China. Our reporting gave few clues about the severity of the disease or its origins. I made a note to check on future coverage. Then, on 7 January, I flew to Berlin for an interview with Chancellor Angela Merkel, a coda to my editorship and a 35-year career at the *FT*.

Germany was the foreign assignment I had always coveted as a young journalist. Despite a fascination with the language and culture going back to my school days, it was not to be. Instead I found myself transferred from Washington to Brussels, a natural perch from which to write about Europe after the Maastricht treaty. Securing that final rendezvous in Berlin was a chance to bid a professional farewell to Europe's foremost statesman but also a reckoning of sorts for the German assignment that never was.

Angela Merkel took over as chancellor in 2005, three weeks after I took over as *FT* editor. The symmetry, her chief spokesman Steffen Seibert told me, ultimately persuaded the chancellor to sit down for an unscripted interview, her first in months. Merkel was guarded but defiant in our near hour-long conversation: Europe was Germany's salvation and this was no time to retreat on European cooperation and (measured) integration. In a world of populists and strongmen, she was doubling down on the EU as (almost) the last liberal democrat standing.

Seven weeks later, the coronavirus pandemic brought the world to a stop. This was not just a bookend to my editorship; it was an emphatic exclamation mark. The fragility of the modern economy and its finely tuned global supply chains was exposed brutally. To be sure, between 2005 and 2020, there were signs that globalisation was in trouble. The financial crisis, mass migration, the rise of national populism and President Trump's weaponisation of trade tariffs: all these trends threatened the free flow of goods, people and ideas which represented the benign face of globalisation. Covid-19 reinforced the negative trends underway.

Something else changed in the spring of 2020. Globalisation was always more than a physical and political phenomenon, it was a mindset: the idea of ubiquitous choice, where the consumer can have it all, on demand, in real time. The pandemic spelt the end of ultra-mobility. In a world of 'social distancing', without a vaccine in sight, the basic modus operandi of a modern economy would have to be rethought, from air travel to office working.

The coronavirus outbreak presented a supreme test of leadership in authoritarian societies as well as liberal democracies. In China, where the virus originated, the regime started with a bungled cover-up. After draconian quarantines backed by extensive state surveillance, the economy slowly began to recover. In Russia, Vladimir Putin's government remained in denial until the rising number of victims and slumping poll ratings forced Moscow to act.

In Germany, Chancellor Merkel, the trained scientist, took early, decisive action and her approval ratings soared, a remarkable comeback from the twilight zone. Other women leaders, from New Zealand to South Korea and Taiwan fared well. In the UK Boris Johnson dithered until he found himself virus-stricken and the economy slumped, a double shock alongside Brexit. President Trump too remained in denial, triggering a sharp decline in the economy which threatened his chances of re-election.

In normal times, the world would look to American leadership in a global crisis, but the US was missing in action. The contrast with the coordinated response to the 2008–9 financial crisis, where Gordon Brown, George Bush, Barack Obama and Nicolas Sarkozy played leading roles, was stark. In America's absence, China attempted to fill the vacuum with economic diplomacy and financial and material assistance. But China had already forfeited the moral high ground and Asian neighbours remained suspicious and wary of its intentions. Europe was too divided, too puny and too preoccupied with its own economic disaster to fill the breach. We lived, truly, in a leaderless world.

Amid political drift and economic collapse, another inconvenient truth stood out. This was the second time in a decade that the state had been obliged to bail out the corporate sector. In 2020, moral blame was much less easily assigned than in the global financial crisis where highly leveraged banks took on dizzying levels of risk, only to be rescued at taxpayers' expense. Twelve years on, the sums involved were far higher. Hundreds of billions of dollars translated into trillions. These sums amounted to debts of a size which could only be reduced seriously by a burst of inflation or sustained economic growth, at a rate more readily associated with emerging markets than advanced western economies.

For the time being, central banks, once again, came to the rescue. The Fed's and the ECB's massive purchase of assets restored a measure of confidence in financial markets, but the real economy risked becoming permanently scarred. Unemployment on a scale not seen since the 1930s remained a serious threat. As after the financial crisis, propping up financial assets risked creating perverse consequences. Risk was being socialised. As my colleague Martin Wolf wrote: central banks used to have the role of taking away the punch-bowl when the party was getting out of hand; now the central bankers were offering a second helping.

In the post-Covid-19 world, there are five potential developments worth considering for business, politics, the world economy and international relations, particularly the crucial balance of power between the US and China and the role of Europe. In each case, the choices which leaders make will shape the future of liberal democracies which thrived under the post-war rules-based order, only to stumble badly in the decade after the financial crisis.

The first development, the most perilous, would see the world turn into a battleground of unregulated competition between the US and China. This would spell a further unravelling of international alliances and a weakening of international institutions such as the UN and the World Trade Organisation. It would not be a new Cold War per se. But the risk of the incumbent superpower America and its strategic rival China falling into the Thucydides Trap of military conflict, as Graham Allison presciently observed, would remain a real one.

A second, more optimistic development would see the big powers understand that they have basic shared interests and a responsibility to manage relations with each other despite different political systems. After Donald Trump's transactional foreign policy, Americans would rediscover its tradition of advancing American ideas and values. The US would halt its retreat from international responsibilities and re-engage with friend and foe to tackle the great issues of the commons: energy and the environment, migration, digital security. As Robert Zoellick has wisely observed in his new history of US diplomacy*, a narrowly defined US nationalism stunts America's true power.

For its part, Europe would redouble efforts to assert its own weight in the world, without being sandwiched by the two superpowers. In the summer of 2020, the pandemic brought the 27 EU member states closer together. Merkel's Germany cast its lot in favour of deeper economic integration, exemplified by the agreement on a €750bn recovery fund which broke the taboo of common borrowing on the financial markets. In future, this financial firepower could be directed towards new projects, such as collective defence, technological research and steps towards a closer political union.

The foreign policy dilemma for the UK, having chosen to abandon membership of the EU, will remain acute. Boris Johnson's government once invoked a 'Global Britain' liberated from the legal and political constraints of Brussels. But trade agreements with individual countries, let alone the collective weight of the EU and the US, will require a hard slog. The UK will likely lean more towards America than Europe and certainly China, but its status as junior partner will be more explicit than ever. At home, Brexit is an opportunity for national renewal but it is the equivalent of a heavy

---

* See *America in the World: A History of U.S. Diplomacy and Foreign Policy* by Robert B. Zoellick, published August 2020.

cold shower: bracing but not ideal for the short-term health of a sickly patient. Nor has the spectre of Scottish independence vanished. A break-up of the United Kingdom would have repercussions far beyond London, Belfast, Cardiff and Edinburgh. For all the talk of decline, the UK has been an important actor in international affairs, from Thatcher through Blair and Brown. England will never replace the UK in weight or standing.

The third current involves reimagining the role of the state and representative government in what used to be called 'the west'. The decline of the party system is a recurrent phenomenon, as is the breakdown between the traditional left/right divisions prevalent during the Cold War. In the UK, as recorded in this book, David Cameron weakened representative government by resorting to referenda and later blocking efforts to reform a bloated upper chamber, the House of Lords. The opposition Labour party has often been complicit. Brexit should be the catalyst to reform political institutions, redraw the settlement between the UK's constituent parts and instil fresh vigour into the state which has been progressively weakened through austerity and neglect. In this respect, if not others, the instincts of agitators for change like Dominic Cummings are not entirely misplaced.

Compared to the UK and US governments, governments in Asia such as those of Singapore and South Korea proved far more effective in deploying the resources of the state to tackle the coronavirus pandemic. Their 'track and trace' systems illustrated the value of professional expertise and investment in high technology. These countries may lean towards authoritarian democracy but they showed themselves to be functioning, modern states capable of providing security and economic progress to their citizens. In the 20th century, the west taught Asia about liberal democracy. In the 21st century, the west should not be tempted by Xi's model of illiberal democracy and the unassailable authority of the communist party; but it has much to learn from Asia in general.

The fourth development involves a reform of capitalism, the engine of wealth creation intrinsic to the survival of liberal democracy. Well before the pandemic struck, the calls for a new social compact were growing. Rather than focusing exclusively on shareholder value, company boards were under pressure to consider other factors such as climate change, diversity and human capital. Boards were obliged to find ways to reduce the gross inequalities which had arisen under the old system. In the new system, as governments seek to pay down their colossal debts, the pressure to redress the balance, through higher taxes, will prove irresistible. The challenge is how to adjust course without returning to the stifling statism of the 1960s and 70s. Whatever the case, a new agenda is needed.

This leads to the fifth development: the ever expanding role of technology. Covid-19 has turbo-charged the internet. Automated working and artificial intelligence will proceed apace, threatening white collar jobs in the same way that industrial robots decimated the blue collar workforce in the 1980s. Other sectors like the travel and hospitality industries will find their business models upended by the emergence of new companies like Zoom and other virtual networking sites. Those that fail to adapt will either be crushed or wither away.

In this new super-networked world, the US tech giants – Amazon, Facebook, Google, Microsoft, Netflix – have seen their market capitalisations grow exponentially under the precept of 'winner takes all'. Yet their very success will leave them exposed, with their super-sized profits a target for those in favour of fiscal redistribution. Their market dominance, reminiscent of the US trusts of the late 19th century, will encourage voices calling for regulation, even break-up. Yet the so-called 'Fangs' have been great engines of dynamism and innovation. Their best defence may be to point to the size and scale of rivals in China, which is determined to overtake the US in the technology arms race and promote their own champions like Alibaba and Tencent. Either way, the seamless fabric of the internet, championed at the turn of the century, is fast eroding as the world divides into opposing camps.

In the middle of the digital revolution, a decade ago, it became fashionable to write off journalism. In the post-Covid-19 world, journalism's mission to explain will never be more important or more challenging. Newspapers will gradually become quaint relics. In their place, digital-first news organisations must find ways to make money but also to be heard above the din of hyperpartisanship. These news providers will depend on sugar daddies, the new Hearsts and Pulitzers. But they will also, hopefully, find support among philanthropic foundations and other sources of funding distinct from advertising. New forms of ownership and collaboration between news organisations will appear, driven by the need to reduce costs and to produce journalism in the most efficient manner possible. This is 'news on demand', delivered directly to the reader at any time, in any form.

C.P. Scott, the long-time editor of the *Guardian*, once famously proclaimed: comment is free but facts are sacred. The coronavirus pandemic has offered a timely reminder of the importance of fact-based science. In a world where politicians are promoting 'alternative facts' – the latest euphemism for propaganda and deceit – journalists have a duty to present the truth or something as close as possible. Factual reporting – not uninformed hyperpartisanship – remains essential to maintain an informed citizenry, on which our democracies depend.

Over more than four decades, as a journalist and editor, I had the privilege of being able to speak the occasional truth to power. My father Frank was right: journalism is not a profession; it is a vocation. This book is a testimony to that mission, and I commend it to the next generation.

ACKNOWLEDGEMENTS

I have been fortunate to have been able to draw on the wisdom and advice of many friends to help me bring this book to fruition, but without the support of one special person it would never have been possible.

Tsuneo Kita, chairman of Nikkei and proprietor of the *FT*, gave his approval for the book, sight unseen. There can be no greater expression of trust. Kita-san and I share the belief that journalism should act as a witness to history. As ever, he is a man true to his word.

I would like to offer a special thanks to Jim MacGregor in New York who read through several drafts and made numerous helpful suggestions, drawing on his deep knowledge of Wall Street and his erstwhile career as a journalist. Marcus Brauchli sharpened the original outline with his metaphorical felt-tip pen. Richard Cohen, with whom I first became friends at the *Washington Post* in the summer of 1985, offered invaluable tips on writing style, gleaned from his many years as a columnist in Washington and New York.

In the UK, I owe a debt of gratitude to Hannah Rothschild and Sir Tom Stoppard for reading early versions of the manuscript and helping me to find my voice. Eden Collinsworth, a fellow author, was generous with advice and tips. Caroline Michel, my agent, has been an indispensable pillar of support and encouragement, never doubting that there was a book to write after editorship.

I owe thanks to Joel Rickett at Penguin Random House, who encouraged me to write 'The Barber Diaries', and to Jamie Joseph, my editor, for showing me how to build a narrative arc and structure, not easy for a journalist more attuned to the short form. Peter James, my copy editor, was a study in vigilance and displayed encyclopaedic knowledge, vital when scrutinising a diary with global reach.

I owe a great debt to Joshua Oliver, my assistant at the *FT*, who provided outstanding support in terms of reading the original drafts and appending the footnotes. Peter Cheek, the *FT*'s chief librarian and researcher, was ever diligent in nailing down articles and references relevant to the book.

In a book of this length, which ranges far and wide over space and time, it is entirely possible that mistakes have crept in. I did not keep a daily diary but I kept extensive notes on key meetings and events, both in written and dictated form. In many cases, I have gone back to original sources to check whether their account tallies with my own. In some cases, this has not been possible. Any errors of fact, if not interpretation, are entirely my own.

As editor rather than author, I would once again like to thank all *FT* colleagues who accompanied me on my trips around the world. I learnt so much from them, and I hope they will one day forgive me for stepping occasionally on their toes.

Many colleagues are mentioned in this book, but I want to extend a special thanks to Jamil Anderlini for guiding me around China, always a tough assignment which he managed with great resourcefulness. I would also like to thank Alex Barker, Peter Spiegel and Tony Barber in Brussels; Tobias

Buck in Madrid and Jerusalem; George Parker, doyen of Westminster political editors; Amy Kazmin and James Lamont in India; Alec Russell in South Africa; John Paul Rathbone in Latin America; Andrew England in the Gulf, Kenya and South Africa; Katrina Manson in Sierra Leone; Gwen Robinson in Myanmar and Japan; Kathrin Hille in Moscow and Kazakhstan; Richard Waters (so many times) in San Francisco and Silicon Valley; Demetri Sevastopulo and Ed Luce in Washington; Tom Braithwaite and Gillian Tett in New York; Henry Foy in Moscow and Almaty; David Pilling in Rwanda, Congo and Japan; William Wallis in Nigeria and Ghana; Najmeh Bozorgmehr in Tehran; Anne-Sylvaine Chassany in Paris; Guy Chazan in Berlin; and Jude Webber in Argentina and Mexico.

I would also like to thank my editors in London, in particular Alice Fishburn and Esther Bintliff at the weekend *Magazine* and Geoff Dyer and Tom O'Sullivan on the *Big Read*. They are brilliant long-form editors. And a special thanks to two indispensable colleagues: Nigel Hanson, an outstanding and extraordinarily diligent in-house lawyer, and Sally Kennedy, my personal assistant for almost 14 years and a model of discretion and sound advice. I spent many rewarding hours with both.

Finally, I would like to thank my family – Dash and Francesca, for putting up with an often absent father, and above all Victoria who has been my counsellor and editor. She will always have the last word.

INDEX